Personal Insolvency Law

Personal Insolvency Law

James Burke
Barrister-at-Law, AITI

Amanda-Jayne Comyn
Barrister-at-Law, AITI, TEP

Bloomsbury Professional

Published by
Bloomsbury Professional
Maxwelton House
41–43 Boltro Road
Haywards Heath
West Sussex
RH16 1BJ

Bloomsbury Professional
The Fitzwilliam Business Centre
26 Upper Pembroke Street
Dublin 2

ISBN 978 1 847664860

British Library Cataloguing-in-Publication Data
A catalogue record for this book is available from the British Library

Typeset by Marie Armah-Kwantreng, Dublin, Ireland
Printed in United Kingdom by
Hobbs the Printers Ltd, Totton, Hampshire

FOREWORD

When the authors asked me to write a foreword for this book, they informed me that it was not 'an academic book on the jurisprudence of Personal Insolvency law, but rather is a guide to the new arrangements available under the new Act ...'.

Well, they may be right about that, but the work is no less valuable for being practical rather than academic. Having read through the text, it is clear that this will be an invaluable textbook for lawyers, Insolvency Practitioners and members of the public. The Personal Insolvency Act 2012 utterly changes the legal landscape in the area of Personal Insolvency. The Act provides new laws, new bodies to implement the laws, new processes and new authorised practitioners to carry out functions under the Act.

We are now entering a world of Debt Relief Notices, Approved Intermediaries, Personal Insolvency Practitioners and the creation of a new monitoring body, the Insolvency Service of Ireland. The authors of this work start with a *tabula rasa*. There is no jurisprudence to fall back on as we enter this brave new world. So what is more useful than to find, in one volume, a complete guide through the new law and its procedures written in a clear and uncomplicated style.

The text is set out in an orderly scheme, taking the reader through the provisions of the Personal Insolvency Act 2012 and describing in great detail the way in which the Act will work, with much practical information about the new bodies and professional administrators who will carry into effect the scheme of the legislation. There is also a very helpful section of appendices setting out the relevant forms and rules that will come into play. In short, this is an invaluable guide for all who work in the area of Personal Insolvency and is likely to become the first reference point for most practitioners in the area.

Mr Justice Brian J McGovern

The High Court

December 2013

CONTENTS

TABLE OF STATUTES

TABLE OF STATUTORY INSTRUMENTS

Constitution of Ireland

European Legislation

Chapter 1

INTRODUCTION

ECONOMIC CRISIS IN IRELAND

The Build Up

[1.01] Ireland's economy was widely seen as one of the most successful in the world, yet it has been among the hardest hit by the global financial crisis. From the mid-1990s to 2007, Ireland enjoyed strong economic growth where there was a rapid convergence of Irish living standards towards those of the world's most successful economies.

There were a number of contributing factors for this growth pattern. These included internal and external elements such as the number of workers in the labour market, the improvement of the educational level of the labour force and the arrival of the EU single market which made Ireland an attractive location for inward investment, especially from the US, and helped boost Irish exports.

From roughly 2002 until 2007, however, this growth dynamic changed in fundamental ways. The Irish economy continued to experience high growth rates, but this was increasingly based on the rapid expansion of credit and an accompanying build-up of personal indebtedness by Irish households. This was fuelled, above all else, by rising property prices. During this period, construction activity grew very strongly, accounting for a much larger share of the economy and employment than was previously the case.

The speculative bubble in property was supported by a surge in bank lending, and the balance sheets of Irish banks grew disproportionately large relative to the size of the economy. The lending appetite of Irish banks was reflected in both a concentration of lending in property and increasingly leveraged lending practices, both of which proved to be highly damaging when the bubble burst.

Some commentators have argued that Irish fiscal policy during this period played a part in exacerbating the imbalances that were building up.

The funding of the Exchequer was largely derived from particular taxes – capital gains tax and stamp duty – both of which were directly attributable to the property bubble. This period also saw rapid increases in prices and wages, which led to an erosion of Ireland's international competitiveness.

The Crash

[1.02] From a global perspective, from August 2007 there were severe tensions in global financial markets. A key event was the collapse of Lehman Brothers, a US investment bank, in September 2008.

As the international financial crisis erupted, Irish banks were left vulnerable and exposed. With falling property prices, banks began to suffer huge losses on their loans. At the same time, short term inter-bank lending, on which Irish banks had become heavily reliant for their funding, became difficult to access. With confidence evaporating, Irish banks began to experience deposit outflows, and there were mounting fears about their ability to access funding from the wholesale money markets.

Responding to these pressures, on 30 September 2008, the Irish government decided to issue a blanket guarantee of the banks' liabilities and to recapitalise the banks using public funds. The large costs of these measures led to an acute deterioration in the government's fiscal position.

Although the government began to implement austerity measures designed to restore sustainability to its public finances, it was facing an uphill struggle, with the measures being seen as closing the stable door after the horse had bolted.

In November 2010 yields on Irish government debt reached an unsustainable nine per cent, which meant that the government was effectively locked out of international bond markets.

The Recovery

[1.03] On 29 November 2010, the Irish government negotiated a financial assistance package with the European Commission, European Central Bank and the International Monetary Fund totalling €85 billion (including a contribution of €17.5 billion from Ireland's own resources). Ireland's bailout partners are collectively known as the Troika. The three main objectives of the Economic Adjustment Programme were:

(a) the immediate strengthening and comprehensive overhaul of the banking sector;

(b) ambitious fiscal adjustment to restore fiscal sustainability with correction of excessive deficit by 2015; and

(c) growth-enhancing reforms, in particular on the labour market, to allow a return to a robust and sustainable growth.

As part of the Economic Adjustment Programme, one of the requirements set out by the Troika was to update Ireland's personal insolvency laws. The development of modern insolvency law by the introduction of the Personal Insolvency Act 2012 ('PIA 2012') is in line with the commitments in the Programme for Government and the EU/IMF Programme of Financial Support for Ireland.

BACKGROUND TO THE PERSONAL INSOLVENCY ACT 2012

[1.04] The Law Reform Commission published a report entitled *Personal Debt Management and Debt Enforcement*[1] which examined several jurisdictions' approach to personal debt. It examined a number of issues amongst which were the different type of debtors and creditors and the effect of write down of debt on financial institutions.

The report also recommended the updating of the Bankruptcy Act 1988 ('BA 1988').

A number of other reports also recommended significant reforms to Ireland's personal insolvency framework. For example, the Inter-Departmental Working Group on

1. *Personal Debt Management and Debt Enforcement* (LRC 100, 2010).

Mortgage Arrears (Keane) Report of October, 2011 recommended that 'the early introduction of new judicial and non-judicial bankruptcy options is vital' and stated that 'without effective bankruptcy legislation the mortgage arrears problem will not be resolved'.

Other comparative jurisdictions are broadly similar in their approach to personal insolvency in that they provide an out of court approach to debt resolution. The PIA 2012 sought to move Ireland in this direction and encompass the approach adopted in these jurisdictions, specifically the Individual Voluntary Arrangement (IVA) process in the UK.

The Minister for Justice and Equality and Defence, Alan Shatter TD, said at the time of the introduction of the Personal Insolvency Bill that:

> this Bill is designed to provide a modern insolvency process in Ireland which addresses the obligations of debtors and the rights of creditors in a proportionate and balanced way having regard to the financial reality of an individual's true circumstances.

Minister Shatter further said:

> I am convinced that new personal insolvency laws including the reform of our bankruptcy law will, in addition to providing new legal remedies, also provide a significant incentive for financial institutions to develop and implement realistic agreements to resolve debt issues with their customers. The provisions relating to a Personal Insolvency Arrangement are specifically designed to facilitate a debtor's continued ownership and occupation of his principal private residence unless the debtor does not wish to do so or the costs of the debtors continuing to reside in it are disproportionately large.

BANKRUPTCY

[1.05] Prior to the PIA 2012, bankruptcy as administered under the BA 1988 was the only statutory scheme which provided a debtor with the possibility of a fresh start. Historically most persons who were made bankrupt remained bankrupt for between twenty to forty years.

The PIA 2012 together with the amendments provided by the Miscellaneous Provisions Acts of 2011 and 2013[2] have amended the BA 1988 and brought it significantly in line with the bankruptcy procedures in the UK. The only significant difference that will still remain following the enactment of the changes in Ireland is the minimum period of bankruptcy which will be three years in Ireland whereas it is one year in the UK.

The reform to the bankruptcy procedure was a crucial development, as Minister Alan Shatter noted that failure to agree a suitable non-judicial debt settlement between debtors and creditors will leave open the option of debt enforcement or judicial bankruptcy.

---

2. Civil Law (Miscellaneous Provisions) Act 2011 and Courts and Civil Law (Miscellaneous Provisions) Act 2013.

These recent amendments to the BA 1988 included the reduction in the period for an automatic discharge from bankruptcy from twelve years[3] to three years[4]. This development moves Ireland to the European norm for such discharge.

Previously the twelve year automatic discharge period meant that the threat of bankruptcy could be used as leverage against debtors, as where a person was made a bankrupt there was effectively no return. There was also a huge stigma attached to being declared bankrupt with some commentators suggesting it was akin to leprosy in biblical times. The economic crisis[5] contributed to a change in peoples' perceptions of persons in financial difficulty due to so many people finding themselves in serious financial trouble. The introduction of the new debt resolution system was much needed and eagerly anticipated, given the increasing necessity to provide a practical equitable solution to ease peoples' financial burdens.

PERSONAL INSOLVENCY ACT 2012

[1.06] The PIA 2012 was introduced to amend the law relating to insolvency having regard to the following objectives:

(a) the need to ameliorate the difficulties experienced by debtors in discharging their indebtedness due to insolvency and thereby lessen the adverse consequences for economic activity in the State;

(b) the need to enable creditors to recover debts due to them by insolvent debtors to the extent that the means of those debtors reasonably permits in an orderly and rational manner; and

(c) the need to enable insolvent persons to resolve their indebtedness (including by determining that debts stand discharged in certain circumstances) in an orderly and rational manner without recourse to bankruptcy, and to thereby facilitate the active participation of such persons in economic activity in the State, to provide for additional mechanisms and arrangements relating to insolvency to facilitate the achievement of those objectives, and to provide for connected matters.

The PIA 2012 provides for the introduction of the following non-judicial debt resolution processes subject to relevant conditions in each case:

(a) a Debt Relief Notice[6] (DRN) to allow for the write-off of qualifying debt up to €20,000, subject to a three-year supervision period;

(b) a Debt Settlement Arrangement[7] (DSA) for the agreed settlement of unsecured debt over five years; and

---

3. Civil Law (Miscellaneous Provisions) Act 2011, Pt 7.
4. PIA 2012, s 157.
5. See para **1.01** above.
6. **Chapter 3** – Debt Relief Notices.
7. **Chapter 4** – Debt Settlement Arrangements.

(c) a Personal Insolvency Arrangement[8] (PIA) for the agreed settlement of secured debt up to €3 million (though this cap can be increased with the consent of all secured creditors) and unsecured debt over six years.

In order to protect the constitutional rights of all concerned provision has been made for Circuit Court oversight of these three new procedures.

Each of these new debt resolution mechanisms has its own rules and procedures. It is possible to be involved in only one of the new mechanisms (DRN, DSA or PIA) or in the bankruptcy process at any one time. If one of these four processes is used, then a debtor will generally have to wait some years before applying to use another.

Each of the new mechanisms may only be used once in a debtor's lifetime (with the exception of bankruptcy – however, it would be unusual for a person to go bankrupt twice).

A debtor who is seeking to use one of the new mechanisms must complete a Prescribed Financial Statement,[9] giving full and honest information about their financial circumstances. A statutory declaration to this effect will also be required to be made by the debtor. It is a requirement under the PIA 2012 that a debtor acts in good faith and co-operates fully with the process. A debtor must also give written consent to the accessing of certain personal data held by banks and other financial institutions so that their financial situation can be verified. Government departments and agencies have the power to release certain information about debtors engaging in the mechanisms.

Where any of the new mechanisms are availed of, the debtor's name and details will be published on a register that is accessible to the public. The success or failure of the process will also be recorded.

The DRN process provides debt relief for people who have virtually no disposable income or assets and no prospect of being able to pay off the debt in the next three years. Where a DRN is issued, it allows for the write-off of qualifying debt up to €20,000, subject to a three-year supervision period. The application for a DRN must be processed through an Approved Intermediary (AI).[10]

A DSA provides for the agreed settlement of unsecured debt with one or more creditors over a period of five years, with a possible agreed extension to six years. A debtor may apply for a DSA where the level of their income, assets and debts would make them ineligible for a DRN. The DSA is a voluntary arrangement and it will have to get the support of creditors representing at least 65 per cent of the total debt in the DSA. The application for a DSA must be processed through a Personal Insolvency Practitioner (PIP).

A PIA provides for the agreed settlement of secured debt up to a limit of €3 million (although this cap may be increased with the consent of all secured creditors) and an unlimited amount of unsecured debt. A PIA will run over a period of six years, with a possible agreed extension to seven years. The application for a PIA must also be processed through a PIP. A PIA is also a voluntary arrangement and will have to get the

8. **Chapter 5** – Personal Insolvency Arrangements.

9. **Appendix 1**.

10. Para **3.30** – Approved Intermediaries.

support of creditors – both secured and unsecured – representing at least 65 per cent of the total debt in the PIA of which over 50 per cent of secured creditors and 50 per cent of unsecured creditors must vote in favour.

[1.07] The PIA 2012 requires debtors and creditors to reach a solution that is realistic. The PIP[11] has a very important role to play in providing a proposal that is both realistic and satisfactory. A properly drafted proposal should provide a debtor with a reasonable standard of living and enable them to deal with their debt without being overburdened with debt. The proposal should provide a satisfactory outcome for creditors and one which would give a better return than if the debtor was made a bankrupt.

The Insolvency Service of Ireland[12] (ISI) is responsible for all matters concerning personal insolvency. Its role includes:

(a) certifying applications for DRNs;
(b) certifying applications for DSAs and PIAs;
(c) developing guidelines for insolvency procedures;
(d) maintaining registers;
(e) authorising AIs;
(f) authorising and regulating PIPs; and
(g) monitoring the operation of the arrangements.

COMPARISON TABLE

[1.08]

Arrangement	**Type of debt covered**	**Value**	**Duration**	**Apply through**
Old Bankruptcy Regime	Unsecured and secured	At least €1,900 (1 creditor) or €1,300 (combined creditors)	12 years	High Court (voluntary declaration or else creditors can petition)
Debt Relief Notice (DRN)	Unsecured (and secured in certain cases)	Up to €20,000	3 years	Approved Intermediary (AI)
Debt Settlement Arrangement (DSA)	Unsecured	No limit	5 years (+1)	Personal Insolvency Practitioner (PIP)
Personal Insolvency Arrangement (PIA)	Unsecured and secured	No limit on unsecured. Up to €3m secured (though cap can increase if agreed)	6 years (+1)	Personal Insolvency Practitioner (PIP)

11. **Chapter 8** – Personal Insolvency Practitioners.
12. **Chapter 2** – Insolvency Service of Ireland.

Arrangement	Type of debt covered	Value	Duration	Apply through
Bankruptcy now[13]	Unsecured and secured	€20,000	3 years	High Court

AUTHORS' COMMENTARY ON PIA 2012

[1.09] The PIA 2012 is a welcomed alternative to the bankruptcy system which previously provided the only solution available to individuals in financial crisis. As noted above, the bankruptcy process was less than an ideal solution for both debtor and creditor given its arduous and lengthy procedure.

The new insolvency processes provided under the PIA 2012 are cognisant of the range of financial difficulties experienced in the current economic climate and the circumstances of both debtors and secured and unsecured creditors. It attempts to strike a balance between the needs of both debtor and creditor with an emphasis on a practical solution being agreed between both parties.

The PIA 2012 has been drafted to be mindful of the range of circumstances that will be dealt with under each of the new mechanisms and extends a broad scope to the ISI and the courts to deal with varying circumstances. The legislation itself will not stand alone, as there is provision for the introduction of regulations by the ISI in respect of various regulatory elements of the PIA 2012. The function of the regulations is to provide further detail on how the requirements under the PIA are to be satisfied and also for the monitoring and regulation of the processes themselves.

The ISI has been active in developing these regulations with a substantial number of regulations already introduced, some of which are set out below:

(a) Guide to Reasonable Living Expenses;

(b) Authorisation and Supervision of AIs and PIPs;

(c) Accounts and Related Matters;

(d) Prescribed Financial Statements;

(e) Procedures for Creditors' Meetings.

The PIA 2012 itself provides for the exercise of a wide discretion by the ISI and the Courts in their roles in the operation of the new mechanisms. This discretion will extend to the ISI and the courts the scope to deal with the changing environment and economic circumstances in which these processes will operate and will provide the opportunity to apply practical solutions in a variety of scenarios.

The PIA 2012 is unique to the processes in other jurisdictions in that it provides a legislative basis for dealing with secured creditors. The PIA 2012 has sought to balance the rights of secured creditors with the needs of the debtor within the remit of the legislation. The secured creditor provisions are the first legislative provisions of their

13. Since 3 December 2013 which is date of Commencement Order commencing PIA 2012, Pt 4.

kind in comparative jurisdictions and the operation of the provisions and the protection of secured creditors and debtors will be a work in progress.

UK SYSTEM

[1.10] In most cases the bankruptcy process in the UK is complete at the end of one year and the debtor will be automatically discharged at the end of this period. This is in contrast to a bankruptcy period of twelve years (awaiting commencement order to reduce this period to three years) in Ireland and six years in Germany. As a direct consequence there has been a vast increase in the number of Irish individuals seeking to be made bankrupt in the UK in recent times.

The application for bankruptcy in the UK by some high profile individuals has resulted in increased public interest and media attention on the bankruptcy process available in the UK.

EC Regulation 1346/2000 (Insolvency Regulation) enabled debtors based within the EU to choose which European country they wished to apply to be made a bankrupt. Effectively it enabled individuals in the EU to forum shop and choose the Member State which provided the easiest or most practical route out of bankruptcy and may even have allowed the debtor to continue to hold a portion of his assets (the most common asset being the pension).

The application of the Insolvency Regulation becomes effective when there is a judgment declaring or adjudicating a debtor bankrupt in a member state. The proceedings are considered opened in the jurisdiction in which the debtor has been declared or adjudicated bankrupt. The Insolvency Regulation requires the courts of all member states to recognise the order of the court adjudicating or declaring the person bankrupt and to recognise all subsequent orders of that court.[14]

Thus if an Irish person is declared a bankrupt in England, all other member states are required to recognise the order adjudicating the person bankrupt and all subsequent orders from that English court which has adjudicated the person bankrupt.

In the UK it is usually sufficient to demonstrate that you have been residing there for at least six months prior to the bringing of the application for bankruptcy. In order for a debtor to substantiate such a claim it will be necessary to provide the court of evidence of the debtor's residence in the UK. The type of evidence that may support such a claim can include items such as a tenancy agreement, utility bills in the debtor's name, payslips and bank or credit card statements for the previous six months.

Historically, applications for a bankruptcy order were short and not scrutinised to any great extent. In recent times the spotlight has been focussed on perceived 'bankruptcy tourism', with the general public consensus that debtors should not be entitled to exit the country in an effort to escape the Irish bankruptcy regime. The media has played a major role in highlighting the flight of debtors to other jurisdictions to declare bankruptcy to avail of perceived softer regimes. The increase in 'bankruptcy tourism' has resulted in judges scrutinising applications in more detail, resulting in more information now being required to persuade a judge of an applicant's UK residency.

14. EC Regulation 1346/2000, art 16.

The main advantages of a UK bankruptcy are:

(a) discharge after a period of 12 months;

(b) established procedure and protocol;

(c) anonymity;

(d) possibility to escape the notice of some creditors;

(e) increased cost to creditor to prove debt;

(f) the bankrupt's pension entitlements are not considered as part of a bankrupt's assets for the purposes of the bankruptcy.

These advantages continue to exist and it will remain to be seen whether the trend for Irish individuals to avail of the UK bankruptcy system will continue in the wake of the PIA 2012.

There is also an alternative insolvency process to bankruptcy in the UK. This alternative process is an Individual Voluntary Arrangement (IVA), which is a legally binding agreement between a debtor and its creditors. An IVA normally lasts five years and during this period the debtor is expected to pay what they can afford outside reasonable living costs. An IVA has to be set up by a licensed professional called an Insolvency Practitioner (IP). All unsecured debts must be declared into an IVA. Following the PIA 2012, the only major difference between an IVA and the PIA process in Ireland is that an IVA does not include secured creditors where a PIA can include secured creditors.

Given the similarities between the processes, it is not expected that the IVA process will be availed of by many Irish individuals.

CONCLUSION

[1.11] The PIA 2012 is to be welcomed – it is certainly a step in the right direction and provides an opportunity for persons in financial difficulty to deal with their debt in a realistic manner.

The authors are of the view that the PIA 2012 should have gone further and brought Ireland into line with the UK by making available an insolvency process that takes a year. It is hoped that this will be considered in the future when the new insolvency processes are fully operational and there are some studies available on their success.

It is also felt that secured creditors are in a strong position and that the provisions in relation to secured creditors may perhaps erode the benefit of the new insolvency processes. The attitude of creditors and debtors cannot yet be ascertained and the future and success of each of the processes will depend on the approach of majority creditors.

The IVA process is a very successful system, as creditors see that the process is more beneficial than making a debtor bankrupt. It is hoped that the success of the IVA system in the UK will be replicated in this jurisdiction.

Chapter 2

INSOLVENCY SERVICE OF IRELAND (ISI)

INTRODUCTION

[2.01] At the time of the publication of the Personal Insolvency Bill 2012, the government announced the establishment of a new State body, the Insolvency Service of Ireland (ISI).

Following this announcement, the ISI, an independent statutory body, was established by the Minister for Justice and Equality, Mr Alan Shatter, TD, on 1 March 2013 under the PIA 2012 and launched on 18 April 2013. Mr Shatter has overall responsibility for the ISI.

The ISI has a key role in the delivery, monitoring and execution of all elements of the Personal Insolvency Act 2012 (PIA 2012). The main function of the ISI is the management and provision of the framework under which each of the insolvency processes outlined in the PIA 2012 will operate. This includes the monitoring of all the insolvency processes, considering the basis for application, processing applications for protective certificates, processing applications for arrangements and keeping all registers up to date. The ISI also performs the function of monitoring, authorising and regulating Approved Intermediaries (AIs) and Personal Insolvency Practitioners (PIPs).

In overseeing the personal insolvency processes the ISI will liaise with appointed debt advisers and the courts system. The ISI is funded by the Exchequer.

The ISI employs between 50 and 70 people and recruitment began at the time of its launch. Mr Lorcan O'Connor was appointed as the director-designate of the Insolvency Service of Ireland by Alan Shatter.

In order to protect the constitutional rights of the citizens engaged in the new insolvency procedures, provision has been made for the oversight of these procedures by the High Court and Circuit Court.

The principal functions of the ISI include:

(a) monitoring of arrangements relating to personal insolvency;

(b) consideration of applications for Debt Relief Notices (DRNs);

(c) maintaining registers of authorised AIs and PIPs;

(d) processing of applications for protective certificates relating to Debt Settlement Arrangements (DSAs) and Personal Insolvency Arrangements (PIAs);

(e) maintaining registers of DRNs, Protective Certificates, DSAs and PIAs;

(f) providing information to the public on workings of the legislation; and

(g) developing policy.

A brief overview of the activity of the ISI since establishment is as follows:

In April 2012 the ISI launched an information campaign about the new debt solutions for insolvent individuals. This involved the publishing of guides explaining the main features of the three new debt reliefs together with detailed sample scenarios and step-by-step guides to aid people in understanding how these new debt reliefs will work. The ISI also launched a website, an information line for the public and guidelines on a reasonable standard of living and reasonable living expenses.

In June 2012 the ISI published regulations governing the authorisation of PIPs and AIs – the people who will be offering the face to face advice and assistance to insolvent debtors. The ISI was involved in the roll out of courses by approved educational bodies for those interested in becoming PIPs and AIs.

In July 2012 the ISI began accepting and processing applications from suitably qualified individuals to act as AIs and PIPs and the Courts and Civil Law (Miscellaneous Provisions) Act 2013 was enacted which contained amendments to the Personal Insolvency Act 2012.

In August 2012 the ISI began authorising AIs and PIPs. This process is set to continue and it is expected that a sufficient number of practitioners will be authorised in due course so that a country-wide network is available to insolvent debtors in the future.

ESTABLISHMENT OF THE ISI

[2.02] The ISI[1] is a body corporate with perpetual succession and with power to:

(a) sue and be sued in its corporate name;

(b) be independent in the exercise of its functions under the PIA 2012;

(c) with the approval of the Minister, given with the consent of the Minister for Public Expenditure and Reform, acquire, hold and dispose of land or an interest in or rights over or in respect of land; and

(d) acquire, hold and dispose of any other property.

Subject to the PIA 2012, the ISI is independent in the exercise of its functions under the PIA 2012, and has all powers that are necessary or expedient for, or incidental to, the performance of those functions.[2]

The seal of the ISI may be authenticated by:

(a) the signature of the director; or

(b) the signature of a member of the staff of the ISI authorised by the ISI to act in that behalf.[3]

Judicial notice is to be taken of the seal of the ISI and every document purporting to be a document made by the ISI and purporting to be sealed with the seal of the ISI authenticated shall be received in evidence and be deemed to be such document without further proof unless the contrary is proved.[4] Any contract or instrument which is not required to be under seal can be entered into or executed on behalf of the ISI by any person generally or specially authorised by the ISI for that purpose.

1. PIA 2012, s 8.
2. PIA 2012, s 8(3).
3. PIA 2012, s 8(4).
4. PIA 2012, s 8(5).

The ISI is to be funded out of moneys provided by the Oireachtas. The amounts provided by the Oireachtas are for the purposes of expenditure by the ISI in the performance of its functions[5] as determined by the Minister with the consent of the Minister for Public Expenditure and Reform.

FUNCTIONS OF THE ISI

[2.03] As noted above, the ISI[6] plays a key role in the delivery, monitoring and execution of all elements of the PIA 2012, with one of the principal roles being the administration of the three insolvency processes. In performing this function, the ISI has a role in certifying or determining an application for a DRN,[7] certifying applications for a DSA[8] or a PIA[9] and referring the relevant documentation to the Circuit Court or the High Court.

The other principal functions of the ISI are to:

(a) monitor the operation of the arrangements relating to personal insolvency provided for in the PIA 2012;

(b) consider applications for DRNs;[10]

(c) process applications for protective certificates in respect of DSAs[11] and PIAs;[12]

(d) maintain the Personal Insolvency Registers (including the DRN Register, Protective Certificate Register, the DSA and PIA Registers and the Register of PIPs and AIs);

(e) provide information to the public on the working of the PIA 2012;

(f) advise the Minister on any matter relating to its functions;

(g) authorise persons to perform the functions of an approved intermediary under the DRN regime;[13]

(h) supervise and regulate persons or classes of persons authorised to perform the function of approved intermediary;[14]

(i) authorise individuals to carry on practice as PIPs;[15]

---

5. PIA 2012, s 21.
6. PIA 2012, s 9.
7. See **Ch 3** – Debt Relief Notices.
8. See **Ch 4** – Debt Settlement Arrangements.
9. See **Ch 5** – Personal Insolvency Arrangements.
10. See **Ch 3** para **3.15**.
11. See **Ch 4** paras **4.13** and **4.14**.
12. See **Ch 5** para **5.13** and **5.14**.
13. See SI 216 /2013 and **Ch 8** – Personal Insolvency Practitioners.
14. PIA 2012, s 9(1)(g) as amended by the Courts and Civil Law (Miscellaneous Provisions) Act 2013, s 45.
15. See **Ch 8** – Personal Insolvency Practitioners.

(j) supervise and regulate persons practising as PIPs;

(ja) subject to s 60(3) Bankruptcy Act 1988, administer the functions of the Official Assignee by the Bankruptcy Act 1988 or any other enactment;[16]

(k) perform such functions as are assigned to the Insolvency Service under Pt 5 of PIA 2012 which deals with PIPs;

(l) prepare and issue guidelines as to what constitutes a reasonable standard of living and reasonable living expenses under s 23 PIA 2012;[17]

(m) arrange for the provision of such education and training, in relation to the performance by them of their functions under the PIA 2012, of AIs, PIPs and other persons, as it thinks fit;

(n) contribute to the development of policy in the area of personal insolvency; and

(o) carry out any other duties and exercise any other powers assigned to it by or under the PIA 2012.

Under the provisions of the PIA 2012, the ISI is also entitled to disseminate, to such extent and in such manner as it considers appropriate, information relating to the services it provides under the PIA 2012.[18] It is also empowered to do anything which it considers necessary or expedient to enable it to perform its functions.[19]

Any function or responsibility of the ISI may be performed through or by the Director or any member of its staff duly authorised in that behalf by the ISI.[20] In addition, the Director or a member of staff of the ISI who performs any of its functions is presumed in any proceedings to have been authorised by it to do so on its behalf, unless the contrary is shown.[21]

COMPOSITION OF THE ISI

[2.04] The ISI[22] comprises the Director of the ISI as appointed and such members of staff of the ISI appointed under Pt 2, PIA 2012.

Director of the ISI

[2.05] The Director of the ISI[23] shall be known, and is referred to in the PIA 2012 and in this chapter, as the Director. Lorcan O'Connor took up his post in October 2012 after

16. Courts and Civil Law (Miscellaneous Provisions) Act 2013, s 38.
17. See **Ch 7** – Reasonable Living Expenses and http://www.isi.gov.ie/en/ISI/Pages/Reasonable_living_expenses.
18. PIA 2012, s 9(2).
19. PIA 2012, s 9(3).
20. PIA 2012, s 9(4).
21. PIA 2012, s 9(5).
22. PIA 2012, s 10.
23. PIA 2012, s 11.

being appointed the director-designate of the Insolvency Service of Ireland by Alan Shatter, the Minister for Justice and Equality.

The Director holds office for such period, not exceeding five years from the date of his or her appointment, or as may be determined by the Minister. A person who has held office as Director shall be eligible for re-appointment but is not entitled to hold office for periods the aggregate of which exceeds ten years.

The Director may be removed or suspended from office for stated reasons by the Minister for Justice and Equality.

The Director shall be appointed by the Minister on the recommendation of the Director of the Public Appointments Service, after a competition for that purpose under s 47 of the Public Service Management (Recruitment and Appointments) Act 2004 has been held on behalf of the Minister, and have the appropriate experience, qualifications, training and expertise for the appointment.[24]

The Director is not entitled to hold any other office or position in respect of which remuneration is payable, or carry on any business, trade or profession without the approval of the Minister.[25]

The responsibilities of the Director include:

(a) the implementation of the policies and decisions of the ISI;

(b) the management and control generally of the ISI's staff, administration and business;

(c) being responsible to the Minister for the performance of his or her functions; and

(d) to perform such other functions (if any) as may be required by the Minister or as may be authorised under the PIA 2012.[26]

The Director with the consent of the Minister is entitled to specify which functions may be performed by such member or members of the staff of the ISI as the Director authorises for that purpose. That member or those members of staff shall be accountable to the Director for the performance of any delegated functions.

The Director is accountable to the Minister for the performance of functions delegated by him or her. The Director may revoke a delegation with the written consent of the Minister.[27]

The Director must provide the Minister with such information, including financial information, in respect of the performance of the Director's functions as the Minister requires.

If the Director dies, resigns, becomes disqualified for or is removed from office, or is temporarily unable to continue to perform his or her functions for any reason, the Minister may designate such member or members of the staff of the ISI to perform the functions of the Director until, in the case of death, an appointment is made of another

24. PIA 2012, s 11(2).
25. PIA 2012, s 11(6).
26. PIA 2012, s 11(3).
27. PIA 2012, s 11(7).

Director or until such time as the Director is able to resume the performance of his or her functions, or the Minister decides to revoke or alter a designation made.[28]

Staff of the ISI

[2.06] The Minister may, after consultation with the ISI, appoint such number of persons to be members of the staff of the ISI[29] as may be approved by the Minister for Public Expenditure and Reform. Following consultation with the ISI, the Minister may, and with the consent of the Minister for Public Expenditure and Reform, determine the grades of the staff of the ISI and the numbers of staff in each grade.

Each appointment shall be on such terms and conditions relating to remuneration as the Minister determines (with the consent of the Minister for Public Expenditure and Reform). The other terms and conditions of the appointments may be determined by the ISI and approved by the Minister with the consent of the Minister for Public Expenditure and Reform.

The ISI is empowered to set superannuation schemes for both the Director and the staff of the ISI[30] with the consent of the Minster and the consent of the Minister for Public Expenditure and Reform.

STRATEGIC PLANS OF THE ISI

[2.07] The ISI as soon as is practicable from the date of establishment, being the 1 March 2013 (but not later than six months after establishment), prepare and submit to the Minister a strategic plan[31] for the ISI for the ensuing three year period. This plan must be approved by the Minister with or without amendment. The requirement is that a strategic plan is made every three years and within six months before the anniversary of the establishment day (ie between 1 September and 1 March).

The strategic plan must comply with any directions issued from time to time by the Minister in respect of the form and manner of the plan's preparation, and set out the key objectives, outputs and related strategies of the ISI, including the use of resources, and, finally, have regard to the need to ensure the most beneficial, effective and efficient use of the ISI's resources.[32]

Once the strategic plan has been approved, the Minister must cause a copy of the strategic plan to be laid before each House of the Oireachtas.

---

28. PIA 2012, s 11(11).
29. PIA 2012, s 12.
30. PIA 2012, s 13.
31. PIA 2012, s 14.
32. PIA 2012, s 14(2).

BUSINESS PLANS OF THE ISI

[2.08] Each year the ISI must both prepare and adopt a business plan in respect of that year and submit the plan to the Minister.[33] The Minister is entitled to change the period for which the business plan must be adopted.

There are certain requirements for the business plan. Each business plan must conform to the following:

(a) be prepared in the form and manner of and in accordance with any directions given by the Minister (including any timescale in which the plan must be submitted to the Minister);

(b) indicate the activities of the ISI for the period to which the business plan relates;

(c) contain estimates of the number of employees of the ISI for the period and the business to which the plan relates;

(d) contain any other information specified by the Minister; and

(e) accord with policies and objectives of the Minister and the government as they relate to the functions of the ISI.

In preparing the business plan, the ISI must have regard to the current strategic plan in operation at the time of making the business plan.[34]

The ISI must submit together with the business plan a statement of its estimate of the income and expenditure relating to the plan that is consistent with the moneys estimated to be available to the ISI for the period to which the business plan relates.[35]

REPORTS BY THE ISI

[2.09] Within four months of the end of the financial year, the ISI has to make a written report (in this section referred to as the 'annual report') to the Minister on the performance of the functions of the ISI during that year.[36]

The financial year is the period between the date of establishment and the following 31 December.

The report will be in the form and shall include information in respect of such matters as the ISI thinks appropriate or as the Minister may direct.

In addition to the final report, the ISI is entitled to make any other reports that it considers appropriate for drawing to the Minister's attention matters relating to the functions of the ISI that have come to its notice and that, in its opinion, should, because of their gravity or other exceptional circumstances, be the subject of a special report to

33. PIA 2012, s 15.

34. PIA 2012, s 15(3).

35. PIA 2012, s 15(4).

36. PIA 2012, s 16.

the Minister. The ISI is also required to make a report on any matter if so requested by the Minister.

The ISI must publish its annual report as soon as it is completed in such form and manner as it considers appropriate.

The ISI is under obligation to give to the Minister any information the Minister may require in respect of the performance by the ISI of its functions and its policies in respect of such performance or any specific document or account prepared by it, or the annual report or any report referred to above.

The annual report must be laid before the House of the Oireachtas by the Minister within twenty-one days of the plan being submitted.[37]

The ISI, as soon as is practicable after copies of the annual report are laid before the Houses of the Oireachtas, must ensure that the plan is published in accordance with such arrangements as the Minister may specify.[38]

ACCOUNTS AND AUDIT OF THE ISI

[2.10] The ISI is obliged to submit estimates of income and expenditure[39] to the Minister in such form, in respect of such periods and at such times as may be specified by the Minister, and provide to the Minister any information which the Minister may require regarding those estimates and also regarding the proposals and plans of the ISI in respect of a period specified by the Minister.[40]

With regard to the keeping of financial records, the ISI must keep in such form and in respect of such accounting periods as may be approved of by the Minister (with the consent of the Minister for Public Expenditure and Reform) all proper and usual accounts of moneys received and spent by the ISI, including an income and expenditure account and a balance sheet[41] and relating to the functions of the Official Assignee under the Bankruptcy Act 1988.[42]

The submission and approval of the accounts[43] will follow the process set out below:

(a) The accounts of the ISI are to be approved by the ISI as soon as practicable (but not later than 3 months after the end of the accounting period to which they relate) and submitted by it to the Comptroller and Auditor General for audit;

(b) A copy of the accounts and the report of the Comptroller and Auditor General on the accounts must then be presented to the Minister as soon as practicable and a copy of the accounts and report must then be laid before each house of the Oireachtas.

37. PIA 2012, s 16(6).
38. PIA 2012, s 16(7).
39. PIA 2012, s 17.
40. PIA 2012, s 17(1).
41. PIA 2012, s 17(2).
42. Courts and Civil Law (Miscellaneous Provisions) Act 2013, s 39.
43. PIA 2012, s 17(3).

The Director will at any time when required by Dáil Éireann give evidence as to the regularity and propriety of the transactions recorded; or prepare any book or record for examination; or give evidence as to the economy and efficiency of the ISI in the use of resources, the systems, procedures and practices employed by the ISI for the purpose of evaluating the effectiveness of its operations, and any matter affecting the ISI referred to in a special report of the Comptroller and Auditor General.[44]

Accounts which are required to be maintained by the Official Assignee under the Bankruptcy Act 1988 in relation to the estates of bankrupts or in respect of unclaimed dividends shall be kept in such a manner that monies or securities or interest accrued or earned thereon in relation to the estates of bankrupts or unclaimed dividends are not intermingled with monies otherwise held by the ISI.[45]

POWER TO CHARGE AND RECOVER FEES

[2.11] The Minister is empowered to make regulations[46] as to the fees to be paid to the ISI and when they fall due in respect of the performance of functions, the provision of services, and the carrying on of its activities and the performance of the functions of the Official Assignee under the Bankruptcy Act 1988.[47]

The power of the ISI to prescribe fees includes the power to provide for exemptions from the payment of fees, or waiving, remitting or refunding fees (in whole or in part), in whatever circumstances or cases.[48]

Any such fees received by the ISI shall be paid into or disposed of for the benefit of the Exchequer in such manner as the Minister for Public Expenditure and Reform directs. These fees may be recovered by the ISI as a simple contract debt in any court of competent jurisdiction. The fee is recoverable from a person by whom the fee is payable and is any amount due and owing to the ISI in respect of a fee charged under this section.

Under SI 246/2013[49] the ISI exercised the powers conferred on it under this section to make the following regulations:

(a) the amount of €1,500 is prescribed as the fee payable to the ISI for the authorisation of a PIP; and

(b) the amount of €1,000 is prescribed as the fee payable to the ISI for the renewal of such authorisation.

44. PIA 2012, s 18.
45. Courts and Civil Law (Miscellaneous Provisions) Act 2013, s 39.
46. PIA 2012, s 20.
47. Courts and Civil Law (Miscellaneous Provisions) Act 2013, s 40.
48. PIA 2012, s 20(2).
49. Personal Insolvency Act 2012 (Personal Insolvency Practitioner Authorisation and Renewal of Prescribed Fees) Regulations 2013 (SI 246/2013).

Under SI 329/2013,[50] the ISI exercised the powers conferred on it and prescribed the following fees:

(a) the amount of €100 is prescribed as the fee payable to the ISI to make an application for a DRN pursuant to s 29(2) PIA 2012;

(b) the amount of €250 is prescribed as the fee payable to the ISI to make an application for a Protective Certificate in a DSA pursuant to s 59(2) PIA 2012;

(c) the amount of €500 is prescribed as the fee payable to the ISI to make an application for a Protective Certificate in a PIA pursuant to s 93(2) PIA 2012.

Under the new s 21A PIA 2012,[51] notwithstanding the Data Protection Act 1988, the ISI is entitled to retain any information or data obtained by it under the PIA 2012 as is necessary for the performance of its functions.

REGISTER OF AIS AND PIPS

[2.12] The ISI is obliged to establish and maintain registers[52] in relation to authorised PIPs and AIs. The Register is in the form determined by the ISI and contains information such as the name, address, area, authorisation number, e-mail address, telephone number and date of authorisation of each authorised PIP or AI.[53]

The ISI is entitled to extend the information on the Register to include other identifying particulars and other information so far as the ISI deem it appropriate (for example – suspension of authorisation of PIP or AI). The Register is available for inspection by the public on the ISI website.[54] The ISI has the responsibility of keeping the Register accurate. A PIP is obliged to notify the ISI where there is incorrect information contained in the Register or where there is a change in the circumstances of the PIP affecting the Register.

REGISTER OF DRNS

[2.13] The information to be contained in the Register of DRNs[55] is as follows:[56]

(a) the appropriate court's record number relating to the DRN;

(b) the alias of the debtor (if any);

(c) the year of the debtor's birth;

50. Personal Insolvency Act 2012 (Prescribed Fees) Regulations 2013 (SI 329/2013).

51. Courts and Civil Law (Miscellaneous Provisions) Act 2013, s 47.

52. PIA 2012, s 162.

53. http://www.isi.gov.ie/en/ISI/Pages/Registers.

54. http://www.isi.gov.ie/en/ISI/Pages/Registers.

55. http://www.isi.gov.ie/en/ISI/Pages/Registers.

56. Personal Insolvency Act 2012 (Additional Information to be Contained in Registers) Regulations 2013 (SI 356/2013).

(d) the start date of the supervision period (being the date on which the issue of the Debt Relief Notice by the appropriate court is recorded by the ISI in the Register of Debt Relief Notices under s 33(4) of the PIA 2012);

(e) the end date of the supervision period (noting that this date is subject to change in accordance with the Act);

(f) the appropriate court, and where this is the Circuit Court, the circuit of the Circuit Court;

(g) the address and telephone and/or email contact details of the ISI.

REGISTER OF PROTECTIVE CERTIFICATES

[2.14] The information to be contained in the Register of Protective Certificates[57] is as follows:[58]

(a) the appropriate court's record number relating to the protective certificate;

(b) the type of arrangement (DSA or PIA) relating to the protective certificate;

(c) the alias of the debtor (if any);

(d) the year of the debtor's birth;

(e) the appropriate court, and where this is the Circuit Court, the circuit of the Circuit Court;

(f) the name, address and telephone and/or email contact details of the relevant PIP;

(g) the address and telephone and/or email contact details of the ISI.

REGISTER OF DSAS

[2.15] The information to be contained in the Register of DSAs[59] is as follows:[60]

(a) the appropriate court's record number relating to the DSA;

(b) the debtor's name;

(c) the alias of the debtor (if any);

(d) the debtor's address;

(e) the year of the debtor's birth;

(f) the date on which the proposed DSA was approved at a creditors' meeting;

57. http://www.isi.gov.ie/en/ISI/Pages/Registers.

58. Personal Insolvency Act 2012 (Additional Information to be Contained in Registers) Regulations 2013 (SI 356/2013).

59. http://www.isi.gov.ie/en/ISI/Pages/Registers.

60. Personal Insolvency Act 2012 (Additional Information to be Contained in Registers) Regulations 2013 (SI 356/2013).

(g) the date on which the coming into effect of the DSA was approved by the appropriate court;

(h) the start date of the DSA (being the date on which the DSA comes into effect);

(i) the scheduled end date of the DSA;

(j) when known, the actual end date of the DSA;

(k) the appropriate court, and where this is the Circuit Court, the circuit of the Circuit Court;

(l) where applicable, the date on which the proposed variation to the DSA was approved at a creditors' meeting;

(m) where applicable, the date on which the coming into effect of the DSA as varied was approved by the appropriate court;

(n) where applicable, the date on which the DSA as varied comes into effect;

(o) the outcome of the DSA, which shall be recorded in the Register of DSAs as one of the following –

  (i) successful completion,

  (ii) early termination by court,

  (iii) failure after six months' arrears default,

  (iv) other failure;

(p) the name, address and telephone and/or email contact details of the relevant PIP;

(q) the address and telephone and/or email contact details of the ISI.

REGISTER OF PIAS

[2.16] The information to be contained in the Register of PIAs[61] is as follows:[62]

(a) the appropriate court's record number relating to the PIA;

(b) the debtor's name;

(c) the alias of the debtor (if any);

(d) the debtor's address;

(e) the year of the debtor's birth;

(f) the date on which the proposed PIA was approved at a creditors' meeting;

(g) the date on which the coming into effect of the PIA was approved by the appropriate court;

(h) the start date of the PIA (being the date on which the PIA comes into effect);

61. http://www.isi.gov.ie/en/ISI/Pages/Registers.

62. Personal Insolvency Act 2012 (Additional Information to be Contained in Registers) Regulations 2013 (SI 356/2013).

(i) the scheduled end date of the PIA;

(j) when known, the actual end date of the PIA;

(k) the appropriate court, and where this is the Circuit Court, the circuit of the Circuit Court;

(l) where applicable, the date on which the proposed variation to the PIA was approved at a creditors' meeting;

(m) where applicable, the date on which the coming into effect of the PIA as varied was approved by the appropriate court;

(n) where applicable, the date on which the PIA as varied comes into effect;

(o) the outcome of the PIA which shall be recorded in the Register of PIAs as one of the following –

    (i) successful completion,

    (ii) early termination by court,

    (iii) failure after six months' arrears default,

    (iv) other failure;

(p) the name, address and telephone and/or email contact details of the relevant PIP;

(q) the address and telephone and/or email contact details of the ISI.

POWER OF ISI TO DEAL WITH DOCUMENTS

[2.17] Where the ISI refuses to renew an authorisation[63] to carry on practice as a PIP or where an authorisation is suspended or revoked and the ISI is of the opinion that adequate arrangements have not been made in relation to the handing over of documents to another PIP, the ISI, by notice in writing given to the PIP, may require the PIP to produce such documents to a person appointed by the ISI.[64]

Where a PIP does not comply with this notice, the ISI may apply to the Circuit Court in a summary manner, on notice to the PIP, for an order requiring the person to comply within a specified period and the court may make the order it deems appropriate.

Where the ISI takes possession of documents under the procedures outlined above, it must serve on the PIP by whom the documents were produced a notice giving particulars of the documents and the date of taking possession thereof and it must make sure reasonable enquiries to ensure that the person taking possession or control of the documents may deal with the documents.

Where a person has been served a notice requiring possession of the documents it may, within 14 days of the receipt of such notice, apply in a summary manner to the Circuit Court for an order directing the ISI to return the documents and the Circuit Court may make such an order or such other order as it deems appropriate.

63. See **Ch 8** – Personal Insolvency Practitioners.

64. PIA 2012, s 175.

Any such application to the Circuit Court shall be made to the judge of that court for the circuit in which the PIP resides or ordinarily carries on within the previous three years' practice as a PIP.

Chapter 3

DEBT RELIEF NOTICES

INTRODUCTION

[3.01] The purpose of a Debt Relief Notice (DRN) is to give relief from debt to people who are in debt and who have little or no disposable income or assets which they could use to pay what they owe. Typical creditors or debts included in a DRN will be credit/store cards; credit union; personal loans or overdrafts; and utility bills.

A DRN provides for the write off of qualifying debts which are not greater than €20,000 for persons with no assets and no income, who are insolvent and have no realistic prospect of being able to pay their debts within the ensuing five years. The period of protection (known as the period of supervision) is for three years and upon completion of a DRN then the specified debtor stands discharged from the specified qualifying debts. This process allows people who have debts of not greater than €20,000 but no assets and no possibility of becoming solvent in the ensuing five years to deal with their debt crisis, providing an opportunity for a clean start. Creditors whose debts are included in the process do not have a say in the process and the only mechanism for objection is during the supervision period.

GENERAL ELIGIBILITY CRITERIA

[3.02]

Qualifying Criteria	**Disqualifying Criteria**
A debtor is insolvent in they are unable to pay their debts in full as they fall due and there is no likelihood of them doing so within three years	25% or more of the debts must not have been incurred during the six months prior to making the application
The debtor's net monthly disposable income is less than €60 after reasonable living expenses (calculated by the Approved Intermediary [AI] on a case by case basis using a standard template)[1]	The debtor must not have used a DRN previously
The debtor's qualifying debts[2] are less than €20,000	The debtor must not have been the subject of a Debt Settlement Arrangement (DSA) or a Personal Insolvency Arrangement (PIA) within the past five years

1. See **Ch 7** – Reasonable Living Expenses.
2. See para **3.04** – Eligibility for Debt Relief Notice.

Qualifying Criteria	Disqualifying Criteria
The debtor must not have assets valued at greater than €400 (one item of jewellery valued at less than €750, one motor vehicle valued at less than €2,000 and reasonably necessary household items, equipment/tools of a business valued at less than €6,000 are disregarded in determining the debtor's assets)	The debtor must not have been the subject of a protective certificate issued in respect of a DSA or PIA in the previous year
The debtor must be domiciled in the Republic of Ireland, or must have ordinarily resided or had a place of business within the Republic of Ireland within the previous year	The debtor must not have entered into certain transactions at less than market value in the previous two years
The debtor must complete a Prescribed Financial Statement (PFS) and have made a statutory declaration of its truth and accuracy	The debtor must not have given preferential treatment to one creditor over another in the previous two years
An AI must have signed a statement of satisfaction as to the debtor's eligibility and the truth and accuracy of the PFS	The debtor must not be bankrupt or subject to a bankruptcy measure or have been discharged from bankruptcy in the previous five years

A STEP-BY-STEP SUMMARY OF THE PROCESS

[3.03]

Step 1 The debtor contacts an AI from the list available on the Insolvency Service of Ireland (ISI) website.[3]

Step 2 The insolvent debtor provides the AI with information on his finances and financial circumstances.

Step 3 The AI meets with the debtor and discusses the debtor's situation and eligibility to apply for a DRN based on the information supplied and gives him advice of his options. The AI will detail the DRN application process and outline the debtor's duties and obligations in the process. The AI should provide written advice setting out their opinion on whether the DRN is the best insolvency arrangement available to the debtor together with any reasons for advising same. In circumstances where the DRN process is not suitable for the debtor, the AI should provide advice on alternative insolvency arrangement options.

Step 4 Once the debtor decides he wishes to proceed then he must indicate this intention in writing to the AI and request that the AI act on the debtor's behalf.

Step 5 The debtor must then provide all his financial information and supporting documentation to the AI whereupon the AI will assist the debtor in completing the Prescribed Financial Statement (PFS). There will be a meeting/series of meetings and/or phone calls with the AI to progress the application.

Step 6 The AI will examine the completed PFS and where it is satisfied that the PFS is true and accurate and that the debtor satisfies the eligibility criteria the AI will provide a statement, inter alia, that he is of the opinion that the DRN would facilitate the debtor becoming solvent in a period of five years or more.

Step 7 The debtor will be required to sign a statutory declaration affirming that the PFS is a complete and accurate statement of the debtor's assets, liabilities, income and expenditure.

Step 8 The debtor will be required to complete and sign the following documentation required to accompany the application for a DRN:

(a) a copy of the statement made by the AI referred to above;

(b) a document signed by the debtor confirming satisfaction with the eligibility criteria for a DRN;

(c) a completed PFS form and statutory declaration;

(d) the prescribed fee of €100;

(e) a schedule of the debtor's creditors and amount owed to each; whether the creditor is a secured creditor or not (if secured, details must be provided of any security); where a debt is an excludable debt, a statement of whether it is a permitted debt;

(f) the debtor's written consent to enable –

(i) the AI to disclose personal data to the ISI,

(ii) the ISI to process the application,

(iii) the ISI to make any necessary enquiries about the debtor, and

(iv) the ISI to disclose the debtor's personal data to the creditors concerned, as required;

(g) A document signed by the debtor stating whether they are aware of any judgment or court order in force against them which relates to any of the debts which are included in the DRN.

Step 9 An application is then made to the ISI by the AI on behalf of the debtor. The ISI can then make enquiries as it deems necessary as to the information and documents provided. Once satisfied that the debtor has complied with the criteria then it can issue a certificate that the application is in order and will forward the application to the Circuit Court.

3. http://www.isi.gov.ie/en/ISI/Pages/Registers.

Step 10 The Circuit Court will review the application and once the court is satisfied that the necessary criteria are satisfied, the application will be approved and the court will issue a DRN.

Step 11 Where the DRN is issued, the ISI will notify the AI of the issue of the DRN. The details of the DRN will be placed on an electronic public Register of Debt Relief Notices.

From the date of the issue of the DRN there will be a three year supervision period. During that time the creditors listed in the DRN cannot pursue the debtor for any debts owed provided they are specified in the DRN. This does not apply to secured creditors.

Any aggrieved debtor or creditor during the DRN process may apply to the court. Where a creditor objects to a debt being included in the DRN, then he can apply to the court to have it excluded.

Once the DRN ceases then the debtor is discharged from the specified qualifying debts.

ELIGIBILITY FOR DEBT RELIEF NOTICE

[3.04] In order to qualify for a DRN the specified debtor must satisfy eligibility criteria as set out in the PIA 2012. The eligibility criteria set down in the PIA 2012 are as follows.

The debtor, on the application date:[4]

Qualifying Debts

Has qualifying debts that amount to €20,000 or less

[3.05] For the purposes of applying for a DRN a qualifying debt is defined as a debt other than an excluded debt and

(a) includes the following:

- (i) credit card debt;
- (ii) an overdraft or an unsecured loan from a bank or other entity regulated by the Central Bank of Ireland which carries on business in the State and is regulated by the Central Bank of Ireland;
- (iii) debt for payment of one or more than one bill in respect of rent, utilities or telephone;
- (iv) liquidated debts incurred by the debtor as surety for another person;

and

(b) includes secured debt,[5] as may be included but shall not affect the right of the secured creditor to enforce or otherwise deal with his security.

4. PIA 2012, s 26.
5. A secured debt means a debt the payment for which is secured by security in or over any asset or property of any kind.

Effectively a qualifying debt is any unsecured debt which is particularised in s 25 PIA 2012 subject to a number of exceptions. It can include secured debt but again this is regulated by s 35(9) and s 46 PIA 2012.

There are two types of debt that may be excluded as qualifying debt and these are divided into two different categories. The first type of debt is an 'excludable debt' which is a debt that requires the consent of a creditor to be included. Once creditor consent is obtained, the debt becomes an included debt. In circumstances where creditor consent has been sought and the creditor does not respond, the creditor will be deemed to have consented and the debt becomes an included debt. The second category of debt is an 'excluded debt' which is a debt that will never form a debt that is part of the DRN process.

Debts excludable as qualifying debts:

(a) any liability arising out of any tax, duty, levy or other charge owed or payable to the State;

(b) any amount payable by the debtor under the Local Government (Charges) Act 2009;

(c) any amount payable by the debtor under the Local Government (Household Charge) Act 2011;

(d) rates due to the local authority (within the meaning of the Local Government Act 2001);

(e) any debt or liability in respect of moneys advanced to the debtor by the Health Service Executive under the Nursing Homes Support Scheme Act 2009;

(f) any debt due by the debtor to any owners' management company in respect of annual service charges under s 18 of the Multi-Unit Developments Act 2011 or contributions due under s 19 of that Act;

(g) any debt or liability of the debtor arising under the Social Welfare Consolidation Act 2005.

Debts that are excluded as qualifying debts:

(h) any liability arising out of a domestic support order;

(i) any liability arising out of damages awarded by a court (or other competent authority) in respect of personal injuries or wrongful death arising from the tort of the debtor;

(j) any debt or liability arising from a loan (or forbearance of a loan) obtained through fraud, misappropriation, embezzlement or fraudulent breach of trust;

(k) any debt or liability of the debtor arising by virtue of a court order made under the Proceeds of Crime Acts 1996 and 2005 or by virtue of a fine ordered to be paid by a court in respect of a criminal offence.

Set Off

[3.06] In determining the amount or value of any asset of a debtor or the amount of any debt due to a creditor, where there are mutual credits or debts as between a debtor and a creditor, one debt or demand may be set off against the other and only the balance found owing shall be considered to be a debt or an asset on one side or the other.[6] The effect of this provision is that it is the net overall figure that the debtor owes the creditor which is included in the DRN process rather than a number of different debts owed by the debtor to the same creditor.

Disposable Income

Has 'net disposable income' of €60 or less a month

[3.07]

(a) 'Net disposable income'[7] means the income available to a debtor after payment of reasonable household expenses and payments in respect of excluded debts (if any), and

(b) when calculating a debtor's disposable income there are a certain number of deductions from the income available to the debtor.

The following income should be included in calculating the debtor's available income –

(i) his salary or wages,

(ii) the welfare benefits (other than child benefit) of which he is in receipt,

(iii) his income from a pension,

(iv) contributions from other household members, and

(v) any other income available to him.

The following deductions (where applicable) should be deducted from the available income calculated above to arrive at the debtor's net disposable income –

(vi) his or her reasonable living expenses,[8]

(vii) income tax payable by the debtor,

(viii) social insurance contributions payable by the debtor,

(ix) payments made by the debtor in respect of excluded debts,

(x) payments made by the debtor in respect of excludable debts that are not permitted debts,

(xi) such other levies and charges on the debtor's income as may be prescribed.

6. PIA 2012, ss 135 and 26(3).
7. PIA 2012, s 26(2)(b) and (5).
8. See **Ch 7** – Reasonable Living Expenses.

Debtor's Assets

Has assets worth €400 or less

[3.08]

(a) In calculating a debtor's assets the value of an asset shall be taken to be its market value irrespective of any mortgage or charge to which it is subject;[9]

(b) The following should be taken into account –

(i) Savings

Set off – When arriving at the value when determining the amount or value of any asset of a debtor or the amount of any debt due to a creditor, where there are mutual credits or debts as between a debtor and a creditor, one debt or demand may be set off against the other and only the balance found owing shall be considered to be a debt or an asset on one side or the other;[10]

(ii) Motor Vehicles

Exclusion – But excluding one motor vehicle belonging to him where that vehicle is reasonably necessary in order for him to carry out his everyday activities and that vehicle is worth €2,000 or less, or where the debtor has a disability and the motor vehicle has been specially designed or adapted for use solely by him[11] (there is no upper limit specified in these exceptional circumstances);

(iii) Shares

(iv) Property (real and personal)

(c) The following should not be taken into account –

(i) the following items to a total value that does not exceed €6,000

(A) essential household equipment and appliances that are reasonably necessary to maintain a reasonable standard of living for the debtor and his or her dependants,

(B) books, tools and other items of equipment used by the debtor that are reasonably necessary in his employment, business or vocation,

(ii) one motor vehicle as set out above,

(iii) one item of personal jewellery to a value not exceeding €750 or such other value as the Minister may prescribe, where the cost of purchase of that item is not included in the qualifying debts,

(iv) where the debtor or his or her dependant is attending a course of primary or second-level education, books, materials and other items of equipment

---

9. PIA 2012, s 26(6).

10. PIA 2012, ss 135 and 26(3).

11. PIA 2012, s 26(6)(c)(iii).

that are reasonably necessary to enable the debtor or that dependant to participate in and complete that course,

(v) where a person is retired and is receiving payments from a pension fund, the payments shall be regarded as income rather than an asset.

Debtor's Domicile

[3.09] The debtor must be domiciled in the State or within one year before the application dated has ordinarily:

(a) resided in the State; or

(b) had a place of business in the State.

Debtor's Insolvency

[3.10] The debtor must be insolvent with no likelihood of becoming solvent within the period of three years commencing on the application date, while maintaining a reasonable standard of living for himself and his or her dependants;

When considering the factors to be taken into account of whether someone is insolvent or not the following must be considered:[12]

(a) the current liabilities of the debtor;

(b) the contingent and prospective liabilities of the debtor and (insofar as ascertainable) the times at which such liabilities will become due for payment; and

(c) the current and prospective assets and income of the debtor; and

(d) any items included in the guidelines issued under s 23 PIA 2012 in relation to reasonable living expenses.[13]

Historical Transactions

[3.11] The debtor must not in the preceding two years have:

(a) entered into a transaction with any person at an undervalue that has materially contributed to the debtor's inability to pay his or her debts (other than any debts due to the person with whom the debtor entered the transaction at an undervalue); or

(b) given preference to any person that has had the effect of substantially reducing the amount available to the debtor for the payment of his or her debts (other than any debts due to the person who received the preference).

12. PIA 2012, s 26(7).

13. See **Ch 7** – Reasonable Living Expenses.

Ineligibility Criteria

[3.12] A debtor is ineligible for a DRN by virtue of matters set out in sub-s (8). A debtor is ineligible for a DRN where:

(a) he has, before the application date been a specified debtor. A 'specified debtor' is defined, pursuant to s 25 of PIA 2012, as a person who has been the subject of a DRN;

(b) he has applied for a protective certificate in that period of 12 months ending on the application date;

(c) he, as a debtor, is, as of the application date, a party to a DSA or a PIA which is in effect;

(d) he, as a debtor, successfully completed a DSA or a PIA within a period of five years ending on the application date, ie five years back from the application date;

(e) he has applied for bankruptcy and the petition concerned has not been adjudicated before the application date;

This section shall not apply where the petition concerned[14] –

(i) has not been presented before the date on which the application for the DRN is determined,

(ii) has been so presented, but proceedings on the petition have been finally disposed of before that date, or

(iii) has been so presented and proceedings in relation to the petition remain before the High Court at that date, but the court has referred the person for the purposes of making an application for a DRN, DSA or PIA;

(f) a creditor has, before the application date, petitioned to make the person bankrupt but the hearing concerned has not yet taken place. This section shall not apply where the petition concerned –

(i) has not been presented before the date on which the application for the DRN is determined,

(ii) has been so presented, but proceedings on the petition have been finally disposed of before that date, or

(iii) has been so presented and proceedings in relation to the petition remain before the court at that date, but the making of an application for a DRN has been consented to by the creditor or the person who presented the petition on the creditor's behalf.

(g) he has, before the application date, been adjudicated bankrupt and the adjudication has not been annulled or discharged;

(h) he is, as of the date of the application, an undischarged bankrupt;

14. PIA 2012, s 26(12).

(i) he is, as of the application date, a discharged bankrupt subject to a bankruptcy payments order;

(j) he is, as a debtor, subject as of the application date to an arrangement under the control of the court under Pt IV of the Bankruptcy Act 1988 (ie a scheme of arrangement);

(k) he has been discharged from bankruptcy within the period of five years ending on the application date.

THE DRN PROCESS

Preliminary Process with AI

[3.13] A debtor who wishes to become a specified debtor shall submit to an AI a written statement disclosing all of the debtor's financial affairs, which statement shall include:[15]

(a) such information in relation to his creditors, his debts and other liabilities and his assets, as may be prescribed; and

(b) such other information as may be prescribed.

Please see below for full details of the financial details to be provided by the debtor.

Once the debtor decides that he wishes to proceed with a DRN application then he must confirm this intention in writing to the AI.[16] The PIA 2012 specifies that once the debtor has made the decision to proceed with the DRN application then he must make full disclosure to the DRN of his financial affairs.[17]

The debtor should provide the PIP with a written statement[18] setting out the following in so far as the debtor can reasonably ascertain and the relevant information is applicable to the debtor:

(a) the full name and address and email or telephone contact details of the debtor's creditors;

(b) a full description of the debtor's debts and other liabilities;

(c) whether each of these debts and other liabilities are secured debts or unsecured debts;

(d) the amount of each debt or other liability (including principal, interest, costs and arrears) due to each of the debtor's creditors at the date of the written statement;

(e) any contingent and prospective debts or other liabilities of the debtor (including any guarantee or similar commitment signed by the debtor in respect of any

15. PIA 2012, s 27.

16. PIA 2012, s 27(3).

17. PIA 2012, s 27(4).

18. Personal Insolvency Act 2012 (Written Statement Disclosing All of the Debtor's Financial Affairs) Regulations 2013 (SI 312/2013).

other person) and the times at which such debts or other liabilities will become due for payment;

(f) a full description of the current and prospective assets of the debtor;

(g) the address or location of these assets;

(h) where the assets comprise real property, whether the debtor's title is freehold, leasehold or other;

(i) whether these assets are held jointly or collectively with any other person and, if held collectively, the debtor's ownership percentage or other interest;

(j) the financial institution and account details where any of these assets are held;

(k) in the case of assets which may give rise to income to the debtor or are shares or other securities, the name and address of the obligor or issuer; and

(l) the purchase date, original cost and current market value of each asset.

A debtor shall provide full details, including any documentary evidence, of the efforts made by him or her to reach an alternative payment arrangement with his or her creditors or any of them where this applies.

A debtor shall also provide full details of his or her monthly income and monthly expenditure for the purposes of the PIA 2012 and such details shall include:

(a) a breakdown as between the different items of income and expenditure;

(b) an averaging of the income and expenditure on a monthly basis where the income is not received or the expenditure made on a monthly basis;

(c) where income or expenditure is received or made other than on an individual basis by the debtor, details of any joint or collective arrangements which apply in respect of such income or expenditure.

The debtor must also give its written consent to the AI to make an enquiry as the AI considers appropriate to verify the value of the debt or other liability disclosed by the debtor and also to the disclosure by the AI of personal data of the debtor to pursue such enquiry.[19]

In respect of the information to be provided by the debtor there is an obligation on the debtor to act in good faith and to co-operate fully in the process.[20]

Furthermore the debtor must:[21]

(a) make full and honest disclosure to the AI of all his assets, income and liabilities and of all other circumstances that are relevant to the process;

(b) comply with any reasonable request from the AI to provide assistance, documents and information, including any debt, tax, employment, business, social welfare or other financial records necessary for the application of the process to the debtor's case or the performance of the AI's functions, and

19. PIA 2012, s 27(4) as amended.

20. PIA 2012, s 27(7).

21. PIA 2012, s 27(8).

ensure that, to the best of his knowledge, the PFS completed is true and accurate.

On receipt of the information provided, the AI shall examine the information provided and he shall assist the debtor in completing the PFS.[22] The AI is entitled to make such enquiry as it considers appropriate to verify the value of the debt or other liability disclosed by the debtor. The debtor who receives such enquiry by the AI must furnish the information within 21 days of the making of the enquiry. Where the debtor does not furnish the information, the AI is entitled to presume the value of the debt or other liability is that disclosed by the debtor.[23]

At this preliminary juncture, the AI is only providing provisional advice as to the debtor's eligibility for the DRN process and full disclosure will only be required on furnishing his views in writing. Once the AI has received all necessary information, the AI must then meet the debtor and at that meeting he must provide the debtor with the following information and advice:[24]

(a) Whether the debtor satisfies the eligibility criteria;

(b) The general effect of making an application for a DRN and the consequences including any adverse consequences for the debtor in the event of him becoming a specified debtor, ie obtaining a DRN;

(c) The other option or options available (if any) to him for addressing his financial difficulties, including, in particular, becoming a party to a DSA, PIA or bankruptcy and the general effect of choosing one or more than one of those options;

(d) The fee of €100 for making a DRN application.[25]

Prescribed Financial Statement (PFS)

[3.14] Every applicant for one of the new arrangements is required to complete a PFS with the help of an Approved Intermediary (AI), for a DRN, or Personal Insolvency Practitioner (PIP), for a DSA or PIA. The PFS will enable the AI or PIP to determine which (if any) one of the three new arrangements is most suitable in any particular case.

The PFS will be used primarily:

(a) to establish the applicant's eligibility for an arrangement;

(b) to form the basis for calculating a sustainable contribution which the applicant will pay to his creditors over the period of the arrangement (for a DSA/PIA); and

(c) to identify those liabilities from which the applicant will be discharged at the end of an arrangement.

---

22. PIA 2012, s 27(5).
23. PIA 2012, s 27(9) and (10) as amended.
24. PIA 2012, s 27(2).
25. Personal Insolvency Act 2012 (Prescribed Fees) Regulations 2013 (SI 329/2013).

The PFS will fully disclose all of the debtor's financial affairs (ie assets, liabilities, income and expenditure).

This is a written statement which shall include full details of the debtor's:

(a) income

(b) expenditure

(c) creditors

(d) debts and other liabilities

(e) assets

(f) additional information which may be required by the ISI

(g) guarantees (if any) given by the debtor in respect of a debt of another person

The actual format of this PFS written statement[26] is now available pursuant to Personal Insolvency Act 2012 (Prescribed Financial Statement) Regulations 2013 (SI 326/2013).

The PFS will be annexed to a statutory declaration which must be witnessed by a notary public, Commissioner for Oaths, Peace Commissioner or a practising solicitor.

On completion of the PFS, the AI must prepare a statement stating that he is of the opinion that:

(a) the information contained in the debtor's PFS is complete and accurate;

(b) the debtor satisfies the eligibility criteria; and

(c) having regard to the debtor's circumstances as set out in the PFS, it is appropriate for the debtor to apply for a DRN as there is a reasonable prospect that the issue of such a notice in respect of the debtor would facilitate the debtor becoming solvent within a period of not more than five years.

An application is then made to the ISI.

Application to the ISI for a DRN

[3.15] An application to the ISI can only be made if a debtor has confirmed in writing to the AI that he wishes to apply for a DRN[27] and the application can only be made by an AI who has provided a statement stating that he believes the information provided is accurate, that the debtor satisfies the eligibility criteria and that it is his belief that the DRN would facilitate the debtor becoming solvent within a period of not more than five years[28] (ie a statement pursuant to s 27(6)).

The application to the ISI shall be in the form prescribed by the ISI under Personal Insolvency Act 2012 (Prescribed Debt Relief Notice Application Form) Regulations

26. See **Appendix 1** – Prescribed Financial Statement: http://www.isi.gov.ie/en/ISI/PFS.pdf/Files/PFS.pdf.
27. PIA 2012, s 27(3).
28. PIA 2012, s 28(1).

2013 (SI 333/2013) [29] and shall be accompanied by the fee prescribed under SI 329/2013[30] of €100 and the following documentation:

(a) a copy of the statement made by the AI (the s 27(6) statement);

(b) a document signed by the debtor confirming that he satisfied the eligibility criteria (as set out in s 26(2));

(c) the PFS;

(d) a statutory declaration by debtor confirming the PFS is a complete and accurate statement of the debtor's assets, liabilities, income and expenditure;

(e) a schedule of the debtor's debts and creditors concerned stating in relation to each such creditor –

   (i) the amount due to that creditor,

   (ii) whether the creditor concerned is a secured creditor and, if so, the details of any security held in respect of the debt concerned;

(f) a consent in writing signed by the debtor confirming that he consents to disclosure and processing of his personal data to and by the ISI and creditors to such an extent as may be necessary in connection with the DRN process;

(g) confirmation by the debtor that the ISI may carry out any verification checks as referred to in s 29;

(h) a document signed by the debtor stating whether, to the best of his knowledge, there is any judgment or court order in force against him which relates to a debt which is a qualifying debt;

(i) such other information about the debtor's affairs (including his creditors, debts, liabilities, income and assets) as may be prescribed (see para **3.13** above).

If an application has been made on behalf of the debtor and the debtor becomes aware of any error in, or omission from, the information supplied to the ISI, in or in support of the application, and any material change in his circumstances between the application date and the date on which the application is determined that would affect the determination of the application then the debtor must notify the AI as soon as practicable.[31] Upon receiving this information the AI must, without delay, furnish the information to the ISI.[32]

Consideration of the Application by the ISI

[3.16] The AI makes the application for a DRN to the ISI and submits the aforementioned documentation. The ISI is entitled to request from the AI any further information that it requires. The ISI can defer further consideration of the application

---

29. See **Appendix 2** – DRN Application Form: http://www.isi.gov.ie/en/ISI/DRN.pdf/Files/DRN.pdf.
30. Personal Insolvency Act 2012 (Prescribed Fees) Regulations 2013 (SI 329/ 2013).
31. PIA 2012, s 29(3).
32. PIA 2012, s 29(4).

until such time as the requested information is required.[33] If the AI fails to provide the information requested by the ISI within 14 days or such longer period as the ISI may permit the application shall be deemed to be withdrawn.

The ISI must make such enquiries as it deems necessary to satisfy itself that the AI is entitled to be an AI and the debtor satisfies the eligibility criteria.[34] When making such enquiries the ISI is entitled to presume that the debtor does satisfy the eligibility criteria if the documents required to be submitted to support a DRN application are submitted and the ISI has no reason to believe that the information supplied in or in support of the application, including any corrections made by the debtor, are incomplete or inaccurate, ie once the documentation is provided the ISI can rely on it unless there is something else that indicates incomplete or inaccurate information. The ISI can make enquiries as it considers appropriate to verify the completeness or accuracy of any matter referred to in the PFS of the debtor in relation to the assets, liabilities, income or expenditure of the debtor.

The ISI can make enquiries in respect of the following:[35]

(a) particulars relating to bank accounts, securities or other accounts held, solely or jointly, by or for the benefit of the debtor with financial institutions or financial intermediaries in the State or abroad;

(b) particulars relating to assets of the debtor and the value of such assets;

(c) particulars of the liabilities of the debtor;

(d) the employment and income of the debtor;

(e) payments received by the debtor from the Department of Social Protection, other departments of State, local authorities or other State bodies or agencies, and whether or not such payments are made as agent or any other person;

(f) taxes or charges imposed by or under statute paid or owed by the debtor, whether within or outside the State, and refunds in respect of such taxes and charges which are or may become due to the debtor.

Even though the ISI can make enquiries in respect of the veracity of information provided, it does not have to make such enquiries if it does not deem it necessary.[36]

Any person that does receive an enquiry from the ISI in this regard shall be under a duty to furnish the information requested as soon as practicable.[37] Information held by the Department of Social Protection, other departments of State, the Revenue Commissioners, local authorities or other State bodies or agencies in relation to a debtor may be furnished to the ISI.

33. PIA 2012, s 30(1).

34. PIA 2012, s 30(3).

35. PIA 2012, s 30(7).

36. PIA 2012, s 30(7).

37. PIA 2012, s 30(8).

Once the ISI is satisfied that the application is in order, having considered all the documentation provided as required, the ISI shall:

(a) issue a certificate to that effect;

(b) furnish that certificate together with a copy of the application and supporting documentation to the appropriate court; and

(c) notify the AI to that effect.

Application to Circuit Court

[3.17] Once the Circuit Court receives the application and accompanying documentation, it shall review the application and documentation and if satisfied that the eligibility criteria specified have been satisfied, it must issue a DRN in respect of the debts specified in the application which the court is satisfied are qualifying debts.[38] If the court is not satisfied that the criteria specified have been fulfilled then it must refuse to issue a DRN.

However when the court is considering the application for a DRN, the court is entitled to seek further information or evidence for the purpose of its arriving at a decision. Section 31(3)(b) PIA 2012 requires that the court holds a hearing when it requires this information and/or evidence and this hearing must be on notice to the ISI and the AI concerned.[39] The hearing that a court holds in such circumstances will normally be held in camera[40] unless the court considers it appropriate to hold it in public.

The registrar of the court will notify the ISI that the court requires a hearing pursuant to s 31(3) PIA 2012. When considering the application the court is entitled to treat a certificate issued by the ISI as evidence of the matters certified. The registrar of the appropriate court[41] shall notify the ISI of the DRN being issued.

CONTENTS OF THE DRN

[3.18] A DRN issued shall specify:[42]

(a) the debtor who is the subject of the notice;

(b) the debts as specified in the application as qualifying debts; and

(c) in relation to each specifying debt –

    (i) the value of the debt on the application date, and

    (ii) the creditor ('specified creditor') to whom it is owed.

38. PIA 2012, s 31(2).
39. PIA 2012, s 31(3).
40. PIA 2012, s 31(4).
41. PIA 2012, s 5(1).
42. PIA 2012, s 32.

Once the ISI receives the notice the ISI must, as soon as practicable:

(a) notify the AI concerned that the DRN has been issued;

(b) send a notice which informs the debtor of the issue of the DRN and that he is a specified debtor –

(i) this notice must inform the specifying debtor of the issue of a DRN in respect of which he is specified debtor and this notice should be accompanied by a copy of the DRN and a statement of the obligations of a specified debtor during the supervision period;

(c) send a notice which informs the specified creditor of the issue of the DRN –

(i) This notice must inform the specified creditor that they are a specified creditor, and the notice must be accompanied by

(A) a copy of the notice,

(B) a statement of the specified qualifying debt or debts of which he is the specific creditor,

(C) a statement of his right to object to the inclusion of a specified qualifying debt of which he is a specified creditor, and

(D) a copy of the completed PFS.

(d) The ISI must also record in the Register of DRNs the following:

(i) the fact that a DRN has been issued,

(ii) the name and address of the specified debtor concerned,

(iii) such other details as it considers appropriate.

A court has power to amend a DRN where it is satisfied that such an amendment is necessary in order to address an ambiguity or rectify an error or omission in the DRN. Such an application is made by the ISI[43] during the supervision period. Any such application shall be on notice to each specified creditor and the debtor.[44]

The Effect of a DRN

[3.19] The DRN shall remain in effect for a period of three years from the date that the DRN has been recorded in the Registry of DRNs.[45] This period is known as the supervision period.

The supervision period may be extended by the court if the ISI applies for an extension and the court is satisfied that such extension is necessary to allow the ISI to:[46]

(a) carry out or complete an investigation that appears to be relevant to the ISI to carry out or complete in arriving at a decision to exercise its powers under this chapter;[47]

43. PIA 2012, s 39.

44. PIA 2012, s 39(2) as amended by the Courts and Civil Law (Miscellaneous Provisions) Act 2013, s 56.

45. PIA 2012, s 35(1).

46. PIA 2012, s 35(2).

47. PIA 2012, s 40.

(b) take any other action it considers necessary (whether as a result of an investigation or otherwise) in relation to the notice concerned.

The court can extend the supervision period where an application is made under any of the following sections:

(a) section 42 – an application by the specified debtor or creditor where they are aggrieved by any act, omission or decision of the ISI in connection with a DRN,

(b) section 43 – a specified creditor objection where he objects to the inclusion, as a qualifying debt, of a debt in respect of which he is a specified debtor,

(c) section 44 – an ISI may apply to the appropriate court to have a DRN terminated;

The power of the court to extend the time is specific to the particular instances set out but the extension is as long as is needed to determine the issues so raised and is not for a specified period, unlike the PIA.

However, despite the power of the court to grant a DRN or an extension of the supervisory period, a DRN shall cease to have effect on the date on which a termination takes effect if an application is successful under ss 42, 43 or 44 PIA 2012, ie where the court, upon hearing the application, grants an order terminating the DRN. A DRN will also cease to have effect where the debtor has successfully paid at least 50 per cent of the value of the specified debts to the ISI in compliance with s 37(2) of the PIA 2012.[48]

The Registrar of the Court shall notify the ISI and the AI where a supervision period has been extended.[49] On receipt of the notification the ISI shall send a notice to the specified debtor and each specified creditor, informing them of the extension,[50] and record the extension in the Register of DRNs.[51]

The ISI can, during the supervision period, carry out an investigation of any matter that appears to it to be relevant to arriving at a decision to exercise its powers.[52] As set above the investigative powers of the ISI entitle it to examine the accounts of the debtor, assets, liabilities, the PFS, any payments received by the State etc.[53]

The Effect of a Supervision Period

[3.20] During the supervision period a specified creditor cannot:[54]

(a) initiate any legal proceedings in relation to a specified debt;

(b) take any step to prosecute any such legal proceedings already initiated;

(c) take any step to secure or recover payment of a specified debt;

48. See para **3.22** below.
49. PIA 2012, s 34(5).
50. PIA 2012, s 34(6)(i).
51. PIA 2012, s 34(6)(ii).
52. PIA 2012, s 40.
53. See para **3.16** – Consideration for Application by ISI.
54. PIA 2012, s 35(1).

(d) execute or enforce a judgment or order of a court or tribunal against the debtor in respect of a specified debt;

(e) take any step to recover goods in the possession or custody of the debtor (whether or not title to the goods is vested in the specified creditor);

(f) contact the specified debtor regarding payment of a specified debt, otherwise than at the request of the debtor;

(g) in relation to an agreement with the specified debtor, by reason only that the debtor is insolvent or that the DRN concerned is in effect –

    (i) terminate or amend that agreement, or

    (ii) claim an accelerated payment, or a forfeiture of a term, under that agreement.

Furthermore a specified creditor shall not, during the supervision period, in respect of a specified debt, apply to proceed with:

(a) a bankruptcy petition relating to the debtor;

(b) a summons under s 8 of the Bankruptcy Act 1988; or

(c) a petition to have the specified debtor concerned adjudicated a bankrupt in respect of a specified qualifying debt.

No other proceedings, execution or other legal process may be commenced or continued against the specified debtor or his property without leave of the court during the supervision period. The court can stay any such proceedings, execution or other legal processes for such period as the court deems appropriate.

The supervision period does not prevent a specified creditor pursuing any person that has guaranteed a debt of the specified debtor. The supervision period does not prohibit a specified creditor from taking action against a person who has jointly contracted with the specified debtor concerned or is jointly liable with that specified debtor to the specified creditor unless that other person has obtained the protection of a DSA or a PIA. The person who has jointly contracted may sue or be sued in respect of the contract without joining the specified debtor[55] unless the other person is under the protection of a DSA or a PIA.

The supervision period is disregarded when reckoning any period for the purposes of a limitation period under the statute of limitations for any proceedings or process in respect of a DRN.[56] It seems that the supervision period is excluded even where a person pursuing the specified debtor is unaware of that debtor being under the protection of a specified debt. Similarly the period for which any judgment against the specified debtor in relation to a specified qualifying debt has effect shall be extended by the period that the DRN is in effect, ie for the duration of the supervision period.[57]

The Deeds of Arrangement Act 1887 does not apply to a DRN.[58]

55. PIA 2012, s 35(5).

56. PIA 2012, s 35(7).

57. PIA 2012, s 35(8).

58. PIA 2012, s 35(9).

The information contained in a DRN registry and any extensions shall remain on the DRN registry for the duration of the supervision period.[59]

During the currency of the supervision period the ISI can apply to the court for directions in relation to a matter arising in connection with a DRN, including the specified debtor's compliance with its obligations.[60] Such an application shall be made by lodgement by the ISI of a notice with the appropriate court and the said application must be on notice to the specified debtor. On foot of such an application the court can:

(a) give the ISI such directions as it thinks fit;

(b) make an order for the enforcement of an obligation of the specified debtor as set out in s 36 PIA 2012;

(c) extend the supervision period concerned;

(d) make an order amending the DRN (subject to the restrictions under s 41(4) PIA 2012 relating to the inclusion of a debt that was not specified in the DRN); or

(e) make such other order as the court thinks fit.

Where the court makes a decision on foot of such an application, the Registrar of the court must notify the ISI of the decision and the ISI, on receipt of such notification, must notify the specified creditors of the decision.[61] However the power of the court to amend a DRN does not include the power to specify in a DRN as a specified qualifying debt any debt that was not included in the schedule of the debtor's debts and creditors or any information provided or documents submitted by the specified debtor or on his behalf for the purposes of his application for that DRN.[62]

GENERAL OBLIGATIONS OF A DEBTOR

[3.21] A specified debtor must inform the ISI, during the supervision period, as soon as practicable:

(a) of any material change in the specified debtor's circumstances, in particular an increase or decrease in the level of his assets, liabilities or income; and

(b) where the specified debtor becomes aware of any inaccuracy or omission in his PFS or any other information provided or documents submitted by him or on his behalf to the ISI.

If a specified debtor, during the supervision period, receives a gift or payment of €500 or more then he must surrender 50 per cent of that gift or payment to the ISI.[63]

59. PIA 2012, s 35(10).

60. PIA 2012, s 41.

61. PIA 2012, s 43(6) as amended by the Courts and Civil Law (Miscellaneous Provisions) Act 2013, s 57.

62. PIA 2012, s 41(4).

63. PIA 2012, s 36(2).

A specified debtor whose income, as stated in the information provided or documents supplied, after the deduction of income tax, social insurance contributions and other levies and charges on the specified debtor's income, during the supervision period increases by €400 or more per month shall surrender to the ISI 50 per cent of that increase.[64] In either of the foregoing instances, if the amount surrendered by the specified debtor equals 50 per cent of the total value of the specified qualifying debts concerned then the sections cease to apply. However any sum paid prior to this level being obtained will be considered in the calculation of the aggregate of the sum paid in consideration of s 37(2).

This cessation of the application of the foregoing sections is a consequence of s 37(2) PIA 2012 taking effect and once there has been at least a 50 per cent discharge of the debt due then the DRN ceases to have effect.

A specified debtor during the supervision period concerned shall not, either alone or with any other person, obtain credit in an amount of more than €650 from any person without informing that person that he is a specified debtor.

PAYMENT OF PORTION OF SPECIFIED DEBT

[3.22] A specified debtor can at any time during the supervision period pay a sum to the ISI. Where the aggregate of the sum paid by the specified debtor is in an amount that is not less than 50 per cent of the value of the specified debts then:[65]

(a) the DRN shall cease to have effect;

(b) his name shall, within three months of the cessation of the DRN or the discharge of his specified qualifying debts, be removed from the register; and

(c) he shall stand discharged from all of the specified qualifying debts.

A sum surrendered by a specified debtor in pursuance of s 36(2) (receipt of a gift) and 36(3) (increase of income) PIA 2012 must be included in the calculation of the aggregate of the sums paid.[66]

This section entitles a debtor to release themselves from a DRN on the payment of 50 per cent of the qualifying debts that form part of the DRN. In applying this section, any monies received by way of gift or any increase in a debtor's income must be included in the DRN as set out above with only the balance available to release the debtor from the DRN on the payment of 50 per cent of the qualifying debts of the DRN.

In reality, it will be unusual for a debtor who is the subject of a DRN to find themselves in a position to pay off 50 per cent of the qualifying debts of the DRN without either having an increase in income or received a gift of monies.

The effect of s 37(3) PIA 2012 is that a debtor would need to receive a gift of twice the value of the outstanding debts to be in a position to pay off 50 per cent of the debts of the DRN. The first 50 per cent will automatically form part of the DRN under the

64. PIA 2012, s 36(3).

65. PIA 2012, s 37(2).

66. PIA 2012, s 37(3).

provisions of s 36(2) PIA 2012 with the remaining amount available to pay off 50 per cent of the balancing debts of the DRN.

TREATMENT BY THE ISI OF THE SUMS RECEIVED

[3.23] Where the AI pays any money to the ISI and not to a specified creditor, it is then up to the ISI to apportion to the funds collected and to distribute them on a *parri passu* basis among the specified creditors.[67] However the ISI shall disregard a debt owed to a specified debtor to the extent that the debt is secured.[68] It would appear that if the debt is more than the secured then it could be argued that this debt can be included as a specified debt as it is unsecured; however, unlike a PIA, there is no mechanism for valuing an asset and ascertaining the unsecured debt. The ISI must, within one month of receipt of payment, transmit to the specified creditor payment of the sum apportioned to that creditor. If, however, the ISI is unable to locate the specified creditor, after reasonable efforts, in order to distribute to it its entitlement then the ISI must apportion on a *pari passu* basis that payment between the existing specified creditors (again this is to the exclusion of any secured creditor).[69] There is no definition of 'reasonable efforts' in respect of locating a specified creditor.

APPLICATION BY PERSON AFFECTED BY THE ISSUE OF A DRN

(1) Where aggrieved by any act, omission or decision of the ISI

[3.24] A specified debtor or creditor may during the supervision period concerned make an application to the appropriate court if he is aggrieved by any act or omission or decision of the ISI in connection with a DRN.

The application must be made by the applicant lodging a notice with the appropriate court, which application must be on notice to the ISI and to other parties to the DRN – ie if the debtor on notice to all the specified creditors and if a creditor on notice to the debtor and all other specified creditors.[70]

On foot of such an application the court can:[71]

(a) dismiss the application;

(b) revoke the whole or part of any act or decision of the ISI;

(c) make an order for the enforcement of an obligation of the specified debtor;

(d) extend the supervision period concerned;

(e) make an order amending the DRN (however s 41(4) PIA 2012 does restrict this power);

(f) make such other order as the court thinks fit.

67. PIA 2012, s 38(1).

68. PIA 2012, s 38(3).

69. PIA 2012, s 38(2).

70. PIA 2012, s 42.

71. PIA 2012, s 42(3).

The court has a generic power to amend the terms of the DRN but the restriction under s 41(4) PIA 2012 ensures that any debt that wasn't a specified debt in the original DRN may not be included by way of amendment by the court.

(2) Where a specifying creditor objects to inclusion of a qualifying debt

[3.25] A specifying creditor can, during the supervision period concerned, make an application to the appropriate court if he objects to the inclusion, as a specified debt, of a debt in respect of which he is a specified creditor. Such an application must be made by the specified creditor lodging a notice of objection with the appropriate court on notice to the ISI and the specified debtor.[72] The objection should specify one of the following grounds:

(a) the specified debtor did not satisfy the eligibility criteria specified when the application was made on his behalf;

(b) one or more of the following applies which causes or has caused a material detriment to the specified creditor –

    (i) a material inaccuracy or omission exists in the specified debtor's PFS or other information provided, or documents submitted, by him or on his behalf for a DRN,

    (ii) the specified debtor failed to comply with his obligations as specified under the PIA 2012,

    (iii) an adjudication in bankruptcy has been made in relation to the specified debtor that has not been annulled or discharged,

    (iv) the specified debtor has, since the coming into effect of the DRN, committed an offence under the PIA 2012,

    (v) the procedural requirements specified, pursuant to the DRN process, have not been complied with.

When a specified creditor objects on this basis then the hearing is to be heard with all due expedition.[73]

Upon such an application by the specified creditor the court has the following remedies available to it:

(a) dismiss the application;

(b) terminate the DRN;

(c) extend the supervision period;

(d) make an order amending the DRN, including the removal of the debt which was the subject of the s 43 application;

(e) make such other order as the court thinks fit.

---

72. PIA 2012, s 50.

73. PIA 2012, s 43(4).

Application by the ISI to have a DRN terminated

[3.26] The ISI may, during the supervision period concerned, apply to the court to have a DRN terminated. The grounds upon which the ISI can make an application to the court are limited as follows:[74]

(a) the specified debtor did not satisfy the eligibility criteria the application was made on his behalf;

(b) a material inaccuracy or omission exists in the specified debtor's PFS or any other information provided, or documents submitted, by him or on his behalf in the making of the application;

(c) the specified debtor failed to comply with his obligation pursuant to the DRN;

(d) an adjudication in bankruptcy has been made in relation to the specified debtor that has not been annulled or discharged;

(e) the specified debtor has, since the coming into effect of the DRN, committed an offence under the PIA 2012;

(f) the procedural requirements as set out under a DRN application were not followed.

Upon such an application by the ISI the court has the following remedies available:[75]

(a) dismiss the application;

(b) terminate the DRN;

(c) extend the supervision period concerned;

(d) make an order for the enforcement of an obligation of the specified debtor;

(e) make such other order as the court thinks fit.

Procedure

[3.27] An application is made by the ISI by lodging a notice with the appropriate court, which notice must be on notice to the specified debtor and each specified creditor. The notice must also be based on one of the grounds outlined above.[76]

EFFECT OF TERMINATION OF A DRN

[3.28] Where a DRN is terminated in the circumstances outlined above, the specified debtor shall, unless the court has ordered otherwise, be liable in full for:

(a) all debts specified in the DRN at the time of its termination as specified qualifying debts; and

---

74. PIA 2012, s 44(3).

75. PIA 2012, s 44(4).

76. PIA 2012, s 26(2).

(b) all arrears, charges and interest that have accrued during the supervision period in relation to those debts.

When calculating the liability of a specified debtor, the debtor shall be given credit in respect of payments made by him.[77]

Where a DRN is terminated, the ISI shall, within three months after the date of the cessation of the supervision period, remove from the Register of DRNs all information recorded in it in respect of the DRN.[78]

Discharge from Specified Qualifying Debts

[3.29] Where the DRN ceases to have effect (other than when terminated as outlined above) the specified debtor shall stand discharged from the specified qualifying debts concerned. The specified debtor also stands discharged from all interest, penalties and other sums which have, since the application date, become payable in relation to those debts.[79]

This is subject to a specified debtor's obligations under s 36(2) and (3) PIA 2012, ie the payment of a gift in excess of €500 or more or income in excess of €400 or more, but is not subject to s 37(2).

A specified debtor is not discharged from the qualifying debts if the DRN has been terminated upon an application being made to the court.

Where a specified debtor stands discharged from the specified qualifying debts, the ISI shall:[80]

(a) remove from the register all information recorded in it in respect of the DRN;

(b) send a notice to the specified creditors informing them of that fact; and

(c) issue to the specified debtor a certificate (called a Debt Relief Certificate) confirming the discharge.

The discharge of the specified debtor under does not release any other person from any liability (whether as partner or co-trustee of the specified debtor or otherwise) from which the specified debtor is discharged or any liability as surety for the specified debtor or as a person in the nature of such a surety.[81]

The discharge of a specified debtor shall not affect the rights of a secured creditor to enforce his security.[82]

77. PIA 2012, s 44.

78. PIA 2012, s 45(4) as amended by the Courts and Civil Law (Miscellaneous Provisions) Act 2013, s 58.

79. PIA 2012, s 46(1).

80. PIA 2012, s 46(2).

81. PIA 2012, s 46(4).

82. PIA 2012, s 46(5).

APPROVED INTERMEDIARIES

Introduction

[3.30] The ISI may authorise a person or a class of person to perform the functions of an AI.[83] An AI is not liable in damages to any person for anything done or omitted to be done when acting (or purporting to act) as an AI.[84] However an AI will be held liable in damages when acting (or purporting to act) as an AI where he acts in bad faith.[85]

Regulations for Authorisation and Supervision of AIs

[3.31] The ISI, with the consent of the Minister, may and, if directed by the Minister to do so and in accordance with the terms of the direction, shall, following consultation with the Minister for Finance and any other person as the ISI deems appropriate or as the Minister directs, by regulations provide for any of the following for the purposes of the authorisation, regulation and supervision of AIs and the protection of debtors and creditors who are or may become specified debtors or specified creditors:

(a) the requirements applicable to—

  (i) the authorisation of persons as approved intermediaries,

  (ii) the dealings of an AI with the ISI;

(b) the requirements to be met in the performance of their functions under this act by AIs including, without limiting the generality of the foregoing, in relation to –

  (i) the public interest,

  (ii) the duties owed to debtors and creditors who are or may become specified debtors or specified creditors,

  (iii) the professional and ethical conduct of AIs,

  (iv) the maintenance of the confidentiality of the information of debtors, and

  (v) creditors who are or may become specified debtors or specified creditors,

  (vi) case management in respect of debtors who are or may become specified debtors,

  (vii) conflicts of interest;

(c) the qualifications (including levels of training, education, expertise and experience) or any other requirements (including required standards of competence) for the authorisation of persons as AIs under this section;

(d) the records, including files and accounts, to be maintained, including in electronic form, by an AI;

(e) the requirements to be met by an AI when handling complaints against that AI;

83. PIA 2012, s 47.

84. PIA 2012, s 47(2).

85. PIA 2012, s 47(3).

(f) any other matter relating to the authorisation, supervision or regulation of approved intermediaries which is incidental to or is considered by the ISI to be necessary or expedient for the said purposes or all or any of the matters referred to above.[86]

The ISI made regulations pursuant to s 3 PIA 2012 relating to the authorisation of AIs[87] (Regulations).

Qualifying criteria and authorisation requirements and standards qualifying criteria

[3.32] The ISI may authorise a person or a class of person to perform the functions of an AI.[88]

A natural person may make an application to the ISI to perform the functions of an AI if he or she can demonstrate to the satisfaction of the ISI that he or she:

(a) has relevant training or experience in the provision of financial advice to persons in arrears;

(b) is sufficiently competent and proficient to undertake the role of an AI under the PIA 2012;

(c) has a clear and comprehensive understanding of the relevant legal, regulatory and financial environment applicable to the role of an AI under the PIA 2012; and

(d) has completed a course of study and passed an exam in relation to the law and practice in the State relating to the insolvency of individuals and in relation to the PIA 2012.

A body corporate may make an application to the ISI to perform the functions of an AI if it can demonstrate to the ISI that it has at least one individual in the organisation that meets the criteria above, and any person within the organisation with responsibility for supervising the work of that individual is competent to so supervise and monitor compliance with the requirements of the PIA 2012 and the Regulations.

An applicant shall demonstrate to the satisfaction of the ISI that he, she or it:

(a) has, or has access to, adequate organisational capability and resources to carry on the practice of an AI under the PIA 2012; and

(b) has submitted a completed application form approved by the ISI together with such supporting information, documentation and mandates as the ISI has requested.

86. PIA 2012, s 47(5) as amended by the Courts and Civil Law (Miscellaneous Provisions) Act 2013, s 60.

87. Personal Insolvency Act 2012 (Authorisation of Approved Intermediaries) Regulations 2013 (SI 216/2013).

88. Personal Insolvency Act 2012 (Authorisation of Approved Intermediaries) Regulations 2013 (SI 216/2013), s 3.

Authorisation

[3.33] An applicant for authorisation as an AI shall submit to the ISI a completed application form[89] together with such supporting documentation as required in that form.

The ISI shall grant authorisations on the basis of the information provided to the ISI during the application process. An applicant shall take all reasonable steps to ensure that the information provided in support of an application is accurate and complete. An applicant shall comply with all requests for further information or clarification that the ISI may issue during the assessment of an application in relation to any aspect of the application and within any time limits as may be specified by the ISI.

Honest, ethical and acting with integrity

[3.34] A natural person applying for an authorisation, and in the case of a body corporate applying for an authorisation, the individual that meets the criteria set out above, must be able to demonstrate to the satisfaction of the ISI that his or her ability to act as an AI under the PIA 2012, or, as the case may be, to provide approved intermediary services on behalf of the body corporate, shall not be adversely affected to a material degree where he or she is, or has been, in any jurisdiction:

(a) subject to any relevant disciplinary proceedings or has been issued a warning, censure, suspension, reprimand or other administrative or judicial sanction or its equivalent;

(b) dismissed, or asked to resign and did resign, from a fiduciary appointment or a position of trust, whether or not remunerated;

(c) a director (or equivalent) of a company that was struck off the register of companies (or its equivalent) by the Registrar of Companies (or its equivalent) on an involuntary basis;

(d) disqualified or restricted from acting as a director in any jurisdiction or has been disqualified from acting in any managerial capacity;

(e) convicted of an offence either of money laundering or terrorist financing (or their equivalents);

(f) been convicted of an offence which could be relevant to the AI's ability to perform his, her or its functions under the PIA 2012;

(g) subject to a finding, judgment or order made against him or her by any court, tribunal or administrative enquiry involving fraud, misrepresentation, dishonesty or breach of trust or is subject to any current proceedings or investigation for fraud, misrepresentation, dishonesty or breach of trust;

(h) in the course of his or her employment or profession been the subject of enforcement action taken by a regulatory authority under applicable law.

---

89. See **Appendix 3** – Application Form for AI: http://www.isi.gov.ie/en/ISI/SI216of13(AI).pdf/Files/SI216of13(AI).pdf.

Organisation and management

[3.35] An applicant must be in a position to demonstrate to the satisfaction of the ISI that he, she or it will have in place appropriate policies, systems, procedures and internal control mechanisms to monitor compliance with his or her or its statutory obligations if authorised by the ISI as an AI. An applicant must be in a position to demonstrate to the satisfaction of the ISI that he, she or it will have effective disaster recovery procedures in place to ensure continuity of his, her or its functions under the PIA 2012 to debtors and creditors if authorised by the ISI as an AI.

The ISI may do anything which is necessary or expedient to monitor an AI's compliance with his or her obligations under the PIA 2012, the Regulations and any further regulations made under the PIA 2012.[90]

The ISI may make payments to an AI in connection with the performance of his functions out of the proceeds of fees charged pursuant to s 20 PIA 2012.

FURTHER INFORMATION

[3.36] The ISI has published 'The Guide to a Debt Relief Notice' and the following other guidelines which are available on their website:

http://www.isi.gov.ie/en/ISI/Pages/Publications

- Debt Relief Notice Scenarios
- Debt Relief Notice Scenario Revenue Involvement
- Debt Relief Notice Step by Step Example

90. PIA 2012, s 47(5A) as amended by the Courts and Civil Law (Miscellaneous Provisions) Act 2013, s 60.

Chapter 4

DEBT SETTLEMENT ARRANGEMENTS

INTRODUCTION

[4.01] A Debt Settlement Arrangement (DSA) is an insolvency process that can be entered into between a debtor and his or her unsecured creditors. A DSA only includes unsecured debt without a limit on the amount of debt.

DSAs are dealt with under Ch 3 of the PIA 2012. The DSA will assist persons who have such income, assets and debts that would fall outside the criteria for a Debt Relief Notice (DRN).[1] The difference between a DRN and a DSA is that a DSA is concerned with debts above €20,000.

A DSA differs from a Personal Insolvency Arrangement (PIA) as it only includes unsecured debts. Unsecured debts are debts where the unsecured creditor would not be entitled to seize specific assets if the debtor fails to meet repayment requirements as that creditor does not hold security over the assets. Secured debts cannot be covered in a DSA.

In brief, where a DSA is considered a Personal Insolvency Practitioner (PIP) would design a plan where the debtor would pay a specified amount to creditors over a five-year period after which the outstanding debts that are part of the DSA would be discharged. A specified proportion of creditors would be required to approve the DSA agreement. Any debts not satisfied within the period would be written off. The DSA must be processed by the Insolvency Service of Ireland (ISI) and approved by the relevant court.[2]

General Eligibility Criteria

[4.02]

Qualifying Criteria	**Disqualifying Criteria**
A debtor is insolvent in they are unable to pay their debts in full as they fall due	25% or more of the debts must not have been incurred during the six months prior to making the application
The debtor has one or more unsecured creditors	The debtor must not be the subject of a DRN now or have been within the previous three years
The debtor must be domiciled in the Republic of Ireland, or must have ordinarily resided or had a place of business within the Republic of Ireland within the previous year	The debtor must not be the subject of a PIA now or have been within the previous five years

1. See **Ch 3** – Debt Relief Notices.
2. See para **4.48**.

Qualifying Criteria	Disqualifying Criteria
The debtor must complete a Prescribed Financial Statement (PFS) and have made a statutory declaration of its truth and accuracy	The debtor must not have been the subject of a DSA previously
The debtor has obtained a statement from the PIP confirming that the PIP is of the following opinion: - the information in the PFS is true and accurate - the debtor is eligible to make a proposal for a DSA - having considered the PFS there is no likelihood of the debtor becoming solvent within the next five years - if the debtor enters the DSA there is a reasonable prospect that they will become solvent within the next five years	The debtor must not be bankrupt or subject to a bankruptcy measure or have been discharged from bankruptcy in the previous five years
	The debtor must not have been the subject of a protective certificate issued in respect of a DSA in the previous year

A STEP-BY-STEP SUMMARY OF THE PROCESS

Initial Steps

[4.03]

Step 1 Having reviewed their circumstances and determining that they are unable to pay their debts as they fall due, the debtor contacts a PIP from the list available on the ISI website.[3]

Step 2 The insolvent debtor provides the PIP with information on his finances and financial circumstances including information on his creditors, debts, liabilities, assets, guarantees and any other financial information.

Step 3 The PIP meets with the debtor and/or discusses the debtor's situation and eligibility to apply for a DSA. The PIP must provide written advice setting out their opinion on whether the DSA is the best insolvency arrangement available to the debtor.

Step 4 Once the debtor decides he wishes to proceed then he must indicate this intention in writing to the PIP and request that the PIP acts on the debtor's behalf.

Step 5 The debtor must then provide all his financial information and supporting documentation to the PIP whereupon the PIP will assist the debtor in completing the PFS. There will be a meeting/series of meetings and/or phone calls with the PIP to progress the application.

Step 6 On completion of the PFS, the PIP will further advise the debtor of their options for addressing their financial difficulties.[4]

Step 7 Once the debtor decides to proceed and apply for a DSA, it must instruct the PIP in writing of its decision. The PIP must notify the ISI of his appointment.

Step 8 The PIP will examine the completed PFS and where it is satisfied that the PFS is true and accurate and that the debtor satisfies the eligibility criteria the PIP will provide a statement which will include, inter alia, a statement that there is no likelihood of the debtor becoming solvent within five years, that he is of the opinion that the DSA would facilitate the debtor becoming solvent in a period of five years or more, that the debtor satisfies the eligibility criteria and that the information in the PFS is true and accurate.[5]

Step 9 The debtor will be required to sign a statutory declaration affirming that the PFS is a complete and accurate statement of the debtor's assets, liabilities, income and expenditure.

Step 10 The debtor will be required to complete and sign the following documentation required to accompany the application for a DSA:

(a) a copy of the statement made by the PIP referred to above;

(b) a document signed by the debtor confirming satisfaction with the eligibility criteria for a DSA;

(c) a completed PFS form and statutory declaration;

(d) a schedule of the debtor's creditors and amount owed to each; whether the creditor is a secured creditor or not (if secured, details must be provided of any security); where a debt is an excludable debt, a statement of whether it is a permitted debt;

(e) the debtor's written consent to enable

(ii) the PIP to disclose personal data to the ISI;

(iii) the ISI to process the application;

(iv) the ISI to make any necessary enquiries about the debtor; and

(v) the ISI to disclose the debtor's personal data to the creditors concerned, as required.

---

3. http://www.isi.gov.ie/en/ISI/Pages/Registers.
4. See **Ch 8** – Personal Insolvency Practitioners.
5. See **Ch 8** – Personal Insolvency Practitioners.

Application for a Protective Certificate

[4.04]

Step 11 When the PIP has obtained all the above signed documents from the debtor then the PIP must notify the ISI of the debtor's intention to propose a DSA and apply on behalf of the debtor for a protective certificate.

Step 12 An application is then made to the ISI by the PIP on behalf of the debtor.

Step 13 Once the court is satisfied that the necessary criteria are fulfilled, the application will be approved and the court will issue a protective certificate, which is valid for a period of seventy days from the date of issue.

Step 14 Where a protective certificate is issued, the ISI will notify the PIP of the issue of the protective certificate. The name, address, date of birth of the debtor and the date of issue of the Protective Certificate will be placed on an electronic public Register of Protective Certificates.

Agreement of a DSA Proposal

[4.05]

Step 15 Once the court has issued the protective certificate, the debtor will liaise with the PIP to prepare a proposal for a DSA. The debtor will be required to make a full disclosure of their living expenses, life plans and any circumstances that may have a bearing on their ability to pay current or future debts.

Step 16 The PIP will liaise with the debtor's creditors when drawing up the proposal for a DSA and will have regard, where relevant, to the creditors' preferences in the terms of the DSA. The PIP will then provide a draft proposal for the DSA which the debtor must review.

Step 17 Where the debtor approves the proposal, the debtor should sign and return the proposal to the PIP together with indicating consent to the calling of a meeting of the creditors to approve the DSA.

Step 18 The PIP must give written notice to the creditors of its appointment as a PIP for the purpose of making a proposal for a DSA. The PIP must invite the creditors to make submissions in respect of the debts concerned and the manner in which they might be dealt with under the DSA. A copy of the debtor's PFS must accompany this notice. The PIP must consider any submissions made by a creditor with particular reference to any previous or existing offers of arrangement made by the creditor to the debtor. The PIP may request that a creditor file a proof of debt with the debt proved in the same manner as a debt of a bankrupt under the Bankruptcy Act 1988.[6] Where a creditor does not comply with the requirement to file a proof of debt, they will not be entitled to vote at the creditors' meeting or share in any distribution that may be made under the DSA.

Step 19 The PIP will call a creditors' meeting[7] with not less than 14 days' written notice of the meeting and the date and time and place at which the meeting will be held. The notice will be accompanied by the following documentation:

(a) completed PFS;

(b) document containing the terms of the proposed DSA;

(c) statement by the PIP confirming his appointment by the debtor and his consent to act, advice to the debtor on the range of insolvency arrangement options, confirmation that the PIP is not aware of any reasonable grounds to believe that the information contained in the PFS is not complete or accurate, and confirmation of the debtor's eligibility for a DSA; and

(d) report by the PIP setting out the outcome for creditors and whether the DSA represents a fair outcome for the creditors and indicating whether the financial outcome for the creditors under the terms of the proposal is likely to be better than the estimated financial outcome for such creditors if the debtor were to be adjudicated bankrupt and an opinion as to whether, in the PIP's opinion, the debtor is likely to be able to comply with the terms of the DSA.

Step 20 Where the DSA has been approved at the creditors' meeting by 65 per cent of the creditors in value, the PIP will notify the creditors and the ISI. The ISI will notify the relevant court and the relevant court will consider the DSA subject to any creditor's objection. The PIP will inform the debtor whether the relevant court has approved the DSA. Where the DSA has been approved, the debtor's name, address, date of birth and the date of the coming into effect of the DSA will be entered in the electronic public Register of DSAs.

The Life of the DSA

[4.06]

Step 21 The PIP will contact the debtor to arrange implementing the terms of the DSA. The debtor will make payments through the PIP during the lifetime of the DSA unless the terms of the DSA provide otherwise.

Step 22 The PIP will monitor the implementation of the DSA during the lifetime of the DSA and must carry out reviews at least once a year. The debtor will be required to complete a PFS as part of the review process. The reviewed PFS will be distributed to creditors by the PIP.

6. See **Appendix 4** – Bankruptcy Act 1988, Sch 1, paras 1–22.

7. PIA 2012, s 2.

Termination of the DSA

[4.07]

Step 23 When the debtor has completed all his obligations under the terms of the DSA for the full term of the DSA he will be considered to have successfully completed the DSA at the end of the DSA term. The PIP will inform the ISI, who will record the successful completion of the DSA on the Register of DSAs. The debtor will be discharged from all debts included in the DSA and is considered solvent.

OVERVIEW OF DSA

[4.08] The DSA is very similar to the Individual Voluntary Arrangement (IVA) in the UK; however the DSA requires more involvement of the courts than the IVA system in the UK.

Application for a DSA can be made by an insolvent debtor who has total unsecured debts of over €20,000 (ie €20,001 upwards). A DSA can only be sought via a PIP, who acts on the debtor's behalf throughout the process.[8] Where there are two or more debtors party to all the debts to be covered by the DSA and each of those debtors satisfies the eligibility criteria, those debtors may jointly propose a DSA.

Once the debtor has provided the necessary information to the PIP and signed the requisite documents then, with the assistance of a PIP,[9] the debtor can apply for a protective certificate. The protective certificate provides the debtor with temporary protection while the DSA is being prepared by preventing creditors from taking any action for the recovery of debts for 70 working days from the date of issue.

Under the DSA scheme, creditors are sent a DSA proposal providing for payments to be made by the debtor for a period of five years. Creditors may agree to this but for further protection there is provision to extend the period of the DSA for a further year.[10]

Payments into the DSA will generally only cover a percentage of what is actually owed. The debtor will stand discharged from any remaining debt included in the DSA once all agreed payments are made.

For the DSA to be accepted, at least 65 per cent of voting creditors must support it. Creditors are accorded voting rights strictly in accordance with the amount of their debts. All creditors are bound by the decision of those creditors who choose to exercise their vote.

Apart from the DRN[11] application, which will be processed by an approved intermediary (AI) and made to the ISI, the other applications must be made on behalf of an insolvent debtor to his or creditors by a PIP.[12] What is proposed is essentially what

8. PIA 2012, ss 48 and 55(2).
9. See **Ch 8** – Personal Insolvency Practitioners.
10. PIA 2012, s 65(2)(a).
11. See **Ch 3** – Debt Relief Notices.
12. See **Ch 8** – Personal Insolvency Practitioners.

amounts to a privatised system. PIPs will have to undergo a licensing or authorisation process which will be administered by the ISI. PIPs will need to be paid for the work carried out. The fees charged will vary depending on a variety of factors such as the complexity of the DSA, the level of debt or the number of creditors. It is submitted by the authors that there must be careful monitoring provisions together with guidelines to ensure the protection of vulnerable over-indebted people from uncontrolled and unfair costs.

The PIA 2012 authorises the ISI to make regulations governing the supervision and authorisation of PIPs. The Personal Insolvency Act 2012 (Authorisation and Supervision of Personal Insolvency Practitioners) Regulations 2013[13] were introduced to fulfil this requirement. Generally speaking, PIPs' fees come out of the sale of debtors' assets and the distribution of debtors' surplus income, subject to the payment in some cases of initial upfront fees to process an application. It is imperative that we don't end up with a system whereby the fees and costs of the PIPs erode the benefit of the new insolvency processes.

It will remain to be seen how the regulation and fee scale of the PIPs will play out in practice.

The system in the UK in relation to PIPs has been replicated in this jurisdiction. In the UK, the fees are approved and fixed by creditors. This method ensures that creditors have some ability to control the fee process and ensure fees remain at an acceptable level and do not erode the benefit of having used this insolvency process. It is understood from the guidance produced by the ISI that this process is to be followed in this jurisdiction whereby creditors will have an opportunity to vote on the fees proposed by the PIP.

REQUIREMENTS FOR DEBTOR ELIGIBILITY

Eligibility Criteria

[4.09] The following criteria must be met in order for a debtor to be eligible to make a proposal for a Debt Settlement Agreement:[14]

(a) that the debtor –

  (i) is domiciled in the State, or

  (ii) within one year before the date of the application for a protective certificate has ordinarily

    (A) resided in the State, or

    (B) had a place of business in the State;

(b) that the debtor is insolvent;

13. Personal Insolvency Act 2012 (Authorisation and Supervision of Personal Insolvency Practitioners) Regulations 2013 (SI 209/2013).

14. PIA 2012, s 57.

(c) that the debtor has completed a PFS and has made a statutory declaration confirming that the statement is a complete and accurate statement of the debtor's assets, liabilities, income and expenditure;

(d) that the PIP has made a statement confirming that the PFS is complete and accurate, that the debtor is eligible to make a proposal, that there is no likelihood of the debtor becoming solvent within the period of five years commencing on the date of the making of the declaration and, having regard to the debtor's circumstances, it is appropriate for the debtor to make a proposal for a DSA as there is a reasonable prospect that the debtor would become solvent within a period of not more than five years;[15]

(e) that the debtor is not –

  (i) an undischarged bankrupt,

  (ii) a discharged bankrupt subject to a bankruptcy payment order,

  (iii) a person who is a specified debtor in respects of DRN,

  (iv) a person who, as a debtor, is subject to a PIA which is in force, or

  (v) a person who, as a debtor, is subject to an arrangement under the control of the court under Pt IV of the Bankruptcy Act 1988;

(f) that the debtor has not –

  (i) been the subject of a protective certificate issued under a DSA less than 12 months prior to the date of the application for a protective certificate,

  (ii) had his or her debts discharged pursuant to a DRN[16] less than three years prior to the date of the application for a protective certificate,

  (iii) had his or her debts discharged pursuant to a PIA[17] less than five years prior to the date of the application for a protective certificate, or

  (iv) been discharged from bankruptcy less than five years prior to the date of the application for a protective certificate.

The factors above shall not apply where the debtor has, on notice to the ISI, made an application to the appropriate court and the court has made an order stating that it is satisfied that the current insolvency of the debtor arises by reason of exceptional circumstances or other factors which are substantially outside the control of the debtor and that it would be just to permit the debtor to make a proposal for a DSA.[18]

A debtor will not be eligible to make a proposal for a DSA where 25 per cent or more of his debts (other than excluded debts and secured debts) were incurred during the period of six months ending on the date on which the application is made for a Protective Certificate.[19]

15. PIA 2012, s 54.
16. See **Ch 3** – Debt Relief Notices.
17. See **Ch 5** – Personal Insolvency Arrangements.
18. PIA 2012, s 57(2).
19. PIA 2012, s 57(3).

A DSA shall not contain any terms that would release the debtor from an excluded debt or otherwise affect such a debt.[20] The DSA should not include any term which would give rise to such a release.

Qualifying Debts

[4.10] A debtor is only entitled to include qualifying debts in the DSA proposal. There are two types of debt that may be excluded as a qualifying debt and these are divided into two different categories. The first type of debt is an 'excludable debt', which is a debt that requires the consent of a creditor to be included. Once creditor consent is obtained, the debt becomes an included debt. In circumstances where creditor consent has been sought and the creditor does not respond, the creditor will be deemed to have consented and the debt becomes an included debt. The second category of debt is an 'excluded debt', which is a debt that will never form a debt that is part of the DSA process.

Debts excludable as qualifying debts (require creditor consent):

(a) any liability arising out of any tax, duty, levy or other charge owed or payable to the State;

(b) any amount payable by the debtor under the Local Government (Charges) Act 2009;

(c) any amount payable by the debtor under the Local Government (Household Charge) Act 2011;

(d) rates due to the local authority (within the meaning of the Local Government Act 2001);

(e) any debt or liability in respect of moneys advanced to the debtor by the Health Service Executive under the Nursing Homes Support Scheme Act 2009;

(f) any debt due by the debtor to any owners' management company in respect of annual service charges under s 18 of the Multi-Unit Developments Act 2011 or contributions due under s 19 of that act,

(g) any debt or liability of the debtor arising under the Social Welfare Consolidation Act 2005;

Debts that are excluded as qualifying debts (never included):

(h) any liability arising out of a domestic support order;

(i) any liability arising out of damages awarded by a court (or another competent authority) in respect of personal injuries or wrongful death arising from the tort of the debtor;

(j) any debt or liability arising from a loan (or forbearance of a loan) obtained through fraud, misappropriation, embezzlement or fraudulent breach of trust;

20. PIA 2012, s 55(4).

(k) any debt or liability of the debtor arising by virtue of a court order made under the Proceeds of Crime Acts 1996 and 2005 or by virtue of a fine ordered to be paid by a court in respect of a criminal offence.

Set Off

[4.11] In determining the amount or value of any asset of a debtor or the amount of any debt due to a creditor, where there are mutual credits or debts as between a debtor and a creditor, one debt or demand may be set off against the other and only the balance found owing shall be considered to be a debt or an asset on one side or the other.[21] The effect of this provision is that it is the net overall figure that the debtor owes the creditor which is included in the DSA process rather than a number of different debts owed by the debtor to the same creditor.

Pensions

[4.12] The treatment of a debtor's pension is split into pension income and pension fund. All pension income received by the debtor or an entitlement to a pension lump sum or income in accordance with the tax code will be treated as an asset or, as applicable, income for the purposes of a DSA. Thus a PIP will consider this income/lump sum when preparing the DSA.

Section 51 PIA 2012 states that where a debtor has an interest in or an entitlement under a relevant pension arrangement, such interest or entitlement of the debtor shall not be treated as an asset of the debtor unless sub-s (2) applies.

Before considering sub-s (2) it is necessary to set out what a 'relevant pension arrangement' is. It means:

(a) a retirement benefits scheme, within the meaning of s 771 of the Taxes Consolidation Act 1997 (TCA 1997), for the time being approved by the Revenue Commissioners;

(b) an annuity contract or a trust scheme or part of a trust scheme for the time being approved by the Revenue Commissioners under s 784 of the TCA 1997;

(c) a PRSA contract, within the meaning of s 787A of the TCA 1997, in respect of a PRSA product, within the meaning of that section;

(d) a qualifying overseas pension plan within the meaning of s 787M of the TCA 1997;

(e) a public service pension scheme within the meaning of s 1 of the Public Service Superannuation (Miscellaneous Provisions) Act 2004;

(f) a statutory scheme, within the meaning of s 770(1) of the TCA 1997, other than a public service pension scheme referred to in para (e);

21. PIA 2012, ss 135 and 26(3).

(g) such other pension arrangement as may be prescribed by the Minister, following consultation with the Ministers for Finance, Social Protection and Public Expenditure and Reform.

Subsection (2) of s 51 PIA 2012 sets out the situation where a debtor receives an income or a lump sum which can then be used by a PIP when formulating a DSA. Where a debtor (a) is entitled at the date of the making of the application for a protective certificate, (b) was entitled at any time before the date of the making of the application for a protective certificate, or (c) will become entitled within six years of the date for the making of the application for a protective certificate in relation to a DSA, performs the act or exercises the option which causes the debtor to receive from or at the request of the person administering that relevant pension arrangement (a) an income or (b) an amount of money other than an income, in accordance with the provisions of the TCA 1997, that debtor shall be considered as being in receipt of such income or amount of money resulting in the income or lump sum being treated as an asset.[22]

The debtor's pension fund will be excluded from any DSA if it is a 'relevant pension arrangement' for the purposes of the PIA 2012. However an Approved Retirement Fund will not come under a 'relevant pension arrangement' and may be included by the PIP when preparing a DSA

There will be an onus on the debtor to be transparent in relation to all historical pension contributions and the PIP will review these. The debtor will continue to be obliged when making an application for a protective certificate to make disclosure of any interest in or entitlement under a relevant pension arrangement in completing the PFS.

Where a creditor or a PIP considers that a debtor has made excessive contributions to a relevant pension arrangement, they can make an application to the appropriate court for the relief. Excessive contributions that were made at any time within three years prior to the making of the application for a protective certificate are to be considered.[23]

Where a court considers that contributions to a relevant pension arrangement were excessive it may:

(a) direct that such part of the contribution concerned (less any tax required to be deducted) be paid by the person administering the relevant pension arrangement to the PIP for distribution amongst the creditors of the debtor, and

(b) make such other order as the court deems appropriate, including an order as to the costs of the application.

When considering whether the contributions being made to the pension were excessive or not it may consider:

(a) whether the debtor made payments to his creditors in respect of debts due to those creditors on a timely basis at or about the time when the debtor made the contribution concerned;

22. PIA 2012, s 51.

23. PIA 2012, s 88.

(b) whether the debtor was obliged to make contributions of the amount or percentage of income as the payments actually made under his terms and conditions of employment and, if so obliged, whether the debtor or a person who as respects the debtor is a connected person could have materially influenced the creation of such obligation;

(c) the amount of the contributions paid including the percentage of total income of the debtor in each tax year concerned which contributions represent;

(d) the amount of the contributions paid in each of the six years prior to the making of the application for a protective certificate on behalf of the debtor, including the percentage of total income of the debtor concerned which such contributions represent in each of those years;

(e) the age of the debtor at the relevant times;

(f) the percentage limits which applied to the debtor in relation to relief from income tax for purposes of making contributions to a relevant pension arrangement in each of the six years prior to the making of the application for a protective certificate on behalf of the debtor; and

(g) the extent of provision made by the debtor in relation to any relevant pension arrangement prior to the making of the contributions concerned.

APPLICATION PROCESS FOR A PROTECTIVE CERTIFICATE

[4.13] Section 59 PIA 2012 sets out the requirements in relation to applications for a protective certificate. The first step for the debtor in this process is to contact a PIP who will assist in advising the debtor in relation to the eligibility requirements, his insolvency options and preparing a PFS.[24] Where a PIP has been instructed to make a proposal for a DSA, the PIP will notify the ISI of the debtor's intention to propose a DSA and apply on the debtor's behalf for a protective certificate.

Information to PIP

[4.14] When the debtor contacts the PIP he must provide him with certain information. In order for a PIP to give initial advice then the debtor is obliged under the PIA 2012 to provide a substantial amount of information. The debtor must provide information in relation to his creditors, debts and liabilities, assets and guarantees and any other financial information as prescribed.[25] The debtor should provide the PIP with a written statement setting out the following (in so far as the debtor can reasonably ascertain and the relevant information is applicable to the debtor):

(a) the full name and address and email or telephone contact details of the debtor's creditors;

---

24. See para **4.16** below.

25. Personal Insolvency Act 2012 (Written Statement Disclosing all of the Debtor's Financial Affairs) Regulations 2013 (SI 312/2013).

(b) a full description of the debtor's debts and other liabilities;

(c) whether each of these debts and other liabilities are secured debts or unsecured debts;

(d) the amount of each debt or other liability (including principal, interest, costs and arrears) due to each of the debtor's creditors at the date of the written statement;

(e) any contingent and prospective debts or other liabilities of the debtor including any guarantee or similar commitment signed by the debtor in respect of any other person and the times at which such debts or other liabilities will become due for payment;

(f) a full description of the current and prospective assets of the debtor;

(g) the address or location of these assets;

(h) where the assets comprise real property, whether the debtor's title is freehold, leasehold or other;

(i) whether these assets are held jointly or collectively with any other person, and if held collectively, the debtor's ownership percentage or other interest;

(j) the financial institution and account details where any of these assets are held;

(k) in the case of assets which may give rise to income to the debtor or are shares or other securities, the name and address of the obligor or issuer; and

(l) the purchase date, original cost and current market value of each asset.

A debtor shall provide a full schedule of his creditors[26] which must contain the following information:

(a) the creditor's legal name;

(b) the creditor's address (being the physical address and, if applicable, electronic address for service of notices and correspondence to the creditor subject to s 134 PIA 2012);

(c) whether the creditor is a connected person in relation to the debtor;

(d) whether the debt concerned is an excludable debt and, if so, whether that debt is a permitted debt;

(e) whether the debt concerned is an excluded debt;

(f) whether some or all of the debt concerned is a preferential debt within and, if so, the preferential amount.

Under Personal Insolvency Act 2012 (Written Statement Disclosing all of the Debtor's Financial Affairs) Regulations 2013 (SI 312/2013),[27] a debtor shall provide full details,

26. Personal Insolvency Act 2012 (Written Statement Disclosing all of the Debtor's Financial Affairs) Regulations 2013 (SI 312/2013).

27. Personal Insolvency Act 2012 (Written Statement Disclosing all of the Debtor's Financial Affairs) Regulations 2013 (SI 312/2013), ss 4 and 5.

including any documentary evidence, of the efforts made by him or her to reach an alternative payment arrangement with his or her creditors or any of them where this applies.

A debtor shall also provide full details of his or her monthly income and monthly expenditure for the purposes of the PIA 2012 and such details shall include:

(a) a breakdown as between the different items of income and expenditure;

(b) an averaging of the income and expenditure on a monthly basis where the income is not received or the expenditure made on a monthly basis;

(c) where income or expenditure is received or made other than on an individual basis by the debtor, details of any joint or collective arrangements which apply in respect of such income or expenditure.

Initial meeting between PIP and Debtor

[4.15] The PIP meets with the debtor and/or discusses the debtor's situation and eligibility to apply for a DSA based on the information supplied and gives him advice of the various insolvency options. The PIP will detail the DSA application process and outline the debtor's duties and obligations in the process and whether the debtor meets the eligibility criteria. The PIP should provide written advice setting out their opinion on whether the DSA is the best insolvency arrangement available to the debtor together with any reasons for advising same. The PIP should provide information on fee arrangements and other conditions of their appointment.

Once the debtor decides he wishes to proceed then he must indicate this intention in writing to the PIP and request that the PIP acts on the debtor's behalf.

The debtor must then provide all his financial information and supporting documentation to the PIP whereupon the PIP will assist the debtor in completing the PFS. There will be a meeting/series of meetings and/or phone calls with the PIP to progress the application.

Prescribed Financial Statement (PFS)

[4.16] Every applicant for one of the new arrangements is required to complete a PFS with the help of a PIP (for a DSA or PIA). The PFS will enable the PIP to determine which (if any) one of the three new arrangements is most suitable in any particular case. The debtor is under an obligation to make full and honest disclosure of his financial affairs and to ensure to the best of his knowledge that the PFS is true, accurate and complete.

The PFS will be used primarily to establish the applicant's eligibility for an arrangement, to form the basis for calculating a sustainable contribution which the applicant will pay to his creditors over the period of the arrangement (for a DSA/PIA) and to identify those liabilities from which the applicant will be discharged at the end of an arrangement.

The PFS will fully disclose all of the debtor's financial affairs (ie assets, liabilities, income and expenditure). It shall include full details of the debtor's:

(a) income;

(b) expenditure;

(c) creditors;

(d) debts and other liabilities;

(e) assets;

(f) additional information which may be required by the ISI;

(g) guarantees (if any) given by the debtor in respect of a debt of another person.

The actual format of this PFS written statement is now available pursuant to Personal Insolvency Act 2012 (Prescribed Financial Statement) Regulations 2013 (SI 326/ 2013).[28]

The PFS will be annexed to a statutory declaration which must be witnessed by a notary public, Commissioner for Oaths, Peace Commissioner or a practicing solicitor.

PIP Advice

[4.17] On completion of the PFS, the PIP will further advise the debtor of their options for addressing their financial difficulties, whether the debtor is eligible for a DSA and, in the PIP's opinion, if a DSA is the most appropriate option.[29]

Once the debtor decides to proceed and apply for a DSA, it must instruct the PIP in writing of its decision. The PIP must notify the ISI of his appointment.

The PIP will examine the completed PFS and where it is satisfied that the PFS is true and accurate and that the debtor satisfies the eligibility criteria the PIP will provide a statement which will include, inter alia, a statement that there is no likelihood of the debtor becoming solvent within five years, that he is of the opinion that the DSA would facilitate the debtor becoming solvent in a period of five years or more, that the debtor satisfies the eligibility criteria and that the information in the PFS is true and accurate.[30]

The debtor will be required to sign a statutory declaration affirming that the PFS is a complete and accurate statement of the debtor's assets, liabilities, income and expenditure.

Application for a Protective Certificate

[4.18] When the PIP has obtained all the above signed documents from the debtor then the PIP must notify the ISI of the debtor's intention to propose a DSA and apply on behalf of the debtor for a protective certificate.

The PIP will apply to the ISI for a protective certificate which will prevent creditors from taking any action against the debtor for 70 days during which time the arrangement is being prepared.

---

28. See **Appendix 1** – Prescribed Financial Statement - http://www.isi.gov.ie/en/ISI/PFS.pdf/Files/PFS.pdf.
29. See **Ch 8** – Personal Insolvency Practitioners.
30. See **Ch 8** – Personal Insolvency Practitioners.

The PIA 2012 sets out that the application for a protective certificate shall be in such form as may be specified by the ISI[31] and shall be accompanied by the fee[32] of €250.

The form of the application for a protective certificate under a DSA has been prescribed by the ISI under the Personal Insolvency Act 2012 (Prescribed Protective Certificate Debt Settlement Arrangement Application Form) Regulations 2013 (SI 332/2013).[33]

The following documents will need to be provided with the application for a protective certification:[34]

(a) the statement of the PIP prepared confirming the PFS;[35]

(b) a document signed by the debtor confirming that he or she satisfies the eligibility criteria for a DSA;

(c) the statutory declaration[36] of the debtor;

(d) the PFS;

(e) the fee of €250 as prescribed under SI 329/2013;[37]

(f) a schedule of the debtor's debts and creditors concerned, stating in relation to each such creditor—

  (i) the amount due to that creditor, and

  (ii) whether the creditor concerned is a secured creditor and, if so, the nature of any security held in respect of the debt concerned;

(g) a consent in writing signed by the debtor confirming that he or she consents to disclosure and processing of his or her personal data to and by the ISI and creditors to such extent as may be necessary in connection with the DSA procedure provided for in the PIA 2012;

(h) confirmation by the debtor that the ISI may carry out any prescribed verification checks.[38]

ISI CONSIDERATIONS

[4.19] The ISI shall be entitled to request any further information it requires from the debtor or PIP and to defer further consideration of the application until such information

31. See **Appendix 5** – DSA Protective Certificate Application Form: http://www.isi.gov.ie/en/ISI/DSA.pdf/Files/DSA.pdf.
32. Personal Insolvency Act 2012 (Prescribed Fees) Regulations 2013 (SI 329/2013).
33. See **Appendix 5** – DSA Protective Certificate Application Form: http://www.isi.gov.ie/en/ISI/DSA.pdf/Files/DSA.pdf.
34. PIA 2012, s 59.
35. See **Ch 8** – Personal Insolvency Practitioners.
36. PIA 2012, s 57(1)(c).
37. Personal Insolvency Act 2012 (Prescribed Fees) Regulations 2013 (SI 329/2013).
38. PIA 2012, s 60.

is furnished to it.[39] Any such information must be provided within 14 days or as long as the ISI shall permit or the application will be deemed to be withdrawn.

The ISI also has further rights in relation to the verification of information provided by both the PIP and the debtor. This will result in additional obligations on the PIP.

The ISI shall make such enquiries as it considers necessary to satisfy itself:

(a) that the PIP is a person entitled to act as a PIP;

(b) having regard to the documents which are required to accompany the application for a protective certificate—

(i) that the debtor satisfies the eligibility criteria for making a proposal for a DSA, and

(ii) the application does not appear to be frivolous or an attempt to frustrate the efforts of creditors to recover debts due to them.

The ISI is also entitled to make such enquiries as it considers necessary to verify the completeness or accuracy of any matter referred to in the PFS of the debtor or in relation to the assets, liabilities, income or expenditure of the debtor.

In addition to the general powers of enquiry that the ISI has it also has the following specific powers of enquiry:[40]

(a) particulars relating to bank accounts, securities accounts or other accounts held, solely or jointly, by or for the benefit of the debtor with financial institutions or financial intermediaries in the State or abroad;

(b) particulars relating to assets of the debtor and the value of such assets;

(c) particulars of the liabilities of the debtor;

(d) the employment and income of the debtor;

(e) payments received by the debtor from the Department of Social Protection or other departments of State or other State bodies or agencies and whether or not such payments are made as agent of any other person;

(f) taxes or charges imposed by or under statute paid or owed by the debtor, whether within or outside the State, and refunds in respect of such taxes and charges which are or may become due to the debtor.

There is a general provision[41] which states that information held by a department of State, the Revenue Commissioners, a local authority or any other State body or agency in relation to a debtor may be furnished to the ISI.

Where the ISI is not satisfied with the application, it shall notify the PIP and request that, within twenty-one days of the notification, to submit a revised application or confirm that the application is withdrawn.

39. PIA 2012, s 60.

40. PIA 2012, s 60(6).

41. PIA 2012, s 60(9).

COURT REFERRAL FOR THE ISSUING OF A PROTECTIVE CERTIFICATE

[4.20] Once the ISI is satisfied that the application is in order it will furnish a certificate to that effect, and furnish that certificate together with a copy of the application and supporting documentation to the appropriate court and notify the PIP to that effect.[42] The only documentation that is not required is the documentation consenting to enquiries by the ISI.

Section 5 PIA 2012 sets out the appropriate court in respect of DSAs. Where the total liabilities of the debtor, determined on the basis of the PFS completed by the debtor, are in excess of €2,500,000, the appropriate court is the High Court with the Circuit Court being the appropriate court in all other circumstances of a DSA. The performance of the functions and the exercise of the powers and jurisdiction shall be within the jurisdiction of the circuit of the Circuit Court in which:

(a) the debtor to whom the application relates is residing at the time of the making of the application or has resided within one year of the time of the making of the application; or

(b) the debtor to whom the application relates has a place of business at the time of the making of the application or has a place of business within one year of the time of the making of the application.

Once the court is in receipt of the application and the supporting documentation, the court shall review the application and documentation and, if satisfied that the eligibility criteria[43] in respect of the debtor have been satisfied and the other relevant requirements relating to an application for the issue of a protective certificate have been met, shall issue a protective certificate.

Section 61(5) PIA 2012 provides the protective certification to be in force for a period of 70 days. There is a possible 40-day extension period on application to the court in the following circumstances:

(a) the debtor and the PIP satisfy the court that they have acted in good faith and with reasonable expedition; and

(b) the court is satisfied that it is likely that a proposal for a DSA which is likely—

  (i) to be accepted by the creditors, and

  (ii) to be successfully completed by the debtor

  will be made if the extension is granted.

The registrar of the appropriate court shall notify the ISI and the PIP concerned where it issues or extends a protective certificate under this section. The ISI shall enter details of the name and address of the debtor, the date of issue of the protective certificate, or the extension of the protective certificate, or the making of an order of the court in relation to a protective certificate, and the date on which the protective certificate ceases,

42. PIA 2012, s 61.

43. PIA 2012, s 61(2).

together with such other details as it considers appropriate, in the Register of Protective Certificates.[44]

Where the protective certificate ceases, the ISI must, within three months of the date of cessation, remove from the Register of Protective Certificates all information recorded by it in respect of the protective certificate.[45]

Once a protective certificate has been issued, it is the responsibility of the PIP to notify each of the creditors specified in the schedule of creditors of the fact of such issue and that the debtor intends to make a proposal for a DSA.[46]

The protective certification issued shall provide the following:

(a) the name of the debtor who is the subject of it;

(b) the debts ('specified debts') which are subject to it; and

(c) the name of each creditor to whom a specified debt is owed; and

(d) contain such other information as may be prescribed.

EFFECT OF THE PROTECTIVE CERTIFICATION

Creditors

[4.21] A creditor to whom notice of the issue of a protective certificate has been given shall not, whilst the protective certificate remains in force:[47]

(a) initiate any legal proceedings in relation to a debt which is a specified debt;

(b) take any step to prosecute legal proceedings already initiated;

(c) execute or enforce a judgment held against the debtor in respect of a specified debt;

(d) take any step to recover goods in the possession or custody of the debtor (whether or not title to the goods is vested in the creditor);

(e) contact the debtor regarding payment of the debt otherwise than at the request of the debtor;

(f) in relation to an agreement with the debtor, including a security agreement, by reason only that the debtor is insolvent or that the protective certificate has been issued—

  (i) terminate or amend that agreement, or

  (ii) claim an accelerated payment, or a forfeiture of a term, under that agreement.

---

44. PIA 2012, s 61(11).

45. PIA 2012, s 61(11) as amended by the Courts and Civil Law (Miscellaneous Provisions) Act 2013, s 65.

46. PIA 2012, s 61(12).

47. PIA 2012, s 62.

Where a creditor has been notified of the granting of a protective certificate, whilst the protective certificate remains in force no bankruptcy petition relating to the debtor may be presented by a creditor or, in a case where the petition has been presented by a creditor, may be proceeded with.

In addition to the specific provision above, there is a general protection[48] afforded to the debtor such that no other proceedings, no enforcement of security and no execution or other legal process may be commenced or continued against the debtor or his or her property, except with the leave of the court and subject to any order the court may make to stay such proceedings, enforcement or execution, for such period as the court deems appropriate pending the outcome of attempts to reach a DSA.

It should be noted that the protective certification does not extend to protect any guarantor of the debts of the debtor or a person who has jointly contracted with the debtor or is jointly liable with the debtor to the creditor and that other person may sue or be sued in respect of the contract without joining the debtor.[49]

The period of protective certification and any extension to this period does not affect any period for the purposes of the Statute of Limitations 1957[50] or period in relation to any proceedings or process (ie the period of protective certification is disregarded). This may be of relevance in the event that a DSA is unsuccessful.

Right of Appeal of Creditor against the Issue of Protective Certification

[4.22] In the event that a creditor is aggrieved by the issue of a protective certificate that creditor may within 14 days of the giving of notice of the issue of the protective certificate to that creditor apply to the appropriate court for an order directing that the protective certificate shall not apply to that creditor.[51]

Notice must be given to the ISI and the relevant PIP and to such other persons as the court may direct of that fact, and the application shall be made in such form as is provided for in the rules of court.[52]

The court shall not make the order directing that the protective certificate shall not apply to that creditor unless it is satisfied that:

(a) failing to give such direction would cause irreparable loss to the creditor which would not otherwise occur; and

(b) no other creditor to whom notice of the protective certificate has been given would be unfairly prejudiced.[53]

48. PIA 2012, s 62(3).
49. PIA 2012, s 62(4) and (5).
50. PIA 2012, s 62(7).
51. PIA 2012, s 63.
52. See para **6.26** – Court Procedures.
53. PIA 2012, s 63(3).

In determining the costs of the application[54] the court shall have regard to the objective that all the parties to such an application should bear their own costs unless to do so would cause a serious injustice to the parties to the application.

Where the court makes an order under this section, the court shall, unless it considers that there are good reasons not to do so, direct the creditor to hold any moneys or other assets recovered in trust for the benefit of the other creditors to whom the protective certificate applies, pending a further direction on the matter by the court.

The court is bound to hear any application[55] by a creditor appealing the protective notification with 'due expedition' but no guidance has been given as to how long this may be.

OBLIGATIONS OF THE PIP IN RESPECT OF THE ISSUANCE OF A PROTECTIVE CERTIFICATE

[4.23] Upon issue of the protective certification there are a number of persons that the PIP[56] must give notice to and are as follows:

(a) give written notice to those creditors that the PIP has been appointed by the debtor for the purpose of making a proposal for a DSA and invite the creditors concerned to make submissions to the PIP regarding the debts concerned and the manner in which the debts might be dealt with as part of a DSA, and such notice shall be accompanied by the debtor's completed PFS;

(b) consider any submissions made by creditors in accordance with the above regarding the debts and the manner in which the debts might be dealt with as part of a DSA, including any submission made by a creditor with respect to previous or existing offers of arrangements made by the creditor to or with the debtor.

In notifying creditors of the issue of a protective certificate, the PIP shall indicate that any creditor who considers some or all of his or her debt to be a preferential debt[57] is required to furnish evidence of the circumstances of how that debt, or part of that debt, is claimed to be a preferential debt within such reasonable period as may be specified, and that in the absence of such evidence the proposal for a DSA may be prepared on the basis that the debt concerned is not a preferential debt.

A PIP may in any case request a creditor to file a proof of debt and the debt shall be proved in the same manner as a debt of a bankrupt is proved under the Bankruptcy Act 1988 and the First Schedule of that act[58] shall apply to the proof of such debts. Any creditor who does not comply with the provisions above is not entitled to vote at a

54. PIA 2012, s 63(4).

55. PIA 2012, s 63(5).

56. PIA 2012, s 64.

57. PIA 2012, s 64(2).

58. See **Appendix 4** – Bankruptcy Act 1988, Sch 1.

meeting relating to the DSA or share in any distribution under the DSA.[59] Any proof of debt filed by such a creditor shall cease to apply.

In applying the First Schedule of the Bankruptcy Act 1988 to proof of debts for these purposes, any reference to the Official Assignee shall be read as a reference to the PIP, and a reference to the bankrupt shall read as a reference to the insolvent debtor to whom the proposal for a DSA relates.

MANDATORY REQUIREMENTS UNDER A DSA

[4.24] In general, the terms of a DSA are the terms to which the debtor agrees, in respect of his debts, which are approved by a majority of the creditors (ie greater than 65 per cent of the voting creditors).[60] In addition to this, there are certain mandatory requirements that must also be met.

The following are the mandatory requirements:

(a) the maximum duration of a DSA shall be 60 months but a DSA may provide that this period may be extended for a further period of not more than 12 months in such circumstances as are specified in the terms of the DSA;

(b) subject to paras (c) and (d), where the debtor performs all of his or her obligations specified in a DSA, he or she shall stand discharged from the remainder of the debts covered by the DSA;

(c) a DSA shall not release the debtor from any of the following debts or liabilities unless the proposed DSA explicitly provides for the compromise of that debt or liability and the relevant creditor for any of the following debts or liabilities has agreed in writing to accept the compromise contained in the DSA (insofar as it applies to that creditor's debt)—

  (i) any liability arising out of a domestic support order,

  (ii) any liability arising out of any tax, duty, levy or other charge owed or payable to the State,

  (iii) any amount payable by the debtor under the Local Government (Charges) Act 2009,

  (iv) any amount payable by the debtor under the Local Government (Household Charge) Act 2011,

  (v) rates to the local authority (within the meaning of the Local Government Act 2001),

  (vi) any debt or liability in respect of moneys advanced to the debtor by the Health Service Executive under the Nursing Homes Support Scheme Act 2009,

  (vii) any debt due by the debtor to any owners' management company in respect of annual service charges under s 18 of the Multi-Unit Developments Act 2011 or contributions due under s 19 of that act,

59. PIA 2012, s 58(2)(a).

60. PIA 2012, s 65.

(viii) any liability arising out of damages awarded by a court (or another competent authority) in respect of personal injuries or wrongful death arising from the tort of the debtor,

(ix) any debt or liability arising from a loan (or forbearance of a loan) obtained through fraud, misappropriation, embezzlement or fraudulent breach of trust;

(d) a DSA shall not release the debtor from any debt or liability arising by virtue of a court order made under the Proceeds of Crime Acts 1996 and 2005 or by virtue of a fine ordered to be paid by a court in respect of a criminal offence;

(e) a DSA shall not require the debtor to sell any of his or her assets that are reasonably necessary for the debtor's employment, business or vocation unless the debtor explicitly consents to such sale;

(f) a DSA shall not contain any terms which would require the debtor to make payments of such an amount that the debtor would not have sufficient income to maintain a reasonable standard of living for the debtor and his or her dependants;

(g) a DSA shall—

(i) make provision for the costs and outlays of the PIP which relate to the application for the DSA and to the ongoing administration of the DSA,

(ii) indicate the likely amount of the costs to be incurred or, where this is not practicable, the basis of how those charges will be calculated, and

(iii) specify the person or persons by whom those costs and charges are payable and the manner in which they are to be paid;

(h) a DSA shall make provision for the manner in which the debtor's debts are to be treated in the event of the death or mental incapacity of the debtor;

(i) a DSA shall not require that the debtor dispose of his or her interest in his or her principal private residence (PPR) or to cease to occupy such residence unless the provisions of s 69(3) PIA 2012[61] apply;

(j) a DSA shall provide that the circumstances of the debtor be reviewed by the PIP at regular intervals which are specified in the DSA (which intervals are not greater than 12 months) during the currency of the DSA;

(k) the review referred to in para (j) shall include the preparation by the debtor of a new PFS, a copy of which, together with a statement by the PIP as to whether he or she considers that statement to be complete and accurate, shall be sent by the PIP to each creditor;

(l) the terms of a DSA shall specify the circumstances where the PIP shall be obliged to propose a variation of the DSA in accordance with s 82 PIA 2012.

---

61. See para **4.28** below – Where debtor does not wish to remain in PPR or where cost of remaining in PPR is disproportionately large.

Guidelines on a Reasonable Standard of Living and Reasonable Living Expenses[62] (Guidelines) have been published by the ISI on the matters outlined above. In addition, for the purposes of a PIP determining whether a debtor would have sufficient income to maintain a reasonable standard of living for the debtor and his or her dependants under the DSA, the PIP shall have regard to these Guidelines and any further guidelines on reasonable expenditure and essential income for debtors published by the ISI.

THE DSA

Terms of the Proposal

[4.25] The terms of proposal for the DSA[63] may include any of the following:

(a) a lump sum payment to creditors, whether provided from the debtor's own resources or from the resources of other persons;

(b) a payment arrangement with creditors;

(c) an agreement by the debtor to transfer some or all of the debtor's property to a person (who may be the PIP) to hold the property in trust for the benefit of the creditors;

(d) a transfer of specified assets of the debtor to creditors generally or to a specified creditor;

(e) a sale of specified assets of the debtor by the PIP and the payment of the proceeds of such sale to creditors.

The DSA shall provide for payments to creditors of the same class to be made on a *pari passu* basis, and where so otherwise provided the DSA shall specify the reasons for such provision being made unless the payments specifically provided to be paid otherwise than *pari passu*.[64] Payments other than the payments specified above may be provided for under the DSA.

Unless provision is made otherwise in the DSA, where a DSA provides for payments to a creditor who had an excludable debt that are greater than the payment that creditor would receive if such payments were made on a *pari passu* basis, the fees, costs and charges shall be payable by the creditor in proportion to the payments received by that creditor.

The payment of moneys or the performance of obligations provided for by a DSA may be secured by a charge or a guarantee given by the debtor or a charge or guarantee given by a person other than the debtor.

62. **Ch 7** – Reasonable Living Expenses and http://www.isi.gov.ie/en/ISI/Pages/Publications.

63. PIA 2012, s 66(2).

64. PIA 2012, s 66(3).

Preferential Debts

[4.26] For the purposes of a DSA, a preferential debt[65] is a debt which if the debtor concerned were a bankrupt would be a debt:

(a) that by virtue of s 81 of the Bankruptcy Act 1988[66] is to be paid in priority to all other debts; or

(b) that by virtue of any other statutory provision is to be included among such debts, shall be paid in full by the debtor unless the creditor concerned otherwise agrees and provision is so made in the terms of the DSA and such debt is in this Chapter referred to as a 'preferred debt', and where those debts are to be paid in full the provisions of s 81 of the Bankruptcy Act 1988 shall apply with all necessary modifications.

In notifying creditors of the issue of a protective certificate, the PIP shall indicate that any creditor who considers some or all of his or her debt to be a preferential debt[67] is required to furnish evidence of the circumstances of how that debt, or part of that debt, is claimed to be a preferential debt within such reasonable period as may be specified, and that in the absence of such evidence the proposal for a DSA may be prepared on the basis that the debt concerned is not a preferential debt. Where a creditor fails to satisfy the PIP that his or her debt is a preferential debt the debt shall be treated as not being a preferential debt for the purposes of a DSA.[68]

Secured Debt

[4.27] There is nothing within the PIA 2012 that affects the right of a secured creditor of the debtor to enforce or otherwise deal with his or her security.[69]

A secured creditor of the debtor may not participate in a DSA with respect to a secured debt.[70]

The debtor or the PIP is not prevented from liaising or sharing information (including a copy of the debtor's PFS and information relating to a proposed or existing DSA) with a secured creditor in connection with a proposed or existing DSA.

A secured creditor shall not be deemed to participate in or otherwise be bound by a DSA as a result of entering into an agreement with the debtor to vary the terms of the secured debt following contact between the secured creditor and debtor or, as applicable, the PIP (including, without limitation, any variation of the terms of the secured debt that would reduce the amounts payable by the debtor in respect of the secured debt for the duration of the DSA).

65. PIA 2012, s 67.

66. See **Appendix 6** – Bankruptcy Act 1988, s 81.

67. PIA 2012, s 67(2).

68. PIA 2012, s 67(3).

69. PIA 2012, ss 68(1) and 62.

70. PIA 2012, s 68(2).

Principal Private Residence

[4.28] In formulating a proposal for a DSA a PIP shall, insofar as reasonably practicable and having regard to the matters referred to below, formulate the proposal on terms that will not require the debtor to dispose of an interest in or cease to occupy his or her principal private residence and the PIP shall consider any appropriate alternatives to such vacation.[71]

A principal private residence is defined as a dwelling in which the debtor ordinarily resides and includes any building or structure, or any vehicle or vessel (whether mobile or not), together with any garden or portion of ground attached to and occupied with the dwelling or otherwise required for the amenity or convenience of the dwelling.

The matters which the PIP must take into consideration in dealing with the principal private residence of the debtor are:

(a) the costs likely to be incurred by the debtor by remaining in occupation of his or her principal private residence (including rent, mortgage loan repayments, insurance payments, owners' management company service charges and contributions, taxes or other charges relating to ownership or occupation of the property imposed by or under statute and necessary maintenance in respect of the principal private residence);

(b) the debtor's income and other financial circumstances as disclosed in the PFS;

(c) the ability of other persons residing with the debtor in the principal private residence to contribute to the costs referred to in para (1) above; and

(d) the reasonable living accommodation needs of the debtor and his or her dependants and, having regard to those needs, the cost of alternative accommodation (including the costs which would necessarily be incurred in obtaining such accommodation).

Where the debtor confirms in writing to the PIP that the debtor does not wish to remain in occupation of his or her principal private residence; or where the PIP has, having discussed the issue with the debtor, formed the opinion that, taking account of the matters referred to above, the costs of continuing to reside in the debtor's principal private residence are disproportionately large, the PIP shall not be required to formulate the proposal for a DSA on terms that will not require the debtor to cease to occupy his or her principal private residence.[72]

A DSA shall not contain terms providing for a disposal of the debtor's interest in the principal private residence unless:[73]

(a) the debtor has obtained independent legal advice in relation to such disposal or, having been advised by the PIP to obtain such legal advice, has declined to do so; and

---

71. PIA 2012, s 69.
72. PIA 2012, s 69(3).
73. PIA 2012, s 69(4).

(b) to the extent that the provisions of the Family Home Protection Act 1976 or the Civil Partnership and Certain Rights and Obligations of Cohabitants Act 2010 apply to the property, all relevant provisions of those acts are complied with.

CREDITORS' MEETING

Calling a Creditors' Meeting

[4.29] Where a PIP has prepared a proposal for a DSA and the debtor has consented to that proposal and the calling of the meeting, the PIP shall arrange for the holding of a meeting.[74] In fixing a venue for a creditors' meeting, the chairperson must have regard to the convenience of the creditors. The meeting shall be scheduled for commencement between 9am and 4pm on a business day.[75]

The venue for the holding of a creditors' meeting shall be situated within the State. The period of notice of the meeting of creditors shall be 14 days, but such period may be waived or abridged where the consent of all the creditors to such waiver or abridgement is given in writing.

The PIP shall send a written notice of a creditors' meeting to each creditor. The written notice shall be in accordance with the regulations made by the Minister[76] and any further regulations pursuant to s 74 PIA 2012.

There are certain provisions which the PIP must observe when calling a meeting. These are as follows:

(a) give creditors at least 14 days' written notice of the meeting and the date on which, and the time and place at which, the meeting will be held;

(b) send, along with the notice referred to in para (a) above, the documents referred to below; and

(c) lodge a copy of the notice referred to in para (a) above and the documents referred to in para (b) above (as set out below) with the ISI.

In the event that the debtor does not consent to the calling of a creditors' meeting before the expiry of the protective certificate, the procedure as respects that debtor making a proposal for a DSA shall be treated as having concluded.[77]

The documents required to be furnished to the creditors and the ISI when calling a creditors' meeting are as follows:

(a) a copy of the PFS;

(b) a document containing the terms of the proposal for a DSA;

---

74. PIA 2012, s 70.

75. Personal Insolvency Act 2012 (Procedures for the Conduct of Creditors' Meetings) Regulations 2013 (SI 335/2013).

76. Personal Insolvency Act 2012 (Procedures for the Conduct of Creditors' Meetings) Regulations 2013 (SI 335/2013).

77. PIA 2012, s 70(4).

(c) a statement by the PIP to the effect that –

(i) he or she has been instructed by the debtor to act as PIP in connection with the DSA procedure, he or she has consented to so act and that he or she is a person entitled to act as a PIP,

(ii) he or she has advised the debtor of the various insolvency options for managing the debtor's financial difficulties,

(iii) he or she is not aware of any reasonable grounds to believe that the information contained in the debtor's PFS is not complete and accurate; and

(iv) he or she is of the opinion[78] that

(A) the debtor satisfies the eligibility criteria for the proposal of a DSA,[79]

(B) the proposed DSA complies with the mandatory requirements referred to in para **4.24** above, and

(C) the proposed DSA does not contain any terms that would release the debtor from an excluded debt, an excludable debt (other than a permitted debt) or a secured debt or otherwise affect such a debt;

(d) a report of the PIP—

(i) describing the outcome for creditors and, having regard to the financial circumstances of the debtor, whether or not the proposed DSA represents a fair outcome for the creditors and indicating, where relevant, how that financial outcome for creditors (whether individually or as a member of a class of creditors) under the terms of the proposal is likely to be better than the estimated financial outcome for such creditors if the debtor were to be adjudicated a bankrupt (having regard to, amongst other things, the estimated costs of the bankruptcy process), and

(ii) indicating whether or not he or she is of the opinion that the debtor is reasonably likely to be able to comply with the terms of the proposed DSA, and that the proposal is an acceptable alternative to bankruptcy for the debtor.

A debtor is under an obligation to inform the PIP if their financial position has materially altered since the completion of the PFS and the sending of the notice.[80] The PIP must assist the debtor in completing a new statement where they believe that the change in the debtor's financial position justifies same. This updated statement will accompany the notice for the creditors' meeting.

---

78. PIA 2012, s 71 as amended by the Courts and Civil Law (Miscellaneous Provisions) Act 2013, s 68.

79. PIA 2012, s 57.

80. PIA 2012, s 71(2).

Conduct of the Creditors' Meeting

[4.30] The conduct of the meeting[81] shall be governed by s 72 PIA 2012 and any regulations made under s 74 PIA 2012.[82]

The PIP may, where he or she is of the opinion that to do so would aid in obtaining approval of a proposed DSA by the creditors, adjourn the meeting and, with the consent in writing of the debtor, shall prepare an amended proposal for a DSA.[83] In the event that an amended proposal for a DSA is prepared the PIP shall, firstly, notify each creditor of the time, date and venue of the adjourned meeting and, secondly, send a copy of the amended proposal to each creditor at least seven days before the day of the adjourned meeting, unless all of the creditors waive the right to receive such period of notice in writing. The provisions set out above at para **4.29** in relation to the calling of a creditors' meeting shall apply, with all necessary modifications, after the adjournment.

An adjournment for the purpose of preparing an amended proposal for a DSA may occur once only in the course of the period of validity of a protective certificate (including any extension of such period).[84]

The proposal for a DSA may, before the proposal has been voted upon, be subject to a proposal for a modification to address an ambiguity or rectify an error in the proposed DSA if the modification has been proposed by a creditor or the PIP and the debtor gives his or her written consent to the modification.[85]

Once the meeting is convened, creditors, having considered a proposal for a DSA, shall vote either by voting in favour or against the approval of the proposed DSA.

The manner in which the voting is conducted is dealt with at para **4.31** below.

In the event that only one creditor is entitled to vote at the creditors' meeting (whether in respect of one or more debts), the requirement to hold a creditors' meeting may be satisfied where the creditor concerned notifies the PIP in writing of that creditor's approval or otherwise of the proposal for a DSA.[86]

Where the proposed DSA is not approved in accordance with the voting procedure outlined below, the DSA procedure shall be deemed to have come to an end, and the protective certificate issued shall cease to have effect.[87] The debtor will become fully liable to all debts including any arrears, charges and interest that have accrued during the continuance of the protective certificate but excluding any amounts paid in respect of those debts during the continuance of the protective certificate.

---

81. PIA 2012, s 72.
82. Personal Insolvency Act 2012 (Procedures for the Conduct of Creditors' Meetings) Regulations 2013 (SI 335/2013).
83. PIA 2012, s 72(2).
84. PIA 2012, s 72(4).
85. PIA 2012, s 72(6).
86. PIA 2012, s 72(8).
87. PIA 2012, s 72(7).

Voting Procedure at the Creditors' Meeting

[4.31] Except in circumstances where the debt owed to the creditor is owed in a currency that is not the currency of the State, the voting rights exercisable[88] by a creditor shall be proportionate to the value of the debt or debts owed by the debtor to that creditor on the date of the issue of the protective certificate concerned.[89]

In addition, a creditor to whom a preferred debt is owed shall not be entitled to vote in respect of that debt at a creditors' meeting unless that creditor has furnished to the PIP a waiver in writing of the creditor's right to have that debt treated as a preferred debt.[90]

A creditor who is a connected person of the debtor may not vote in favour of a proposal for a DSA at a creditors' meeting. A person is connected with another person where:[91]

(a) a person is connected with an individual if that person is a relative (brother, sister, parent, spouse or civil partner of the person or a child of the person or of the spouse or civil partner) of the individual;

(b) a person, in his or her capacity as a trustee of a trust, is connected with an individual who or any of whose children or as respects whom anybody corporate which he or she controls is a beneficiary of the trust;

(c) a person is connected with any person with whom he or she is in partnership;

(d) a company is connected with another person if that person has control of it or if that person and persons connected with that person together have control of it;

(e) any two or more persons acting together to secure or exercise control of a company shall be treated in relation to that company as connected with one another and with any person acting on the directions of any of them to secure or exercise control of the company.

With the exception of proxies, which are dealt with below, only the person who appears to the PIP to be the person to whom the debt is owed (or an agent acting on behalf of that person) shall be entitled to receive notices required to be sent to a creditor or to vote at the creditors' meeting.

Each creditor participating at a creditors' meeting at which a vote is held shall be entitled, in respect of each debt owed to such creditor, to vote once only in respect of the relevant resolution. Upon request by the chairperson, he or she shall vote without undue delay by stating to the chairperson whether he or she is in favour of or against the relevant resolution (or words to the like effect).[92]

88. PIA 2012, s 73.
89. PIA 2012, s 73(2)
90. PIA 2012, s 73(3).
91. PIA 2012, s 73(4).
92. Personal Insolvency Act 2012 (Procedures for the Conduct of Creditors' Meetings) Regulations 2013 (SI 335/2013).

Votes at a creditors' meeting may be given either personally or by proxy. Every notice summoning a creditors' meeting shall be accompanied by an instrument under which a creditor may appoint a proxy to attend such meeting and vote on such creditor's behalf[93] or in such form as the chairperson may allow. An instrument appointing a proxy shall be completed in writing under the hand of the creditor or, if such creditor is a company or other body corporate, under the hand of the secretary or other person duly authorised by the company or other body corporate. Each completed instrument appointing a proxy shall be delivered to the office of the PIP no later than 4pm on the last working day before the creditors' meeting is to be held. The chairperson may accept a validly appointed proxy which has been delivered as set out above.

Where a creditor abstains from voting then that shall not be counted as a vote.

No resolution shall be passed at any meeting save for a single resolution approving a DSA or a variation of a DSA.[94]

A proposal for a DSA shall be considered as having been approved by a creditors' meeting held under this Chapter where creditors, representing not less than 65 per cent in value of the creditors present and voting, have voted in favour of the proposal.[95]

Where no creditor votes, the proposed DSA shall be deemed to have been approved under this section.[96]

There is provision under s 74 PIA 2012 for the Minster to make regulations relating to the conduct of the creditors' meeting. The Personal Insolvency Act 2012 (Procedures for the Conduct of Creditors' Meetings) Regulations 2013 (SI 335/2013) has been enacted and the contents of same have been set out above.

STEPS FOLLOWING APPROVAL OF THE PROPOSAL FOR DSA

PIP

[4.32] Following approval of the proposal for a DSA, the PIP[97] shall as soon as practicable after the meeting has concluded notify the ISI and each creditor concerned and enclose with that notification a certificate with the result of the vote taken at the creditors' meeting, identifying the number of votes, in value, of the creditors present and voting in favour and against the proposed DSA, and a copy of the approved DSA and a statement by the PIP that he or she is of the opinion that; the debtor satisfies the eligibility criteria for the proposal of a DSA, the proposed DSA complies with the mandatory requirements referred to in para **4.24** above, and the proposed DSA does not contain any terms that would release the debtor from an excluded debt, an excludable debt (other than a permitted debt) or a secured debt or otherwise affect such a debt.

---

93. See **Appendix 7** – Creditor Proxy Form: http://www.isi.gov.ie/en/ISI/Creditors_meeting.pdf/Files/Creditors_meeting.pdf

94. Personal Insolvency Act 2012 (Procedures for the Conduct of Creditors' Meetings) Regulations 2013 (SI 335/2013).

95. PIA 2012, s 73(8).

96. PIA 2012, s 73(9).

97. PIA 2012, s 75(1).

The PIP shall also send a notice to each creditor indicating that he or she may make objection to the coming into effect of the DSA by lodging a notice of objection with the appropriate court, within fourteen days of the date of the sending of that notice.[98]

ISI

[4.33] On receipt of a notification by the PIP, the ISI[99] shall record the approval in the Register of DSAs and notify the appropriate court and furnish to that court a copy of the notification and the DSA. Where the notification of the PIP is received by the ISI before the expiry of the period of the protective certificate, such protective certificate shall continue in force until the DSA comes into effect or all objections lodged with the appropriate court have been determined by the court.

On receipt of a notification by it from the court, the ISI shall register the DSA in the Register of DSAs, and the DSA shall have effect upon being so registered.[100]

Creditor

[4.34] A creditor who lodges a notice of objection with the appropriate court shall at the same time send a copy of the notice of objection to both the ISI, and the PIP.[101]

The grounds on which objection may be made to the coming into effect of the DSA are those set out below. Pending the determination by the appropriate court of the objection made by a creditor, the protective certificate shall continue to have full effect.[102] The Courts Service shall make appropriate endeavours to facilitate the early hearing of the objection lodged having regard to the continuation in force of the protective certificate pending determination of the objection.[103] Where the appropriate court upholds the objection to the DSA, the DSA procedure shall be deemed to have come to an end together with the period of protection under the protective certificate.

The grounds on which a DSA may be challenged by a creditor are limited to the following matters:[104]

(a) that the debtor has by his or her conduct within the two years prior to the issue of the protective certificate arranged his or her financial affairs primarily with a view to being or becoming eligible to apply for a DSA or a PIA;

(b) the procedural requirements specified in the PIA 2012 were not followed;

(c) a material inaccuracy or omission exists in the debtor's statement of affairs (based on the PFS) which causes a material detriment to the creditor;

(d) the debtor, when the DSA was proposed, did not satisfy the eligibility criteria;

---

98. PIA 2012, s 75(2).
99. PIA 2012, s 76.
100. PIA 2012, s 78(6).
101. PIA 2012, s 75(3).
102. PIA 2012, s 77(2).
103. PIA 2012, s 77(3).
104. PIA 2012, s 87.

(e) the DSA unfairly prejudices the interests of a creditor;

(f) the debtor has committed an offence under this act;

(g) the debtor had entered into a transaction with a person at an undervalue within the preceding three years that has materially contributed to his or her inability to pay his or her debts (other than any debts due to the person with whom the debtor entered the transaction at an undervalue);

(h) the debtor had given a preference to a person within the preceding three years that had the effect of substantially reducing the sum available for distribution to the creditors (other than any debts due to the person who received the preference).

A debtor enters into a transaction with a person at an undervalue if he or she makes a gift to that person or he or she otherwise enters into a transaction with that person on terms that provide for him or her to receive no consideration; or he or she enters into a transaction with that person and the value of which, in money or money's worth, is significantly greater than the value, in money or money's worth, of the consideration provided by the person.

A debtor gives a preference to a person if that person is one of the debtor's creditors to whom a qualifying debt is owed or is a surety or guarantor for any such debt, and the debtor does anything (including the grant of security) or suffers anything to be done which (in either case) has the effect of putting that person into a position which, in the event that a DSA is made in relation to the debtor, will be better than the position he or she would have been in if that thing had not been done.

Court

[4.35] Where no objection is lodged by a creditor with the appropriate court[105] within 14 days of the giving of the notice, the court shall, where it is satisfied that the eligibility criteria in relation to the debtor have been satisfied and that the requisite percentage of creditors has approved the proposal for a DSA, approve the coming into effect of the DSA.[106]

In the event that a creditor lodges an objection with the appropriate court and the matter is determined by the court on the basis that the objection should not be allowed, the court shall, where it is satisfied that the eligibility criteria in relation to the debtor have been satisfied and that the requisite percentage of creditors has approved the proposal for a DSA, approve the coming into effect of the DSA.[107]

Where the appropriate court, for the purpose of its arriving at a decision, requires:

(a) further information, it may request the ISI to provide this information, and the ISI shall provide the information requested to the court and to the PIP concerned;

105. PIA 2012, s 78.

106. PIA 2012, s 78(1).

107. PIA 2012, s 78(2).

(b) further information or evidence, it may hold a hearing, which hearing shall be on notice to the ISI and the PIP concerned.

The court is entitled to accept the certificate of the PIP and the statement of the PIP referred to at para **4.32** above[108] as evidence that such eligibility criteria have been satisfied. The court may accept the certificate issued by the PIP concerned as evidence that the requisite percentage of creditors has approved the proposal for a DSA.[109]

Where the court approves the coming into effect of the DSA it shall arrange for the ISI to be notified in accordance with rules of court.[110] Please see **Ch 6** – Court Procedures for detailed information on the court procedures to be followed.

On receipt of a notification by it from the court, the ISI shall register the DSA in the Register of DSAs, and the DSA shall have effect upon being so registered.[111]

EFFECT OF DSA

[4.36] A DSA having been registered in the Register of DSAs shall have effect according to its terms and remain in effect until it is completed in accordance with its terms or the terms of any variation made or it is terminated in accordance with the DSA provisions.[112]

Where a DSA is in operation the debtor and every creditor who was entitled to vote at the creditors' meeting, regardless of whether such creditor voted to approve the proposal for the DSA, shall be bound by the terms of it.[113]

A creditor is subject to certain restrictions once a DSA becomes effective.[114] The creditor cannot:

(a) initiate any legal proceedings in relation to a specified debt;

(b) take any step to prosecute such legal proceedings already initiated;

(c) take any step to secure or recover payment of a specified debt;

(d) execute or enforce a judgment or order of a court or tribunal against the debtor in respect of a specified debt;

(e) take any step to recover goods in the possession or custody of the debtor (whether or not title to the goods is vested in the creditor);

(f) otherwise initiate contact with the debtor in respect of payment of a specified debt;

108. PIA 2012, s 78(5) as amended by the Courts and Civil Law (Miscellaneous Provisions) Act 2013, s 73.

109. PIA 2012, s 78(4).

110. PIA 2012, s 78(5).

111. PIA 2012, s 78(6).

112. PIA 2012, s 79.

113. PIA 2012, s 79(2).

114. PIA 2012, s 79(3).

(g) in relation to an agreement with the debtor, including a security agreement, by reason only that the debtor is insolvent or that a DSA is in effect—

(i) terminate or amend that agreement, or

(ii) claim an accelerated payment, or a forfeiture of a term, under that agreement.

Furthermore, while a DSA is in effect a creditor of that debtor shall not apply for the issue of a summons under s 8 of the Bankruptcy Act 1988 or present a petition to have the debtor concerned adjudicated a bankrupt in respect of a debt covered by the DSA.[115]

A creditor is not precluded from taking an action as respects a person who has jointly contracted with the debtor or is jointly liable with the debtor to the creditor and that other person may sue or be sued in respect of the contract without joining the debtor.[116]

The period in which the DSA is in effect shall be disregarded for the purpose of any applicable limitation period in relation to any proceedings or process to which this section applies (including any limitation period under the Statute of Limitations 1957).[117] Equally, the period for which any judgment against the debtor in relation to a debt which is the subject of a DSA has effect (whether under statute or rule of court) shall, subject to the provisions of this Act, be extended by the period that the DSA is in effect.[118]

OPERATION OF THE TERMS OF THE DSA

[4.37] In general terms, a debtor or creditor who is party to that DSA shall perform his or her obligations in accordance with its terms.[119] Unless otherwise provided for under the terms of the DSA, the following general terms should be followed. Any payments to creditors under the DSA will be made by the PIP. The PIP shall transmit payments received to each of the creditors in the agreed proportion on a timely basis. Regular contact with the debtor should be maintained and the PIP should request such reports and conduct such reviews as may be required, but such review shall in any event be carried out at least once in every period of 12 months.

Where the debtor has defaulted or appears likely to default in his or her obligations under the DSA, the PIP should discuss the matter with the debtor and should monitor implementation of the DSA.

Where the circumstances of the debtor have changed in a material respect, the PIP shall provide information to the debtor regarding his or her right or obligation to initiate an application to vary the DSA.[120] A material change in the debtor's circumstances includes an increase or decrease in the level of the debtor's assets, liabilities or income

115. PIA 2012, s 79(5).
116. PIA 2012, s 79(6).
117. PIA 2012, s 79(8).
118. PIA 2012, s 79(9).
119. PIA 2012, s 80.
120. PIA 2012, s 82.

which would affect the debtor's ability to make repayments under the DSA. In addition to this, where the circumstances of a debtor have changed to such an extent that a variation in the terms of a DSA is appropriate, the PIP shall take the necessary steps to initiate a variation of the DSA as set out below.[121]

The PIP shall deal with the property of the debtor in accordance with the DSA. The PIP shall not charge fees or seek to recover expenses incurred unless those fees and expenses are in accordance with the terms of the DSA.

The PIP is obliged to respond in a timely manner to requests for information regarding the operation of the DSA from the ISI, the debtor and the creditors.

The PIP shall maintain complete and accurate records of account of the moneys received from the debtor and the moneys disbursed to the creditors and such moneys shall while in the possession and control of the PIP be maintained in an account in the State with a bank authorised to carry on business in the State, which account is used solely for the purposes of receiving payments from the debtor and transmitting such payments to creditors (after the deduction of any fees or expenses payable to the PIP permitted to be made).[122]

GENERAL DUTIES AND OBLIGATIONS OF THE DEBTOR

[4.38] A debtor who participates in any DSA process is under an obligation to act in good faith and, in his or her dealings with the PIP concerned, to make full disclosure to that PIP of all of his or her assets, income and liabilities and of all other circumstances that are reasonably likely to have a bearing on the ability of the debtor to make payments to his or her creditors.[123]

A debtor who participates in any part of the DSA process of applying for or operating a DSA shall co-operate fully in the process, and in particular comply with any reasonable request from the PIP to provide assistance, documents and information necessary for the application of the process to the debtor's case or the carrying out of the PIP's functions, including any debt, tax, employment, business, social welfare or other financial records.

The debtor is obliged under this section to inform the PIP as soon as reasonably practicable of any material change in the debtor's circumstances, particularly an increase or decrease in the level of the debtor's assets, liabilities or income, which would affect the debtor's ability to make repayments under the DSA.

A debtor in respect of whom a DSA is in effect shall not, either alone or with any other person, obtain credit in an amount of more than €650 from any person without informing that person that he or she is subject to a DSA.

A debtor in respect of whom a DSA is in effect shall not transfer, lease, grant security over or otherwise dispose of any interest in property above a value of €650[124]

121. See para **4.40** below.
122. See **Ch 8** – Personal Insolvency Practitioners.
123. PIA 2012, s 81.
124. Personal Insolvency Act 2012 (Value Above which a Debtor Must not Transfer, Lease, Grant Security Over, or Otherwise Dispose of an Interest in Property) Regulations 2013 (SI 330/2013).

otherwise than in accordance with the terms of the DSA. A debtor shall inform the PIP as soon as reasonably practicable after becoming aware of any inaccuracy or omission in the debtor's statement of affairs based on the PFS.

Finally, a debtor who participates in a DSA shall not pay to creditors any additional payments separate to the DSA in respect of debts covered in the DSA.

VARIATION OF A DSA

[4.39] A DSA like any other legal agreement may be varied in accordance with its terms.[125] Where the DSA is silent, the following applies in relation to the variation of the terms.

PIP

[4.40] A PIP, whether on his or her own initiative or on a request made by a debtor or creditor in the circumstances outlined at para **4.41** below, shall propose a variation of a DSA where:

(a) the PIP is concerned that there has been a material change in the debtor's circumstances which would affect his or her ability to make repayments under the DSA, and

(b) the PIP is satisfied that there is a reasonable prospect that the variation that addresses the circumstances would be approved.

A material change in the debtor's circumstances is generally an increase or decrease in the level of the debtor's assets, liabilities or income, which would affect the debtor's ability to make repayments under the DSA.

The PIP shall, within 21 days of receipt of a request by a debtor or creditor pursuant to para **4.41** below, decide whether further enquiry is required. The PIP may request such further information as he or she requires for the person making the request and shall make such enquiries as is necessary to arrive at a decision. Where the PIP is satisfied that the conditions at para **4.40** above are met the PIP shall without delay:

(a) with the debtor's assistance, require a debtor to complete a new PFS;

(b) formulate a proposal for a variation;

(c) seek the written consent of the debtor to the proposal and to the calling of a creditors' meeting for the purpose of considering the proposal; and

(d) where consent has been given, arrange for the holding of a creditors' meeting.

Debtor or Creditor

[4.41] A debtor or creditor who is bound by a DSA may request that a PIP propose a variation to a DSA which request shall be:

(a) in writing;

125. PIA 2012, s 82 as amended by the Courts and Civil Law (Miscellaneous Provisions) Act 2013, s 75.

(b) accompanied by information or evidence to support the assertion that there has been a material change in the debtor's circumstances; and

(c) accompanied by the written consent of the person making the request to the –

(i) making of an enquiry by the PIP, and

(ii) disclosure by the PIP of personal data of the person to the extent necessary for such an enquiry.

Creditors' Meeting

[4.42] When calling a creditors' meeting for this purpose, the PIP shall give creditors at least 14 days' written notice of the meeting and the date on which, and the time and place at which, the meeting will be held. The PIP will also send, along with the notice, a written proposal for the variation of the DSA, a report of the PIP describing the outcome for the creditors and debtor under the terms of the proposal and indicating whether the PIP is of the opinion that the debtor will comply with the varied terms of the proposal and a copy of the PFS. The PIP shall lodge a copy of the notice and the proposal with the ISI.

A creditors' meeting under this section shall be conducted in the usual procedure as set out at para **4.29** above. The creditors at the creditors' meeting shall vote in the prescribed manner either in favour of the approval of the proposal for the variation or against the approval of the proposal for the variation.

The only slight variation to the voting for the variation of a DSA is that the value of a creditor's vote at the meeting shall be calculated by reference to the value of the creditor's debts on the date on which the vote takes place.

Where the proposal is not approved or a court upholds a creditor's objection to the variation, then the terms of the original DSA will continue in effect without being subject to the variation. In this event, the entitlement of the PIP to propose another variation is not prejudiced.[126]

Any unreasonable refusal by the debtor to consent to the proposal for a variation or the calling of a creditors' meeting shall be grounds for an application to terminate the DSA. The following grounds shall be considered reasonable grounds for refusal by the debtor to vary the terms of the DSA:

(a) where there has been an increase in the debtor's income, to make additional payments in excess of 50 per cent of the increase in his or her income available to him or her after the following deductions (where applicable) are made:

(i) income tax,

(ii) social insurance contributions,

(iii) payments made by him or her in respect of excluded debts,

(iv) payments made by him or her in respect of excludable debts that are not permitted debts,

(v) such other levies and charges on income as may be prescribed, or

126. Courts and Civil Law (Miscellaneous Provisions) Act 2013, s 82(10)(b).

(b) to make a payment amounting to more than 50 per cent of the value of any property acquired by the debtor after the coming into effect of the DSA that is proposed to be varied, unless receipt of that property had been anticipated by the terms of that DSA.

Following approval of the variation, the PIP shall as soon as practicable notify the ISI and each creditor concerned of the fact, and enclose with that notification a copy of the DSA as varied. On receipt of this notification, the ISI shall record the variation in the Register of DSAs.

The variation will take effect immediately upon its being recorded and shall remain in effect until the DSA as varied is completed in accordance with its terms, is terminated in accordance with the PIA 2012 or is further varied in accordance with this section.

Finally, a variation to a DSA shall, while it is in effect, be binding upon the debtor and each creditor who was entitled to vote at the meeting held under this section, regardless of whether such creditor voted to approve that variation.

TERMINATION OF DSA

Creditors' Meeting

[4.43] A DSA may be terminated at a meeting of creditors.[127] The PIP (whether on his or her own initiative or at the request of a creditor) may call a meeting of creditors to be held in accordance with this section where it reasonably appears to that PIP that there has been a material change in the debtor's circumstances which would affect his or her ability to make repayments under the DSA, or the debtor participated in the DSA process in the knowledge that he or she did not satisfy the eligibility criteria to make a proposal for a DSA.

When calling a creditors' meeting to be held under this section, the PIP shall give creditors at least 14 days' written notice of the meeting and the date on which, and the time and place at which, the meeting will be held and lodge a copy of the notice with the ISI.

The creditors' meeting and voting will follow the usual procedure set out at para **4.29** above. The only variation is that the voting will be in accordance with the value of a creditor's vote at the meeting and shall be calculated by reference to the value of the creditor's debts on the date on which the vote takes place.

The PIP is under the usual obligations to notify the ISI and each creditor of the approval of the termination of the DSA. The ISI will record the termination in the Register of DSAs. The termination of a DSA shall take effect immediately upon its being so recorded.

Application to Court

[4.44] In the limited circumstances set out below, a creditor or a PIP may, at any time during the operation of a DSA, apply to the appropriate court to have that DSA

127. PIA 2012, s 82(4).

terminated.[128] Please see **Ch 6** – Court Procedures for detailed information on the court procedures to be followed.

The grounds of termination are limited to the following:

(a) a material inaccuracy or omission exists in the debtor's PFS, which causes a material detriment to the creditor;

(b) the debtor did not satisfy the eligibility criteria to enter the DSA process when he or she initiated the process;

(c) the debtor did not comply with the duties and obligations imposed on him or her under the DSA process;

(d) the debtor has since the coming into effect of the DSA committed an offence under this act;

(e) the debtor is in arrears with his or her payments for a period of not less than three months;

(f) the debtor has failed to carry out any action necessary to enable a term of the DSA have effect;

(g) the debtor has unreasonably refused to consent to a variation of the DSA.

In determining whether a debtor is in arrears with his or her payments for a period of not less than three months the following applies:

(a) at the beginning of the three-month period ending immediately before the day on which the application was made, one or more than one payment in respect of the debts became due and payable by the debtor under the DSA; and

(b) throughout that three-month period the debtor was in arrears in respect of any or all of those payments.

On hearing the application the court may dismiss the application, terminate the DSA or order the PIP to propose a variation of the DSA.

Where a court makes a decision, the Registrar of the court shall notify the ISI of the decision who will notify the PIP and specified creditors of the decision. Where the court decides to terminate a DSA, the ISI shall on receipt of the notification of the decision record the fact of the termination in the Register of DSAs.[129]

Automatic Termination – Six Months' Arrears

[4.45] Where the debtor is in arrears with his or her payments for a period of six months, the DSA shall be deemed to have failed and shall terminate where a creditor or the PIP notifies the ISI of such default. Where the ISI receives such a notification of default, it shall record the failure of the DSA in the Register of DSAs.[130]

128. PIA 2012, s 83.

129. PIA 2012, s 83(3) as amended by the Courts and Civil Law (Miscellaneous Provisions) Act 2013, s 76.

130. PIA 2012, s 84.

A debtor is in arrears with his or her payments for a period of six months on a given date if at the beginning of the six-month period ending immediately before that date one or more than one payment in respect of a debt became due and payable by the debtor under the DSA, and at no time during that six-month period were any obligations in respect of those payments discharged.

Effect of Premature Termination of DSA

[4.46] Where a DSA has been deemed to come to an end, has failed or has terminated prematurely,[131] the debtor shall thereupon be liable in full for all debts covered by the DSA (including any arrears, charges and interest that have accrued during the continuance of the DSA but excluding any amounts paid in respect of those debts during the continuance of the DSA), unless the terms of the DSA provide otherwise or the appropriate court has made an order otherwise.

This is effective regardless of any prejudice to the validity of any act done or property disposed of in accordance with the DSA.

Where a DSA has terminated under para **4.43**, the ISI shall, within three months after the date on which the DSA would have terminated, remove from the Register of DSAs all information in respect of the DSA.[132]

COMPLETION OF THE DSA

[4.47] Upon the expiration of the DSA, and where the debtor has complied with his or her obligations under the DSA, the PIP shall notify the debtor, creditors and the ISI.[133] Where the debtor has complied with his or her obligations under the DSA, the debtor stands discharged from the debts specified in the DSA. The ISI shall record the successful completion of the DSA in the Register of DSAs and within three months remove all information recorded in the Register of DSAs in respect of that DSA.[134]

RULES OF COURT

[4.48] Please see **Ch 6** – Court Procedures[135] for the details of the court procedures to be followed in a DSA.

131. PIA 2012, s 85.

132. PIA 2012, s 85 as amended by the Courts and Civil Law (Miscellaneous Provisions) Act 2013, s 77.

133. PIA 2012, s 86.

134. PIA 2012, s 86(3) as amended by the Courts and Civil Law (Miscellaneous Provisions) Act 2013, s 78.

135. para **6.20**.

Appropriate Court

[4.49] Section 5 PIA 2012 sets out the appropriate court in respect of DSAs. Where the total liabilities of the debtor, determined on the basis of the PFS completed by the debtor, are in excess of €2,500,000, the appropriate court is the High Court, with the Circuit Court being the appropriate court in all other circumstances of a DSA. The performance of the functions and the exercise of the powers and jurisdiction shall be within the jurisdiction of the circuit of the Circuit Court in which:

(a) the debtor to whom the application relates is residing at the time of the making of the application or has resided within one year of the time of the making of the application; or

(b) the debtor to whom the application relates has a place of business at the time of the making of the application or has a place of business within one year of the time of the making of the application.

FURTHER INFORMATION

[4.50] The ISI has published 'The Guide to a Debt Settlement Arrangement' and the following other guidelines which are available on their website:

http://www.isi.gov.ie/en/ISI/Pages/Publications

- Debt Settlement Arrangement Scenarios
- Debt Settlement Arrangement Scenario Revenue Involvement
- Debt Settlement Arrangement Step by Step Example

Chapter 5

PERSONAL INSOLVENCY ARRANGEMENTS

INTRODUCTION

[5.01] A Personal Insolvency Arrangement (PIA) is an insolvency process that can be entered into between a debtor and his or her secured and unsecured creditors. A PIA allows an eligible debtor to reach agreement with its unsecured and secured creditors in relation to the settlement of and/or the restructuring of its debts.

PIAs are dealt with under Ch 4 of the PIA 2012. The PIA will assist persons who have such income, assets and debts that would fall outside the criteria for a Debt Relief Notice (DRN)[1] and a Debt Settlement Arrangement (DSA).[2] A PIA will allow a debtor to include secured debt subject to a cap of €3,000,000 unless all secured creditors consent to the inclusion of a higher amount.

The type of debts that can be included in a PIA are principal private residence (PPR) loans, investment property loans, buy to let mortgages/loans, personal guarantees, personal loans, credit union loans, business/commercial loans and credit card loans.

The difference between a DRN and a PIA is that a DRN is concerned with unsecured debts below €20,000 whereas a PIA includes secured debts to a value of €3,000,000 and an unlimited amount of unsecured debts.

A PIA differs from a DSA as a PIA includes secured debts. Secured debts cannot be covered in a DSA. Secured debt is a debt backed or secured by an asset. Unsecured debts are debts where the unsecured creditor would not be entitled to seize specific assets if the debtor fails to meet repayment requirements as that creditor does not hold security over the assets.

In brief, where a PIA is considered, a Personal Insolvency Practitioner (PIP) would design a plan where the debtor would pay a specified amount to creditors over a six-year period after which the outstanding unsecured debts that are part of the PIA would be discharged. Secured debts can be restructured under a PIA (eg to provide for payments for a certain period or a write-down of a portion of negative equity). Depending on the terms of the PIA, the debtor may be released from a secured debt at the end of the PIA period or the secured debt can continue to be payable by the debtor after the term of the PIA (possibly on restructured terms).

A specified proportion of creditors would be required to approve the PIA. The PIA must be processed by the Insolvency Service of Ireland (ISI) and approved by the relevant court.[3]

1. See **Ch 3** – Debt Relief Notices.
2. See **Ch 4** – Debt Settlement Arrangements.
3. See para **6.01**.

GENERAL ELIGIBILITY CRITERIA

[5.02]

Qualifying Criteria	Disqualifying Criteria
A debtor is insolvent in they are unable to pay their debts in full as they fall due	25% or more of the debts must not have been incurred during the six months prior to making the application
The debtor has at least one secured creditor holding security over Irish property or assets	The debtor must not be the subject of a DRN now or have been within the previous three years
The debtor's secured debts are not in excess of €3,000,000[4]	The debtor must not be the subject of a DSA now or have been within the previous five years
The debtor must have cooperated under a mortgage arrears process for a period of six months with its secured creditor in respect of its PPR with the result that no alternative repayment scheme was agreed or the secured creditor confirmed it would not put such arrangement in place[5]	The debtor must not have previously been the subject of a PIA
The debtor must be domiciled in the Republic of Ireland, or must have ordinarily resided or had a place of business within the Republic of Ireland within the previous year	The debtor must not be bankrupt or subject to a bankruptcy measure or have been discharged from bankruptcy in the previous five years
The debtor must complete a Prescribed Financial Statement (PFS) and have made a statutory declaration of its truth and accuracy	The debtor must not have been the subject of a protective certificate issued in respect of a PIA in the previous year
The debtor has obtained a statement from the PIP confirming that the PIP is of the following opinion: the information in the PFS is true and accurate the debtor is eligible to make a proposal for a PIA having considered the PFS there is no likelihood of the debtor becoming solvent within the next five years	

4. Where all secured creditors consent, the €3,000,000 cap may be increased.

Qualifying Criteria	Disqualifying Criteria
if the debtor enters the PIA there is a reasonable prospect that they will become solvent within the next five years	

A STEP-BY-STEP SUMMARY OF THE PROCESS

Applying for a Protective Certificate

[5.03]

Step 1 Having reviewed their circumstances and determining that they are unable to pay their debts as they fall due, the debtor contacts a PIP from the list available on the ISI website.[6]

Step 2 The insolvent debtor provides the PIP with information on his finances and financial circumstances including information on his creditors, debts, liabilities, assets, guarantees and any other financial information.

Step 3 The PIP meets with the debtor and/or discusses the debtor's situation and eligibility to apply for a PIA based on the information supplied and gives him advice on the various insolvency options. The PIP will detail the PIA application process and outline the debtor's duties and obligations in the process and whether the debtor meets the eligibility criteria. The PIP should provide written advice setting out their opinion on whether the PIA is the best insolvency arrangement available to the debtor together with any reasons for advising same. The PIP should provide information on fee arrangements and other conditions of their appointment.

Step 4 Once the debtor decides he wishes to proceed then he must indicate this intention in writing to the PIP and request that the PIP act on the debtor's behalf. The PIP should confirm in writing that the PIP is willing to act as a PIP for the particular debtor.

Step 5 The debtor must then provide all his financial information and supporting documentation to the PIP whereupon the PIP will assist the debtor in completing the PFS. There will be a meeting/series of meetings and/or phone calls with the PIP to progress the application.

Step 6 On completion of the PFS, the PIP will further advise the debtor of their options for addressing their financial difficulties, whether the debtor is eligible for a PIA and in the PIP's opinion if a PIA is the most appropriate option.[7]

---

5. Mortgage arrears process includes that provided for in the Central Bank of Ireland's Code of Conduct on Mortgage Arrears (www.centralbank.ie). This condition does not apply if the PIP believes that, even if the debtor were to enter such arrangement, it is unlikely that the debtor would become solvent with a period of five years.

Step 7 Once the debtor decides to proceed and apply for a PIA, it must instruct the PIP in writing of its decision. The PIP must notify the ISI of his appointment.

Step 8 The PIP will examine the completed PFS and, where it is satisfied that the PFS is true and accurate and that the debtor satisfies the eligibility criteria, the PIP will provide a statement, inter alia, that there is no likelihood of the debtor becoming solvent within five years, that he is of the opinion that the PIA would facilitate the debtor becoming solvent in a period of five years or more, that the debtor satisfies the eligibility criteria and that the information in the PFS is true and accurate.[8]

Step 9 The debtor will be required to sign a statutory declaration affirming that the PFS is a complete and accurate statement of the debtor's assets, liabilities, income and expenditure.

Step 10 The debtor will be required to complete and sign the following documentation required to accompany the application for a PIA:

(a) a copy of the statement made by the PIP referred to above;

(b) a document signed by the debtor confirming satisfaction with the eligibility criteria for a PIA;

(c) a completed PFS form and statutory declaration;

(d) a schedule of the debtor's creditors and amount owed to each; whether the creditor is a secured creditor or not (if secured, details must be provided of any security); where a debt is an excludable debt, a statement of whether it is a permitted debt;

(e) debtor's written statement confirming cooperation for a period of at least six months with its secured creditor in respect of their PPR and confirmation of no agreement for an alternative repayment plan agreement or secured creditor's written confirmation of their unwillingness to enter into an alternative arrangement (the PIP may advise that this statement is not required in circumstances where the PIP makes a statement that, even if an alternative arrangement is entered, it is unlikely that the debtor would become solvent within a period of five years);

(f) the debtor's written consent to enable –

(i) the PIP to disclose personal data to the ISI,

(ii) the ISI to process the application,

(iii) the ISI to make any necessary enquiries about the debtor, and

---

6. http://www.isi.gov.ie/en/ISI/Pages/Registers.
7. See **Ch 8** – Personal Insolvency Practitioners.
8. See **Ch 8** – Personal Insolvency Practitioners.

(iv) the ISI to disclose the debtor's personal data to the creditors concerned, as required.

Application for a Protective Certificate

[5.04] [9]

Step 11 An application is then made to the ISI by the PIP on behalf of the debtor. The ISI can then make enquiries as it deems necessary as to the information and documents provided. Once satisfied that the debtor has complied with the criteria then it can issue a certificate that the application is in order and will forward the application to the appropriate court[9] (ie Circuit Court or High Court).

Step 12 The appropriate court will review the application and once the court is satisfied that the necessary criteria are satisfied, the application will be approved and the court will issue a protective certificate, which is valid for a period of 70 days from the date of issue.

Step 13 Where a protective certificate is issued, the ISI will notify the PIP of the issue of the protective certificate. The name, address and date of birth of the debtor and the date of issue of the protective certificate will be placed on an electronic public Register of Protective Certificates.

Agreement to a PIA Proposal

[5.05]

Step 14 Once the court has issued the protective certificate, the debtor will liaise with the PIP to prepare a proposal for a PIA. The debtor will be required to make a full disclosure of their living expenses, life plans and any circumstances that may have a bearing on their ability to pay current or future debts.

Step 15 The PIP will liaise with the debtor's creditors when drawing up the proposal for a PIA and will have regard, where relevant, to the preferences in the terms of the PIA. In the case of secured debts, the market value of the security can be determined by agreement between the debtor, the PIP and the relevant secured creditor, or in the absence of agreement an independent valuer can be appointed. The PIP will then provide a draft proposal for the PIA which the debtor must review.

Step 16 Where the debtor approves the proposal, the debtor should sign and return the proposal to the PIP together with indicating consent to the calling of a meeting of the creditors to approve the PIA.

9. Where the liabilities of the debtor on the basis of the PFS are in excess of €2,500,000, the PIA is in jurisdiction of the High Court with all other PIAs in the jurisdiction of the Circuit Court. Please see Ch 6 – Court Procedures.

Step 17 The PIP must give written notice to the creditors of its appointment as a PIP for the purpose of making a proposal for a PIA. The PIP must invite the creditors to make submissions in respect of the debts concerned and the manner in which they might be dealt with under the PIA. A copy of the debtor's PFS must accompany this notice. The PIP must consider any submissions made by a creditor with particular reference to any previous or existing offers of arrangement made by the creditor to the debtor. The PIP may request that a creditor file a proof of debt with the debt proved in the same manner as a debt of a bankrupt under Bankruptcy Act 1988.[10] Where a creditor does not comply with the requirement to file a proof of debt, they will not be entitled to vote at the creditors' meeting or share in any distribution that may be made under the PIA.

Step 18 The PIP will call a creditors' meeting[11] with not less than 14 days' written notice of the meeting and the date and time and place at which the meeting will be held. The notice will be accompanied by the following documentation:

(a) completed PFS,

(b) document containing the terms of the proposed PIA,

(c) statement by the PIP confirming his appointment by the debtor and his consent to act, advice to debtor on the range of insolvency arrangement options, confirmation that the PIP is not aware of any reasonable grounds to believe that the information contained in the PFS is not complete or accurate, and confirmation of the debtor's eligibility for a PIA, and

(d) report by the PIP setting out the outcome for creditors and whether the PIA represents a fair outcome for the creditors and indicating whether the financial outcome for the creditors under the terms of the proposal is likely to be better than the estimated financial outcome for such creditors if the debtor were to be adjudicated bankrupt and an opinion as to whether, in the PIP's opinion, the debtor is likely to be able to comply with the terms of the PIA.

Step 19 Where the PIA has been approved at the creditors' meeting by being accepted by a majority of voting creditors representing not less than 65 per cent of the total amount of the debtor's debts due to creditors participating in the meeting of which at least 50 per cent of the secured creditors entitled to vote have voted in favour and of the unsecured creditors entitled to vote at least 50 per cent have voted in favour, the PIP will notify the creditors and the ISI. The ISI will notify the relevant court and the relevant court will consider the PIA subject to any creditor's objection. The PIP will inform the debtor whether the relevant court has approved the PIA.

---

10. **Appendix 4** – the Bankruptcy Act 1988, Sch 1, paras 1–22.

11. PIA 2012, s 106.

Step 19 (contd) Where the PIA has been approved, the debtor's name, address, date of birth and the date of the coming into effect of the PIA will be entered in the electronic public Register of PIAs.

During the PIA Period

[5.06]

Step 20 The PIP will contact the debtor to arrange implementing the terms of the PIA. The debtor will make payments through the PIP during the lifetime of the PIA unless the terms of the PIA provide otherwise.

Step 21 The PIP will monitor the implementation of the PIA during the lifetime of the PIA and must carry out reviews at least once a year. The debtor will be required to complete a PFS as part of the review process. The reviewed PFS will be distributed to creditors by the PIP.

Termination of the PIA

[5.07]

Step 22 When the debtor has completed all its obligations under the terms of the PIA for the full term of the PIA they will be considered to have successfully completed the PIA at the end of the PIA term. The PIP will inform the ISI, who will record the successful completion of the PIA on the Register of PIAs. The debtor will be discharged from the unsecured debts included in the PIA and the secured debts to the extent specified in the PIA and will now be considered solvent.

OVERVIEW OF PIA

[5.08] Application for a PIA can be made by an insolvent debtor who has total unsecured debts of over €20,000 (ie €20,001 upwards) and secured debts of less than €3,000,000. The limit of €3,000,000 on the secured debts can be increased where there is consent among all secured creditors. A PIA can only be sought via a PIP, who acts on the debtor's behalf throughout the process. Where there are two or more debtors party to all the debts to be covered by the PIA and each of those debtors satisfies the eligibility criteria, those debtors may jointly propose a PIA.

There is further provision in the PIA 2012[12] for a PIA to be administered in common by a PIP with one or more other PIAs, where in the opinion of the PIP:

(a) the PIAs can reasonably be administered in common because of the financial relationship between the debtors;

12. PIA 2012, s 89.

(b) the terms of the PIAs specify in sufficient detail how the administration will operate including –

(i) the treatment of the joint and individual assets and the treatment of joint and individual debts,

(ii) whether the approval of one PIA is contingent on the approval of the other PIA,

(iii) the effect of the failure or early termination of one PIA on the other PIA – in particular, as to whether it is a condition of each PIA that for it to be considered as having been successfully completed other PIAs are also required to have been successfully completed, and

(iv) where a joint payment is to be received from two or more debtors, how that payment is to be apportioned between the creditors under each PIA.

With the assistance of a PIP,[13] the debtor can apply for a protective certificate while the PIA is being prepared. A protective certificate prevents creditors from taking any action for the recovery of debts for 70 working days from the date of issue.[14] There is provision for this time to be extended by a further 40 days subject to certain conditions.[15] There is further provision for this period to be extended by another 40 days where a PIP has been replaced in accordance with the PIA 2012.[16]

Under this scheme creditors are sent a PIA proposal providing for payments to be made by the debtor for a period of six years. Creditors may agree to this but for further protection there is provision to extend the period of the PIA for a further year.

Payments into the PIA will generally only cover a percentage of what is actually owed. Any remaining debt, once all agreed payments are made, will be legally written off. Any arrangement in relation to a secured debt will be in accordance with the terms of the PIA.

For the PIA to be accepted, a majority of voting creditors, representing not less than 65 per cent of the total amount of the debtor's debts due to creditors, participating in the meeting, of which at least 50 per cent of the secured creditors entitled to vote have voted in favour and at least 50 per cent of the unsecured creditors entitled to vote have voted in favour.[17] Creditors are accorded voting rights strictly in accordance with the amount of their debts. The value of the secured debts is the lesser of the market value[18] of the security concerned or the amount of debt secured on the security on the date of issue of the protective certificate.[19] All creditors entitled to vote are bound by the decision of those creditors who choose to exercise their vote.

13. See **Ch 8** – Personal Insolvency Practitioners.
14. PIA 2012, s 95(5).
15. PIA 2012, s 96(6).
16. PIA 2012, s 96(7).
17. PIA 2012, s 110.
18. PIA 2012, s 105(6).
19. PIA 2012, s 110(2).

Apart from the DRN[20] application, which will be processed by an AI and made to the ISI, the other applications must be made on behalf of an insolvent debtor to his or creditors by a PIP.[21] What is proposed is essentially what amounts to a privatised system. PIPs will have to undergo a licensing or authorisation process which will be administered by the ISI. PIPs will need to be paid for the work carried out. The fees charged will vary depending on a variety of factors such as the complexity of the PIA, the level of debt or the number of creditors. It is submitted by the authors that there must be careful monitoring provisions together with guidelines to ensure the protection of vulnerable over-indebted people from uncontrolled and unfair costs.

The PIA 2012 authorises the ISI to make regulations governing the supervision and authorisation of PIPs. The Personal Insolvency Act 2012 (Authorisation and Supervision of Personal Insolvency Practitioners) Regulations 2013[22] were introduced to fulfil this requirement. Generally speaking, PIPs' fees come out of the sale of debtors' assets and the distribution of debtors' surplus income, subject to the payment in some case of initial upfront fees to process an application. It is imperative that we don't end up with a system whereby the fees and costs of the PIPs erode the benefit of the new insolvency processes.

It will remain to be seen how the regulation and fee scale of the PIPs will play out in practice.

The system in the UK in relation to PIPs has been replicated in this jurisdiction. In the UK, the fees are approved and fixed by creditors. This method ensures that creditors have some ability to control the fee process and ensure fees remain at an acceptable level and do not erode the benefit of having used this insolvency process. It is understood from the guidance produced by the ISI that this process is to be followed in this jurisdiction, whereby creditors will have an opportunity to vote on the fees proposed by the PIP.

REQUIREMENTS FOR DEBTOR ELIGIBILITY

Eligibility Criteria

[5.09] The following criteria must be met in order for the debtor to be eligible to make a proposal for a PIA:[23]

(a) that the aggregate of the debts which are secured debts is less than €3,000,000, subject to this limit not applying where all secured creditors consent to removing the limit;

(b) that the debtor—

(i) is domiciled in the State, or

---

20. See **Ch 3** – Debt Relief Notices.
21. See **Ch 8** – Personal Insolvency Practitioners.
22. Personal Insolvency Act 2012 (Authorisation and Supervision of Personal Insolvency Practitioners) Regulations 2013 (SI 209/2013).
23. PIA 2012, s 91.

(ii) within one year before the date of the application for a protective certificate has ordinarily

(A) resided in the State, or

(B) had a place of business in the State;

(c) that at least one of the creditors is a secured creditor holding security over an interest in property of the debtor situate in the State (personal or real property);

(d) that the debtor is insolvent;

(e) that the debtor has completed a PFS and has made a statutory declaration confirming that the statement is a complete and accurate statement of the debtor's assets, liabilities, income and expenditure;

(f) that the debtor has made a declaration in writing that he or she has cooperated for a period of at least six months with his or her creditors who are secured creditors as respects the debtor's PPR in accordance with any process relating to mortgage arrears operated by the secured creditors and approved or required by the Central Bank of Ireland and which process relates to the secured debt concerned and that notwithstanding such cooperation the debtor has not been able to agree an alternative repayment arrangement with the secured creditor or that secured creditor has confirmed in writing their unwillingness to enter into an alternative repayment arrangement. This criteria will not apply where the PIP confirms in writing that, having regard to the PFS, it is the belief of the PIP that if the debtor were to enter an alternative repayment arrangement with the secured creditor, the debtor would be unlikely to become solvent within the period of five years commencing on the date of that PIP confirmation;[24]

(g) that the PIP has issued a certificate to the effect that, having considered the PFS completed by the debtor and having considered the matters before issuing a certification, in his or her opinion there is no likelihood of the debtor becoming solvent within the period of five years commencing on the date of the making of the declaration;[25]

Before issuing a certification, the PIP must consider the following[26] –

(i) the current liabilities of the debtor,

(ii) the contingent and prospective liabilities of the debtor and (insofar as is ascertainable) the times at which such liabilities will become due for payment, and

(iii) the current and prospective assets and income of the debtor.

(h) that the debtor has made a statutory declaration declaring that he or she has not been able to agree an alternative repayment arrangement with his or her creditors, or that his or her creditors have confirmed to the debtor in writing their unwillingness to enter into an alternative repayment arrangement;

---

24. PIA 2012, s 91(2).
25. PIA 2012, s 54.
26. PIA 2012, s 52(2).

The above criterion shall not apply where the relevant PIP confirms in writing that, having regard to the financial circumstances of the debtor as disclosed in the PFS completed by the debtor and when the factors before issuing a certification are considered, it is the belief of that PIP that if the debtor were to have entered into an alternative repayment arrangement with the creditors concerned, the debtor would be unlikely to become solvent within the period of five years commencing on the date of the PIP giving that confirmation.

(i) that the debtor is not –

 (i) an undischarged bankrupt,

 (ii) a discharged bankrupt subject to a bankruptcy payment order,

 (iii) a person who is a specified debtor in respect of a DRN,

 (iv) a person who, as a debtor, is subject to a PIA which is in force, or

 (v) a person who, as a debtor, is subject to an arrangement under the control of the court under Pt IV of the Bankruptcy Act 1988;

(j) that the debtor has not –

 (i) been the subject of a protective certificate issued under a PIA less than 12 months prior to the date of the application for a protective certificate,

 (ii) had his or her debts discharged pursuant to a DRN[27] less than three years prior to the date of the application for a protective certificate,

 (iii) had his or her debts discharged pursuant to a DSA[28] less than five years prior to the date of the application for a protective certificate, or

 (iv) been discharged from bankruptcy less than five years prior to the date of the application for a protective certificate.

The factors above shall not apply where the debtor has, on notice to the ISI, made an application to the appropriate court and the court has made an order stating that it is satisfied that the current insolvency of the debtor arises by reason of exceptional circumstances or other factors which are substantially outside the control of the debtor and that it would be just to permit the debtor to make a proposal for a PIA.[29] Exceptional circumstances as referred to in s 91(3) PIA 2012 are not defined and so it will be left up to the court to determine what constitutes exceptional circumstances.

A PIA shall not contain any terms that would release the debtor from an excluded debt or otherwise affect such a debt.[30] The PIA should not include any term which would give rise to such a release.

27. See **Ch 3** – Debt Relief Notices.

28. See **Ch 4** – Debt Settlement Arrangements.

29. PIA 2012, s 91(3).

30. PIA 2012, s 89(6).

Qualifying Debts

[5.10] A debtor is only entitled to include qualifying debts in the PIA proposal. There are two types of debt that may be excluded as a qualifying debt and these are divided into two different categories. The first type of debt is an 'excludable debt', which is a debt that requires the consent of a creditor to be included. Once creditor consent is obtained, the debt becomes an included debt. In circumstances where creditor consent has been sought and the creditor does not respond, the creditor will be deemed to have consented and the debt becomes a permitted or included debt. The second category of debt is an 'excluded debt', which is a debt that will never form a debt that is part of the PIA process.

Debts excludable as qualifying debts (require creditor consent):

(a) any liability arising out of any tax, duty, levy or other charge owed or payable to the State;

(b) any amount payable by the debtor under the Local Government (Charges) Act 2009;

(c) any amount payable by the debtor under the Local Government (Household Charge) Act 2011;

(d) rates due to the local authority (within the meaning of the Local Government Act 2001);

(e) any debt or liability in respect of moneys advanced to the debtor by the Health Service Executive under the Nursing Homes Support Scheme Act 2009;

(f) any debt due by the debtor to any owners' management company in respect of annual service charges under s 18 of the Multi-Unit Developments Act 2011 or contributions due under s 19 of that Act;

(g) any debt or liability of the debtor arising under the Social Welfare Consolidation Act 2005;

Debts that are excluded as qualifying debts (never included):

(h) any liability arising out of a domestic support order;

(i) any liability arising out of damages awarded by a court (or another competent authority) in respect of personal injuries or wrongful death arising from the tort of the debtor;

(j) any debt or liability arising from a loan (or forbearance of a loan) obtained through fraud, misappropriation, embezzlement or fraudulent breach of trust;

(k) any debt or liability of the debtor arising by virtue of a court order made under the Proceeds of Crime Acts 1996 and 2005 or by virtue of a fine ordered to be paid by a court in respect of a criminal offence.

Set Off

[5.11] In determining the amount or value of any asset of a debtor or the amount of any debt due to a creditor, where there are mutual credits or debts as between a debtor and a creditor, one debt or demand may be set off against the other and only the balance found owing shall be considered to be a debt or an asset on one side or the other.[31] The effect of this provision is that it is the net overall figure that the debtor owes the creditor which is included in the PIA process rather than a number of different debts owed by the debtor to the same creditor.

Pensions

[5.12] The treatment of a debtor's pension is split into pension income and pension fund. All pension income received by the debtor or an entitlement to a pension lump sum or income in accordance with the tax code will be treated as an asset or, as applicable, income for the purposes of a PIA. Thus a PIP will consider this income/lump sum when preparing the PIA.

Section 51 PIA 2012 states that where a debtor has an interest in or an entitlement under a relevant pension arrangement, such interest or entitlement of the debtor shall not be treated as an asset of the debtor unless sub-s (2) applies.

Before considering sub-s (2) it is necessary to set out what a 'relevant pension arrangement' is. It means:

(a) a retirement benefits scheme, within the meaning of s 771 of the Taxes Consolidation Act 1997 (TCA 1997), for the time being approved by the Revenue Commissioners;

(b) an annuity contract or a trust scheme or part of a trust scheme for the time being approved by the Revenue Commissioners under s 784 of the TCA 1997;

(c) a PRSA contract, within the meaning of s 787A of the TCA 1997, in respect of a PRSA product, within the meaning of that section;

(d) a qualifying overseas pension plan within the meaning of s 787M of the TCA 1997;

(e) a public service pension scheme within the meaning of s 1 of the Public Service Superannuation (Miscellaneous Provisions) Act 2004;

(f) a statutory scheme, within the meaning of s 770(1) of the TCA 1997, other than a public service pension scheme referred to in para (e);

(g) such other pension arrangement as may be prescribed by the Minister, following consultation with the Ministers for Finance, Social Protection and Public Expenditure and Reform.

Subsection (2) of s 51 PIA 2012 sets out the situation where a debtor receives an income or a lump sum which can then be used by a PIP when formulating a PIA. Where a debtor (a) is entitled at the date of the making of the application for a protective certificate, (b) was entitled at any time before the date of the making of the application for a protective certificate or (c) will become entitled within six years of the date for the making of the application for a protective certificate in relation to a DSA, performs the act or exercises the option which causes the debtor to receive from or at the request of the person

31. PIA 2012, ss 135 and 26(3).

administering that relevant pension arrangement (a) an income, or (b) an amount of money other than an income, in accordance with the provisions of the TCA 1997, that debtor shall be considered as being in receipt of such income or amount of money resulting in the income or lump sum being treated as an asset.[32]

The debtor's pension fund will be excluded from any PIA if it is a 'relevant pension arrangement' for the purposes of the PIA 2012. However an Approved Retirement Fund will not come under a 'relevant pension arrangement' and may be included by the PIP when preparing a PIA

There will be an onus on the debtor to be transparent in relation to all historical pension contributions and the PIP will review these. The debtor will continue to be obliged, when making an application for a protective certificate to make disclosure of any interest in or entitlement under a relevant pension arrangement in completing the PFS.

Where a creditor or a PIP considers that a debtor has made excessive contributions to a relevant pension arrangement, they can make an application to the appropriate court for the relief. Excessive contributions that were made at any time within three years prior to the making of the application for a protective certificate are to be considered.[33]

Where a court considers that contributions to a relevant pension arrangement were excessive it may:

(a) direct that such part of the contribution concerned (less any tax required to be deducted) be paid by the person administering the relevant pension arrangement to the PIP for distribution amongst the creditors of the debtor and

(b) make such other order as the court deems appropriate, including an order as to the costs of the application.

When considering whether the contributions being made to the pension were excessive or not it may consider:

(a) whether the debtor made payments to his creditors in respect of debts due to those creditors on a timely basis at or about the time when the debtor made the contribution concerned;

(b) whether the debtor was obliged to make contributions of the amount or percentage of income as the payments actually made under his terms and conditions of employment, and if so obliged, whether the debtor or a person who as respects the debtor is a connected person could have materially influenced the creation of such obligation;

(c) the amount of the contributions paid including the percentage of total income of the debtor in each tax year concerned which contributions represent;

(d) the amount of the contributions paid in each of the six years prior to the making of the application for a protective certificate on behalf of the debtor, including the percentage of total income of the debtor concerned which such contributions represent in each of those years;

---

32. PIA 2012, s 51.
33. PIA 2012, s 88.

(e) the age of the debtor at the relevant times;

(f) the percentage limits which applied to the debtor in relation to relief from income tax for purposes of making contributions to a relevant pension arrangement in each of the six years prior to the making of the application for a protective certificate on behalf of the debtor; and

(g) the extent of provision made by the debtor in relation to any relevant pension arrangement prior to the making of the contributions concerned.

APPLICATION PROCESS FOR A PROTECTIVE CERTIFICATE

[5.13] Section 93 PIA 2012 sets out the requirements in relation to applications for a protective certificate. The first step for the debtor in this process is to contact a PIP who will assist in advising the debtor in relation to the eligibility requirements, his insolvency options and in preparing a PFS.[34] Where a PIP has been instructed to make a proposal for a PIA, the PIP will notify the ISI of its appointment and the debtor's intention to propose a PIA and apply on the debtor's behalf for a protective certificate.

Information to PIP

[5.14] When the debtor contacts the PIP he must provide him with certain information. In order for a PIP to give initial advice then the debtor is obliged under the PIA 2012 to provide a substantial amount of information. The debtor must provide information in relation to his creditors, debts and liabilities, assets and guarantees and any other financial information as prescribed.[35]

The debtor should provide the PIP with a written statement[36] setting out the following in so far as the debtor can reasonably ascertain and the relevant information is applicable to the debtor:

(a) the full name and address and email or telephone contact details of the debtor's creditors;

(b) a full description of the debtor's debts and other liabilities;

(c) whether each of these debts and other liabilities are secured debts or unsecured debts;

(d) the amount of each debt or other liability (including principal, interest, costs and arrears) due to each of the debtor's creditors at the date of the written statement;

(e) any contingent and prospective debts or other liabilities of the debtor (including any guarantee or similar commitment signed by the debtor in respect of any

34. See para **5.16** below.

35. Personal Insolvency Act 2012 (Written Statement Disclosing all of the Debtor's Financial Affairs) Regulations 2013 (SI 312/2013).

36. Personal Insolvency Act 2012 (Written Statement Disclosing all of the Debtor's Financial Affairs) Regulations 2013 (SI 312/2013).

other person) and the times at which such debts or other liabilities will become due for payment;

(f) a full description of the current and prospective assets of the debtor;

(g) the address or location of these assets;

(h) where the assets comprise real property, whether the debtor's title is freehold, leasehold or other;

(i) whether these assets are held jointly or collectively with any other person, and if held collectively, the debtor's ownership percentage or other interest;

(j) the financial institution and account details where any of these assets are held;

(k) in the case of assets which may give rise to income to the debtor or are shares or other securities, the name and address of the obligor or issuer; and

(l) the purchase date, original cost and current market value of each asset.

A debtor shall provide a full schedule of his creditors[37] which must contain the following information:

(a) the creditor's legal name;

(b) the creditor's address (being the physical address and, if applicable, electronic address for service of notices and correspondence to the creditor subject to s 134 PIA 2012);

(c) whether the creditor is a connected person in relation to the debtor;

(d) whether the debt concerned is an excludable debt and, if so, whether that debt is a permitted debt

(e) whether the debt concerned is an excluded debt;

(f) whether some or all of the debt concerned is a preferential debt within and, if so, the preferential amount.

Under Personal Insolvency Act 2012 (Written Statement Disclosing all of the Debtor's Financial Affairs) Regulations 2013 (SI 312/2013),[38] a debtor shall provide full details, including any documentary evidence, of the efforts made by him or her to reach an alternative payment arrangement with his or her creditors or any of them where this applies.

A debtor shall also provide full details of his or her monthly income and monthly expenditure for the purposes of the PIA 2012 and such details shall include:

(a) a breakdown as between the different items of income and expenditure;

---

37. Personal Insolvency Act 2012 (Written Statement Disclosing all of the Debtor's Financial Affairs) Regulations 2013 (SI 312/2013).

38. Personal Insolvency Act 2012 (Written Statement Disclosing all of the Debtor's Financial Affairs) Regulations 2013 (SI 312/2013), ss 4 and 5.

(b) an averaging of the income and expenditure on a monthly basis where the income is not received or the expenditure made on a monthly basis;

(c) where income or expenditure is received or made other than on an individual basis by the debtor, details of any joint or collective arrangements which apply in respect of such income or expenditure.

Initial meeting between PIP and Debtor

[5.15] The PIP meets with the debtor and/or discusses the debtor's situation and eligibility to apply for a PIA based on the information supplied and gives him advice of the various insolvency options. The PIP will detail the PIA application process and outline the debtor's duties and obligations in the process and whether the debtor meets the eligibility criteria. The PIP should provide written advice setting out their opinion on whether the PIA is the best insolvency arrangement available to the debtor together with any reasons for advising same. The PIP should provide information on fee arrangements and other conditions of their appointment.

Once the debtor decides he wishes to proceed then he must indicate this intention in writing to the PIP and request that the PIP acts on the debtor's behalf.

The debtor must then provide all his financial information and supporting documentation to the PIP whereupon the PIP will assist the debtor in completing the PFS. There will be a meeting/series of meetings and/or phone calls with the PIP to progress the application.

Prescribed Financial Statement (PFS)

[5.16] Every applicant for one of the new arrangements is required to complete a PFS with the help of a PIP (in respect of a DSA or PIA). The PFS will enable the PIP to determine which (if any) one of the three new arrangements is most suitable in any particular case.

The PFS will be used primarily:

(a) to establish the applicant's eligibility for an arrangement;

(b) to form the basis for calculating a sustainable contribution which the applicant will pay to his creditors over the period of the arrangement (for a DSA/PIA); and

(c) to identify those liabilities from which the applicant will be discharged at the end of an arrangement.

The PFS will fully disclose all of the debtor's financial affairs (ie assets, liabilities, income and expenditure).

This is a written statement which shall include full details of the debtor's:

(a) income;

(b) expenditure;

(c) creditors;

(d) debts and other liabilities;

(e) assets;

(f) additional information which may be required by the ISI;

(g) guarantees (if any) given by the debtor in respect of a debt of another person.

The actual format of this PFS written statement is now available pursuant to Personal Insolvency Act 2012 (Prescribed Financial Statement) Regulations 2013 (SI 326/2013).[39]

The PFS will be annexed to a statutory declaration which must be witnessed by a notary public, Commissioner for Oaths, Peace Commissioner or a practicing solicitor.

PIP Advice

[5.17] On completion of the PFS, the PIP will further advise the debtor of their options for addressing their financial difficulties, whether the debtor is eligible for a PIA and, in the PIP's opinion, if a PIA is the most appropriate option.

Once the debtor decides to proceed and apply for a PIA, it must instruct the PIP in writing of its decision. The PIP must notify the ISI of his appointment.

The PIP will examine the completed PFS and where it is satisfied that the PFS is true and accurate and that the debtor satisfies the eligibility criteria, the PIP will provide a statement which will include, inter alia, a statement that there is no likelihood of the debtor becoming solvent within five years, that he is of the opinion that the PIA would facilitate the debtor becoming solvent in a period of five years or more, that the debtor satisfies the eligibility criteria and that the information in the PFS is true and accurate.

The debtor will be required to sign a statutory declaration affirming that the PFS is a complete and accurate statement of the debtor's assets, liabilities, income and expenditure.

Application for a Protective Certificate

[5.18] When the PIP has obtained all the above signed documents from the debtor then the PIP must notify the ISI of the debtor's intention to propose a PIA and apply on behalf of the debtor for a protective certificate.

The PIP will apply to the ISI for a protective certificate which will prevent creditors from taking any action against the debtor for 70 days[40] during which time the arrangement is being prepared.

The form of the application for a protective certificate under a PIA has been prescribed by the ISI under Personal Insolvency Act 2012 (Prescribed Protective Certificate Personal Insolvency Arrangement Application Form) Regulations 2013 (SI 332/2013).[41]

---

39. **Appendix 1** – Prescribed Financial Statement: http://www.isi.gov.ie/en/ISI/PFS.pdf/Files/PFS.pdf.

40. PIA 2012, s 95(5).

41. **Appendix 8** – PIA Protective Certificate Application Form: http://www.isi.gov.ie/en/ISI/PIA.pdf/Files/PIA.pdf.

There is provision for the protective certificate period to be extended for a further 40 days on application to the court by the PIP. The court may extend the period where:

(a) the debtor and the PIP satisfy the court that they have acted in good faith and with reasonable expedition, and

(b) the court is satisfied that it is likely that a proposal for a PIA is likely to –

 (i) be accepted by creditors, and

 (ii) be successfully completed by the debtor.

In circumstances where a replacement PIP has been appointed,[42] there is provision for the protective certificate period to be extended for a further 40 days[43] (ie an additional 40 days to the issue period of 70 days and the further 40-day period referred to above) on an application by that replacement PIP to the appropriate court. The court may extend the period where:

(a) the replacement PIP has been appointed in accordance with the provisions of the PIA 2012,[44] and

(b) the court is satisfied that the extension is necessary to enable the replacement PIP to perform its functions under the PIA 2012.

The PIA 2012 sets out that the application for a protective certificate shall be in the form[45] specified by the ISI and shall be accompanied by a fee of €500.[46]

In addition to the prescribed fee of €500, the following documents will need to be provided with the application for a protective certificate:[47]

(a) the statement of the PIP prepared confirming the PFS;[48]

(b) a document signed by the debtor confirming that he or she satisfies the eligibility criteria for a PIA;

(c) the statutory declaration[49] of the debtor;

(d) the fee of €500 as prescribed under SI 329/2013;[50]

(e) the PFS;

(f) the declaration of the debtor declaring that he or she has cooperated for a period of at least six months with his or her creditors who are secured creditors as

42. PIA 2012, s 49(9).

43. PIA 2012, s 95(6).

44. PIA 2012, s 49(9).

45. **Appendix 8** – PIA Protective Certificate Application Form: http://www.isi.gov.ie/en/ISI/PIA.pdf/Files/PIA.pdf.

46. Personal Insolvency Act 2012 (Prescribed Fees) Regulations 2013 (SI 329/2013).

47. PIA 2012, s 93(2) as amended by the Courts and Civil Law (Miscellaneous Provisions) Act 2013, s 80.

48. See **Ch 8** – Personal Insolvency Practitioners.

49. PIA 2012, s 91(1)(g).

50. Personal Insolvency Act 2012 (Prescribed Fees) Regulations 2013 (SI 329/2013).

respects the debtor's PPR in accordance with any process relating to mortgage arrears operated by the secured creditors and approved or required by the Central Bank of Ireland and which process relates to the secured debt concerned and that notwithstanding such cooperation the debtor has not been able to agree an alternative repayment arrangement with the secured creditor or that secured creditor has confirmed in writing their unwillingness to enter into an alternative repayment arrangement;

(g) a schedule of the debtor's debts and creditors concerned, stating in relation to each such creditor—

(i) the amount due to that creditor, and

(ii) whether the creditor concerned is a secured creditor and, if so, the nature of any security held in respect of the debt concerned;

(h) a consent in writing signed by the debtor confirming that he or she consents to disclosure and processing of his or her personal data to and by the ISI and creditors to such extent as may be necessary in connection with the PIA procedure provided for in the PIA 2012;

(i) confirmation by the debtor that the ISI may carry out any prescribed verification checks.[51]

ISI CONSIDERATIONS

[5.19] The ISI shall be entitled to request any further information it requires from the debtor or PIP and to defer further consideration of the application until such information is furnished to it.[52] Any such information must be provided within 14 days or as long as the ISI shall permit or the application will be deemed to be withdrawn.

The ISI also has further rights in relation to the verification of information provided by both the PIP and the debtor. This will result in additional obligations on the PIP. The ISI shall make such enquiries as it considers necessary to satisfy itself:

(a) that the PIP is a person entitled to act as a PIP;

(b) having regard to the documents which are required to accompany the application for a protective certificate—

(i) that the debtor satisfies the eligibility criteria for making a proposal for a PIA, and

(ii) the application does not appear to be frivolous or an attempt to frustrate the efforts of creditors to recover debts due to them.

The ISI is entitled to rely on the documents lodged with the ISI in ascertaining the debtor's eligibility criteria for a PIA where the ISI has no reason to believe that the information supplied in or in support of the application is incorrect or incomplete.[53]

51. PIA 2012, s 94.
52. PIA 2012, s 94.
53. PIA 2012, s 94(4).

The ISI is also entitled to make such enquiries as it considers necessary to verify the completeness or accuracy of any matter referred to in the PFS of the debtor or in relation to the assets, liabilities, income or expenditure of the debtor.[54]

In addition to the general powers of enquiry that the ISI has it also has the following specific powers of enquiry:[55]

(a) particulars relating to bank accounts, securities accounts or other accounts held, solely or jointly, by or for the benefit of the debtor with financial institutions or financial intermediaries in the State or abroad;

(b) particulars relating to assets of the debtor and the value of such assets;

(c) particulars of the liabilities of the debtor;

(d) the employment and income of the debtor;

(e) payments received by the debtor from the Department of Social Protection or other Departments of State or other State bodies or agencies and whether or not such payments are made as agent of any other person;

(f) taxes or charges imposed by or under statute paid or owed by the debtor, whether within or outside the State, and refunds in respect of such taxes and charges which are or may become due to the debtor.

There is a general provision[56] which states that information held by a department of State, the Revenue Commissioners, a local authority or any other State body or agency in relation to a debtor may be furnished to the ISI.

COURT REFERRAL FOR THE ISSUING OF A PROTECTIVE CERTIFICATE

[5.20] Once the ISI is satisfied that the application is in order it will furnish a certificate to that effect[57] and furnish that certificate together with a copy of the application and supporting documentation to the appropriate court and notify the PIP to that effect.[58] Where the ISI is not satisfied with the application, it shall notify the PIP and request that, within 21 days of the notification, to submit a revised application or confirm that the application is withdrawn.[59]

Section 5 PIA 2012 sets out the appropriate court in respect of PIAs. Where the total liabilities of the debtor, determined on the basis of the PFS completed by the debtor, are in excess of €2,500,000, the appropriate court is the High Court with the Circuit Court being the appropriate court in all other circumstances of a PIA. The performance of the

54. PIA 2012, s 94(5).

55. PIA 2012, s 94(6).

56. PIA 2012, s 94(9).

57. PIA 2012, s 95.

58. PIA 2012, s 95(1).

59. PIA 2012, s 95(1)(b).

functions and the exercise of the powers and jurisdiction shall be within the jurisdiction of the circuit of the Circuit Court in which:

(a) the debtor to whom the application relates is residing at the time of the making of the application or has resided within one year of the time of the making of the application, or

(b) the debtor to whom the application relates has a place of business at the time of the making of the application or had a place of business within one year of the time of the making of the application.

Once the court is in receipt of the application and the supporting documentation, the court shall review the application and documentation and, if satisfied that the eligibility criteria[60] in respect of the debtor have been satisfied and the other relevant requirements relating to an application for the issue of a protective certificate have been met, shall issue a protective certificate.

Section 95(5) PIA 2012 provides the protective certificate to be in force for a period of 70 days. There is a possible 40-day extension period[61] on application to the court in the following circumstances:

(a) the debtor and the PIP satisfy the court that they have acted in good faith and with reasonable expedition, and

(b) the court is satisfied that it is likely that a proposal for a PIA which is likely—

(i) to be accepted by the creditors, and

(ii) to be successfully completed by the debtor

will be made if the extension is granted.

In circumstances where a replacement PIP has been appointed,[62] there is provision for the protective certificate period to be extended for a further 40 days[63] (ie a further 40 days to the issue period of 70 days and the additional 40-day period referred to above) on an application by that replacement PIP to the appropriate court. The court may extend the period where:

(a) the replacement PIP has been appointed in accordance with the provisions of the PIA 2012;[64] and

(b) the court is satisfied that the extension is necessary to enable the replacement PIP to perform its functions under the PIA 2012.

The registrar of the appropriate court shall notify the ISI and the PIP concerned where it issues or extends a protective certificate under this section. The ISI shall enter details of the name and address of the debtor, the date of issue of the protective certificate, or the making of an order of the court in relation to a protective certificate, and the date on

60. PIA 2012, s 95(2).

61. PIA 2012, s 95(5).

62. PIA 2012, s 49(9).

63. PIA 2012, s 95(6).

64. PIA 2012, s 49(9).

which the protective certificate ceases, together with such other details as it considers appropriate, in the Register of Protective Certificates.[65]

Where the protective certificate ceases, the ISI must within three months of the date of cessation remove from the Register of Protective Certificates all information recorded by it in respect of the protective certificate.[66]

Once a protective certificate has issued, it is the responsibility of the PIP to notify each of the creditors specified in the schedule of creditors of the fact of such issue and that the debtor intends to make a proposal for a PIA.[67]

The protective certificate issued shall provide the following:

(a) the name of the debtor who is the subject of it;

(b) the debts ('specified debts') which are subject to it; and

(c) the name of each creditor to whom a specified debt is owed; and

(d) contain such other information as may be prescribed.

EFFECT OF THE PROTECTIVE CERTIFICATE

Creditors

[5.21] A creditor[68] to whom notice of the issue of a protective certificate has been given shall not, whilst the protective certificate remains in force:[69]

(a) initiate any legal proceedings in relation to a debt which is a specified debt;

(b) take any step to prosecute legal proceedings already initiated;

(c) execute or enforce a judgment held against the debtor in respect of a specified debt;

(d) take any step to recover goods in the possession or custody of the debtor (whether or not title to the goods is vested in the creditor);

(e) contact the debtor regarding payment of the debt otherwise than at the request of the debtor;

(f) in relation to an agreement with the debtor, including a security agreement, by reason only that the debtor is insolvent or that the protective certificate has been issued—

 (i) terminate or amend that agreement, or

 (ii) claim an accelerated payment, or a forfeiture of a term, under that agreement.

---

65. PIA 2012, s 95(11).

66. PIA 2012, s 95(11)(b) as amended by the Courts and Civil Law (Miscellaneous Provisions) Act 2013, s 81.

67. PIA 2012, s 95(12).

68. PIA 2012, s 96(1).

69. PIA 2012, s 96.

Where a creditor has been notified of the granting of a protective certificate, whilst the protective certificate remains in force no bankruptcy petition relating to the debtor may be presented by a creditor, or in a case where the petition has been presented by a creditor, may be proceeded with.

In addition to the specific provision above, there is a general protection[70] afforded to the debtor such that no other proceedings, no enforcement of security and no execution or other legal process may be commenced or continued against the debtor or his or her property, except with the leave of the court and subject to any order the court may make to stay such proceedings, enforcement or execution for such period as the court deems appropriate pending the outcome of attempts to reach a PIA. This is relevant where a creditor claims not to be on notice of the issue of the protective certificate.

It should be noted that the protective certificate does not extend to protect any guarantor of the debts of the debtor or a person who has jointly contracted with the debtor or is jointly liable with the debtor to the creditor and that other person may sue or be sued in respect of the contract without joining the debtor.[71]

The period of the protective certificate and any extension to this period does not affect any period for the purposes of the Statute of Limitations 1957[72] or period in relation to any proceedings or process (ie the protective certificate period is disregarded). This may be of relevance in the event that a PIA is unsuccessful.

Right of Appeal of Creditor against the Issue of the Protective Certificate

[5.22] In the event that a creditor is aggrieved by the issue of a protective certificate that creditor may within 14 days of the giving of notice of the issue of the protective certificate to that creditor apply to the appropriate court for an order directing that the protective certificate shall not apply to that creditor.[73]

Notice must be given to the ISI and the relevant PIP and to such other persons as the court may direct of that fact, and the application shall be made in such form as is provided for in the rules of court.[74]

The court shall not make the order directing that the protective certificate shall not apply to that creditor unless it is satisfied that:

(a) failing to give such direction would cause irreparable loss to the creditor which would not otherwise occur, and

(b) no other creditor to whom notice of the protective certificate has been given would be unfairly prejudiced.[75]

70. PIA 2012, s 96(3).

71. PIA 2012, s 96(4) and (5).

72. PIA 2012, s 96(7).

73. PIA 2012, s 96.

74. See **Ch 6** – Court Procedures.

75. PIA 2012, s 97(3).

In determining the costs of the application[76] the court shall have regard to the objective that all the parties to such an application should bear their own costs unless to do so would cause a serious injustice to the parties to the application.

Where the court makes an order under this section, the court shall, unless it considers that there are good reasons not to do so, direct the creditor to hold any moneys or other assets recovered in trust for the benefit of the other creditors to whom the protective certificate applies, pending a further direction on the matter by the court.

The court is bound to hear any application[77] by a creditor appealing the protective notification with 'due expedition' but no guidance has been given as to how long this may be.

Obligations of PIP

[5.23] Upon issue of the protective certificate there are a number of persons that the PIP must give notice to as follows:[78]

(a) give written notice to creditors that the PIP has been appointed by the debtor for the purpose of making a proposal for a PIA and invite the creditors concerned to make submissions to the PIP regarding the debts concerned and the manner in which the debts might be dealt with as part of a PIA, and such notice shall be accompanied by the debtor's completed PFS;

(b) consider any submissions made by creditors in accordance with the above regarding the debts and the manner in which the debts might be dealt with as part of a PIA, including any submission made by a creditor with respect to previous or existing offers of arrangements made by the creditor to or with the debtor.

In notifying creditors of the issue of a protective certificate, the PIP shall indicate that any creditor who considers some or all of his or her debt to be a preferential debt[79] is required to furnish evidence of the circumstances of how that debt, or part of that debt, is claimed to be a preferential debt within such reasonable period as may be specified, and that in the absence of such evidence the proposal for a PIA may be prepared on the basis that the debt concerned is not a preferential debt.

A PIP may in any case request a creditor to file a proof of debt and the debt shall be proved in the same manner as a debt of a bankrupt is proved under the Bankruptcy Act 1988 and the First Schedule of that Act[80] shall apply to the proof of such debts. Any creditor who does not comply with the provisions above is not entitled to vote at a meeting relating to the PIA or share in any distribution under the PIA.[81] Where any subsequent proof of debt is filed by such a creditor they shall be entitled to vote at a

76. PIA 2012, s 97(4).
77. PIA 2012, s 97(5).
78. PIA 2012, s 98.
79. PIA 2012, s 98(2).
80. **Appendix 4** – Bankruptcy Act 1988, Sch 1.
81. PIA 2012, s 98(2)(b).

meeting related to the PIA and share in a distribution under the PIA without prejudice to the fact that those restrictions applied while the proof of debt was outstanding.[82]

In applying the First Schedule of the Bankruptcy Act 1988 to proof of debts for these purposes, any reference to the Official Assignee shall be read as a reference to the PIP, and a reference to the bankrupt shall read as a reference to the insolvent debtor to whom the proposal for a PIA relates.

MANDATORY REQUIREMENTS UNDER A PIA

[5.24] In general, the terms of a PIA[83] are the terms to which the debtor agrees which are approved by a majority of the creditors (ie representing not less than 65 per cent of the total amount of the debtor's debts due to creditors participating in the meeting of which at least 50 per cent of the secured creditors entitled to vote have voted in favour and of the unsecured creditors entitled to vote at least 50 per cent have voted in favour). In addition to this, there are certain mandatory requirements that must also be met:

(a) the PIA will clearly specify which debts are secured debts and which debts are unsecured debts;

(b) the maximum duration of a PIA shall be 72 months but a PIA may provide that this period may be extended for a further period of not more than 12 months in such circumstances as are specified in the terms of the PIA;

(c) where the debtor performs all of his or her obligations specified in a PIA, he or she shall stand discharged from the remainder of the unsecured debts covered by the PIA and discharged from the secured debts to the extent specified under the terms of the PIA;

(d) a PIA shall not release the debtor from any debt or liability arising by virtue of a court order made under the Proceeds of Crime Acts 1996 and 2005 or by virtue of a fine ordered to be paid by a court in respect of a criminal offence;

(e) a PIA shall not require the debtor to sell any of his or her assets that are reasonably necessary for the debtor's employment, business or vocation unless the debtor explicitly consents to such sale;

(f) a PIA shall not contain any terms which would require the debtor to make payments of such an amount that the debtor would not have sufficient income to maintain a reasonable standard of living for the debtor and his or her dependants;

(g) a PIA shall—

    (i) make provision for the costs and outlays of the PIP which relate to the matters referred to in relation to the application for a PIA and to the ongoing administration of the PIA,

    (ii) indicate the likely amount of the costs to be incurred or, where this is not practicable, the basis of how those charges will be calculated, and

82. PIA 2012, s 98(2)(c).

83. PIA 2012, s 99.

(iii) specify the person or persons by whom those costs and charges are payable and the manner in which they are to be paid;

(h) a PIA shall make provision for the manner in which the debtor's debts are to be treated in the event of the death or mental incapacity of the debtor;

(i) a PIA shall not require that the debtor dispose of his or her interest in his or her principal private residence or to cease to occupy such residence unless the provisions of s 104(3)[84] apply;

(j) a PIA shall provide that the circumstances of the debtor be reviewed by the PIP at regular intervals which are specified in PIA (which intervals are not greater than 12 months) during the currency of the PIA;

(k) the review referred to in para (j) shall include the preparation by the debtor of a new PFS, a copy of which, together with a statement by the PIP as to whether he or she considers that statement to be complete and accurate, shall be sent by the PIP to each creditor;

(l) a PIA shall provide for the manner in which security held by a secured creditor is to be treated; and

(m) the terms of a PIA shall specify the circumstances where the PIP shall be obliged to propose a variation of the PIA[85] in accordance with s 119 PIA 2012.

Guidelines on a Reasonable Standard of Living and Reasonable Living Expenses[86] have been published by the ISI on the matters outlined above. In addition, for the purposes of a PIP determining whether a debtor would have sufficient income to maintain a reasonable standard of living for the debtor and his or her dependants under the PIA, the PIP shall have regard to these guidelines and any further guidelines on reasonable expenditure and essential income for debtors published by the ISI.

PIA

Terms of the Proposal

[5.25] The terms of the proposal for the PIA[87] may include any or more of the following:

(a) a lump sum payment to creditors, whether provided from the debtor's own resources or from the resources of other persons;

(b) a payment arrangement with creditors;

(c) an agreement by the debtor to transfer some or all of the debtor's property to a person (who may be the PIP) to hold the property in trust for the benefit of the creditors;

---

84. See para **5.34** below: where debtor does not wish to remain in PPR or where cost of remaining in PPR is disproportionately large.

85. See para **5.41** below.

86. **Ch 7** – Reasonable Living Expenses and http://www.isi.gov.ie/en/ISI/Pages/Publications.

87. PIA 2012, s 100(2).

(d) a transfer of specified assets of the debtor to creditors generally or to a specified creditor;

(e) a sale of specified assets of the debtor by the PIP and the payment of the proceeds of such sale to creditors;

(f) in respect of secured debts, an arrangement for the treatment of the security and the satisfaction or restructuring of the secured debt.

The PIA shall provide for payments to creditors of the same class to be made on a *pari passu* basis, and where so otherwise provided the PIA shall specify the reasons for such provision being made unless the payments specifically provided to be paid otherwise than *pari passu*.[88] Payments other than the payments specified above may be provided for under the PIA.

Unless provision is made otherwise in the PIA, where a PIA provides for payments to a creditor who had an excludable debt that are greater than the payment that creditor would receive if such payments were made on a *pari passu* basis, the fees, costs and charges shall be payable by the creditor in proportion to the payments received by that creditor.

The payment of moneys or the performance of obligations provided for by a PIA may be secured by a charge or a guarantee given by the debtor or a charge or guarantee given by a person other than the debtor.[89]

Preferential Debts

[5.26] For the purposes of a PIA, a preferential debt[90] is a debt which if the debtor concerned were a bankrupt would be a debt:

(a) that by virtue of s 81 of the Bankruptcy Act 1988[91] is to be paid in priority to all other debts, or

(b) that by virtue of any other statutory provision is to be included among such debts, shall be paid in full by the debtor unless the creditor concerned otherwise agrees and provision is so made in the terms of the PIA and such debt is in this chapter referred to as a 'preferred debt', and where those debts are to be paid in full the provisions of s 81 of the Bankruptcy Act 1988 shall apply with all necessary modifications.

In notifying creditors of the issue of a protective certificate, the PIP shall indicate that any creditor who considers some or all of his or her debt to be a preferential debt[92] is required to furnish evidence of the circumstances of how that debt, or part of that debt, is claimed to be a preferential debt within such reasonable period as may be specified, and that in the absence of such evidence, the proposal for a PIA may be prepared on the

88. PIA 2012, s 100(3).
89. PIA 2012, s 100(5).
90. PIA 2012, s 101.
91. **Appendix 4** – Bankruptcy Act 1988, s 81.
92. PIA 2012, s 101(2).

basis that the debt concerned is not a preferential debt. Where a creditor fails to satisfy the PIP that his or her debt is a preferential debt the debt shall be treated as not being a preferential debt for the purposes of a PIA.[93]

Secured Debt

Treatment of Security in PIA

[5.27] Where a secured creditor has been notified by the PIP that a protective certificate has issued in respect of the debtor, the secured creditor must furnish to the PIP an estimate, made in good faith, of the market value of the security and the creditor may also indicate a preference as to how the secured creditor wishes to have the security and secured debt[94] treated under the PIA.[95]

In formulating a proposal for a PIA, the PIP shall have regard to the valuation of the security and the protection of the secured creditor under s 103 PIA 2012 and also to the preference indicated by the secured creditor to the extent that the PIP feels it reasonable to do so.

The terms of the PIA may provide for the manner in which the security for the secured debt is treated including:

(a) the sale or any other disposition of the property or asset the subject of the security;

(b) the surrender of the security to the debtor; or

(c) the retention of the secured creditor of the security.[96]

Any failure by the secured creditor to furnish a valuation and/or an indication of a preference for how the security be treated within the period specified by the PIP or such further period as may be agreed shall not prevent the PIP from formulating a proposal for a PIA.[97]

Where there is a sale or other disposal of the secured property and the value of the property is less than the amount due in respect of the secured debt, then the balance due to the secured creditor shall abate in equal proportion to the unsecured debts in the PIA and shall be discharged with them on completion of the obligations specified in the terms of the PIA.[98]

In addition to the foregoing, the terms of the PIA may also provide one or more of the following in relation to the secured debt:[99]

---

93. PIA 2012, s 101(3).
94. PIA 2012, s 102.
95. PIA 2012, s 102(1).
96. PIA 2012, s 102(3).
97. PIA 2012, s 102(4).
98. PIA 2012, s 102(5).
99. PIA 2012, s 102(6).

(a) that the debtor pay interest and only part of the capital amount of the secured debt to the secured creditor for a specified period of time which shall not exceed the duration of the PIA;

(b) that the debtor make interest-only payments on the secured debt for a specified period of time which shall not exceed the duration of the PIA;

(c) that the period over which the secured debt was to be paid or the time or times at which the secured debt was to be repaid be extended by a specified period of time;

(d) that the secured debt payments due to be made by the debtor be deferred for a specified period of time which shall not exceed the duration of the PIA;

(e) that the basis on which the interest rate relating to the secured debt be changed to one that is fixed, variable or at a margin above or below a reference rate;

(f) that the principal sum due on the secured debt be reduced provided that the secured creditor be granted a share in the debtor's equity in the property the subject of the security;

(g) that the principal sum due on the secured debt be reduced but subject to a condition that where the property the subject of the security is subsequently sold for an amount greater than the value attributed to that property for the purposes of the PIA, the secured creditor's security will continue to cover such part of the difference between the attributed value and the amount for which the property is sold as is specified in the PIA;

(h) that arrears of payments existing at the inception of the PIA and payments falling due during a specified period thereafter be added to the principal amount due in respect of the secured debt; and

(i) that the principal sum due in respect of the secured debt be reduced to a specified amount.

A creditor who has registered a judgment mortgage against a debtor more than three months before the issuing of a protective certificate is a secured creditor for the purposes of a PIA.[100]

The secured creditor shall provide proof of the existence and nature of the security where requested by the PIP, in default of which the PIP may treat the debt as unsecured.[101]

Where the market value of the security held by the secured creditor is less than 10 per cent of the amount of that secured debt, the creditor can elect by notice in writing to the PIP to be treated as an unsecured creditor. Where the PIP receives notice of such an election by a secured creditor, the PIP shall formulate the proposal for the PIA on terms providing for the surrender of the security to the debtor and shall treat the creditor as an unsecured creditor for the purposes of the PIA. It is an entitlement of a secured creditor and more often the case that a secured creditor would elect to be treated as an unsecured

100. PIA 2012, s 102(7) as amended by the Courts and Civil Law (Miscellaneous Provisions) Act 2013, s 83.

101. PIA 2012, s 102(8).

creditor in situations where the security has no real value. It is therefore unclear why this 10 per cent threshold provision has been included.

Where the secured creditor consents in writing to the inclusion of terms of the PIA providing for the surrender to the debtor of the security, that creditor shall be treated as an unsecured creditor and shall be only entitled to vote as such at the creditors' meeting.[102]

Where a PIA includes terms providing for the reduction of debt (including principal, interest and arrears) secured by the security as at the date of the issue of the protective certificate to a specified amount, the terms of the PIA shall include a term providing that the amount of the reduction shall:

(a) rank equally with and abate in proportion to the unsecured debts of the PIA; and

(b) be discharged with those unsecured debts on completion of the obligations specified in the PIA.[103]

There is nothing within the PIA 2012 that affects the right of a secured creditor of the debtor to enforce or otherwise deal with his or her security.[104]

Protection of Secured Creditor

[5.28] Where a secured asset is sold or disposed of under the terms of a PIA, the amount paid to the secured creditor shall be at least:

(a) the value of the security; or

(b) the amount of the debt (including principal, interest and arrears) secured by the security at the date of the issue of the protective certificate.

Where a secured creditor retains a security and agrees to a reduction of the principal sum due in respect of the security, the amount of the reduced principal shall not be an amount less than the value of the security as valued under the PIA 2012,[105] unless otherwise agreed by the secured creditor.

Where a secured creditor retains a security and agrees to a reduction of the principal sum due in respect of the security, the terms of the PIA shall include terms providing that the reduction of the principal sum is subject to the condition that in the event the property which is the subject of the security is sold or otherwise disposed of for an amount or at a value greater than the value attributed to the security as valued under the PIA 2012 (ie any uplift in the value of the property from the date of entering the PIA and the date of sale), the debtor shall pay to the secured creditor an amount additional to the reduced principal sum calculated in accordance with the lesser of the following:

(a) the entire of the difference between the value of the property on disposition and the value attributed to the security as valued under the PIA 2012; and

---

102. PIA 2012, s 108(4).

103. PIA 2012, s 102(11).

104. PIA 2012, ss 102(1) and 62.

105. PIA 2012, s 105 – see para **5.29**.

(b) the amount of the reduction in the principal sum due in respect of the secured debt under the PIA; or

(c) such greater amount as is provided for under the terms of the PIA.

Any payment made during the PIA attributable to the reduction in principal shall be deducted from the balancing payment[106] as set out above.

Any increase in the value of the property attributable to improvements made to the property or other measures taken to enhance the value of the property subsequent to the valuation of the property for the purposes of the PIA shall be disregarded in any of the calculations relating to the reduction of principal on a secured debt.[107] This shall not apply unless consent of the secured creditor was obtained prior to carrying out the improvements to the property and which consent cannot be unreasonably withheld by the secured creditor.

Any additional amount to be paid shall stand secured in the same manner and with the same priority as the principal sum.[108]

The obligation to pay the additional amount shall cease on the expiry of 20 years commencing on the date on which the PIA came into effect and the date on which the debtor is scheduled or permitted to fully discharge the amount secured by the security and does so discharge that indebtedness.[109] Unless a debtor discharges the full amount of the security to the secured creditor they will be liable for the balancing payment for a period of 20 years from the date of the PIA.

The provisions in the PIA 2012 relating to the reduction of a principal sum of a secured debt amount to a clawback on the write-off of any secured debt. The effect of the provision is that where a secured property is sold following an agreement to reduce the principal, any uplift in the value of the property may be payable to the secured creditor subject to certain conditions. The clawback period may run for a maximum of 20 years following the date of the PIA.

There has been much debate about these provisions. It is thought that the provisions erode the benefit of a PIA as the result of these clawback provisions is that the period of the PIA, where there is a write down of principal on a secured property, is in reality 20 years rather than the intended six- or seven-year period envisioned under the original format of the legislation.

PIPs will need to ensure that debtors are made fully aware of these provisions where there is a write-down of the principal of a secured debt.

Another issue raised by these clawback provisions is the question of whether the additional payment crystallised on the sale or disposal of the property is the responsibility of the PIP or the debtor. There is also the question of whether the terms of the PIA are not concluded until the expiration of the clawback period. This is not clear from the legislation and some clarification in this regard would be welcomed. It is the authors' view that a PIP should ensure that their responsibilities in respect of any

106. PIA 2012, s 103(7).

107. PIA 2012, s 103(5).

108. PIA 2012, s 103(10).

109. PIA 2012, s 103(12).

additional payment that becomes due and payable are clarified within the terms of the PIA.

The practical implications of these provisions will remain to be seen but the authors wonder whether the benefits of the PIA insolvency process are greatly reduced by the inclusion of these clawback provisions. Debtors' attitudes to the inclusion and implications of these provisions will be demonstrated by the number of debtors who opt to use the PIA insolvency process.

Valuation of Security

[5.29] The value of the security in respect of a secured debt shall be the market value of the security determined by agreement between the debtor, secured creditor and PIP.[110] Where the PIP does not agree to the secured creditor's valuation estimate, the debtor, the secured creditor and the PIP must agree to endeavour to agree to the market value having regard to the following:

(a) the type of property the subject of the security;

(b) the priority of the security;

(c) the costs of disposing of the property the subject of the security;

(d) the price at which similar property to that which is the subject of the security has been sold within the 12 months prior to the issue of the protective certificate;

(e) the date of the most recent valuation or transaction with respect to the property the subject of the security and the value attributed to the property in respect of that valuation or transaction;

(f) the value attributed to the property the subject of the security in the debtor's accounting records (if any);

(g) the value attributed to the security in the secured creditor's accounting records (if any);

(h) whether the market for the type of property the subject of the security is or has been subject to significant changes in conditions;

(i) data made available to the public by the Property Services Regulatory Authority pursuant to Pt 12 of the Property Services (Regulation) Act 2011 and which relate to property similar to the property the subject of the security; and

(j) any relevant statistical index relating to the valuation of the same or similar types of property as the property the subject of the security.

In the absence of any agreement, the debtor, secured creditor and PIP will appoint an independent expert to determine the market value of the security having regard to the aforementioned matters.[111] Where the parties cannot agree to an independent expert, any of them may refer the matter to the ISI, which shall appoint an appropriate independent

110. PIA 2012, s 105(1).

111. PIA 2012, s 105(3).

expert to determine the market value of the security.[112] The creditor and PIP shall carry 50 per cent of the costs each of obtaining an independent expert,[113] with the amount paid by the PIP treated as an outlay of the PIA.

The term 'market value' in relation to property as the subject of the security shall mean the price which that property might reasonably be expected to fetch on a sale in the open market.[114] In all other circumstances, it means the amount that might reasonably be expected to be available to discharge that secured debt, in whole or in part, following the realisation of that security after deducting all relevant costs and expenses in relation to the realisation of that security. The agreement of what constitutes relevant costs and expenses may be the subject of discussion between the parties and may in reality be difficult to agree.

In determining the market value of a security, the PIP, the debtor, the secured creditor and any independent valuer are entitled to assume, in the absence of any clear evidence to the contrary, that the market value of the security which is a first charge is the lesser of:

(a) an amount equal to the market value of the property the subject of the security; or

(b) unless the nature of the security and the property concerned would make it unreasonable to do so, an amount equal to the market value of the property the subject of the security *less* an adjustment to that value as respects the costs and expenses which would normally be necessarily incurred by a secured creditor in the realisation of a security of a similar kind to that of the security concerned, provided that the adjustment is no greater than 10 per cent of the market value of the property the subject of the security.[115]

Again, the agreement of what constitutes costs and expenses normally incurred in the realisation of a security may be difficult in practice. For example, a secured creditor may feel the inclusion of legal expenses incurred in realising the security is reasonable whereas the debtor may not.

Principal Private Residence

[5.30] In formulating a proposal for a PIA a PIP shall, insofar as reasonably practicable, and having regard to the matters referred to below, formulate the proposal on terms that will not require the debtor to dispose of an interest in or to cease to occupy his or her principal private residence[116] and the PIP shall consider any appropriate alternatives to such vacation.

112. PIA 2012, s 105(4).
113. PIA 2012, s 105(7).
114. PIA 2012, s 105(6).
115. PIA 2012, s 105(9).
116. PIA 2012, s 104.

A principal private residence is defined[117] as a dwelling in which the debtor ordinarily resides and includes any building or structure, or any vehicle or vessel (whether mobile or not), together with any garden or portion of ground attached to and occupied with the dwelling or otherwise required for the amenity or convenience of the dwelling.

The matters which the PIP must take into consideration in dealing with the principal private residence of the debtor are:

(a) the costs likely to be incurred by the debtor by remaining in occupation of his or her principal private residence (including rent, mortgage loan repayments, insurance payments, owners' management company service charges and contributions, taxes or other charges relating to ownership or occupation of the property imposed by or under statute and necessary maintenance in respect of the principal private residence);

(b) the debtor's income and other financial circumstances as disclosed in the PFS;

(c) the ability of other persons residing with the debtor in the principal private residence to contribute to the costs referred to in para (1) above; and

(d) the reasonable living accommodation needs of the debtor and his or her dependants and having regard to those needs the cost of alternative accommodation (including the costs which would necessarily be incurred in obtaining such accommodation).

Where the debtor confirms in writing to the PIP that the debtor does not wish to remain in occupation of his or her principal private residence; or where the PIP has, having discussed the issue with the debtor, formed the opinion that, taking account of the matters referred to above, the costs of continuing to reside in the debtor's principal private residence are disproportionately large, the PIP shall not be required to formulate the proposal for a PIA on terms that will not require the debtor to cease to occupy his or her principal private residence.[118]

A PIA shall not contain terms providing for a disposal of the debtor's interest in the principal private residence unless:[119]

(a) the debtor has obtained independent legal advice in relation to such disposal or, having been advised by the PIP to obtain such legal advice, has declined to do so; and

(b) to the extent that the provisions of the Family Home Protection Act 1976 or the Civil Partnership and Certain Rights and Obligations of Cohabitants Act 2010 apply to the property that all relevant provisions of those acts are complied with.

117. PIA 2012, s 1.

118. PIA 2012, s 104.

119. PIA 2012, s 104(4).

CREDITORS' MEETING

Calling a Creditors' Meeting

[5.31] Where a PIP has prepared a proposal for a PIA and the debtor has consented to that proposal and the calling of the meeting, the PIP shall arrange for the holding of a meeting.[120] In fixing a venue for a creditors' meeting, the chairperson must have regard to the convenience of the creditors. The meeting shall be scheduled for commencement between 9am and 4pm on a business day.[121]

The venue for the holding of a creditors' meeting shall be situated within the State. The period of notice of the meeting of creditors shall be 14 days, but such period may be waived or abridged where the consent of all the creditors to such waiver or abridgement is given in writing.

The PIP shall send a written notice of a creditors' meeting to each creditor. The written notice shall be in accordance with the regulations made by the Minister[122] which have yet to be released and it is not known when this will be at the time of writing.

There are certain provisions which the PIP must observe when calling a meeting. These are as follows:

(a) give creditors at least 14 days' written notice of the meeting and the date on which, and the time and place at which, the meeting will be held;

(b) send, along with the notice referred to in para (a) above, the documents referred to below; and

(c) lodge a copy of the notice referred to in para (a) above and the documents referred to in para (b) above (as set out below) with the ISI.

In the event that the debtor does not consent to the calling of a creditors' meeting before the expiry of the protective certificate, the procedure as respects that debtor making a proposal for a PIA shall be treated as having concluded.[123]

The documents required to be furnished to the creditors and the ISI when calling a creditors' meeting are as follows:

(a) a copy of the PFS;

(b) a document containing the terms of the proposal for a PIA;

(c) a statement by the PIP that he or she is of the opinion[124] that –

   (i) the debtor satisfies the eligibility criteria for the proposal of a PIA,[125]

---

120. PIA 2012, s 106.

121. Personal Insolvency Act 2012 (Procedures for the Conduct of Creditors' Meetings) Regulations 2013 (SI 335/2013).

122. PIA 2012, s 111.

123. PIA 2012, s 107(3).

124. PIA 2012, s 107(1)(c) as amended by the Courts and Civil Law (Miscellaneous Provisions) Act 2013, s 84.

125. PIA 2012, s 57.

(ii) the proposed PIA complies with the mandatory requirements referred to in para **5.24** above, and

(iii) the proposed PIA does not contain any terms that would release the debtor from an excluded debt, an excludable debt (other than a permitted debt) or a secured debt or otherwise affect such a debt;

(d) a statement by the PIP to the effect that –

(i) he or she has been instructed by the debtor to act as a PIP in connection with the PIA procedure, he or she has consented to so act and that he or she is a person entitled to act as a PIP,

(ii) he or she has advised the debtor of the various insolvency options for managing the debtor's financial difficulties,

(iii) he or she is not aware of any reasonable grounds to believe that the information contained in the debtor's PFS is not complete and accurate, and

(iv) he or she is of the opinion that the debtor satisfies the eligibility criteria for the proposal of a PIA;[126]

(e) a report of the PIP—

(i) describing the outcome for creditors and, having regard to the financial circumstances of the debtor, whether or not the proposed PIA represents a fair outcome for the creditors, and indicating, where relevant, how that financial outcome for creditors (whether individually or as a member of a class of creditors) under the terms of the proposal is likely to be better than the estimated financial outcome for such creditors if the debtor were to be adjudicated a bankrupt (having regard to, amongst other things, the estimated costs of the bankruptcy process), and

(ii) indicating whether or not he or she is of the opinion that the debtor is reasonably likely to be able to comply with the terms of the proposed PIA, and that the proposal is an acceptable alternative to bankruptcy for the debtor.

A debtor is under obligation to inform the PIP if their financial position has materially altered since the completion of the PFS and the sending of the notice.[127] The PIP must assist the debtor in completing a new statement where they believe that the change in the debtor's financial position justifies same. This updated statement will accompany the notice for the creditors' meeting.

Conduct of the Creditors' Meeting

[5.32] The conduct of the meeting shall be governed by s 109 PIA 2012 and any regulations made under s 111 PIA 2012.[128]

126. PIA 2012, s 91.

127. PIA 2012, s 107(2).

128. PIA 2012, s 109.

The PIP may, where he or she is of the opinion that to do so would aid in obtaining approval of a proposed PIA by the creditors, adjourn the meeting and, with the consent in writing of the debtor, shall prepare an amended proposal for a PIA.[129] In the event that an amended proposal for a PIA is prepared the PIP shall, firstly, notify each creditor of the time, date and venue of the adjourned meeting, and secondly, send a copy of the amended proposal to each creditor, at least seven days before the day of the adjourned meeting, unless all of the creditors waive the right to receive such period of notice in writing. The provisions set out above at para **5.31** in relation to the calling of a creditors' meeting shall apply, with all necessary modifications, after the adjournment.

An adjournment for the purpose of preparing an amended proposal for a PIA may occur once only in the course of the period of validity of a protective certificate (including any extension of such period).[130]

The proposal for a PIA may, before the proposal has been voted upon, be subject to a proposal for a modification to address an ambiguity or rectify an error in the proposed PIA if the modification has been proposed by a creditor or the PIP and the debtor gives his or her written consent to the modification.[131]

Once the meeting is convened, creditors, having considered a proposal for a PIA, shall vote either by voting in favour or against the approval of the proposed PIA. The manner in which the voting is conducted is dealt with at para **5.33** below.

In the event that only one creditor is entitled to vote at the creditors' meeting (whether in respect of one or more debts), the requirement to hold a creditors' meeting may be satisfied where the creditor concerned notifies the PIP in writing of that creditor's approval or otherwise of the proposal for a PIA.[132]

Where the proposed PIA is not approved in accordance with the voting procedure outlined below, the PIA procedure shall be deemed to have come to an end, and the protective certificate issued shall cease to have effect.[133] The debtor will become fully liable to all debts including any arrears, charges and interest that have accrued during the continuance of the protective certificate but excluding any amounts paid in respect of those debts during the continuance of the protective certificate.

Voting Procedure at the Creditors' Meeting

[5.33] The voting rights exercisable by a creditor at a creditors' meeting[134] to consider a proposal for a PIA shall be proportionate to the amount of the debt due by the debtor to the creditor on the day the protective certificate is issued. In the case of a secured debt where:

(a) the value held by a creditor who is a secured creditor is determined to be less than the amount of the secured debt due to the creditor on the day the protective certificate is issued; and

129. PIA 2012, s 109(2).
130. PIA 2012, s 109(4).
131. PIA 2012, s 109(6).
132. PIA 2012, s 109(8).
133. PIA 2012, s 109(7).
134. PIA 2012, s 108.

(b) the proposed PIA provides for all or part of that secured debt to –

(i) rank equally with and abate in equal proportion to the unsecured debts covered by the PIA and

(ii) be discharged with those unsecured debts on completion of the obligations under the PIA,

then the relevant portion of that secured debt shall be treated as unsecured and the creditor concerned may vote in respect of the relevant portion of that debt as an unsecured creditor.[135]

Where the secured creditor consents in writing to the inclusion of terms of the PIA providing for the surrender to the debtor of the security, that creditor shall be treated as an unsecured creditor and shall be only entitled to vote as such at the creditors' meeting.[136]

Each creditor participating at a creditors' meeting at which a vote is held shall be entitled, in respect of each debt owed to such creditor, to vote once only in respect of the relevant resolution. Upon request by the chairperson, he or she shall vote without undue delay by stating to the chairperson whether he or she is in favour of or against the relevant resolution (or words to the like effect).[137]

A creditor who is a connected person of the debtor may not vote in favour of a proposal for a PIA at a creditors' meeting:[138]

(a) a person is connected with an individual if that person is a relative (brother, sister, parent, spouse or civil partner of the person or a child of the person or of the spouse or civil partner) of the individual;

(b) a person, in his or her capacity as a trustee of a trust, is connected with an individual who or any of whose children or as respects whom any body corporate which he or she controls is a beneficiary of the trust;

(c) a person is connected with any person with whom he or she is in partnership;

(d) a company is connected with another person if that person has control of it or if that person and persons connected with that person together have control of it;

(e) any two or more persons acting together to secure or exercise control of a company shall be treated in relation to that company as connected with one another and with any person acting on the directions of any of them to secure or exercise control of the company.

Where only one creditor is entitled to vote at the creditors' meeting, the requirement to hold a meeting shall be satisfied where that creditor notifies the PIP in writing of that

135. PIA 2012, s 108(3).

136. PIA 2012, s 108(4).

137. Personal Insolvency Act 2012 (Procedures for the Conduct of Creditors' Meetings) Regulations 2013 (SI 335/2013).

138. PIA 2012, s 108(5).

creditor's approval or otherwise of the PIA.[139] Where no creditor votes the terms of the PIA will be deemed to have been approved.[140]

Where a creditor abstains from voting then that shall not be counted as a vote.

No resolution shall be passed at any meeting save for a single resolution approving a PIA or a variation of a PIA.[141]

Votes at a creditors' meeting may be given either personally or by proxy. Every notice summoning a creditors' meeting shall be accompanied by an instrument under which a creditor may appoint a proxy to attend such meeting and vote on such creditor's behalf[142] or in such form as the chairperson may allow. An instrument appointing a proxy shall be completed in writing under the hand of the creditor or, if such creditor is a company or other body corporate, under the hand of the secretary or other person duly authorised by the company or other body corporate. Each completed instrument appointing a proxy shall be delivered to the office of the PIP no later than 4pm on the last working day before the creditors' meeting is to be held. The chairperson may accept a validly appointed proxy which has been delivered as set out above.

A proposed PIA shall be considered as having been approved where:

(a) a majority of creditors representing not less than 65 per cent in value of the creditors present and voting, have voted in favour of the proposal;

(b) creditors representing more than 50 per cent of the value of the secured debts due to the creditors who are –

 (i) entitled to vote and

 (ii) have voted

 at the meeting as secured creditors have voted in favour of the proposal, and

(c) creditors representing more than 50 per cent of the value of the unsecured debts due to the creditors who are –

 (i) entitled to vote and

 (ii) have voted

 at the meeting as unsecured creditors have voted in favour of the proposal.

The value of the secured debt shall be the lesser of the market value of the security as determined under the provisions outlined at para **5.27** above or the amount of the debt secured by the security on the day the protective certificate is issued.[143]

There is provision under s 74 PIA 2012 for the Minister to make regulations relating to the conduct of the creditors' meeting. Personal Insolvency Act 2012 (Procedures for

139. PIA 2012, s 108(6).

140. PIA 2012, s 108(8).

141. Personal Insolvency Act 2012 (Procedures for the Conduct of Creditors' Meetings) 2013 (SI 335/2013).

142. **Appendix 7** – Creditor Proxy Form: http://www.isi.gov.ie/en/ISI/Creditors_meeting.pdf/Files/Creditors_meeting.pdf.

143. PIA 2012, s 110.

the Conduct of Creditors' Meetings) Regulations 2013 (SI 335/2013) was enacted governing various items such as voting by proxy and abstention from voting, all detailed above.

STEPS FOLLOWING APPROVAL OF THE PROPOSAL FOR A PIA

PIP

[5.34] Following approval of the proposal for a PIA, the PIP[144] shall as soon as practicable after the meeting has concluded notify the ISI and each creditor concerned and enclose with that notification a certificate with the result of the vote taken at the creditors' meeting, identifying the number of votes, in value of the creditors present and voting, in favour and against the proposed PIA and a copy of the approved PIA. The PIP shall also include a statement that he or she is of the opinion that:

(a) the debtor satisfies the eligibility criteria for the proposal of a PIA;

(b) the proposed PIA complies with the mandatory requirements referred to in para **5.24** above; and

(c) the proposed PIA does not contain any terms that would release the debtor from an excluded debt, an excludable debt (other than a permitted debt) or a secured debt or otherwise affect such a debt.[145]

The PIP shall also send a notice to each creditor indicating that he or she may make objection to the coming into effect of the PIA by lodging a notice of objection with the appropriate court, within 21 days of the date of the sending of that notice.[146]

ISI

[5.35] On receipt of a notification by the PIP, the ISI[147] shall record the approval in the Register of PIAs and notify the appropriate court and furnish to that court a copy of the PIA. Where the notification of the PIP is received by the ISI before the expiry of the period of the protective certificate, such protective certificate shall continue in force until the PIA comes into effect or all objections lodged with the appropriate court have been determined by the court.

On receipt of a notification by it from the court, the ISI shall register the PIA in the Register of PIAs, and the PIA shall have effect upon being so registered.[148]

144. PIA 2012, s 112(1).

145. PIA 2012, s 112(1)(c) as amended by the Courts and Civil Law (Miscellaneous Provisions) Act 2013, s 85.

146. PIA 2012, s 112(2).

147. PIA 2012, s 113 as amended by the Courts and Civil Law (Miscellaneous Provisions) Act 2013, s 85.

148. PIA 2012, s 113.

Creditor

[5.36] A creditor who lodges a notice of objection with the appropriate court shall at the same time send a copy of the notice of objection to both the ISI and the PIP.[149]

The grounds on which objection may be made to the coming into effect of the PIA are those set out below. Pending the determination by the appropriate court of the objection made by a creditor, the protective certificate shall continue to have full effect.[150] The Courts Service shall make appropriate endeavours to facilitate the early hearing of the objection lodged having regard to the continuation in force of the protective certificate pending determination of the objection.[151] Where the appropriate court upholds the objection to the PIA, the PIA procedure shall be deemed to have come to an end, and the protective certificate shall cease to have effect.

The grounds on which a PIA may be challenged by a creditor are limited to the following matters:[152]

(a) that the debtor has by his or her conduct within the two years prior to the issue of the protective certificate arranged his or her financial affairs primarily with a view to being or becoming eligible to apply for a PIA or a DSA;

(b) the procedural requirements specified in the PIA 2012 were not followed;

(c) a material inaccuracy or omission exists in the debtor's statement of affairs (based on the PFS) which causes a material detriment to the creditor;

(d) the debtor, when the PIA was proposed, did not satisfy the eligibility criteria;

(e) the PIA unfairly prejudices the interests of a creditor;

(f) the debtor has committed an offence under the PIA 2012;

(g) the debtor had entered into a transaction with a person at an undervalue within the preceding three years that has materially contributed to his or her inability to pay his or her debts (other than any debts due to the person with whom the debtor entered the transaction at an undervalue);

(h) the debtor had given a preference to a person within the preceding three years that had the effect of substantially reducing the sum available for distribution to the creditors (other than any debts due to the person who received the preference).

A debtor enters into a transaction with a person at an undervalue if he or she makes a gift to that person or he or she otherwise enters into a transaction with that person on terms that provide for him or her to receive no consideration; or he or she enters into a transaction with that person and the value of which, in money or money's worth, is significantly greater than the value, in money or money's worth, of the consideration provided by the person.

149. PIA 2012, s 114(3).

150. PIA 2012, s 113(2).

151. PIA 2012, s 114(2).

152. PIA 2012, s 120.

A debtor gives a preference to a person if that person is one of the debtor's creditors to whom a qualifying debt is owed or is a surety or guarantor for any such debt, and the debtor does anything (including the grant of security) or suffers anything to be done which (in either case) has the effect of putting that person into a position which, in the event that a PIA is made in relation to the debtor, will be better than the position he or she would have been in if that thing had not been done.

Court

[5.37] Where no objection is lodged by a creditor with the appropriate court within 14 days of the giving of the notice, the court[153] shall, where it is satisfied that the eligibility criteria in relation to the debtor have been satisfied and that the requisite percentage of creditors has approved the proposal for a PIA, approve the coming into effect of the PIA.[154]

In the event that a creditor lodges an objection with the appropriate court and the matter is determined by the court on the basis that the objection should not be allowed, the court shall, where it is satisfied that the eligibility criteria in relation to the debtor have been satisfied and that the requisite percentage of creditors has approved the proposal for a PIA, approve the coming into effect of the PIA.[155]

Where the appropriate court, for the purpose of its arriving at a decision, requires:

(a) further information, it may request the ISI to provide this information, and the ISI shall provide the information requested to the court and to the PIP concerned, or

(b) further information or evidence, it may hold a hearing, which hearing shall be on notice to the ISI and the PIP concerned.[156]

The court is entitled to accept the certificate of the PIP and the statement of the PIP referred to at para **5.34** above[157] as evidence that such eligibility criteria have been satisfied. The court may accept the certificate issued by the PIP concerned as evidence that the requisite percentage of creditors has approved the proposal for a PIA.[158]

Where the court approves the coming into effect of the PIA it shall arrange for the ISI to be notified in accordance with rules of court.[159] Please see **Ch 6** – Court Procedures for detailed information on the court procedures to be followed.

On receipt of a notification by it from the court, the ISI shall register the PIA in the Register of PIAs, and the PIA shall have effect upon being so registered.[160]

153. PIA 2012, s 115.
154. PIA 2012, s 115(1).
155. PIA 2012, s 115(2).
156. PIA 2012, s 115(3)(b) as amended by the Courts and Civil Law (Miscellaneous Provisions) Act 2013, s 87.
157. PIA 2012, s 115(5) as amended by the Courts and Civil Law (Miscellaneous Provisions) Act 2013, s 87.
158. PIA 2012, s 78(4).
159. PIA 2012, s 115(5).
160. PIA 2012, s 115(6).

EFFECT OF PIA

[5.38] A PIA having been registered in the Register of PIAs shall have effect according to its terms and remain in effect until it is completed in accordance with its terms or the terms of any variation made, or it is terminated in accordance with the PIA provisions.[161]

Where a PIA is in effect the debtor and every creditor who was entitled to vote at the creditors' meeting, regardless of whether such creditor voted to approve the proposal for the PIA, shall be bound by the terms of it.[162]

A creditor is subject to certain restrictions once a PIA becomes effective.[163] The creditor cannot:

(a) initiate any legal proceedings in relation to a specified debt;

(b) take any step to prosecute such legal proceedings already initiated;

(c) take any step to secure or recover payment of a specified debt;

(d) execute or enforce a judgment or order of a court or tribunal against the debtor in respect of a specified debt;

(e) take any step to recover goods in the possession or custody of the debtor, unless title to the goods is vested in the creditor;

(f) otherwise initiate contact with the debtor in respect of payment of a specified debt;

(g) in relation to an agreement with the debtor, including a security agreement, by reason only that the debtor is insolvent or that a PIA is in effect—

    (i) terminate or amend that agreement, or

    (ii) claim an accelerated payment, or a forfeiture of a term, under that agreement.

Furthermore, while a PIA is in effect, a creditor of that debtor shall not apply for the issue of a summons under s 8 of the Bankruptcy Act 1988 or present a petition to have the debtor concerned adjudicated a bankrupt in respect of a debt covered by the PIA.[164]

A creditor is not precluded from taking an action as respects a person who has jointly contracted with the debtor or is jointly liable with the debtor to the creditor and that other person may sue or be sued in respect of the contract without joining the debtor.[165] This does not apply where the PIA is also in effect as respects the other person.[166]

The period of time in which the PIA is in effect is disregarded for the purpose of any applicable limitation period in relation to any proceedings or process to which this section applies (including any limitation period under the Statute of Limitations 1957).

161. PIA 2012, s 116.
162. PIA 2012, s 116(2).
163. PIA 2012, s 116(3).
164. PIA 2012, s 116(5).
165. PIA 2012, s 116(6).
166. PIA 2012, s 116(7).

Equally, the period for which any judgment against the debtor in relation to a debt which is the subject of a PIA has effect (whether under statute or rule of court) shall, subject to the provisions of the PIA 2012 be extended by the period that the PIA is in effect.[167]

A creditor is not precluded from taking an action against a guarantor of a debtor where the debtor's guaranteed debts form part of the specified debts of the PIA.[168]

OPERATION OF THE TERMS OF PIA

[5.39] In general terms, a debtor or creditor who is party to that PIA shall perform his or her obligations in accordance with its terms.[169] Unless otherwise provided the following general terms should be followed. Any payments to creditors under the PIA will be made by the PIP. The PIP shall transmit payments received to each of the creditors in the agreed proportion on a timely basis. Regular contact with the debtor should be maintained and the PIP should request such reports and conduct such reviews as may be required, but such review shall in any event be carried out at least once in every period of 12 months.

Where the debtor has defaulted or appears likely to default in his or her obligations under the PIA, the PIP should discuss the matter with the debtor and should monitor implementation of the PIA.

Where the circumstances of the debtor have changed in a material respect the PIP shall provide information to the debtor regarding his or her right or obligation to initiate an application to vary the PIA.[170] In addition to this, where the circumstances of a debtor have changed to such an extent that a variation in the terms of a PIA is appropriate, the PIP shall take the necessary steps to initiate a variation of the PIA as set out below.

The PIP shall deal with the property of the debtor in accordance with the PIA. The PIP shall not charge fees or seek to recover expenses incurred unless those fees and expenses are in accordance with the terms of the PIA.

The PIP is obliged to respond in a timely manner to requests for information regarding the operation of the PIA from the ISI, the debtor and the creditors.

The PIP shall maintain complete and accurate records of account of the moneys received from the debtor and the moneys disbursed to the creditors and such moneys shall while in the possession and control of the PIP be maintained in an account in the State with a bank authorised to carry on business in the State, which account is used solely for the purposes of receiving payments from the debtor and transmitting such payments to creditors (after the deduction of any fees or expenses payable to the PIP permitted to be made).[171]

167. PIA 2012, s 116(9).
168. PIA 2012, s 116(10).
169. PIA 2012, s 117.
170. PIA 2012, s 117.
171. See **Ch 8** – Personal Insolvency Practitioners.

GENERAL DUTIES AND OBLIGATIONS OF THE DEBTOR

[5.40] A debtor who participates in any process is under an obligation to act in good faith, and in his or her dealings with the PIP concerned to make full disclosure to that PIP of all of his or her assets, income and liabilities and of all other circumstances that are reasonably likely to have a bearing on the ability of the debtor to make payments to his or her creditors.[172]

A debtor who participates in any part of the process of applying for or operating a PIA shall co-operate fully in the process, and in particular comply with any reasonable request from the PIP to provide assistance, documents and information necessary for the application of the process to the debtor's case or the carrying out of the PIP's functions, including any debt, tax, employment, business, social welfare or other financial records.

The debtor is obliged under this section to inform the PIP as soon as reasonably practicable of any material change in the debtor's circumstances, particularly an increase or decrease in the level of the debtor's assets, liabilities or income, which would affect the debtor's ability to make repayments under the PIA.

A debtor in respect of whom a PIA is in effect shall not, either alone or with any other person, obtain credit in an amount of more than €650 from any person without informing that person that he or she is subject to a PIA.

A debtor in respect of whom a PIA is in effect shall not transfer, lease, grant security over or otherwise dispose of any interest in property above a prescribed value of €650[173] otherwise than in accordance with the terms of the PIA. A debtor shall inform the PIP as soon as reasonably practicable after becoming aware of any inaccuracy or omission in the debtor's statement of affairs based on the PFS.

Finally, a debtor who participates in a PIA shall not pay to creditors any additional payments separate to the PIA in respect of debts covered in the PIA.

VARIATION OF A PIA

[5.41] A PIA like any other legal agreement may be varied in accordance with its terms.[174] Section 119 PIA 2012 as amended by s 89 of the Courts and Civil Law (Miscellaneous Provisions) Act 2013 provides for specific instances when the PIA can be varied. It should be noted that a variation does not include an extension of the period of the PIA. A PIA can only be extended by a maximum period of 12 months pursuant to the PIA 2012.[175]

172. PIA 2012, s 118.

173. Personal Insolvency Act 2012 (Value Above which a Debtor Must not Transfer, Lease, Grant Security Over, or Otherwise Dispose of an Interest in Property) Regulations 2013 (SI 330/2013).

174. PIA 2012, s 119 as amended by the Courts and Civil Law (Miscellaneous Provisions) Act 2013, s 89.

175. PIA 2012, s 99(2)(b).

PIP

[5.42] A PIP, whether on his or her own initiative or on a request made by a debtor or creditor in the circumstances outlined at para **5.43** below, shall propose a variation of a PIA where:

(a) the PIP is concerned that there has been a material change in the debtor's circumstances[176] which would affect his or her ability to make repayments under the PIA, and

(b) the PIP is satisfied that there is a reasonable prospect that the variation that addresses the circumstances would be approved.

The PIP shall, within 21 days of receipt of a request by a debtor or creditor pursuant to para **5.43** below, decide whether further enquiry is required. The PIP may request such further information as he or she requires for the person making the request and shall make such enquiries as is necessary to arrive at a decision. Where the PIP is satisfied that the conditions at para **5.42** above are met the PIP shall without delay:

(a) with the PIP's assistance, require a debtor to complete a new PFS;

(b) formulate a proposal for a variation;

(c) seek the written consent of the debtor to the proposal and to the calling of a creditors' meeting for the purpose of considering the proposal; and

(d) where consent has been given, arrange for the holding of a creditors' meeting.

Debtor or Creditor

[5.43] A debtor or creditor who is bound by a PIA may request that a PIP propose a variation to a PIA which request shall be:

(a) in writing;

(b) accompanied by information or evidence to support the assertion that there has been a material change in the debtor's circumstances; and

(c) accompanied by the written consent of the person making the request to the –

 (i) making of an enquiry by the PIP, and

 (ii) disclosure by the PIP of personal data of the person to the extent necessary for such an enquiry.

Any unreasonable refusal by the debtor to consent to the proposal for a variation or the calling of a creditors' meeting shall be grounds for an application to terminate the PIA.

---

176. Material change in debtor's circumstances means a change to the debtor's circumstances that would materially affect his or her ability to make payments, or otherwise perform his or her obligations under the PIA, and includes an increase or decrease in the debtor's assets, liabilities or income.

The following grounds shall be considered reasonable grounds for refusal by the debtor to vary the terms of the PIA:

(a) where there has been an increase in the debtor's income, to make additional payments in excess of 50 per cent of the increase in his or her income available to him or her after the following deductions (where applicable) are made –

  (i) income tax,

  (ii) social insurance contributions,

  (iii) payments made by him or her in respect of excluded debts,

  (iv) payments made by him or her in respect of excludable debts that are not permitted debts,

  (v) such other levies and charges on income as may be prescribed;

  or

(b) to make a payment amounting to more than 50 per cent of the value of any property acquired by the debtor after the coming into effect of the PIA that is proposed to be varied, unless receipt of that property had been anticipated by the terms of that PIA.

Creditors' Meeting

[5.44] When calling a creditors' meeting for this purpose, the PIP shall give creditors at least 14 days' written notice of the meeting and the date on which, and the time and place at which, the meeting will be held. The PIP will also send, along with the notice, a written proposal for the variation of the PIA, a report of the PIP describing the outcome for the creditors and debtor under the terms of the proposal and indicating whether the PIP is of the opinion that the debtor will comply with the varied terms of the proposal, and a copy of the PFS. The PIP shall lodge a copy of the notice and the proposal with the ISI.

In order to vary the terms of the PIA, the approval of creditors[177] is required in addition to the written consent of the debtor. The approval of the creditors shall be at a creditors' meeting where:

(a) a majority of creditors, representing not less than 65 per cent in value of the creditors present and voting, have voted in favour of the proposal;

(b) creditors representing more than 50 per cent of the value of the secured debts due to the creditors who are –

  (i) entitled to vote and

  (ii) have voted

  at the meeting as secured creditors have voted in favour of the proposal, and

177. PIA 2012, s 119(4).

(c) creditors representing more than 50 per cent of the value of the unsecured debts due to the creditors who are –

(i) entitled to vote and

(ii) have voted

at the meeting as unsecured creditors have voted in favour of the proposal.

Where the variation is approved at a creditors' meeting, it shall be binding on every creditor who was entitled to vote at the meeting. The conduct of the creditors' meeting and the notification requirements of the variation on the ISI and PIP shall be the same as the requirements on the original approval of the terms of the PIA.[178]

Unless otherwise specified in the terms of the PIA, the following applies in relation to the variation of the terms:[179]

(a) In the event that the PIP is concerned that there has been a material change in the debtor's circumstances which would affect his or her ability to make repayments under the PIA, the PIP (whether on his or her own initiative or at the request of a creditor) may call a meeting of creditors.

(b) When calling a creditors' meeting for this purpose, the PIP shall give creditors at least 14 days' written notice of the meeting and the date on which, and the time and place at which, the meeting will be held. The PIP will also send along with the notice a written proposal for the variation of the PIA and lodge a copy of the notice and the proposal with the ISI.

(c) A creditors' meeting under this section shall be conducted in the usual procedure as set out at para **5.31** above. The creditors at the creditors' meeting shall vote in the prescribed manner either in favour of the approval of the proposal for the variation or against the approval of the proposal for the variation.

An unsecured debt is a debt that is unsecured on the date of the creditors' meeting notwithstanding the fact that it may have been a secured debt when the vote for the proposal for the PIA was held.[180]

For the purposes of the voting at the creditors' meeting the voting shall be the same as those applying at the creditors' meeting to approve the terms of the PIA set out above unless a debt has been discharged under the terms of the PIA at the date of the calling of the creditors' meeting to consider the variation.[181]

Following approval of the variation, the PIP shall as soon as practicable notify the ISI and each creditor concerned of the fact, and enclose with that notification a copy of the PIA as varied. On receipt of this notification, the ISI shall record the variation in the Register of PIAs.

178. Paras **5.34** to **5.40** above.

179. PIA 2012, s 119(7).

180. PIA 2012, s 119(8)(l) as amended by the Courts and Civil Law (Miscellaneous Provisions) Act 2013, s 89.

181. PIA 2012, s 119(8).

The variation will take effect immediately upon its being recorded and shall remain in effect until the PIA, as varied, is completed in accordance with its terms, is terminated in accordance with the PIA 2012 or is further varied in accordance with the provisions above.

The grounds on which the variation to a PIA may be challenged by a creditor are limited to the following matters:[182]

(a) that the debtor has by his or her conduct within the two years prior to the issue of the protective certificate arranged his or her financial affairs primarily with a view to being or becoming eligible to apply for a PIA or a DSA;

(b) the procedural requirements specified in the PIA 2012 were not followed;

(c) a material inaccuracy or omission exists in the debtor's statement of affairs (based on the PFS) which causes a material detriment to the creditor;

(d) the debtor, when the PIA was proposed, did not satisfy the eligibility criteria;

(e) the PIA unfairly prejudices the interests of a creditor;

(f) the debtor has committed an offence under the PIA 2012;

(g) the debtor had entered into a transaction with a person at an undervalue within the preceding three years that has materially contributed to his or her inability to pay his or her debts (other than any debts due to the person with whom the debtor entered the transaction at an undervalue);

(h) the debtor had given a preference to a person within the preceding three years that had the effect of substantially reducing the sum available for distribution to the creditors (other than any debts due to the person who received the preference).

TERMINATION OF PIA

Application to Court

[5.45] In the limited circumstances set out below, a creditor or a PIP may, at any time during the operation of a PIA, apply to the appropriate court to have that PIA terminated.[183] Please see **Ch 6** – Court Procedures for detailed information on the court procedures to be followed.

The grounds of termination are limited to the following:

(a) a material inaccuracy or omission exists in the debtor's PFS, which causes a material detriment to the creditor;

(b) the debtor did not satisfy the eligibility criteria to enter the PIA process when he or she initiated the process;

(c) the debtor did not comply with the duties and obligations imposed on him or her under the PIA process;

182. PIA 2012, s 120.

183. PIA 2012, s 122.

(d) the debtor has since the coming into effect of the PIA committed an offence under this act;

(e) the debtor is in arrears with his or her payments for a period of not less than three months;

(f) the debtor has failed to carry out any action necessary to enable a term of the PIA have effect;

(g) the debtor has unreasonably refused to consent to a variation of the PIA.

In determining whether a debtor is in arrears with his or her payments for a period of not less than three months the following applies:

(a) at the beginning of the three-month period ending immediately before the day on which the application was made, one or more than one payment in respect of the debts became due and payable by the debtor under the PIA, and

(b) throughout that three-month period the debtor was in arrears in respect of any or all of those payments.

On hearing the application the court may dismiss the application, terminate the PIA, or order the PIP to propose the variation of the PIA. On a termination of the PIA by the court, the ISI shall, on receipt of the notification, record the fact of the termination in the Register of PIAs.[184]

Automatic Termination – Six Months' Arrears

[5.46] Where the debtor is in arrears with his or her payments for a period of six months[185] the PIA shall be deemed to have failed and shall terminate where a creditor or the PIP notifies the ISI of such default. Where the ISI receives such a notification of default, it shall record the failure of the PIA in the Register of PIAs.

A debtor is in arrears with his or her payments for a period of six months on a given date if at the beginning of the six-month period ending immediately before that date one or more than one payment in respect of a debt became due and payable by the debtor under the PIA, and at no time during that six-month period were any obligations in respect of those payments discharged.

Effect of Premature Termination of PIA

[5.47] Where a PIA has been deemed to come to an end, has failed or has terminated prematurely,[186] the debtor shall thereupon be liable in full for all debts covered by the PIA (including any arrears, charges and interest that have accrued during the continuance of the PIA but excluding any amounts paid in respect of those debts during

184. PIA 2012, s 122(5) as amended by the Courts and Civil Law (Miscellaneous Provisions) Act 2013, s 90.

185. PIA 2012, s 123.

186. PIA 2012, s 124.

the continuance of the PIA), unless the terms of the PIA provide otherwise or the appropriate court has made an order otherwise.

This is effective regardless of any prejudice to the validity of any act done or property disposed of in accordance with the PIA.

Where a PIA has terminated in the manner set out above, the ISI shall, within three months after the date on which the PIA would have terminated, remove from the Register of PIAs all information in respect of the PIA.[187]

COMPLETION OF THE PIA

[5.48] Upon the expiration of the PIA, and where the debtor has complied with his or her obligations under the PIA, the PIP shall notify the debtor, creditors and the ISI.[188] Where the debtor has complied with his or her obligations under the PIA, the debtor stands discharged from the unsecured debts specified in the PIA. The debtor shall not be discharged from its secured debts except to the extent provided for under the terms of the PIA. The ISI shall record the successful completion of the PIA in the Register of PIAs and within three months remove all information recorded in the Register of PIAs in respect of that PIA.[189]

RULES OF COURT

[5.49] Please see **Ch 6** – Court Procedures[190] for the details of the court procedures to be followed in a PIA.

Appropriate Court

[5.50] Section 5 PIA 2012 sets out the appropriate court in respect of PIAs. Where the total liabilities of the debtor, determined on the basis of the PFS completed by the debtor, are in excess of €2,500,000 the appropriate court is the High Court with the Circuit Court being the appropriate court in all other circumstances of a PIA. The performance of the functions and the exercise of the powers and jurisdiction shall be within the jurisdiction of the circuit of the Circuit Court in which:

(a) the debtor to whom the application relates is residing at the time of the making of the application or has resided within one year of the time of the making of the application, or

187. PIA 2012, s 124(2) as amended by the Courts and Civil Law (Miscellaneous Provisions) Act 2013, s 92.

188. PIA 2012, s 125 as amended by the Courts and Civil Law (Miscellaneous Provisions) Act 2013, s 92.

189. PIA 2012, s 125(4).

190. Para **6.10**.

(b) the debtor to whom the application relates has a place of business at the time of the making of the application or has a place of business within one year of the time of the making of the application.

FURTHER INFORMATION

[5.51] The ISI have published 'The Guide to a Personal Insolvency Arrangement' and the following other guidelines which are available on their website:

http://www.isi.gov.ie/en/ISI/Pages/Publications

- Personal Insolvency Arrangement Scenario Split Mortgage
- Personal Insolvency Arrangement Scenarios
- Personal Insolvency Arrangement Scenario Revenue Involvement
- Personal Insolvency Arrangement Step by Step Example.

Chapter 6

COURT PROCEDURES

INTRODUCTION

[6.01] Section 5 PIA 2012 sets out the appropriate court in respect of Debt Settlement Arrangements[1] (DSAs) and Personal Insolvency Arrangements[2] (PIAs). Where the total liabilities of the debtor, determined on the basis of the Prescribed Financial Statement[3] (PFS) completed by the debtor, are in excess of €2,500,000, the appropriate court is the High Court with the Circuit Court being the appropriate court in all other circumstances of a DSA and PIA. Any application to the court in respect of a Debt Relief Notice[4] (DRN) is within the jurisdiction of the Circuit Court.

In determining which is the appropriate Circuit Court, the performance of the functions and the exercise of the powers and jurisdiction shall be within the jurisdiction of the circuit of the Circuit Court in which:

(a) the debtor to whom the application relates is residing at the time of the making of the application or has resided within one year of the time of the making of the application; or

(b) the debtor to whom the application relates has a place of business at the time of the making of the application or has a place of business within one year of the time of the making of the application.

FILING BY ELECTRONIC MEANS

[6.02] Order 76A Rules of the Superior Court (RSC)[5] and Order 73 Circuit Court (CC) Rules[6] (together referred to as the Rules) both provide for the filing of documents by electronic means. This is one of the first court procedures which specifically set out the process for filing by electronic means and, given this fact, the authors have set out the relevant provisions in detail. It should be noted that the Rules do not specifically require documents to be filed electronically but make provision for electronic filing in certain circumstances.

A proper officer for the purposes of the Circuit Court Rules is the County Registrar attached to that office, and in any other case the combined court office manager for that office and for the purposes of the Rules of the Superior Courts is the proper officer of the Central Office.

1. See **Ch 4** – Debt Settlement Arrangements.
2. See **Ch 5** – Personal Insolvency Arrangements.
3. **Appendix 1** – Prescribed Financial Statement.
4. See **Ch 3** – Debt Relief Notices.
5. Rules of the Superior Court (RSC), Ord 76A r 4.
6. Circuit Court (CC) Rules, Ord 73 r 4.

The proper office for the purposes of the Superior Courts is the Central Office.

The proper office for the purposes of the Circuit Court is the office of the appropriate Circuit Court Office in which:

(a) the debtor to whom the application relates is residing at the time of the making of the application or has resided within one year of the time of the making of the application; or

(b) the debtor to whom the application relates has a place of business at the time of the making of the application or has a place of business within one year of the time of the making of the application.

The relevant Circuit Court offices are as follows:

Circuit	Office
Dublin	Circuit Court (Civil) Office, Dublin
Cork	Circuit Court Office, Cork
Northern	Combined Court Office, Monaghan
Midland	Combined Court Office, Tullamore
Eastern	Circuit Court Office, Trim
South Eastern	Combined Court Office, Kilkenny
South Western	Combined Court Office, Ennis
Western	Combined Court Office, Castlebar

Conditions for Electronic Filing

[6.03] The Rules provide that the proper officer must be satisfied in respect of the intending electronic user (referred to as the User):

(a) that the hardware and other equipment, any data storage media and communications protocol to be employed by the user when delivering, filing, lodging or receiving documents or information by electronic means are compatible with, and otherwise suitable for use in conjunction with, the corresponding equipment, media and protocols used or employed in or in respect of the proper office;

(b) that the User will use such naming conventions, electronic mail addresses, passwords, electronic signatures, electronic seals, digital signatures, protocols, unique identification codes or references or other means of authenticating documents delivered, filed or lodged by electronic means as may be required by the proper officer to assure the security and authenticity of such documents (and the proper officer may, for that purpose, require the provision to it of the names, specimen signatures and other particulars of the individuals authorised to act on behalf of the User);

(c) that the User will use such firewall, anti-virus tool or other devices or applications, if any, as may be required by the proper officer to avoid damage to any information system used in the Proper Office;

(d) that the User will take such steps and use such practice or protocol as may be specified by the proper officer to ensure that harmful, deleterious or offensive material does not enter any information system used in the Proper Office;

(e) that the User will format and organise and, where necessary, identify, code, index or produce in printed form documents to be delivered, filed, lodged or received by electronic means in any manner required by these Rules or by the proper officer.

In ensuring the conditions above are complied with, the proper officer may enter into any agreement or protocol with one or more persons (including one or more electronic users), or may publish any requirements which must be met in order to satisfy it, the conditions or any such guidelines for compliance with the conditions.

In addition to the above and in accordance with s 140(2)(b) PIA 2012 which provides for the transmission of documents by electronic means:

(a) a document transmitted by the ISI; and

(b) a certificate referred to in r 11(3) or r 20(3) RSC and r 19(3) and 28(3) CC Rules (notification to creditors by PIP) transmitted by a Personal Insolvency Practitioner (PIP) who is an electronic user by electronic means to an information system used in the proper office shall be authenticated, and the identity of the person in whose name it has issued shall be verified, by being–

  (i) transmitted from an information system or e-mail address of the ISI or PIP concerned, accepted for these purposes by the proper officer, or

  (ii) transmitted to the information system used in the Proper Office using a password issued for this purpose by the proper officer, without the need for the incorporation in the document of a signature of the person in whose name it has issued.

Where the proper officer determines that an electronic user is not complying with a condition (or part of any condition) specified above which he has required that user to comply with, he may revoke or modify an authorisation or requirement in respect of that user.

Electronic Filing

[6.04] Subject to compliance by the electronic user concerned with one or more of the conditions specified at para **6.03** above, or the whole or part of any one or more of such conditions as the proper officer may notify to it or him:

(a) the proper officer may—

  (i) authorise or require the ISI and

  (ii) authorise any personal insolvency practitioner, debtor, creditor or other party to proceedings under the PIA 2012 (or any solicitor acting for any such party) to deliver, file or lodge to or with the court by electronic means any document which may be delivered, filed or lodged and any application which may be made to the court in any proceedings or category of proceedings under the PIA 2012 or the Rules or in any stage or step in such proceedings;

(b) any originating document, judgment, order or determination of the court (including any judgment, order or determination entered in or issuing from the Proper Office) in such proceedings or category of proceedings which may under PIA 2012 or the Rules be issued by or on behalf of the court or the Proper Office, may be issued to an electronic user by being transmitted by electronic means; and

(c) any other document or information which may in such proceedings or category of proceedings be transmitted under the PIA 2012 or the Rules to the electronic user concerned by or on behalf of the court the Proper Office may be transmitted to an electronic user by electronic means.

An electronic user shall deliver, file or lodge documents by electronic means by such one or more of the following methods as may be provided in or for the Proper Office for the purpose of:

(a) transmitting the same in the form of an electronic document or other structured electronic data (which may include any electronic attachment in portable document format [pdf] or other format specified by the proper officer) to an information system used in the Proper Office for that purpose, and in a manner and in such form as may be specified by the proper officer; or

(b) transmitting the same (including any electronic attachment) to such electronic mail address as may be specified by the proper officer (provided that nothing shall invalidate the effect of any document transmitted to any other electronic mail address but actually received in the Proper Office).

Documents or information to be delivered by the court to an electronic user may be:

(a) transmitted in the form of an electronic document or other structured electronic data to an information system of the user, in a manner and in such form as may be specified by the proper officer; or

(b) made available to the electronic user on an information system used in the Proper Office to which the electronic user concerned has secure access; or

(c) transmitted to the electronic mail address of that user referred to in para **6.03(b)** (provided that nothing in this condition shall invalidate the effect of any document transmitted to any other electronic mail address but actually received by that user).

Originating Document: An originating document in proceedings under PIA 2012 submitted for issue by electronic means in accordance with the Rules shall be issued when it has been assigned a record number. A notice of motion in proceedings under the PIA 2012 submitted for issue by electronic means in accordance with the Rules shall be issued when it has been assigned a return date. The documents required to be filed together with any originating document shall be transmitted by electronic means as a set of files, in portable document format (pdf) or other format specified by the proper officer.

Statutory Declaration or Affidavit: Where a statutory declaration or affidavit is submitted for filing by electronic means in accordance with the Rules, unless otherwise permitted by the proper officer, the statutory declaration or affidavit and all exhibits thereto, in appropriate sequence, shall be transmitted in portable document format (pdf) or other format specified by the proper officer.

Issued Notice of Motion or Originating Document: Where an originating document or a notice of motion is issued in accordance with the preceding provisions of the Rules:

(a) a print or copy of the originating document or notice of motion as transmitted for issue shall, when issued, be treated, in accordance with s 140(3) PIA 2012, as the original of that document; and

(b) the proper officer may certify any printed version of such document as a certified copy of the original.

Retention of Documents: Where a statutory declaration or affidavit is filed by delivery by electronic means in accordance with the preceding provisions set out above, the statutory declaration or affidavit bearing the original manuscript signature of the deponent shall be retained for a period of seven years from the date of swearing thereof by the person who has filed the same by electronic means, subject to any order or direction of the court.

Authentication: Any order or protective certificate made or issued by the court in proceedings under the PIA 2012 shall be authenticated by the incorporation therein of the record number of the proceedings concerned.

Non-Electronic Users: Where –

(a) a party to proceedings under the PIA 2012 who wishes to deliver, file or lodge a document to which the Rules relate is not an electronic user, or

(b) a party to proceedings under the PIA 2012 wishes to deliver, file or lodge a document to which the Rules relate as part of a stage or step in the proceedings for which that party is not an electronic user, or

(c) for any reason, any arrangement for the transmission of documents or information between the Proper Office and an electronic user by electronic means has not been provided or is for the time being unavailable or ineffective,

documents to which the Rules apply may be delivered, filed or lodged by delivering to or filing or lodging with the Proper Office a print of the document concerned (which, in the case of a document which requires to be signed, shall bear an original manuscript signature) together with a copy thereof in accordance with and by any means permitted by the provisions of the Rules of the Superior Courts 1986 and the Circuit Court Rules 2001 (as amended) other than these Rules.

HIGH COURT RULES

General

[6.05] Statutory Instrument (SI) 316/2013 entitled 'Rules of the Superior Courts (Personal Insolvency) 2013' introduced Order 76A into the Rules of the Superior Courts 1986 (as amended) (RSC) to give effect to the provisions of the Personal Insolvency Act 2012 (PIA 2012).

(a) All proceedings will be issued out of the Central Office being the proper office and any document required will be lodged or filed in the Central Office.

(b) The Central Office may authorise or require the ISI, any PIP,[7] any debtor, any creditor or any other party to the proceedings to deliver, file or lodge any document with the court by electronic means.[8]

(c) The rules and procedure which apply to a DSA and a PIA shall equally apply to the notification and consideration of a variation of a DSA and a PIA and any objections in relation to either insolvency procedure.

(d) The court may, where satisfied that no prejudice would be suffered by any person, of its own motion and without hearing for the purpose:

   (i) cancel any order, notice, certificate or other document which has issued for or on behalf of the court in error; or

   (ii) without limiting the entitlement of any party or person to make an application under Order 28, r 11 RSC (correction of clerical mistakes), correct any clerical mistake in any order, notice, certificate or other document which has issued for or on behalf of the court, or any error arising therein from any accidental slip or omission.

(e) Where any party may be affected thereby, the court may cause the matter to be listed on notice to that party, and having heard that party may:

   (i) cancel any order, notice, certificate or other document which has issued for or on behalf of the court in error; or

   (ii) without limiting the entitlement of any party or person to make an application under Order 28, r 11 RSC (correction of clerical mistakes), correct any clerical mistake in any order, notice, certificate or other document which has issued for or on behalf of the court, or any error arising therein from any accidental slip or omission.

High Court Case Management of Personal Insolvency Arrangements

[6.06] The court can on any of the dates set out below, where it has not determined the matter on that date and it considers it necessary to do so, give such direction (as detailed below) and make such orders for the further conduct of the matter as appear convenient for the determination of the matter.

---

7. See **Ch 8** – Personal Insolvency Practitioners.
8. See para **6.31** below.

On any of the following dates:

(a) the return date of a notice of motion issued under any of the following rules of Order 78A RSC –

(i) (r 8) application by PIP to extend the period of a protective certificate period in a DSA,

(ii) (r 9) application for leave during the period of a protective certificate period to commence or continue legal proceedings against the debtor,

(iii) (r 10) application by creditor aggrieved by the issue of the protective certificate,

(iv) (r 13) application by PIP or creditor to terminate the DSA,

(v) (r 14) application by PIP or creditor in relation to excessive pension contributions by debtor,

(vi) (r 17) application by PIP to extend the period of a protective certificate period in a PIA,

(vii) (r 18) application for leave during the period of a protective certificate period to commence or continue legal proceedings against the debtor,

(viii) (r 19) application by creditor aggrieved by the issue of the protective certificate,

(ix) (r 22) application by PIP or creditor in relation to excessive pension contributions by debtor,

(x) (r 23) application by PIP or creditor to terminate the DSA, or,

(b) the date on which any DSA and any objections thereto has or have been entered for initial consideration by the court; or

(c) the date on which any PIA and any objections thereto has or have been entered for initial consideration by the court;

or on any adjournment from such date, the court may, if it does not hear and determine the application, objections or request for approval concerned on that date, and where it considers it necessary to do so, give such direction and make such orders for the further conduct of the matter as appear convenient for the determination of the matter in a manner which is just, expeditious and likely to minimise the costs of the proceedings.

These directions can, where appropriate, include:

(a) directions as to the service of notice of the matter on any other person, including mode of service and the time allowed for such service (and the court may for that purpose adjourn the hearing or further hearing of the matter to a date specified);

(b) directions as to the filing and delivery of any further affidavits by any party or parties;

(c) orders fixing time limits;

(d) directions as to the production of documents to other parties or the furnishing of additional documents or evidence to the court;

(e) directions as to the exchange of memoranda between or among the parties for the purpose of the agreeing by the parties or the fixing by the court of any issues of fact or law to be determined in the proceedings, or orders fixing such issues;

(f) a direction that the matter be determined on oral evidence, where it appears to the court that the matter is likely to involve a substantial dispute of fact or it is otherwise necessary or desirable in the interests of justice (and the court may for that purpose make orders and give directions in relation to the exchange of pleadings or points of claim or defence between the parties);

(g) directions as to the furnishing by the parties to the court and delivery of written submissions;

(h) directions as to the publication of notice of the hearing of the matter and the giving of notice in advance of such hearing to any person other than a party to the proceedings who desires to be heard on the hearing of the matter.

The court may hear any application for relief of an interlocutory nature on any of the following dates:

(a) the return date of a notice of motion issued under any of the following rules of Order 78A RSC –

   (i) (r 8) application by PIP to extend the period of a protective certificate period in a DSA,

   (ii) (r 9) application for leave during the period of a protective certificate period to commence or continue legal proceedings against the debtor,

   (iii) (r 10) application by creditor aggrieved by the issue of the protective certificate,

   (iv) (r 13) application by PIP or creditor to terminate the DSA,

   (v) (r 14) application by PIP or creditor in relation to excessive pension contributions by debtor,

   (vi) (r 17) application by PIP to extend the period of a protective certificate period in a PIA,

   (vii) (r 18) application for leave during the period of a protective certificate period to commence or continue legal proceedings against the debtor,

   (viii) (r 19) application by creditor aggrieved by the issue of the protective certificate,

   (ix) (r 22) application by PIP or creditor in relation to excessive pension contributions by debtor,

   (x) (r 23) application by PIP or creditor to terminate the DSA, or

(b) the date on which any DSA and any objections thereto has or have been entered for initial consideration by the court; or

(c) the date on which any PIA and any objections thereto has or have been entered for initial consideration by the court.

CIRCUIT COURT RULES

General

[6.07] SI 317/2013 entitled 'Circuit Court Rules (Personal Insolvency) 2013' introduced Order 73 into the Circuit Court Rules 2001 (as amended) (CC Rules).

(a) All proceedings will be issued out of the appropriate Circuit Court Office being the proper office and any document required will be lodged or filed in that Circuit Court Office:

Circuit	Office
Dublin	Circuit Court (Civil) Office, Dublin
Cork	Circuit Court Office, Cork
Northern	Combined Court Office, Monaghan
Midland	Combined Court Office, Tullamore
Eastern	Circuit Court Office, Trim
South Eastern	Combined Court Office, Kilkenny
South Western	Combined Court Office, Ennis
Western	Combined Court Office, Castlebar

(b) The Proper Office may authorise or require the ISI, any PIP, any debtor, any creditor or any other party to the proceedings to deliver, file or lodge any document with the court by electronic means.[9]

(c) The rules and procedure which apply to a DSA and a PIA shall equally apply to the notification and consideration of a variation of a DSA and a PIA and any objections thereto.

(d) The court, where satisfied that no prejudice would be suffered by any person, of its own motion and without hearing for the purpose may:

(i) cancel any order, notice, certificate or other document which has issued for or on behalf of the court in error; or

(ii) without limiting the entitlement of any party or person to make an application under Order 65, r 3 (correction of clerical mistakes), correct any clerical mistake in any order, notice, certificate or other document which has issued for or on behalf of the court, or any error arising therein from any accidental slip or omission.

(e) Where any party may be affected thereby, the court may cause the matter to be listed on notice to that part, and having heard that party may:

(i) cancel any order, notice, certificate or other document which has issued for an on behalf of the court in error, or

9. See para **6.02** above.

(ii) without limiting the entitlement of any party or person to make an application under Order 65, r 3 CC Rules (correction of clerical mistakes), correct any clerical mistake in any order, notice, certificate or other document which has issued for or on behalf of the court, or any error arising therein from any accidental slip or omission.

Circuit Court Case Management of Personal Insolvency Arrangements

[6.08] On any of the following dates:

(a) the return date of a notice of motion issued under any of the following rules under Order 73 CC Rules –

(i) (r 7) application by PIP to extend the supervision period in a DRN,

(ii) (r 8) application for leave during the supervision period to commence or continue legal proceedings against the debtor,

(iii) (r 9) application by ISI to amend a DRN,

(iv) (r 10) application by ISI for a direction of the court in respect of a DRN,

(v) (r 11) application by specified debtor or creditor during the supervision period where aggrieved by the issue of the protective certificate,

(vi) (r 12) application by aggrieved creditor during the supervision period against the inclusion of a debt,

(vii) (r 13) application by PIP or creditor to terminate the DRN,

(viii) (r 16) application by PIP to extend the period of the protective certificate in a DSA,

(ix) (r 17) application for leave during the protective certificate period in a DSA to commence or continue legal proceedings against the debtor,

(x) (r 18) application by aggrieved creditor of the issue of the protective certificate in a DSA,

(xi) (r 21) application by PIP or creditor to terminate the DSA,

(xii) (r 22) application by PIP or creditor in relation to excessive pension contributions by debtor,

(xiii) (r 25) application by PIP to extend the period of the protective certificate in a PIA,

(xiv) (r 26) application for leave during the protective certificate period in a PIA to commence or continue legal proceedings against the debtor,

(xv) (r 27) application by aggrieved creditor of the issue of the protective certificate in a PIA,

(xvi) (r 31) application by PIP or creditor in relation to excessive pension contributions by debtor,

(xvii) (r 32) application by PIP or creditor to terminate the PIA.

(b) the date on which any DSA and any objections thereto has or have been entered for initial consideration by the court; or

(c) the date on which any PIA and any objections thereto has or have been entered for initial consideration by the court;

or on any adjournment from such date, the court may, if it does not hear and determine the application, objections or request for approval concerned on that date, and where it considers it necessary to do so, give such direction and make such orders for the further conduct of the matter as appear convenient for the determination of the matter in a manner which is just, expeditious and likely to minimise the costs of the proceedings.

These directions can, where appropriate, include:

(a) directions as to the service of notice of the matter on any other person, including mode of service and the time allowed for such service (and the court may for that purpose adjourn the hearing or further hearing of the matter to a date specified);

(b) directions as to the filing and delivery of any further affidavits by any party or parties;

(c) orders fixing time limits;

(d) directions as to the production of documents to other parties or the furnishing of additional documents or evidence to the court;

(e) directions as to the exchange of memoranda between or among the parties for the purpose of the agreeing by the parties or the fixing by the court of any issues of fact or law to be determined in the proceedings, or orders fixing such issues;

(f) a direction that the matter be determined on oral evidence, where it appears to the court that the matter is likely to involve a substantial dispute of fact or it is otherwise necessary or desirable in the interests of justice (and the court may for that purpose make orders and give directions in relation to the exchange of pleadings or points of claim or defence between the parties);

(g) directions as to the furnishing by the parties to the court and delivery of written submissions;

(h) directions as to the publication of notice of the hearing of the matter and the giving of notice in advance of such hearing to any person other than a party to the proceedings who desires to be heard on the hearing of the matter.

On any of the dates outlined above, the court may hear any application for relief of an interlocutory nature.

SERVICE

[6.09] As the proceedings in respect of DRNs, DSAs and PIAs are under all commenced by way of originating documents, the usual procedure under the relevant Court Rules as to the service of an originating document applies.

Order 9 r 2 RSC provides that service of an originating document must be effected by way of personal service. Personal service for these purposes is effected by delivering in person a copy of the originating document to the person to be served and showing him the original or duplicate original.[10]

All other applications are brought in the proceedings and the service of same is set out under Order 121 r 1 RSC which provides that service shall be effected by leaving the document or a copy thereof (as may be appropriate) at, or sending the document or a copy thereof (as may be appropriate) by registered prepaid post to, the residence or place of business in the State of the person to be served or the place of business in the State of the solicitor (if any) acting for him in the proceedings to which the document relates.

Order 11 r 5 Circuit Court Rules 2001 (as amended) provides that service of an originating document may be effected by:

(a) he sending of the originating document by registered prepaid post in an envelope addressed to the person to be served at his last known residence or place of business in the State and the document may be posted by the person on whose behalf it purports to be issued or a person authorised by him in that behalf;

(b) personal service (by a Summons Server or other person) upon the person to be served.

Order 11 r 6 Circuit Court Rules 2001 (as amended) provides that personal service of an originating document upon the person may be effected by delivering a copy of the originating document to the person personally wherever he is to be found within the jurisdiction. Where it appears by affidavit that the person is personally within the jurisdiction and that due and reasonable diligence has been exercised in endeavouring to effect personal service, service of the originating document may be effected by delivering a copy thereof at the person's place of residence within the jurisdiction to the husband or wife of the person or to some relative of the defendant over the age of 16 years and apparently resident there or at the person's place of business or employment or office within the jurisdiction to some employee of the person over the age of 16 years.

All other applications are brought in the proceedings and the service of same is set out under Order 11 r 17 Circuit Court Rules 2001 (as amended) which provides that service shall be effected by leaving the document or a copy thereof (as may be appropriate) at, or sending the document or a copy thereof (as may be appropriate) by registered prepaid post to, the residence or place of business in the State of the person to be served or the place of business in the State of the solicitor (if any) acting for him in the proceedings to which the document relates.

DEBT RELIEF NOTICE

[6.10] An application to the court in respect of a DRN is within the jurisdiction of the Circuit Court. The determination of the appropriate Circuit Court in which any application is to be brought is set out at para **6.01** above.

10. Rules of the Superior Court (RSC), Ord 9 r 3.

Originating Document: The Form 52A, as prescribed by the ISI, is the originating document for the proceedings concerning the DRN.[11] All further applications under the PIA 2012 concerning the DRN in respect of the debtor concerned shall be brought in the proceedings commenced by the submission of that application and the documents and information as set above.

Application to Court for a DRN

[6.11] The documents to be submitted to the relevant court office are:[12]

(a) the application for a DRN on behalf of the debtor concerned;

(b) the certificate of the ISI (in Form 52A[13] in the Schedule) to the effect that the relevant DRN application is in order; and

(c) the supporting documentation for the DRN application, other than the documents referred to in s 29(2)(e) and (f) PIA 2012, ie the debtor's written consent to the disclosure to the ISI).

The Form 52A, as prescribed by the ISI is the originating document for the proceedings concerning the DRN.[14] All further applications under the PIA 2012 concerning the DRN in respect of the debtor concerned shall be brought in the proceedings commenced by the submission of that application and the documents and information as set above.

First Court Date: On the date first fixed for the consideration of the application for a decision of a DRN, the following are not required to attend –

(a) the ISI,

(b) the AI,

(c) the debtor.

The court deals with the application without the attendance of any of the interested parties.

The options open to the court when having considered the application are the following:

(a) **Issue:** if the court is satisfied that the criteria specified in s 26(2) PIA 2012 (ie the eligibility criteria) have been satisfied, then the court may issue a DRN. The issue of a DRN will be in Form 52B[15] in the Schedule of Forms in accordance with s 31(2)(a) PIA 2012;

(b) **Refuse to issue:** if the court is not satisfied that the criteria specified in s 26(2) PIA 2012 has not been satisfied, then the court may refuse the application to issue a DRN;

---

11. Circuit Court (CC) Rules, Ord 73 r (6)(2).
12. Circuit Court (CC) Rules, Ord 73 r 6(1).
13. See **Appendix 9** – Circuit Court Form No 52A.
14. Circuit Court (CC) Rules, Ord 73 r (6)(2).
15. See **Appendix 10** – Form No 52B.

(c) **Adjourn the application:** the court may adjourn the application and direct the registrar of the court to request the ISI to clarify any matter in the documentation provided or to provide any documentation which appears to the court to have been omitted; or

(d) **Direct a hearing to be held:** the court, where it requires further information or evidence for the purpose of arriving at a decision under s 31(2) PIA 2012, may direct that a hearing be held. This hearing shall be on notice to the ISI and the AI.

Where the court directs a hearing, the court shall direct the registrar of the court to include in the notification to the ISI the time and place fixed for the hearing. The court may direct the registrar to include in the notification:[16]

(a) an indication of the nature of the information or evidence which the court requires and the persons who are likely to be able to provide such information or evidence; and

(b) notice of whether any evidence the court requires shall be given by way of affidavit.

Withdrawal of the DRN Application of authorisation

[6.12] Where the ISI has sought a decision of the court for consideration of the DRN application and the AI wishes to withdraw, the AI shall notify the ISI in writing of the withdrawal.[17] The ISI must, as soon as practicable, upon receipt of the notification of withdrawal, notify the court of the withdrawal of the application.[18]

Application to extend the supervision period

[6.13] An application to extend the supervision period by the ISI must be made by an ex-parte motion.[19] The reasons for the extension must be identified when making the application. It would appear that these reasons can be set out in the motion and any documentation being relied upon should also be submitted. The documentation can also be submitted by electronic means. The rules do not require an affidavit to support this application; however an affidavit may be necessary if the court so requires.[20]

Application for leave during the supervision period

[6.14] Section 35(3) PIA 2012 requires an application to the court for the continuance, commencement, execution or any other legal process in respect of a debtor who is under supervision.[21]

16. Circuit Court (CC) Rules, Ord 73 r 6(4).
17. Circuit Court (CC) Rules, Ord 73 r 6(5).
18. Circuit Court (CC) Rules, Ord 73 r 6(5).
19. Circuit Court (CC) Rules, Ord 73 r 7.
20. Circuit Court (CC) Rules, Ord 73 r 7.
21. Circuit Court (CC) Rules, Ord 73 r 8.

An application for leave during the supervision period concerned, to commence or continue other proceedings, execution or other legal process in respect of a specified qualifying debt against the specified debtor or his/her property, shall:

(a) in the case of proceedings to be commenced or continued *other than* before a judge of the relevant circuit be brought by way of an originating notice of motion;

(b) in the case of proceedings sought to be commenced *before* a judge of the relevant circuit be brought by way of an originating notice of motion; and

(c) in the case of proceedings which it is sought to continue before the judge of the relevant circuit in which the DRN has been issued then it should be brought by originating notice of motion.

The motion must be brought by the person seeking such relief to continue, commence, execute or deal with any other proceedings.

The motion must be accompanied by a grounding affidavit which sets out the reasons why such leave is sought and it must be sworn by the person seeking the relief.

Service: The motion papers together with the grounding affidavit shall be served on the following –

(a) the debtor concerned,

(b) the AI,

(c) the ISI,

(d) any other person who the court directs should be served.

The papers must be served on these persons not less than 21 days before the date first fixed for the hearing of the motion unless otherwise directed by the court.[22]

The Hearing of the Motion: The ISI and the AI shall not be required to attend on the date first fixed for the hearing of the motion nor shall they be required to attend on any date to which such motion is adjourned unless directed by the court.

Application to Amend a DRN

[6.15] An application to amend a DRN by the ISI must be brought by way of a motion on notice.[23] The notice must identify the amendment sought and the ambiguity, error or omission sought to be addressed. The motion should also be accompanied by any documents relied upon (attached by electronic means where authorised or required.)

Service[24]: The notice of motion and a copy of the grounding affidavit shall be served on the specified debtor and each specified creditor concerned.

22. Circuit Court (CC) Rules, Ord 73 r 8.
23. Circuit Court (CC) Rules, Ord 73 r 9.
24. Circuit Court (CC) Rules, Ord 73 r 9(2).

The motion and grounding affidavit must be served not less than 21 days before the date first fixed for the hearing of the motion.

Application for Directions in Relation to a DRN

[6.16] An application by the ISI for directions[25] in relation to a matter arising in connection with a DRN[26] shall be brought by way of a notice of motion. The motion must be grounded by an affidavit sworn by a person duly authorised in that behalf by the ISI.

The motion must specify the particular directions and other reliefs, if any, that are being sought pursuant to s 41(3) PIA 2012.

The affidavit must contain the following:

(a) where relevant to the directions and reliefs sought, include evidence of any alleged non-compliance by the specified debtor concerned with an obligation under s 36 PIA 2012; and

(b) set out the facts or circumstances which it is alleged justify the giving of any particular directions sought, and set out the basis of the deponent's belief as to the existence of those facts or circumstances.

Service[27]: The motion and a copy of the grounding affidavit must be served on the specified debtor concerned not less than 21 days before the date first fixed for the hearing of the motion.

Replying Affidavit[28]: The specified debtor shall be at liberty to file and serve a replying affidavit setting out:

(a) concisely the grounds of any opposition to the application; and

(b) verifying any facts relied on in opposing the application.

Service of Replying Affidavit: The replying affidavit must be served on the ISI not later than seven days before the return date of the notice of motion.

Application to Court by Person Affected

[6.17] A specified debtor or creditor can apply to the court during the supervision period concerned where they are aggrieved by any act, omission or decision of the ISI in connection with a DRN.[29]

This application must be brought by notice of motion in the proceedings, grounded on an affidavit sworn by or on behalf of the specified debtor or creditor. The notice of motion and the grounding affidavit must be lodged with the appropriate court.[30]

25. Circuit Court (CC) Rules, Ord 73 r 10.
26. PIA 2012, s 41.
27. Circuit Court (CC) Rules, Ord 73 r 10(4).
28. Circuit Court (CC) Rules, Ord 73 r 10(5).
29. Circuit Court (CC) Rules, Ord 73 r 11 and PIA 2012, s 42.
30. PIA 2012, s 42(2).

The notice of motion must specify the particular reliefs sought under s 42 of PIA 2012.

The grounding affidavit must set out the following:

(a) particulars of any act, omission or decision of the ISI which is the subject of the application;

(b) the facts or circumstances which it is alleged authorise or entitle the applicant to the relief sought; and

(c) set out the basis of the deponent's belief as to the existence of those facts or circumstances.

Service: The notice of motion and a copy of the grounding affidavit must be served on each of the following persons –

(a) the ISI,

(b) where the applicant is a specified creditor, to the specified debtor and the other specified creditors,

(c) where the applicant is a specified debtor, to the specified creditors.

The notice of motion and the copy of the grounding affidavit must be served on the relevant persons not later than 21 days before the date first fixed for the hearing of the motion.

Replying Affidavit: Each person served with the notice of motion and a copy of the grounding affidavit shall be at liberty to file and serve a replying affidavit.

The replying affidavit shall contain the following:

(a) it must set out concisely the grounds of any opposition to the application; and

(b) it must verify any facts relied on in opposing the application.

The replying affidavit must be served on the moving party and on every other person served with notice of the application not later than seven days before the return date of the notice of motion.[31] There is no further provision within the rules or the PIA 2012 to file a supplemental affidavit at this stage; however one would assume that normal court procedure would apply whereby any party could apply to the court to file a supplemental affidavit or however the court so directs.

Objection by Creditor to the Inclusion of a Debt

[6.18] A specified creditor can apply to the court, during the supervision period concerned, where they object to the inclusion of a debt in respect of which they are a specified creditor.[32]

The application is brought by way of a notice of motion grounded on an affidavit sworn by or on behalf of the specified creditor.

The notice of motion must specify the grounds of objection, which are:

31. Circuit Court (CC) Rules, Ord 73 r 11(5).

32. Circuit Court (CC) Rules, Ord 73 r 12 and PIA 2012, s 43.

(a) the specified debtor did not satisfy the eligibility criteria specified when the application was made on his behalf;

(b) one or more of the following applies which causes or has caused a material detriment to the specified creditor –

(i) a material inaccuracy or omission exists in the specified debtor's PFS or other information provided, or documents submitted, by him or on his behalf for a DRN,

(ii) the specified debtor failed to comply with his obligations as specified under the PIA 2012,

(iii) an adjudication in bankruptcy has been made in relation to the specified debtor that has not been annulled or discharged,

(iv) The specified debtor has, since the coming into effect of the DRN, committed an offence under the PIA 2012,

(v) The procedural requirements specified, pursuant to the DRN process, have not been complied with.

The notice of motion must also set out the relief that is sought as set out in s 43(5) PIA 2012 which are:

(a) it may dismiss the application; or

(b) terminate the DRN;

(c) extend the supervision period;

(d) make an order amending the DRN, including the removal of the debt which was the subject of the s 43 application;

(e) make such other order as the court thinks fit.

The grounding affidavit must:

(a) set out the facts or circumstances which it is alleged establish the grounds of objection concerned; and

(b) the facts or circumstances which it is alleged authorise or entitle the applicant to the relief sought; and

(c) set out the basis of the deponent's belief as to the existence of those facts or circumstances.

Service: The notice of motion and a copy of the grounding affidavit must be served on the following –

(a) the ISI,

(b) the specified debtor.

The motion and affidavit must be served not later than 21 days before the date first fixed for the hearing of the motion.

Replying Affidavit: Each person served with the notice of motion and a copy of the grounding affidavit shall be at liberty to file and serve a replying affidavit.

The replying affidavit shall contain the following –

(a) it must set out concisely the grounds of any opposition to the application, and

(b) it must verify any facts relied on in opposing the application.

The replying affidavit must be served on the moving party and on every other person served with notice of the application not later than seven days before the return date of the notice of motion.[33] There is no further provision within the rules or the PIA 2012 to file a supplemental affidavit at this stage; however one would assume that normal court procedure would apply whereby any party could apply to the court to file a supplemental affidavit or however the court so directs.

Application to Have a DRN terminated

[6.19] The ISI can apply to the court to have a DRN terminated.[34] The application must be brought by notice of motion of the ISI which motion must be grounded on an affidavit sworn by a person duly authorised by the ISI.

The motion must specify the grounds on which the application is made, which are the following:

(a) the specified debtor did not satisfy the eligibility criteria when the application was made on his behalf;

(b) a material inaccuracy or omission exists in the specified debtor's PFS or any other information provided, or documents submitted by him or on his behalf in the making of the application;

(c) the specified debtor failed to comply with his obligation pursuant to the DRN;

(d) an adjudication in bankruptcy has been made in relation to the specified debtor that has not been annulled or discharged;

(e) the specified debtor has, since the coming into effect of the DRN, committed an offence under the PIA 2012;

(f) the procedural requirements as set out under a DRN application were not followed.

The motion must also specify the particular remedy that it is seeking. The following remedies are available:[35]

(a) dismiss the application;

(b) terminate the DRN;

(c) extend the supervision period concerned;

(d) make an order for the enforcement of an obligation of the specified debtor;

(e) make such other order as the court thinks fit.

---

33. Circuit Court (CC) Rules, Ord 73 r 13.

34. PIA 2012, s 44.

35. PIA 2012, s 44(4).

The grounding affidavit must:[36]

(a) set out the facts or circumstances which it is alleged establish the grounds of objection concerned; and

(b) set out the facts or circumstances which it is alleged authorise or entitle the applicant to the relief sought; and

(c) set out the basis of the deponent's belief as to the existence of those facts or circumstances.

Service: The notice of motion and a copy of the grounding affidavit must be served on the following –

(a) the ISI,

(b) the specified debtor.

The motion and affidavit must be served not later than 21 days before the date first fixed for the hearing of the motion.[37]

Replying Affidavit: The specified debtor[38] served with the notice of motion and a copy of the grounding affidavit shall be at liberty to file and serve a replying affidavit (together with exhibits).

The replying affidavit shall contain the following –

(a) it must set out concisely the grounds of any opposition to the application, and

(b) it must verify any facts relied on in opposing the application.

The replying affidavit must be served on the moving party and on every other person served with notice of the application not later than seven days before the return date of the notice of motion.[39] There is no further provision within the rules or the PIA 2012 to file a supplemental affidavit at this stage however one would assume that normal court procedure would apply whereby any party could apply to the court to file a supplemental affidavit or however the Court so directs.

Replying Affidavits in support: Each specified creditor served with notice of the application is at liberty to file and serve an affidavit.

The replying affidavit shall contain the following:

(a) it must set out concisely the grounds of any support or opposition (as the case may be) to the application; and

(b) it must verify any facts relied on in opposing the application.

The replying affidavit must be served on the moving party and on every other person served with notice of the application not later than seven days before the return date of the notice of motion[40]. There is no further provision within the rules or the PIA 2012 to

36. Circuit Court (CC) Rules, Ord 73 r 13(3).
37. Circuit Court (CC) Rules, Ord 73 r 13(4).
38. Circuit Court (CC) Rules, Ord 73 r 13(5).
39. Circuit Court (CC) Rules, Ord 73 r 13(5).
40. Circuit Court (CC) Rules, Ord 73 r 13(6).

file a supplemental affidavit at this stage; however one would assume that normal court procedure would apply whereby any party could apply to the court to file a supplemental affidavit or however the court so directs.

DEBT SETTLEMENT ARRANGEMENTS

[6.20] Originating Document: The application for the protective certificate shall be in the form prescribed by the ISI[41] and shall form the originating document in the proceedings concerning the DSA in respect of the debtor concerned. All further applications concerning the DSA in respect of the debtor concerned shall be brought in the proceedings commenced by the submission of that application. The only exception to this is an application seeking leave to commence proceedings against the debtor during the course of the protective certificate.[42]

Exceptional Circumstances

[6.21] An application by a debtor to the court, on notice to the ISI, to make a proposal for a DSA in circumstances where a debtor would not ordinarily be entitled to make such a proposal for any of the following reasons:

(a) been the subject of a protective certificate issued under a DSA less than 12 months prior to the date of the application for a protective certificate;

(b) had his or her debts discharged pursuant to a DRN less than three years prior to the date of the application for a protective certificate;

(c) had his or her debts discharged pursuant to a PIA less than five years prior to the date of the application for a protective certificate; or

(d) been discharged from bankruptcy less than five years prior to the date of the application for a protective certificate

shall be made by notice of motion grounded on an affidavit of the debtor. The court may direct that notice of the application is given by the debtor to any person as the court directs.

Where the court is satisfied that the current insolvency of the debtor arises by reason of exceptional circumstances or other factors which are substantially outside the control of the debtor and that it would be just to permit the debtor to make a proposal for a DSA, the court may make an order stating that the criterion set out at para **6.22** below preventing an application for a DSA shall not apply to the debtor.

41. **Appendix 5** – Application Form DSA.

42. See para **6.25** below.

Protective Certificate – DSA

Issue of Protective Certificate in a DSA

[6.22] The ISI may seek a decision of the court in respect of an application for a protective certificate in a DSA pursuant to s 61(2) PIA 2012 by submitting to the Central Office:

(a) the application for a protective certificate made to the ISI by the PIP on behalf of the debtor pursuant to s 59 PIA 2012;

(b) a certificate of the ISI (Form No 51[43] or Form No 52A[44]) to the effect that the application for a protective certificate is in order; and

(c) any supporting documentation to the application for a protective certificate by the PIP.

The application for the protective certificate shall be in the form prescribed by the ISI[45] and shall form the originating document in the proceedings concerning the DSA in respect of the debtor concerned. All further applications concerning the DSA in respect of the debtor concerned shall be brought in the proceedings commenced by the submission of that application.

First Court Date: On the date first fixed for the consideration of the application, the ISI, the PIP concerned and the debtor shall not be required to attend and the court, having considered the application, may –

Satisfied:

(a) if satisfied that the eligibility criteria have been satisfied and the other relevant requirements relating to an application for the issue of a protective certificate have been met, issue a protective certificate in accordance with Form No 52[46] or Form 52C;[47]

Not satisfied:

(b) if not satisfied that the eligibility criteria have been satisfied and/or the other relevant requirements relating to an application for a protective certificate have not been met, may refuse the application for a protective certificate;

(c) adjourn the consideration of the application and direct the Proper Officer of the court to request the ISI to clarify any matter in the documentation provided or to provide any documentation which appears to the court to have been omitted; or

43. **Appendix 11** – High Court Form No 51.
44. **Appendix 9** – Circuit Court Form No 52A.
45. **Appendix 5** – Application Form DSA.
46. **Appendix 12** – High Court Form No 52.
47. **Appendix 13** – Circuit Court Form No 52C.

(d) where it requires further information or evidence for the purpose of arriving at a decision to issue a protective certificate, direct that a hearing be held, which hearing shall be on notice to the ISI and the PIP.

Where such a hearing is directed, the court shall direct the Registrar to include in the notification to the ISI the time and place fixed for the hearing and may direct the Registrar to include in the notification:

(a) an indication of the nature of the information or evidence which the court requires for the purposes of its arriving at a decision and the persons likely to provide such information; and

(b) notice of whether the evidence required may be given by way of affidavit.

Withdrawal of Application for Protective Certificate

[6.23] Where a PIP withdraws an application for a protective certificate on behalf of a debtor, it must notify the ISI in writing of the withdrawal and the ISI shall, as soon as is practicable, notify the court of such withdrawal.

The application to withdraw must be made before the protective certificate is issued.

Extension of Protective Certificate

[6.24] An application to extend the period of the protective certificate shall be made by the PIP to the court by way of a notice of motion in the proceedings, setting out the reasons for the extension sought. There is no requirement for a grounding affidavit; however the court may require delivery of an affidavit where it considers it just and necessary to do so. The notice of motion must be served on the ISI.

The ISI is not required to appear at the date fixed for the hearing of the motion nor at any adjourned date, save by direction of the court.

Creditors

Leave to Issue Legal Proceedings during Protective Certificate Period

[6.25] Where an application is made to the court pursuant to s 62(3) PIA 2012 for leave, whilst a protective certificate is in force, to commence or continue other proceedings, execution or other legal process in respect of a specified debt against a debtor or his or her property, the person seeking such relief shall make an application grounded on an affidavit sworn by or on behalf of that person setting out the reasons why such relief is sought.

Application: the application shall –

(a) in the case of an application to commence proceedings, be brought by originating notice of motion, or

(b) in the case of an application to continue proceedings or for execution or other legal process, be brought by notice of motion in the proceedings which it is sought to continue or in which leave for execution or other process is sought.

Service: The originating notice of motion or notice of motion together with a copy of the grounding affidavit shall be served on the debtor, the PIP and the ISI, and any other person who the court directs should be served, not less than 21 days before the date first fixed for hearing unless otherwise directed by the court.

There is no requirement for the ISI or the PIP to attend on the hearing date or any such adjourned date, unless otherwise ordered by the court.

Aggrieved Creditor

[6.26] Application: An application may be made to the Court under s 63 PIA 2012 by a creditor who is aggrieved by the issue of a protective certificate and shall be brought by way of notice of motion in the proceedings of the protective certificate concerned, grounded on an affidavit sworn by or on behalf of the creditor.

The notice of motion must specify the date on which notice of the issue of the protective certificate was given to the creditor concerned and the grounds of the application.

Grounding Affidavit: The affidavit shall set out the facts and circumstances which it is alleged establish the grounds concerned and authorise or entitle the applicant to the relief sought and the basis of the deponent's belief as to the existence of those facts or circumstances.

Service: The notice of motion and a copy of the grounding affidavit shall be served on the ISI and the PIP, and any other person who the court directs should be served, not less than 21 days before the date first fixed for hearing of the motion.

Replying Affidavit: Each person served with the notice of motion and a copy of the grounding affidavit shall be at liberty to file and serve a replying affidavit setting out concisely the grounds for any opposition to the application and verifying any facts relied on in opposing the application, and a copy of such affidavit together with any exhibits thereto shall be served upon the moving party and upon every other person with notice of the application before the return date of the notice of motion. There is no further provision within the rules or the act to file a supplemental affidavit at this stage; however one would assume that normal court procedure would apply whereby any party could apply to the court to file a supplemental affidavit or however the court so directs.

Creditor Notice of Objection

[6.27] Following the approval of a DSA at a creditors' meeting, the PIP shall as soon as is practicable after the meeting has concluded, notify the ISI and each creditor concerned and enclose with that notification:

(a) a certificate with the result of the vote taken at the creditors' meeting, identifying the number of votes, in value of the creditors present and voting, in favour and against the proposed DSA; and

(b) a copy of the approved DSA.

The PIP shall, in addition to the documents referred to above, also send a notice to each creditor indicating their entitlement pursuant to s 75(3) PIA 2012 to lodge a Notice of Objection with the appropriate court within 14 days of the date of the sending of that notice.

The Notice of Objection must be in Form No 53[48] or Form 52D[49] and shall:

(a) include the record number of the proceedings;

(b) state when the notice under s 75(2) PIA 2012 was sent to the creditor by the PIP (if known) and when the said notice was received by the creditor;

(c) specify succinctly the grounds, set out in s 87 PIA 2012, on which objection is made to the coming into effect of the DSA; and

(d) confirm the amount of the debt due to the creditor concerned.

Approval of DSA

Notice of Approval of DSA to Court

[6.28] On receipt of the notification of approval of a DSA at a creditors' meeting from a PIP, the ISI must notify the court in accordance with Form No 54[50] or Form No 52E[51] and it shall be accompanied by:

(a) a true copy of the certificate with the result of the vote taken at the creditors' meeting, which shall be in Form No 55[52] or Form No 52F;[53]

(b) a true copy of the approved DSA; and

(c) a true copy of the statement of eligibility of the debtor, which shall be in Form No 56[54] or Form No 52G.[55]

Following such notification to the court, a certificate of the PIP certifying the date or dates on which every notice to creditors was sent shall be furnished to the ISI and shall promptly be lodged in court by the ISI.

On receipt of the notification of approval of the DSA at the creditors' meeting by the court, the proper officer of the court shall enter the DSA and any objections thereto for initial consideration by the court on a date which is not less than 14 days after the date of the sending by the PIP of the notice of entitlement to object to the creditors or the date of receipt by the court of a copy of the DSA concerned, whichever appears to be the later, and shall notify the ISI, the PIP and any creditor who has lodged an objection to the coming into effect of the DSA.

48. **Appendix 14** – High Court Form No 53.
49. **Appendix 15** – Circuit Court Form No 52D.
50. **Appendix 16** – High Court Form No 54.
51. **Appendix 17** – Circuit Court Form No 52E.
52. **Appendix 18** – High Court Form No 55.
53. **Appendix 19** – Circuit Court Form No 52F.
54. **Appendix 20** – High Court Form No 56.
55. **Appendix 21** – Circuit Court Form No 52G.

Initial Consideration: On the date fixed for the initial consideration by the court of the DSA, the court shall give directions and make orders for the determination of any objections (if it does not hear the objections on that date).

Where no objection has been lodged by a creditor within the prescribed timeframe or the objection is heard by the court on the date of the initial consideration and not allowed, the court:

(a) if satisfied that the requirements relating to the notification to the creditors of their right of objection have been satisfied, shall approve the coming into effect of the DSA;

(b) if not satisfied with the notification of the creditors of their right of objection, shall refuse the application to approve the coming into effect of the DSA;

(c) may adjourn the further consideration of the DSA to a date fixed by the court and direct the Registrar of the court to request the ISI to provide such further information as is specified by the court; or

(d) where the court requires such further information or evidence for the purpose of arriving at a decision to approve the coming into effect of the DSA, the court shall direct that a hearing be held, which hearing shall be on notice to the ISI and the PIP.

Hearing: Where the court directs a hearing, the court shall direct the Registrar to include in the notification to the ISI and the PIP the time and place fixed for the hearing, and may direct the Registrar to include in the notification –

(a) an indication of the nature of the information or evidence which the court requires for the purpose of its arriving at a decision and the persons who are likely to be able to provide such information or evidence, and

(b) notice of whether any evidence required may be given by way of affidavit.

Termination of DSA by PIP or Creditor

[6.29] A PIP or creditor may bring an application to terminate a DSA at any time during the arrangement on any of the following grounds:

(a) a material inaccuracy or omission exists in the debtor's PFS, which causes a material detriment to the creditor;

(b) the debtor, when the DSA was proposed, did not satisfy the eligibility criteria required;

(c) the debtor did not comply with the duties and obligations imposed on him or her under the DSA process;

(d) the debtor has since the coming into effect of the DSA committed an offence under the PIA 2012;

(e) the debtor is in arrears with his or her payments for a period of not less than three months;

(f) the debtor has failed to carry out any action necessary to enable a term of the DSA to have effect;

(g) the debtor has unreasonably refused to consent to a variation of the DSA.

On the hearing of such an application the court can do any of the following:

(a) dismiss the application;

(b) terminate the DSA; or

(c) order the PIP to propose the variation of the DSA.

Application: An application to terminate a DSA by a PIP or creditor in the circumstances outlined above is made by way of notice of motion in the proceedings, grounded on an affidavit sworn by or on behalf of the moving party.

The notice of motion shall specify the grounds on which the application is made and the particular relief sought.

Grounding Affidavit: The affidavit shall set out the facts or circumstances which it is alleged establish the grounds set out in the notice of motion and authorise or entitle the moving party to the relief sought and set out the basis of the deponent's belief as to the existence of those facts or circumstances.

Service: The notice of motion and a copy of the grounding affidavit shall be served on the debtor, and on any other person who the court directs should be served, not less than 21 days before the date first fixed for hearing of the motion, unless otherwise ordered by the court.

Replying Affidavit: The debtor shall be at liberty to file and serve a replying affidavit setting out concisely the grounds of any opposition to the application verifying any facts relied on in opposing the application, and a copy of such affidavit (and any exhibits) shall be served upon the moving party not later than seven days before the return date of the notice of motion. There is no further provision within the rules or the PIA 2012 to file a supplemental affidavit at this stage; however one would assume that normal court procedure would apply whereby any party could apply to the court to file a supplemental affidavit or however the court so directs.

Where a court makes an order terminating the DSA, the debtor shall be liable in full for all debts covered by the DSA (including arrears, charges and interest that have accrued during the DSA period but excluding any amounts paid in respect of those debts during the DSA period) unless the terms of the DSA provide otherwise or the court makes an order otherwise.

Where the court makes an order terminating the DSA on application by the PIP or a creditor, an application for an order against full liability of the debtor for all debts covered by the DSA may be made without a motion for that purpose, provided that the court may direct that the same be heard on affidavit.

Where a DSA terminates through the debtor falling into arrears with his or her payments under the DSA for a period of longer than six months, then an application for any order of the court against full liability of the debtor for all debts covered by the DSA shall be made by notice of motion grounded on an affidavit. The notice of motion and a copy of the grounding affidavit shall be served on the ISI and on any other person who the court directs should be served.

Excessive Pension Contributions

[6.30] Where a debtor has entered into a DSA which is in force and a creditor or PIP considers that a debtor has made excessive pension contributions to a relevant pension arrangement, the creditor or PIP may make an application to the court. The court may direct either of the following:

(a) that such part of the contribution concerned (less any tax required to be deducted) be paid by the person administering the relevant pension arrangement to the PIP for distribution amongst the creditors of the debtor; and

(b) make such other order as the court deems appropriate, including an order as to the costs of the application.

Application: An application must be made by way of notice of motion in the proceedings of the protective certificate, grounded on an affidavit sworn by or on behalf of the moving party. The notice of motion must specify the reliefs sought as outlined above.

Grounding Affidavit: The affidavit shall set out the facts or circumstances which it is alleged establish the grounds set out in the notice of motion and authorise or entitle the moving party to the relief sought and set out the basis of the deponent's belief as to the existence of those facts or circumstances.

Service: The notice of motion and a copy of the grounding affidavit shall be served on the debtor and on any other person who the court directs should be served not less than 21 days before the date first fixed for hearing of the motion, unless otherwise ordered by the court.

Replying Affidavit: The debtor shall be at liberty to file and serve a replying affidavit setting out concisely the grounds of any opposition to the application verifying any facts relied on in opposing the application, and a copy of such affidavit (and any exhibits) shall be served upon the moving party not later than seven days before the return date of the notice of motion. There is no further provision within the rules or the PIA 2012 to file a supplemental affidavit at this stage; however one would assume that normal court procedure would apply whereby any party could apply to the court to file a supplemental affidavit or however the court so directs.

PERSONAL INSOLVENCY ARRANGEMENT

[6.31] Originating Document: The application for the protective certificate shall be in the form prescribed by the ISI[56] and shall form the originating document in the proceedings concerning the PIA in respect of the debtor concerned. All further applications concerning the PIA in respect of the debtor concerned shall be brought in

56. See **Ch 5** – Personal Insolvency Arrangements.

the proceedings commenced by the submission of that application. The only exception to this is in respect of an application seeking leave to commence proceedings against the debtor during the period of the protective certificate.[57]

Exceptional Circumstances

[6.32] An application by a debtor to the court, on notice to the ISI, to make a proposal for a PIA in circumstances where a debtor would not ordinarily be entitled to make such a proposal for any of the following reasons:

(a) been the subject of a protective certificate issued under a DSA less than 12 months prior to the date of the application for a protective certificate;

(b) had his or her debts discharged pursuant to a DRN less than three years prior to the date of the application for a protective certificate;

(c) had his or her debts discharged pursuant to a PIA less than five years prior to the date of the application for a protective certificate; or

(d) been discharged from bankruptcy less than five years prior to the date of the application for a protective certificate

shall be made by notice of motion grounded on an affidavit of the debtor. The court may direct that notice of the application is given by the debtor to any person as the court may direct.

Where the court is satisfied that the current insolvency of the debtor arises by reason of exceptional circumstances or other factors which are substantially outside the control of the debtor and that it would be just to permit the debtor to make a proposal for a PIA, the court may make an order stating that the criteria set out at (i) to (iv) above preventing an application for a PIA shall not apply to the debtor.

Protective Certificate – PIA

Issue of Protective Certificate in a PIA

[6.33] The ISI may seek a decision of the court in respect of an application for a protective certificate in a PIA pursuant to s 61(2) PIA 2012 by submitting to the Central Office:

(a) the application for a protective certificate made to the ISI by the PIP on behalf of the debtor pursuant to s 93 PIA 2012;

(b) a certificate of the ISI (Form No 51[58] or Form No 52A[59]) to the effect that the application for a protective certificate is in order; and

(c) any supporting documentation to the application for a protective certificate by the PIP.

57. See para **6.36** below.

58. **Appendix 11** – High Court Form No 51.

59. **Appendix 9** – Circuit Court Form No 52A.

Application: The application for the protective certificate shall be in the form prescribed by the ISI[60] and shall form the originating document in the proceedings concerning the PIA in respect of the debtor concerned. All further applications concerning the PIA in respect of the debtor concerned shall be brought in the proceedings commenced by the submission of that application.

First Court Date: On the date first fixed for the consideration of the application, the ISI, the PIP concerned and the debtor shall not be required to attend and the court, having considered the application, may –

Satisfied:

(a) if satisfied that the eligibility criteria have been satisfied and the other relevant requirements relating to an application for the issue of a protective certificate have been met, issue a protective certificate in accordance with Form No 57[61] or Form No 54H;[62]

Not satisfied:

(b) if not satisfied that the eligibility criteria have been satisfied and the other relevant requirements relating to an application for a protective certificate have been met, may refuse the application for a protective certificate;

(c) adjourn the consideration of the application and direct the Proper Officer of the court to request the ISI to clarify any matter in the documentation provided or to provide any documentation which appears to the court to have been omitted; or

(d) where it requires further information or evidence for the purpose of arriving at a decision to issue a protective certificate, direct that a hearing be held, which hearing shall be on notice to the ISI and the PIP.

Hearing: Where such a hearing is directed, the court shall direct the Registrar to include in the notification to the ISI the time and place fixed for the hearing, and may direct the Registrar to include in the notification –

(a) an indication of the nature of the information or evidence which the court requires for the purposes of its arriving at a decision and the persons likely to provide such information, and

(b) notice of whether the evidence required may be given by way of affidavit.

Withdrawal of Application for Protective Certificate

[6.34] Where a PIP withdraws an application for a protective certificate on behalf of a debtor, it must notify the ISI in writing of the withdrawal and the ISI shall, as soon as is practicable, notify the court of such withdrawal.

60. See **Ch 5** – Personal Insolvency Arrangements.
61. **Appendix 22** – High Court Form No 57.
62. **Appendix 23** – Circuit Court Form No 52H.

The application to withdraw must be made before the protective certificate is issued.

Extension of Protective Certificate

[6.35] An application to extend the period of the protective certificate shall be made by the PIP to the court by way of a notice of motion in the proceedings, setting out the reasons for the extension sought. There is no requirement for a grounding affidavit; however the court may require delivery of an affidavit where it considers it just and necessary to do so. The notice of motion must be served on the ISI.

The ISI is not required to appear at the date fixed for the hearing of the motion nor at any adjourned date, save by direction of the court.

Creditors

Leave to Issue Legal Proceedings during Protective Certificate Period

[6.36] Where an application is made to the court pursuant to s 96(3) PIA 2012 for leave, whilst a protective certificate is in force, to commence or continue other proceedings, execution or other legal process in respect of a specified debt against a debtor or his or her property, the person seeking such relief shall make an application grounded on an affidavit sworn by or on behalf of that person setting out the reasons why such relief is sought.

Application: The application shall –

(a) in the case of an application to commence proceedings, be brought by originating notice of motion, or

(b) in the case of an application to continue proceedings or for execution or other legal process, be brought by notice of motion in the proceedings which it is sought to continue or in which leave for execution or other process is sought.

Service: The originating notice of motion or notice of motion together with a copy of the grounding affidavit shall be served on the debtor, the PIP and the ISI, and any other person who the court directs should be served, not less than 21 days before the date first fixed for hearing unless otherwise directed by the court.

There is no requirement for the ISI or the PIP to attend on the hearing date or any such adjourned date, unless otherwise ordered by the court.

Aggrieved Creditor

[6.37] An application may be made to the court under s 97 PIA 2012 by a creditor who is aggrieved by the issue of a protective certificate.

Application: The application shall be brought by way of notice of motion in the proceedings of the protective certificate concerned, grounded on an affidavit sworn by or on behalf of the creditor.

The notice of motion must specify the date on which notice of the issue of the protective certificate was given to the creditor concerned and the grounds of the application.

Grounding Affidavit: The affidavit shall set out the facts and circumstances which it is alleged establish the grounds concerned and authorise or entitle the applicant to the relief sought and the basis of the deponent's belief as to the existence of those facts or circumstances.

Service: The notice of motion and a copy of the grounding affidavit shall be served on the ISI and the PIP, and any other person who the court directs should be served, not less than 21 days before the date first fixed for hearing of the motion.

Replying Affidavit: Each person served with the notice of motion and a copy of the grounding affidavit shall be at liberty to file and serve a replying affidavit setting out concisely the grounds for any opposition to the application and verifying any facts relied on in opposing the application, and a copy of such affidavit together with any exhibits thereto shall be served upon the moving party and upon every other person with notice of the application before the return date of the notice of motion. There is no further provision within the rules or the PIA 2012 to file a supplemental affidavit at this stage; however one would assume that normal court procedure would apply whereby any party could apply to the court to file a supplemental affidavit or however the court so directs.

Creditor Notice of Objection

[6.38] Following the approval of a PIA at a creditors' meeting the PIP shall, as soon as is practicable after the meeting has concluded, notify the ISI and each creditor concerned and enclose with that notification:

(a) a certificate with the result of the vote taken at the creditors' meeting, identifying the number of votes, in value of the creditors present and voting, in favour and against the proposed PIA; and

(b) a copy of the approved PIA.

The PIP shall, in addition to the documents referred to above, also send a notice to each creditor indicating their entitlement pursuant to s 112(3) PIA 2012 to lodge a Notice of Objection with the appropriate court within 14 days of the date of the sending of that notice.

The Notice of Objection must be in Form No 53[63] or Form No 52D[64] and shall:

(a) include the record number of the proceedings;

(b) state when the notice under s 112(2) of the act was sent to the creditor by the PIP (if known) and when the said notice was received by the creditor;

(c) specify succinctly the grounds, set out in s 120 PIA 2012, on which objection is made to the coming into effect of the PIA, and

(d) confirm the amount of the debt due to the creditor concerned.

63. **Appendix 14** – High Court Form No 53.

64. **Appendix 15** – Circuit Court Form No 52D.

Approval of PIA

Notice of Approval of PIA to Court

[6.39] On receipt of the notification of approval of a PIA at a creditors' meeting from a PIP, the ISI must notify the court in accordance with Form No 54[65] or Form No 52E[66] and it shall be accompanied by:

(a) a true copy of the certificate with the result of the vote taken at the creditors' meeting, which shall be in Form No 55[67] or Form No 52F;[68]

(b) a true copy of the approved PIA; and

(c) a true copy of the statement of eligibility of the debtor, which shall be in Form No 56[69] or Form No 52G.[70]

Following such notification to the court, a certificate of the PIP certifying the date or dates on which every notice to creditors was sent shall be furnished to the ISI and shall promptly be lodged in court by the ISI.

On receipt of the notification of approval of the PIA at the creditors' meeting by the court, the proper officer of the court shall enter the PIA and any objections thereto for initial consideration by the court on a date which is not less than 14 days after the date of the sending by the PIP of the notice of entitlement to object to the creditors or the date of receipt by the court of a copy of the PIA concerned, whichever appears to be the later, and shall notify the ISI, the PIP and any creditor who has lodged an objection to the coming into effect of the PIA.

Initial Consideration: On the date fixed for the initial consideration by the court of the PIA, the court shall give directions and make orders for the determination of any objections (if it does not hear the objections on that date).

Where no objection has been lodged by a creditor within the prescribed timeframe, or the objection is heard by the court on the date of the initial consideration and not allowed, the court:

(a) if satisfied that the requirements relating to the notification to the creditors of their right of objection have been satisfied, shall approve the coming into effect of the PIA;

(b) if not satisfied with the notification of the creditors of their right of objection, shall refuse the application to approve the coming into effect of the PIA;

(c) may adjourn the further consideration of the PIA to a date fixed by the court and direct the Registrar of the court to request the ISI to provide such further information as is specified by the court; or

---

65. **Appendix 16** – High Court Form No 54.
66. **Appendix 17** – Circuit Court Form No 52E.
67. **Appendix 18** – High Court Form No 55.
68. **Appendix 19** – Circuit Court Form No 52F.
69. **Appendix 20** – High Court Form No 56.
70. **Appendix 21** – Circuit Court Form No 52G.

(d) where the court requires such further information or evidence for the purpose of arriving at a decision to approve the coming into effect of the PIA, the court shall direct that a hearing be held, which hearing shall be on notice to the ISI and the PIP.

Hearing: Where the court directs a hearing, the court shall direct the Registrar to include in the notification to the ISI and the PIP the time and place fixed for the hearing, and may direct the Registrar to include in the notification –

(a) an indication of the nature of the information or evidence which the court requires for the purpose of its arriving at a decision and the persons who are likely to be able to provide such information or evidence, and

(b) notice of whether any evidence required may be given by way of affidavit.

Termination of PIA by PIP or Creditor

[6.40] A PIP or creditor may bring an application to terminate a PIA at any time during the arrangement on any of the following grounds:

(a) a material inaccuracy or omission exists in the debtor's PFS, which causes a material detriment to the creditor;

(b) the debtor, when the PIA was proposed, did not satisfy the eligibility criteria required;

(c) the debtor did not comply with the duties and obligations imposed on him or her under the PIA process;

(d) the debtor has since the coming into effect of the PIA committed an offence under the PIA 2012;

(e) the debtor is in arrears with his or her payments for a period of not less than three months;

(f) the debtor has failed to carry out any action necessary to enable a term of the PIA to have effect;

(g) the debtor has unreasonably refused to consent to a variation of the PIA.

On the hearing of such an application the court can do any of the following:

(a) dismiss the application;

(b) terminate the PIA; or

(c) order the PIP to propose the variation of the PIA.

Application: An application to terminate a PIA by a PIP or creditor in the circumstances outlined at (a) to (g) above is made by way of notice of motion in the proceedings, grounded on an affidavit sworn by or on behalf of the moving party.

The notice of motion shall specify the grounds on which the application is made and the particular relief sought.

Grounding Affidavit: The affidavit shall set out the facts or circumstances which it is alleged establish the grounds set out in the notice of motion and authorise or entitle the moving party to the relief sought and set out the basis of the deponent's belief as to the existence of those facts or circumstances.

Service: The notice of motion and a copy of the grounding affidavit shall be served on the debtor, and on any other person who the court directs should be served, not less than 21 days before the date first fixed for hearing of the motion, unless otherwise ordered by the court.

Replying Affidavit: The debtor shall be at liberty to file and serve a replying affidavit setting out concisely the grounds of any opposition to the application, verifying any facts relied on in opposing the application, and a copy of such affidavit (and any exhibits) shall be served upon the moving party not later than seven days before the return date of the notice of motion. There is no further provision within the rules or PIA 2012 to file a supplemental affidavit at this stage; however one would assume that normal court procedure would apply whereby any party could apply to the court to file a supplemental affidavit or however the court so directs.

Where the court makes an order terminating the arrangement, the debtor shall be liable in full for all debts covered by the PIA (including arrears, charges and interest that have accrued during the PIA period but excluding any amounts paid in respect of those debts during the PIA period) unless the terms of the PIA provide otherwise or the court makes an order otherwise.

Where the court makes an order terminating the PIA on application by the PIP or a creditor, an application for an order against full liability of the debtor for all debts covered by the PIA may be made without a motion for that purpose, provided that the court may direct that the same be heard on affidavit.

Where a PIA terminates through the debtor falling into arrears with his or her payments under the PIA for a period of longer than six months, then an application for any order of the court against full liability of the debtor for all debts covered by the PIA shall be made by notice of motion grounded on an affidavit. The notice of motion and a copy of the grounding affidavit shall be served on the ISI and on any other person who the court directs should be served.

Excessive Pension Contributions

[6.41] Where a debtor has entered into a PIA which is in force and a creditor or PIP considers that a debtor has made excessive pension contributions to a relevant pension arrangement, the creditor or PIP may make an application to the court. The court may:

(a) direct that such part of the contribution concerned (less any tax required to be deducted) be paid by the person administering the relevant pension arrangement to the PIP for distribution amongst the creditors of the debtor, and

(b) make such other order as the court deems appropriate, including an order as to the costs of the application.

Application: An application must be made by way of notice of motion in the proceedings of the protective certificate, grounded on an affidavit sworn by or on behalf of the moving party. The notice of motion must specify the reliefs sought as outlined above.

Grounding Affidavit: The affidavit shall set out the facts or circumstances which it is alleged establish the grounds set out in the notice of motion and authorise or entitle the moving party to the relief sought and set out the basis of the deponent's belief as to the existence of those facts or circumstances.

Service: The notice of motion and a copy of the grounding affidavit shall be served on the debtor, and on any other person who the court directs should be served, not less than 21 days before the date first fixed for hearing of the motion, unless otherwise ordered by the court.

Replying Affidavit: The debtor shall be at liberty to file and serve a replying affidavit setting out concisely the grounds of any opposition to the application, verifying any facts relied on in opposing the application, and a copy of such affidavit (and any exhibits) shall be served upon the moving party not later than seven days before the return date of the notice of motion. There is no further provision within the rules or the PIA 2012 to file a supplemental affidavit at this stage; however one would assume that normal court procedure would apply whereby any party could apply to the court to file a supplemental affidavit or however the court so directs.

PERSONAL INSOLVENCY PRACTITIONER – COMPLAINTS PROCEDURE

Appeal to High Court of a Determination by the Complaints Committee of a Minor Sanction

[6.42] Any appeal to the High Court by a PIP against a finding of the Complaints Committee (with the exception of when the Complaints Committee has referred the matter to the High Court on a major sanction) shall be made in accordance with Order 84C RSC which deals with the procedure in Statutory Appeals.[71]

The following procedures will apply to any such appeal:

Application

[6.43]

(a) The referral shall be made by way of Originating Notice of Motion entitled in the matter of the provision of the enactment pursuant to which the application is made[72] and shall additionally be entitled on the application of the applicant.

(b) The originating notice of motion shall specify the particular relief sought against each respondent and the particular provision or provisions of the relevant enactment authorising the granting of each such relief.

(c) The originating notice of motion shall contain the names and addresses of the appellant and of each respondent. The notice of motion shall specify the relief

71. PIA 2012, s 183.

72. PIA 2012, s 183.

sought, and the particular provision or provisions of the relevant enactment authorising the granting of such relief.

(d) Where the appeal to the High Court is on a point of law, the notice of motion shall state concisely the point of law on which the appeal is made.

(e) Where the court may grant relief consequential upon or in addition to determining the appeal, the notice of motion shall state concisely the consequential or additional relief sought.

The notice of motion shall be issued –

(a) not later than 21 days following the giving of notice of the deciding body's decision, or

(b) within such further period as the court, on application made to it by the intending appellant, may allow where the court is satisfied that there is good and sufficient reason for extending that period and that the extension of the period would not result in an injustice being done to any other person concerned in the matter. Any such application must be made by motion on notice to any person who shall be a respondent to the appeal and to any other person who the court directs shall be given notice of such application.

An application for an extension of time may be made outside the 21-day period.

Grounding Affidavit

[6.44] The notice of motion shall be grounded upon an affidavit sworn by or on behalf of the appellant which shall:

(a) contain a description of the appellant, including particulars sufficient to explain the standing of the appellant to appeal, and, where the deponent is not the appellant, the authority of the deponent to make the affidavit on behalf of the appellant;

(b) if the appellant is acting in any representative capacity, or relief is sought against any respondent in a representative capacity, state the capacity of the appellant or, as the case may be, the respondent;

(c) state the authority of the deciding body to make the decision, determination or direction from which appeal is made;

(d) state the interest of any respondent and of any other person given notice of the appeal in the decision, determination or direction from which appeal is made;

(e) exhibit –

(i) a copy of any application made to the Complaints Committee,

(ii) save where the appeal is on a point of law only, the evidence and any other material adduced to the deciding body, and copies of all relevant correspondence and documents passing between the appellant and the Complaints Committee,

(iii) any official record and, if relevant, any other record of the proceedings before the Complaints Committee,

(iv) a copy of the decision, determination or direction made or given (as the case may be) by the Complaints Committee;

(f) save where the appeal is on a point of law only, set out the facts or circumstances relevant to the making of the decision, determination or direction from which appeal is made (including any act or omission of the principal respondent complained of) which it is alleged support the granting of the appeal in respect of the decision, determination or direction or of any consequential or additional relief sought; and

(g) set out the basis of the deponent's belief as to the existence of the facts or circumstances referred to in the preceding paragraph.

Replying Affidavit

[6.45] Any respondent intending to oppose the application shall file in the Central Office a statement setting out concisely the grounds for such opposition and, if any facts are relied on therein, an affidavit verifying such facts, in which event a copy of such statement and such affidavit (if any) shall be served upon the applicant and upon every other respondent before the return date of the notice of motion.

The applicant shall be at liberty to file a further affidavit replying to any matter verified in an affidavit of a respondent, in which event a copy of such affidavit shall be served upon each respondent within 14 days of the service upon him of the respondent's statement of opposition and verifying affidavit.

In any case where reference is made in an affidavit to a document exhibited previously in an affidavit of any party, the document concerned shall not be further exhibited, but shall be identified by the exhibit reference used in relation to that document in the previous affidavit.

An affidavit giving the names and addresses of, and the places and dates of service on, all persons who have been served with the notice of motion, grounding affidavit and exhibits (if any) shall be filed by the applicant before the motion is heard. If any person who ought under Order 84C RSC to have been served has not been so served, the affidavit shall state that fact and the reason for it.

Return Date

[6.46] On the return date of any notice of motion pursuant to Order 84C RSC concerning an appeal on a point of law only (or on any adjournment of such hearing), the court shall give such directions and make such orders, including the fixing of time limits, for the conduct of the proceedings as appears convenient for the determination of the proceedings in a manner which is just, expeditious and likely to minimise the costs of those proceedings, which may include:

(a) directions as to the service of notice of the appeal on any other person including mode of service and the time allowed for such service (and may for that purpose adjourn the hearing of the notice of motion or further hearing of same to a date specified);

(b) directions as to the filing and delivery of any further affidavits by any party or parties;

(c) directions as to the furnishing by the parties to the court and delivery of written submissions.

On the return date of any notice of motion pursuant to Order 84C RSC concerning an appeal other than an appeal on a point of law only (or on any adjournment of such hearing), the court shall give directions and make orders for the conduct of the proceedings as appear convenient for the determination of the proceedings in a manner which is just, expeditious and likely to minimise the costs of those proceedings, which may include:

(a) directions as to the service of notice of the appeal on any other person including mode of service and the time allowed for such service (and may for that purpose adjourn the hearing of the notice of motion or further hearing of same to a date specified);

(b) directions as to the filing and delivery of any further affidavits by any party or parties;

(c) directions as to the furnishing by the parties to the court and delivery of written submissions on any issue which arises as to the proper scope of the appeal or as to the matter which ought to be before the court on the hearing of the appeal, and directions as to the hearing and determination of any such issue;

(d) orders fixing time limits;

(e) a direction that the appeal be determined by way of plenary hearing, where it appears to the court that the subject matter of the appeal is likely to involve a substantial dispute of fact or it is otherwise necessary or desirable in the interests of justice (and the court may for that purpose make such orders and give such directions in relation to the exchange of pleadings or points of appeal or reply between the parties);

(f) directions as to discovery;

(g) directions as to the furnishing by the parties to the court and delivery of written submissions;

(h) directions as to the exchange of memoranda between or among the parties for the purpose of the agreeing by the parties or the fixing by the court of any issues of fact or law to be determined in the proceedings on the appeal or orders fixing such issues;

(i) an order for the hearing of the proceedings at the same time as or immediately following another cause or matter pending in the High Court.

On the return date of any notice of motion pursuant to Order 84C RSC (or on any adjournment from such date), the court may, where it appears just and proper, make orders for relief of an interlocutory nature, whether in the nature of an injunction or otherwise.

Save where the court otherwise directs, any evidence in proceedings to which Order 84C RSC relates shall be given on affidavit.

Where the court considers it appropriate, having regard to the nature of the proceedings, it may adjourn the proceedings to enable one or more of the parties to make an application pursuant to r 4(2) of Order 63A RSC to the Judge of the Commercial List for an order entering the appeal as proceedings in the Commercial List.

Referral to the High Court of a determination by the Complaints Committee of a Major Sanction

[6.47] Any referral to the High Court in circumstances where the Complaints Committee have determined that the sanction is a major sanction shall be made in accordance with Order 84B RSC which provides for the procedure in Statutory Applications.[73]

The following procedures shall apply to any such referral:

Application

[6.48]

(a) The referral shall be made by way of Originating Notice of Motion entitled in the matter of the provision of the enactment pursuant to which the application is made[74] and shall additionally be entitled on the application of the applicant.

(b) The originating notice of motion shall specify the particular relief sought against each respondent and the particular provision or provisions of the relevant enactment authorising the granting of each such relief.

(c) Where a determination of or decision or opinion on any question, or the giving of any direction is sought in the application, the notice of motion shall state as concisely as is reasonably possible the question or direction concerned.

(d) The originating notice of motion (or, as the case may be, the motion) shall be grounded upon an affidavit sworn by or on behalf of the applicant which shall:

  (i) contain a description of the applicant, including particulars sufficient to explain the standing of the applicant to move the application under the relevant provision of the enactment and, where the deponent is not the applicant, the authority of the deponent to make the affidavit on behalf of the applicant;

  (ii) if the applicant is acting in any representative capacity, or relief is sought against any respondent in a representative capacity, state the capacity of the applicant or, as the case may be, the respondent;

73. PIA 2012, s 182(12).

74. PIA 2012, s 182(12).

(iii) set out the facts or circumstances which it is alleged authorise or entitle the applicant to make, or justify the applicant in making, the application and which support the granting of the relief sought; and

(iv) set out the basis of the deponent's belief as to the existence of the facts or circumstances referred to in the preceding paragraph.

Grounding Affidavit

[6.49] The grounding affidavit shall exhibit copies of all correspondence and documents passing between the applicant and each respondent (if any), or otherwise issuing from any of them, relevant to the matter or matters in respect of which relief is sought. Subject to any direction the court may give, such copies shall be incorporated in a single exhibit, in which event they shall be indexed and numbered sequentially in chronological order.

Any respondent intending to oppose the application shall file in the Central Office a statement setting out concisely the grounds for such opposition and, if any facts are relied on therein, an affidavit verifying such facts, in which event a copy of such statement and such affidavit (if any) shall be served upon the applicant and upon every other respondent before the return date of the notice of motion.

Replying Affidavit

[6.50] The applicant shall be at liberty to file a further affidavit replying to any matter verified in an affidavit of a respondent, in which event a copy of such affidavit shall be served upon each respondent within 14 days of the service upon him of the respondent's statement of opposition and verifying affidavit.

In any case where reference is made in an affidavit to a document exhibited previously in an affidavit of any party, the document concerned shall not be further exhibited but shall be identified by the exhibit reference used in relation to that document in the previous affidavit.

An affidavit giving the names and addresses of, and the places and dates of service on, all persons who have been served with the notice of motion, grounding affidavit and exhibits (if any) shall be filed by the applicant before the motion is heard. If any person who ought under Order 84B RSC to have been served has not been so served, the affidavit shall state that fact and the reason for it.

Save where the court otherwise directs, any evidence in proceedings to which Order 84B RSC relates shall be given on affidavit.

Return Date

[6.51] On the return date of the notice of motion (or on any adjournment from such date), the court shall give directions and make orders for the conduct of the proceedings as appear convenient for the determination of the proceedings in a manner which is just, expeditious and likely to minimise the costs of those proceedings which, where appropriate, may include:

(a) directions as to the service of notice of the application on any other person, including mode of service and the time allowed for such service (and the court may for that purpose adjourn the hearing of the notice of motion or further hearing of such application to a date specified);

(b) directions as to the filing and delivery of any further affidavits by any party or parties;

(c) orders fixing time limits;

(d) directions as to discovery;

(e) directions as to the exchange of memoranda between or among the parties for the purpose of the agreeing by the parties or the fixing by the court of any issues of fact or law to be determined in the proceedings on the application, or orders fixing such issues;

(f) a direction that the application be determined by way of plenary hearing, where it appears to the court that the subject matter of the application is likely to involve a substantial dispute of fact or it is otherwise necessary or desirable in the interests of justice (and the court may for that purpose make orders and give directions in relation to the exchange of pleadings or points of claim or defence between the parties);

(g) directions as to the furnishing by the parties to the court and delivery of written submissions;

(h) directions as to the publication of notice of the hearing of the application and the giving of notice in advance of such hearing to any person other than a party to the proceedings who desires to be heard on the hearing of the application.

On the return date of the notice of motion (or on any adjournment from such date), the court may, where it deems fit, hear any application for relief of an interlocutory nature, whether in the nature of an injunction or otherwise.

Chapter 7

REASONABLE LIVING EXPENSES

INTRODUCTION

[7.01] The Insolvency Service of Ireland (ISI) is required by s 23 PIA 2012 to prepare and issue guidelines as to what constitutes a reasonable standard of living and reasonable living expenses.

Initial guidelines ('Guide to Reasonable Living Expenses'[1] – referred to as Guidelines for this chapter) were published as part of the launch of the ISI's information campaign in April 2013 and updated in June 2013. With the kind permission of the ISI, the information contained in this chapter is taken directly from these Guidelines.

Under s 23 PIA 2012, the ISI is obliged to have regard to a number of matters, including the Consumer Price Index (CPI), in preparing the Guidelines. Since the April publication of the Guidelines, the Vincentian Partnership for Social Justice updated its research to reflect CPI information to March 2013. Resulting from this, in June 2013 the ISI published updated Guidelines to ensure that practitioners are using the most up-to-date information available. These updated Guidelines also address an anomaly that had been contained in the original guide in respect of food costs within two-parent families.

The ISI is required under the PIA 2012 to issue guidelines at intervals of such length as it considers appropriate, once the interval is not more than one year.

The Guidelines are relevant to the assessment of a debtor's eligibility for a DRN, the formulation of DSA and PIA proposals and the court's making of a bankruptcy payment order. The Guidelines are intended to give direction to Approved Intermediaries (AIs) and guidance to Personal Insolvency Practitioners (PIPs) in assessing, for relevant provisions of the PIA 2012, what may be considered 'reasonable' in the context of a standard of living and living expenses.

Under the model developed by the ISI, reasonable living expenses are the expenses a person necessarily incurs in achieving a reasonable standard of living, this being one which meets a person's physical, psychological and social needs.

Reasonable living expenses will vary depending on a number of factors such as the particular composition of a household and the need for a car. Beyond that, when determining reasonable living expenses, provision needs to be made for reasonable housing costs in terms of rent or mortgage payments as well as for reasonable payments in respect of childcare where this expense arises.

It should be noted that the figures used in the Guidelines have unique application to personal insolvency and are not intended to be used for purposes other than the stated purposes of these Guidelines under the Personal Insolvency Act 2012.

1. http://www.isi.gov.ie/en/ISI/Pages/Reasonable_living_expenses.

OVERVIEW OF GUIDELINES

Introduction

[7.02] The ISI model allows for food for a nutritionally balanced diet, clothing, personal care, health, household goods, household services, communications, social inclusion and participation, education, transport, household energy, childcare, insurance and modest allowances for savings and contingencies.

Under the ISI model, a 'reasonable standard of living' does not mean that a person should live at a luxury level but neither does it mean that a person should only live at subsistence level. The ISI states that a debtor should be able to participate in the life of the community, as other citizens do. It should be possible for the debtor

> to eat nutritious food … to have clothes for different weather and situations, to keep the home clean and tidy, to have furniture and equipment at home for rest and recreation, to be able to devote some time to leisure activities, and to read books, newspapers and watch television.[2]

It is the view of the ISI that 'reasonable living expenses' are the expenses a person will necessarily incur in achieving a reasonable standard of living which fulfils these criteria.

The use of the ISI model satisfies the requirement contained in s 23 PIA 2012 to have regard to differences in the size and composition of households. The cost of a child, for example, varies according to the age of the child and this is taken into account under the ISI model. So too is the requirement to facilitate the social inclusion of debtors and their dependants and their active participation in the economic activity of the State.

Where either a DSA or a PIA is proposed, the reasonable living expenses become part of the insolvency proposal put to the creditors at the creditors' meeting. As such, the decision on the reasonableness or otherwise of living expenses will be a matter for the creditors to determine on a case-by-case basis with the PIP acting to facilitate debtors and creditors in working out an arrangement acceptable to both.

Set Costs

[7.03] In the Guidelines, the costs attributed to a household are termed 'set costs'.[3] To these are added the reasonable costs of housing, childcare and special circumstances where they arise. This produces the total for reasonable living expenses for any given household.

Childcare

[7.04] A significant expense connected with employment arises where childcare[4] is needed, particularly at the first two stages of childhood, ie infancy and pre-school. Where childcare costs are paid they are added to the total for set costs.

---

2. Nordenankur, 'More Than a Minimum Budget in Sweden' in *Money Matters – Reference Budgets for Social Inclusion*, European Consumer Debt Network (No 6, 2009), p 8.
3. See paras **7.28** for more detail.
4. See para **7.14** for more detail.

Housing

[7.05] Housing[5] can also be a significant expense. In considering what constitutes reasonable and sustainable accommodation expenditure in an individual case, the rent or mortgage payments of an individual should be assessed taking into account the factors outlined in the Guidelines.

Special Circumstances

[7.06] The differing needs of persons, having regard to matters such as their age, health and whether they have a physical, sensory, mental health or intellectual disability, can be accommodated by a debtor specifying reasonable costs which arise as a consequence of ill-health, age or disability under this category of special circumstances.[6] This category may also be used where a debtor has persons other than his or her minor children financially dependent on him or her, such as where the debtor is contributing financially to the care of an adult dependant such as, for example, an elderly relative or a college-going child.

Tables

[7.07] There are a number of tables[7] produced in the Guidelines which enable the calculation of the minimum set costs on the basis of the composition of the household. These tables have been replicated at para **7.17** of this chapter with the kind permission of the ISI.

LEGISLATIVE REQUIREMENTS

[7.08] Section 9 PIA 2012 lists amongst the principal functions of the ISI the preparation and issuance of guidelines as to what constitutes a reasonable standard of living and reasonable living expenses as required under s 23 PIA 2012.

Section 23(1) PIA 2012 provides that guidelines must be prepared and issued by the ISI for the purposes of ss 26, 65(4) and 99(4) PIA 2012 and s 85D (as inserted by s 157 of the act) of the Bankruptcy Act 1988.

Section 23 PIA 2012 requires the ISI to hold consultations on these guidelines and specifies certain factors which are to be taken into account in preparing the guidelines.

Section 23(3) PIA 2012 requires the ISI to have regard to:

(a) such measures and indicators of poverty set out in Government policy publications on poverty and social inclusion as the ISI considers appropriate;

(b) such official statistics (within the meaning of the Statistics Act 1993) and surveys relating to household income and expenditure published by the Central Statistics Office as the ISI considers appropriate;

---

5. See para **7.13** for more detail.
6. See para **7.15** for more detail.
7. See Ch 9 of 'Guide to Reasonable Living Expenses' and para **7.09** for more detail.

(c) the Consumer Price Index (All Items) published by the Central Statistics Office or any equivalent index published from time to time by that office;

(d) such other information as the ISI considers appropriate for the performance of its functions under this section;

(e) differences in the size and composition of households, and the differing needs of persons, having regard to matters such as their age, health and whether they have a physical, sensory, mental health or intellectual disability; and

(f) the need to facilitate the social inclusion of debtors and their dependants and their active participation in economic activity in the State.

DETAILED REVIEW OF GUIDE TO REASONABLE LIVING EXPENSES

[7.09] Under the ISI model, reasonable living expenses are the expenses a person necessarily incurs in achieving a reasonable standard of living, this being one which meets a person's physical, psychological and social needs. The reasonable living expenses have been broken down into a number of different components and are detailed below.

General Principles in Determining Reasonable Living Expenses

[7.10] As a general principle, the ISI wishes to see debtors retaining the autonomy to make their own choices as to what is best for them, though necessarily within the constraints of reasonableness and the overall expenditure limits. Thus, while the advisory focus groups have decided that cable or satellite television subscriptions are not necessary and that allowance for a Saorview approved set-top box or television is sufficient, a debtor may choose to retain such a subscription by prioritising it within his or her budget. So long as an applicant for one of the three new personal insolvency processes under the PIA 2012 comes within the overall headline figure for reasonable living expenses, the ISI will not be prescriptive in terms of what the applicant can or cannot spend their money on.

Only where an applicant spends in excess of what is considered to be reasonable under these Guidelines will it become necessary for the AI or PIP to look at his or her spending across the categories of expenditure.

The figures produced in the Guidelines are on a monthly basis so as to conform to the requirement to qualify for a DRN that the debtor has less than €60 net disposable income a month.

Housing costs have been kept out of the expenditure categories within the ISI model of reasonable living expenses. Given the number and variety of housing situations possible, the ISI considers this item is best treated by including the actual accommodation costs of an applicant where these are reasonable. Under the provisions for either a DSA or a PIA, a PIP is to have regard to the costs likely to be incurred by the debtor by remaining in occupation of his or her principal private residence. Where the PIP forms the opinion that the costs of continuing to reside in the debtor's principal private residence are disproportionately large he or she will not be required to formulate a proposal on the basis of the debtor continuing to occupy the property.

An applicant seeking a DRN will generally not be the owner of the property in which he or she is living, given the eligibility requirement that the assets of an applicant, including real property, must be worth no more than €400.

Regardless of whether the debtor owns or rents their principal private residence, the same principle should apply that he or she should only have to consider surrendering the property where the costs of continuing to reside in it are disproportionately large as may occur, for example, where the size of the property exceeds the needs of the debtor and his or her dependants. The ISI considered it appropriate at the time of making the Regulations to avoid being overly prescriptive in setting out reasonable housing costs, choosing instead to specify matters to which a PIP or an AI should have regard in determining the reasonableness of the housing costs of a debtor.

Childcare costs are also subject to variance depending on how much childcare is required and who is providing the childcare. Accordingly, childcare costs, like housing costs, have not been included in the set costs. The reasonable cost of childcare will rather be added to the set costs. The Guidelines contain guidance to AIs and PIPs on factors to consider in assessing the reasonableness of childcare costs.

Household Composition

[7.11] Reasonable needs are determined on the basis of the household composition (ie number of persons in the household) and the reasonable needs of the particular household type. Once these reasonable needs are established, each item is then costed to derive a figure representing reasonable living expenses.

Need for a Car

[7.12] The household will not normally need a car where the applicant lives in an urban location with adequate public transport links. Where public transport is not adequate to meet the needs of the household, the AI or PIP should choose the vehicle option based on the needs of the household (needs, not wants). A car will be required where a debtor needs it to travel to and from work. Where a car is not included, the ISI model includes costs associated with the use of public transport.

Housing Costs

[7.13] Housing can also be a significant expense. In considering what constitutes a reasonable and sustainable accommodation expenditure in an individual case, the AI or PIP shall have regard to the following matters:

(a) the costs likely to be incurred by the debtor by remaining in occupation of his or her current accommodation;

(b) the ability of other persons residing with the debtor to contribute to the costs of maintaining the debtor's current accommodation; and

(c) the reasonable living accommodation needs of the debtor and his or her dependants and, having regard to those needs, the cost of alternative accommodation.

In forming an opinion on the reasonable living accommodation needs of the debtor and his or her dependants, the AI or PIP shall take into consideration the size and composition of the household, and the differing needs of persons having regard to the matters set out in s 23(3)(e) of PIA 2012.

The AI or PIP, in assessing the reasonableness of the existing housing costs of the debtor and the cost of alternative accommodation, may draw on his or her knowledge of the local housing market and on such publicly available data sources as he or she considers appropriate. These sources may include the Central Statistics Office Rental Indices, the Private Residential Tenancies Board (PRTB) databases, the Residential Property Price Register produced by the Property Services Regulatory Authority (PSRA), the quarterly Daft.ie Rental Reports and leading websites advertising properties for rent or sale. The AI or PIP should support his or her assessment as to the reasonableness of housing and childcare costs by reference to the matters he or she has taken into account in arriving at his or her opinion.

Childcare Costs

[7.14] A significant expense connected with employment arises where childcare is needed, particularly at the first two stages of childhood, ie infancy and pre-school.

Under the ISI model, childcare costs are brought in under 'other costs'. This means that reasonable costs incurred for childcare – as with housing costs – are added to the total for set costs to produce the final figure for reasonable living expenses.

Where childcare is paid for, the reasonableness of this expense should be considered by the AI or PIP taking into account the hours of childcare needed, the type of childcare (eg crèche, childminder, etc) and the typical cost of childcare in the debtor's locality. Proof in the form of receipts, bank statements or similar may have to be sought where childcare costs appear excessive. Where applicable, the Early Childhood Care and Education (ECCE) Scheme, which provides a free year of childcare and early education for children of pre-school age, should be deducted when calculating childcare costs, given that each of the new arrangements continues over a number of years.

For the purposes of the Guidelines, infant means a child between the ages of zero and two years old inclusive, pre-school means a child three years of age, primary school means a child between the ages of four and 11 years old inclusive and secondary school means a child between the ages of 12 and 18 years old inclusive.

Child Benefit is deducted from the set costs for each child. Child Benefit is paid at the same rate for the first three children in a household and the rate increases for the fourth child.

Special Circumstances

[7.15] The PIA 2012 contains a requirement to take account of the differing needs of persons, having regard to matters such as their age, health and whether they have a physical, sensory, mental health or intellectual disability. Given the number of possible variables, and the individual nature of physical and mental health conditions and disabilities, the ISI states that it believes this aspect is best addressed through making allowance in these guidelines for a debtor to specify reasonable costs which arise as a consequence of ill-health or disability.

The PIP may request that the debtor provide appropriate documentation in support of extra expenses related to disability, for example evidence from a professional, such as a doctor or disability service, to support a claim for allowances in respect of special circumstances.

The category of special circumstances may also be used where a debtor has persons other than his or her minor children financially dependent on him or her, such as where the debtor is contributing financially to the care of an adult dependant such as, for example, an elderly relative or a college-going child. The PIP may request that the debtor provide documentation in support of these expenses prior to recognising under this category the additional costs incurred in such cases.

Categories of Reasonable Living Expenses

[7.16] The headline figure for reasonable living expenses[8] is made up of 15 main categories, namely:

(a) Food

(b) Clothing

(c) Personal Care

(d) Health

(e) Household Goods

(f) Household Services

(g) Communications

(h) Education

(i) Household Energy

(j) Insurance

(k) Savings and Contingencies

(l) Social Inclusion and Participation

(m) Transport

(n) Housing

(o) Childcare

8. Guide to Reasonable Living Expenses – http://www.isi.gov.ie/en/ISI/Pages/Reasonable_living_expenses.

TABLE OF REASONABLE LIVING EXPENSES[9]

[7.17]

Expenditure category	**A guide to what is included in each expenditure category**	**For a single adult of working age living alone this comes to a monthly total of:**
Food	The expenditure on food is based on a balanced, nutritious diet. The consensual budget standards model is premised on a healthy lifestyle	€250.98
Clothing	Clothing and footwear for all seasons, including accessories	€35.34
Personal Care	Personal hygiene and grooming items	€33.06
Health	Medications and visits to the GP, optician, dentist etc. It also includes small items such as plasters, antiseptic and over-the-counter medicines	€31.34
Household Goods	Furniture, appliances, cleaning products, etc. Single adults of working age living in an urban area are assumed to be living in a rented furnished studio apartment	€26.38
Household Services	Vital household related services such as waste charges, getting an annual boiler service and having chimneys swept	€27.54
Communications	Telephone, postage and basic internet, including an internet dongle/wireless connection at €4.42 per week and phone related costs of €4.71 per week	€41.21
Education	This category includes uniforms, books and stationery where applicable and also adult education	€23.72
Transport	The cost of a car is allowed where public transport is inadequate to get to work, school and the local shop	€149.70 – public transport €237.79 – car (where necessary)
Household Energy	Electricity and home heating fuel	€60.37 – electricity €70.80 – heating

9. Guide to Reasonable Living Expenses – http://www.isi.gov.ie/en/ISI/Pages/Reasonable_living_expenses.

Expenditure category	A guide to what is included in each expenditure category	For a single adult of working age living alone this comes to a monthly total of:
Insurance	Home insurance and also car insurance where a car is needed. Note that the ISI model does not ordinarily include private health insurance though this may be included in some circumstances where warranted	€12.25 – home contents €24.25 – car insurance
Savings and Contingencies	Savings and life assurance (for households with dependants). For a single person, savings at €5 a week are assumed as is €5 a week to be put aside for contingencies and emergencies	€43.38
Social Inclusion and Participation	At €29 a week, the minimum considered necessary for participation and inclusion. It includes sports activities and social events such as visits to the cinema. The ISI model does not factor in the cost of a holiday	€126.10
Housing	The cost of renting or making mortgage payments	Variable – subject to PIP or AI assessing cost to be reasonable
Childcare	The cost of full or part-time childcare. This is dependent on the employment status of the adults in the household as well as the age of the child	Variable – subject to PIP or AI assessing cost to be reasonable

DEBT RELIEF NOTICE

[7.18] Section 26(2)(b) of PIA 2012 provides that to be eligible for a DRN[10] the debtor must have net disposable income, calculated in accordance with sub-s (5), of €60 or less a month. The PIA 2012 sets out the basis on which net disposable income is to be calculated. Essentially it is the income available to the debtor less specified deductions.

Calculation of Net Disposable Income

[7.19] All of the income and expenditure items outlined in the table below, other than reasonable living expenses, are a matter of fact. What is 'reasonable' is an objective standard, but one open to interpretation.

As contemplated by s 23(3)(e) of PIA 2012, it may vary from one person to another but it is fundamental to achieving fairness and consistency in evaluating eligibility for DRNs that reasonable living expenses be as objective as possible. It would clearly be wrong to penalise the frugal by making it easier for a debtor to pass the test for net

10. See para **3.13**.

disposable income simply by spending more of his or her money on anything he or she considers reasonable.

Calculation Formula

[7.20] Income - Expenditure = Net Disposable Income

Items that constitute income and expenditure have been classified in the table below.

Income	Expenditure
	Reasonable living expenses
Welfare benefits (other than child benefit)	Income tax payable
	Social insurance contributions
Contributions from other household members	Payments of excluded debts
Any other income	Payments of excludable debts that are not permitted debts
	Such other levies and charges on the debtor's income as may be prescribed

DEBT SETTLEMENT ARRANGEMENTS AND PERSONAL INSOLVENCY ARRANGEMENTS

[7.21] Section 65(2)(d) of PIA 2012 provides that a DSA must not contain any terms which would require the debtor to make payments of an amount that the debtor would not have sufficient income to maintain a reasonable standard of living for himself or herself and his or her dependants.

Section 65(4) of PIA 2012 specifies that, in determining whether a debtor would have a sufficient income to maintain a reasonable standard of living for the debtor and his or her dependants, regard shall be had to the provisions of the Guidelines.

Section 99(2)(e) and (4) of PIA 2012 contain corresponding provisions in respect of a PIA.

The importance for individuals in financial difficulty, who are also in employment, to be given some incentive to continue working has been highlighted. A reduction to the income level which that individual would have if he or she were to be unemployed and in receipt of social welfare could take away the incentive to go to work. In the context of working debtors entering into DSAs and PIAs, those individuals should be able to retain some of the money they are earning before the balance of their income goes to discharge their debt.

The PIPs will need to engage with creditors and debtors in order to ensure that workable arrangements are put in place. Creditors have an interest in getting all, or at least a portion, of their debts repaid and so have an interest in the debtor being at work, getting a financial benefit from working and thereby having the ability to pay off a greater amount of his or her debts over a period of time than might otherwise be the case if they were not at work.

A balance will have to be struck between the allocation of earnings to creditors and their retention by the debtor. This will vary from individual to individual, depending on personal circumstances, family situation, debt levels, income, health and a range of other issues.

Ultimately, where either a DSA or a PIA is proposed, the decision on the reasonableness or otherwise of living expenses will be a matter for the creditors to determine on a case-by-case basis in accordance with the voting thresholds set out in s 73[11] or, as applicable, s 110[12] of PIA 2012. This is subject to the provision that the debtor will not be required to make payments of such an amount that he or she would not have sufficient income to maintain a reasonable standard of living. Where a PIP has put forward a proposal which contains unrealistic or disproportionate living expenses there is a likelihood that creditors will vote against acceptance of the arrangement on that basis.

DISTINGUISHING BETWEEN DRN, DSA AND PIA[13]

[7.22]

DRN	**DSA and PIA**
Strict application of the reasonable living expenses model in determining the eligibility of an applicant	Ultimately, it is a matter for the PIP to determine an acceptable level of reasonable living expenses and for creditors to agree on this and vote in favour of it
To be eligible the applicant must have €60 or less in net disposable income a month	PIA 2012 requires that the debtor have sufficient income to maintain a reasonable standard of living. Accordingly, reasonable living expenses should not be at a level below that proposed under the Guidelines
Actual expenditure would not give reasonable results. An objective standard must be set	Reasonable living standards may be higher than the Guidelines propose where acceptable to creditors. This may occur where creditors can see value for themselves in incentivising the debtor

STEP PROCESS IN DETERMINING REASONABLE LIVING EXPENSES

[7.23] The costs attributed to a typical household in the Guidelines are termed set costs. To these are added the reasonable costs of housing, childcare and special circumstances where these arise. This produces the total for reasonable living expenses for the household. Please see the table at **7.17** which details the types of expenses that may be included in the set costs of a household.

---

11. DSA.
12. PIA.
13. Guide to Reasonable Living Expenses – http://www.isi.gov.ie/en/ISI/Pages/Reasonable_living_expenses.

Step 1 – Determine set costs on basis of household composition using tables (see paras **7.03**, **7.10**, **7.11**, **7.12** and **7.17**)

Step 2 – Determine housing costs depending on circumstances of debtor (see paras **7.05**, **7.13** and **7.17**)

Step 3 – Determine childcare costs depending on circumstances of debtor (see paras **7.04**, **7.06** and **7.17**)

Step 4 – Determine special circumstances depending on circumstances of debtor (see paras **7.06**, **7.15** and **7.17**)

Start:	Set Costs Total
Add:	Housing Costs
Add:	Childcare Costs
Add:	Special Circumstances Costs
Total:	Reasonable Living Expenses

Step 1 – Set Costs: Household Composition

[7.24] The AI or PIP should begin by selecting the set of tables (See para **7.28** below) which best fits the situation of the applicant based on household composition, ie whether or not the applicant is the only adult in the household and whether or not the applicant has children.

The set costs of a household are compiled by totalling the costs for each individual in the household.

Where only one adult resides in the household, the reasonable living expenses for that adult and any dependants will be fully attributed to that adult.

Where two adults reside in the household then it will be presumed that the reasonable living expenses of the household are split equally between them, though a debtor may rebut this presumption and produce evidence to show that he or she pays a different proportion of these reasonable living expenses.

Where adults reside together in a house-sharing arrangement, the reasonable living expenses of the debtor should be based on those of a single person. In such cases, the AI or PIP should assess the reasonableness of the rent based on the portion which the debtor pays rather than the rent of the property.

For households with children, the AI or PIP should first identify the costs for the adult(s). To this is then added the cost for the first child. These should correspond to the age group of that child. This step is repeated for each subsequent child.

Where there are three or more children in the household, an adjustment will need to be made to capture the additional costs associated with the larger households. These tables enable the calculation of the minimum set costs for single adult households, for households with couples and no children, and for two-parent and one-parent households with one or more children.

Set Costs: Need for a Motor Vehicle

[7.25] If the household does not have a motor vehicle and does not need a motor vehicle this will usually mean the applicant lives in an urban location with adequate public transport links.

The AI or PIP should choose the vehicle option based on the needs of the household (needs, not wants). Where a car or motor vehicle is not included, the model includes costs associated with the use of public transport.

Step 2 and Step 3 – Reasonable Costs of Housing and Childcare

[7.26] Under the ISI model, childcare costs and housing costs are added to the total for set costs to produce the final figure for reasonable living expenses.

Where childcare or housing costs are paid for, the AI or PIP should assess the reasonableness of these expenses.

The AI or PIP should support his or her assessment as to the reasonableness of childcare and housing costs by reference to the matters he or she has taken into account in arriving at this opinion.

Step 4 – Special Circumstances

[7.27] The **PIA 2012** contains a requirement to take account of the differing needs of persons, having regard to matters such as their age, health and whether they have a physical, sensory, mental health or intellectual disability. Given the number of possible variables, and the individual nature of physical and mental health conditions and disabilities, the ISI believes this aspect is best addressed through making allowance in these guidelines for a debtor to specify reasonable costs which arise as a consequence of ill-health, age or disability.

The category of special circumstances may also be used where a debtor has persons other than his or her minor children financially dependent on him or her, such as where the debtor is contributing financially to the care of an adult dependant such as, for example, an elderly relative or a college-going child.

TABLES OF REASONABLE LIVING EXPENSES[14]

Index of Tables[15]

[7.28]

14. Tables taken from http://www.isi.gov.ie/en/ISI/Pages/Reasonable_living_expenses.
15. Guide to Reasonable Living Expenses – http://www.isi.gov.ie/en/ISI/Pages/Reasonable_living_expenses.

Table 5.	Two adult household, one or more children, no vehicle
Table 6.	Two adult household, one or more children, vehicle
Table 7.	Two adult household, no vehicle
Table 8.	Two adult household, vehicle

Table 1. One Adult Household, No Vehicle

[7.29]

SINGLE ADULT, WORKING AGE (LIVING ALONE) *Jun 2013* MONTHLY June 2013	NO CAR NEEDED
Total set costs	€933.14
OTHER COSTS	
Housing	
Special circumstances	
Reasonable living expenses	

Set Cost Breakdown – for Informational Purposes Only:

[7.30]

Food	€250.98
Clothing	€35.34
Personal Care	€33.06
Health	€31.34
Household Goods	€26.38
Household Services	€27.54
Communications	€41.21
Social Inclusion & Participation	€126.10
Education	€23.72
Transport (Public)	€149.70
Household Electricity	€60.37
Home Heating	€70.80
Personal Costs	€0.97
Home Insurance	€12.25
Car Insurance	€0.00
Savings & Contingencies	€43.38
Total monthly set costs	**€933.14**

Table 2. One Adult Household, Vehicle

[7.31]

SINGLE ADULT, WORKING AGE (LIVING ALONE) *Jun 2013*	
Total set costs	€1,045.48
OTHER COSTS	
Housing	
Special circumstances	
Reasonable living expenses	

Set Cost Breakdown – for Informational Purposes Only:

[7.32]

Food	€250.98
Clothing	€35.34
Personal Care	€33.06
Health	€31.34
House hold Goods	€26.38
Household Services	€27.54
Communications	€41.21
Social Inclusion & Participation	€126.10
Education	€23.72
Transport (Private)	€237.79
House hold Electricity	€60.37
Home Heating	€70.80
Personal Costs	€0.97
Home Insurance	€12.25
Car Insurance	€24.25
Saving s & Contingencies	€43.38
Total monthly set costs	**€1,045.48**

Table 3. One Adult Household, One or More Children, No Vehicle

[7.33]

ONE ADULT HOUSEHOLD *Jun 2013*						NO CAR NEEDED	
		Child Age Groups				***Adjustment if more than two children***	
	Adult	Infant	Pre-school	Primary	Secondary	Third Child	Fourth Child
Total before deductions	€939.71	€372.26	€208.52	€349.37	€562.16	€10.81	€10.27
LESS child benefit	€0.00	-€130.00	-€130.00	-€130.00	-€130.00	€0.00	-€10.00
Total set costs	**€939.71**	**€242.26**	**€78.52**	**€219.37**	**€432.16**	**€10.81**	**€0.27**

OTHER COSTS

Childcare	
Housing	
Special circumstances	
Reasonable living expenses	

Set Cost Breakdown – for Informational Purposes Only:

[7.34]

		Child Age Groups			
	Adult	Infant	Pre-School	Primary	Secondary
Food	€222.51	€135.44	€105.11	€162.43	€215.88
Clothing	€35.33	€71.99	€21.86	€29.90	€54.44
Personal Care	€31.40	€46.51	€6.09	€11.74	€36.43
Health	€29.20	€35.98	€18.85	€18.60	€24.50
Household Goods	€62.37	€45.58	€11.78	€13.17	€16.04
Household Services	€27.54	€0.00	€0.00	€0.00	€0.00
Communications	€41.07	€0.00	€0.00	€0.00	€20.48
Social Inclusion & Participation	€99.31	€7.72	€10.04	€49.58	€93.33
Education	€10.34	€0.00	€0.00	€29.16	€66.27
Transport (Public)	€125.00	€0.00	€12.25	€12.25	€12.25
House hold Electricity	€86.08	€6.30	€0.00	€0.00	€0.00

Home Heating	€91.45	€0.00	€0.00	€0.00	€0.00
Personal Costs	€0.95	€1.05	€0.85	€0.85	€0.85
Home Insurance	€17.59	€0.00	€0.00	€0.00	€0.00
Car Insurance	€0.00	€0.00	€0.00	€0.00	€0.00
Saving s & Contingencies	€59.57	€21.69	€21.69	€21.69	€21.69
Total before deductions	€939.71	€372.26	€208.52	€349.37	€562.16
LESS child benefit	€0.00	-€130.00	-€130.00	-€130.00	-€130.00
Total monthly set costs	**€939.71**	**€242.26**	**€78. 52**	**€219.37**	**€432.16**

Table 4. One adult household, one or more children, vehicle

[7.35]

ONE ADULT HOUSEHOLD *Jun 2013*						PRIVATE CAR NEEDED	
		Child Age Groups				***Adjustment if more than 2 children***	
MONTHLY	Adult	Infant	Pre-School	Primary	Secondary	Third Child	Fourth Child
Total before deductions	€1,091.15	€372.26	€196.27	€337.12	€549.91	€10.81	€52.72
LESS child benefit	€0.00	-€130.00	-€130.00	-€130.00	-€130.00	€0.00	-€10.00
Total set costs	**€1,091.15**	**€242.26**	**€66.27**	**€207.12**	**€419.91**	**€10.81**	**€42.72**

OTHER COSTS	
Childcare	
Housing	
Special circumstances	
Reasonable Living Expenses	

Set Cost Breakdown – for Informational Purposes Only:

[7.36]

		Child Age Groups			
	Adult	Infant	Pre-school	Primary	Secondary
Food	€222.51	€135.44	€105.11	€162.43	€215.88
Clothing	€35.33	€71.99	€21.86	€29.90	€54.44
Personal Care	€31.40	€46.51	€6.09	€11.74	€36.43

Health	€29.20	€35.98	€18.85	€18.60	€24.50
House hold Goods	€62.37	€45.58	€11.78	€13.17	€16.04
Household Services	€27.54	€0.00	€0.00	€0.00	€0.00
Communications	€41.07	€0.00	€0.00	€0.00	€20.48
Social Inclusion & Participation	€99.31	€7.72	€10.04	€49.58	€93.33
Education	€10.34	€0.00	€0.00	€29.16	€66.27
Transport (Private)	€250.04	€0.00	€0.00	€0.00	€0.00
Household Electricity	€86.08	€6.30	€0.00	€0.00	€0.00
Home Heating	€91.45	€0.00	€0.00	€0.00	€0.00
Personal Costs	€0.95	€1.05	€0.85	€0.85	€0.85
Home Insurance	€17.59	€0.00	€0.00	€0.00	€0.00
Car Insurance	€26.40	€0.00	€0.00	€0.00	€0.00
Savings & Contingencies	€59.57	€21.69	€21.69	€21.69	€21.69
Total before deductions	€1,091.15	€372.26	€196.27	€337.12	€549.91
LESS child benefit	€0.00	-€130.00	-€130.00	-€130.00	-€130.00
Total monthly set costs	**€1,091.15**	**€242.26**	**€66.27**	**€207.12**	**€419.91**

Table 5. Two Adult Household, One or More Children, No Vehicle

[7.37]

TWO ADULT HOUSEHOLD *Jun 2013*						NO CAR NEEDED	
		Child Age Groups					
MONTHLY	Couple	Infant	Pre-School	Primary	Secondary	Third Child	Fourth Child
Total before deductions	€1,360.30	€372.26	€208.52	€349.37	€562.16	€10.81	€10.27
LESS child benefit	€0.00	-€130.00	-€130.00	-€130.00	-€130.00	€0.00	-€10.00
Total set costs	**€1,360.30**	**€242.26**	**€78.52**	**€219.37**	**€432.16**	**€10.81**	**€0.27**

OTHER COSTS	
Childcare	
Housing	
Special circumstances	
Reasonable Living Expenses	

Set Cost Breakdown – for Informational Purposes Only:

[7.38]

		Child Age Groups			
	Couple	Infant	Pre–school	Primary	Secondary
Food	€283.21	€135.44	€105.11	€162.43	€215.88
Clothing	€66.73	€71.99	€21.86	€29.90	€54.44
Personal Care	€64.90	€46.51	€6.09	€11.74	€36.43
Health	€45.17	€35.98	€18.85	€18.60	€24.50
Household Goods	€67.63	€45.58	€11.78	€13.17	€16.04
Household Services	€27.54	€0.00	€0.00	€0.00	€0.00
Communications	€61.56	€0.00	€0.00	€0.00	€20.48
Social Inclusion & Participation	€158.02	€7.72	€10.04	€49.58	€93.33
Education	€10.34	€0.00	€0.00	€29.16	€66.27
Transport (Public)	€250.00	€0.00	€12.25	€12.25	€12.25
Household Electricity	€112.39	€6.30	€0.00	€0.00	€0.00
Home Heating	€114.46	€0.00	€0.00	€0.00	€0.00
Personal Costs	€1.91	€1.05	€0.85	€0.85	€0.85
Home Insurance	€17.59	€0.00	€0.00	€0.00	€0.00
Car Insurance	€0.00	€0.00	€0.00	€0.00	€0.00
Savings & Contingencies	€78.85	€21.69	€21.69	€21.69	€21.69
Total before deductions	€1,360.30	€372.26	€208.52	€349.37	€562.16
LESS child benefit	€0.00	-€130.00	-€130.00	-€130.00	-€130.00
Total monthly set costs	**€1,360.30**	**€242.26**	**€78.52**	**€219.37**	**€432.16**

Table 6. Two Adult Household, One or More Children, Vehicle

[7.39]

TWO ADULT HOUSEHOLD *Jun 2013*						PRIVATE CAR NEEDED	
		Child Age Groups				***Adjustment if more than two children***	
MONTHLY	Couple	Infant	Pre-School	Primary	Secondary	Third Child	Fourth Child
Total before deductions	€1,407.50	€372.26	€196.27	€337.12	€549.91	€10.81	€52.72
LESS child benefit	€0.00	-€130.00	-€130.00	-€130.00	-€130.00	€0.00	-€10.00
Total set costs	**€1,407.50**	**€242.26**	**€66.27**	**€207.12**	**€419.91**	**€10.81**	**€42.72**

OTHER COSTS	
Childcare	
Housing	
Special circumstances	
Reasonable Living Expenses	

Set Cost Breakdown – for Informational Purposes Only:

[7.40]

		Child Age Groups			
	Couple	Infant	Pre-school	Primary	Secondary
Food	€283.21	€135.44	€105.11	€162.43	€215.88
Clothing	€66.73	€71.99	€21.86	€29.90	€54.44
Personal Care	€64.90	€46.51	€6.09	€11.74	€36.43
Health	€45.17	€35.98	€18.85	€18.60	€24.50
Household Goods	€67.63	€45.58	€11.78	€13.17	€16.04
Household Services	€27.54	€0.00	€0.00	€0.00	€0.00
Communications	€61.56	€0.00	€0.00	€0.00	€20.48
Social Inclusion & Participation	€158.02	€7.72	€10.04	€49.58	€93.33
Education	€10.34	€0.00	€0.00	€29.16	€66.27
Transport (Private)	€250.50	€0.00	€0.00	€0.00	€0.00
Household Electricity	€112.39	€6.30	€0.00	€0.00	€0.00
Home Heating	€114.46	€0.00	€0.00	€0.00	€0.00
Personal Costs	€1.91	€1.05	€0.85	€0.85	€0.85
Home Insurance	€17.59	€0.00	€0.00	€0.00	€0.00
Car Insurance	€46.70	€0.00	€0.00	€0.00	€0.00
Savings & Contingencies	€78.85	€21.69	€21.69	€21.69	€21.69
Total before deductions	€1,407.50	€372.26	€196.27	€337.12	€549.91
LESS child benefit	€0.00	-€130.00	-€130.00	-€130.00	-€130.00
Total monthly set costs	**€1,407.50**	**€242.26**	**€66.27**	**€207.12**	**€419.91**

Table 7. Two Adult Household, No Vehicle

[7.41]

TWO ADULT HOUSEHOLD (NO CHILDREN)	
Jun 2013	
MONTHLY	NO CAR NEEDED
Total set costs	€1,496.26

OTHER COSTS	
Housing	
Special circumstances	
Reasonable Living Expenses	

Set Cost Breakdown – for Informational Purposes Only:

[7.42]

Food	€369.37
Clothing	€67.00
Personal Care	€73.70
Health	€49.39
Household Goods	€30.71
Household Services	€27.54
Communications	€61.70
Social Inclusion & Participation	€232.47
Education	€38.13
Transport (Public)	€287.05
Household Electricity	€73.30
Home Heating	€106.65
Personal Costs	€1.93
Home Insurance	€12.25
Car Insurance	€0.00
Savings & Contingencies	€65.07
Total monthly set costs	**€1,496.26**

Table 8. Two adult household, vehicle

[7.43]

TWO ADULT HOUSEHOLD (NO CHILDREN) MONTHLY	CAR NEEDED
Total set costs	€1,473.29
OTHER COSTS	
Housing	
Special circumstances	
Reasonable living expenses	

Set Cost Breakdown – for Informational Purposes Only:

[7.44]

Food	€369.37
Clothing	€67.00
Personal Care	€73.70
Health	€49.39
Household Goods	€30.71
Household Services	€27.54
Communications	€61.70
Social Inclusion & Participation	€232.47
Education	€38.13
Transport (Private)	€238.26
Household Electricity	€73.30
Home Heating	€106.65
Personal Costs	€1.93
Home Insurance	€12.25
Car Insurance	€25.82
Savings & Contingencies	€65.07
Total monthly set costs	€1,473.29

EXAMPLES ILLUSTRATING THE APPLICATION OF REASONABLE LIVING EXPENSES

Ger – DRN

[7.45] This example is designed to show how these guidelines link into the assessment of a debtor's eligibility for a DRN.[16]

Ger is a 23-year-old single male living alone in a city centre flat which he rents privately at a cost of €600 a month. He doesn't have or need a car. He is in full-time employment and his take home pay is €1,550 a month. He has credit card debt of €11,000 and owes a credit union another €6,000. He is finding it impossible to make the monthly payments on top of his rent and all his other bills and wonders if he can get a DRN.

Ger should look at the eligibility criteria on the ISI website before visiting an AI. He can get a list of AIs from the ISI website. Amongst other matters, the AI will check whether Ger meets the eligibility criteria of having €60 or less disposable income each month.

16. Examples taken from http://www.isi.gov.ie/en/ISI/Pages/Reasonable_living_expenses.

The AI will use Table 1 (one adult household, no vehicle) which shows the monthly set costs to be €933.14. To this is added Ger's rent of €600 a month, having been assessed as reasonable by the AI, making his reasonable living expenses €1,533.14.

The AI will make the following calculation:

Monthly income after income tax and social insurance contributions		€1,550.00
Total set costs	€933.14	
Rent / mortgage	€600.00	
Childcare	None	
Special circumstances	None	
Reasonable living expenses	€1,533.14	€1,533.14
Net disposable income		€16.86

Since the net disposable income is less than €60 a month, the eligibility criteria in respect of net disposable income is satisfied. The AI will assess whether Ger meets all of the other eligibility criteria. If he does the AI will advise him of his options which may result in Ger requesting the AI to assist him in making an application for a DRN.

Emma – DSA

[7.46] This example is designed to show how the application of these guidelines may demonstrate that a debtor is ineligible to apply for a DRN and that, in such circumstances, a DSA may remain a possibility for the insolvent debtor.

Emma is self-employed on a part-time basis as an insurance broker and earns €2,500 after tax a month. She is a single mother with a daughter aged five who needs paid childcare on the days Emma works. Emma rents privately and pays €300 a month as rent. She needs a car to transport her daughter to school and to get to her job. She has a 2002 Fiat Punto worth €1,800 which she owns outright. Fees for part-time childcare come to €500 a month. Emma has a personal loan from her bank with an outstanding balance of €18,200. She is finding it difficult to make the repayments and seeks advice.

Emma should look at the eligibility criteria for DRNs and DSAs on the ISI website before proceeding. From the information on the website she can calculate her reasonable living expenses and work out her net disposable income. As this does not meet the eligibility criteria for a DRN, Emma will need to contact a PIP rather than an AI. Emma should obtain the details of registered PIPs from the ISI website and contact one of them.

The PIP will use Table 4 (One adult household, one or more children, vehicle), which shows the monthly set costs to be €1,298.27. This is made up of €1,091.15 for the adult and €207.12 for the child. To this is added €500 a month, being the cost of part-time childcare, and the €300 a month Emma pays in rent which the PIP has assessed as reasonable. Emma's reasonable living expenses come to €2,098.27.

The PIP will make the following calculation:

Monthly income after income tax and social insurance		€2,500.00
Total set costs	€1,298.27	

Rent/mortgage	€300.00	
Childcare	€500.00	
Special circumstances	None	
Reasonable living expenses	€2,098.27	€2,098.27
Net disposable income		€401.73

* Child benefit payments are not included.

Emma's net disposable income at €401.73 a month is above the €60 limit. On this basis, she is not eligible for a DRN but a DSA may be a possibility.

The PIP, in formulating a proposal to Emma's creditors, might suggest that all of her income in excess of the base level of reasonable living expenses be paid to creditors for year one. For year two, as an incentive to keep with the arrangement, the PIP might put forward that Emma retain an additional €25 a month with similar increases in subsequent years. It will be for creditors to decide if this is acceptable during negotiations with the PIP and ultimately at the point in time that they are asked to vote on the proposal.

Don and Aoife – DRN

[7.47] This example is designed to show how these guidelines are applied in the case of a couple where only one of them is in receipt of income and bears all of the reasonable living expenses of the household.

Don and Aoife are a married couple in their twenties living in accommodation provided by their local authority for which they pay €65 a month. Neither is employed at the moment but Don is seeking work and receiving jobseeker's allowance. They do not have a car. They have two children: twins aged three. Don is in arrears on a personal loan he took out with a bank two years ago when he was working. The outstanding balance is just over €12,000. He cannot see where he can get the money to pay off his creditors and thinks that a DRN might be an answer.

Don should look at the eligibility criteria on the ISI website before visiting an AI. He can get a list of AIs from the ISI website. Amongst other matters, the AI will check whether Don meets the eligibility criteria of having €60 or less net disposable income each month.

Don receives €188 in jobseeker's allowance plus a payment of €124.80 in respect of Aoife who is a Qualified Adult. In addition, he receives a total of €59.60 a week in Qualified Child Increase payments. Child benefit payments are not included. His total reckonable income comes to €372.40 a week or €1,619.32 a month.

Using Table 5 (two adult household, one or more children, no vehicle) the AI will take set costs of €1,360.30 for the two adults and add €157.04 for the two children (€78.52 for a pre-school child multiplied by two). To this is added €65 for their housing costs, having been assessed as reasonable by the AI, giving reasonable living expenses of €1,582.34 a month for the household.

The AI will make the following calculation:

Monthly income after income tax and social insurance		€1,619.32
Total set costs	€1,517.34	
Rent mortgage	€65.00	
Childcare	None	
Reasonable living expenses	€1,582.34	€1,582.34
Net disposable income		€36.98

* Child benefit payments are not included.

Normally, with two adults in the household, the reasonable living expenses are assumed to be split evenly between them both. In this case, Don explains to the AI that he receives the only income coming into the household and that he pays all the household expenses in full. Here, the reasonable living expenses are allowed in full against his income.

For Don's application, this means income of €1,619.32 less reasonable living expenses of €1,582.34, giving a net disposable income of €36.98. This is less than €60 and so satisfies the test for net disposable income. The AI will assess whether he meets all of the other eligibility criteria. If he does the AI will advise him of his options which may result in Don requesting the AI to assist him in making an application for a DRN.

Mary and Michael – DRN

[7.48] This example is designed to show how these guidelines are applied in the case of a couple where there is more than one income and the reasonable living expenses of the household are split between the couple.

Mary and Michael are a married couple in their twenties living in accommodation provided by the local authority for which they pay €100 a month. Neither is employed at the moment but both are seeking work and both are in receipt of jobseeker's allowance. They do not have a car. They have one child aged three. Mary has a credit card with an outstanding balance of €14,000. She cannot see where she can get the money to pay off her creditors and thinks that a DRN might be an answer.

Mary should look at the eligibility criteria on the ISI website before visiting an AI. She can get a list of AIs from the ISI website. Amongst other matters, the AI will check to see if Mary meets the eligibility criteria of having €60 or less net disposable income each month.

Mary receives €188 a week in jobseeker's allowance. Her total reckonable income comes to €817.49 a month.

Using Table 5 (two adult household, one or more children, no vehicle) the total set costs for the household are €1,438.82 a month. This is made up of €1,360.30 for the two adults and €78.52 for a child of pre-school age. To this is added €100 for their housing costs, these having been assessed as reasonable by the AI. The total reasonable living expenses for the household are €1,538.82.

The usual presumption is that where there are two adults in the household the reasonable living expenses are split evenly between them. This presumption will be applied here since Michael also receives a jobseeker's allowance payment. The reasonable living expenses assigned against Mary's income are thus half those of the household or €769.41.

The AI will make the following calculation:

Monthly income after income tax and social insurance		€817.49
Total set costs	€1,438.82	
Rent/mortgage	€100.00	
Childcare	None	
Special circumstances	None	
Reasonable living expenses for the household	€1,538.82	
Reasonable living expenses (half for Mary)		€769.41
Net disposable income		€48.08

* Child benefit payments are not included.

For Mary's application, this means income of €817.49 less reasonable living expenses of €769.41, giving a net disposable income of €48.08. This is less than €60 and so satisfies the test for net disposable income. The AI will assess whether she meets all of the other eligibility criteria. If she does the AI will advise her of her options which may result in Mary requesting the AI to assist her in making an application for a DRN.

Conor – PIA

[7.49] This example is designed to show how these guidelines are applied in the case of a debtor who is living beyond his or her means.

Conor is employed as an accountant and takes home €4,000 a month. He is single and lives in an apartment which he bought in 2006 for €280,000 but which is now valued at about €160,000. The outstanding mortgage balance is now €258,000 and the monthly payment is €1,200. He also has a mortgage with an outstanding balance of €210,000 on a buy-to-let property which is unoccupied. Conor has a personal loan from a bank with an outstanding balance of €39,000 and outstanding balances totalling €22,000 on three credit cards. He owns outright a car worth €25,000. His discretionary spending leaves him little money to pay his debts. He is hoping that a PIA or DSA can solve his financial problems.

Conor should look at the information on both DSAs and PIAs available on the ISI website before visiting a PIP. He can get a list of PIPs from the ISI website.

Using Table 2 (one adult household, vehicle), the total set costs for the household are €1,045.48 a month. To this is added the €1,200 which Conor pays in mortgage payments which the PIP has assessed as reasonable having regard to the criteria on pages 11–12. Conor's reasonable living expenses come to €2,245.48.

The PIP will make the following calculation:

Monthly income after income tax and social insurance contributions		€4,000.00
Total set costs	€1,045.48	
Mortgage – reduced payment under the proposal	€1,200.00	
Childcare	None	
Special circumstances	None	
Reasonable living expenses	€2,245.48	€2,245.48
Net disposable income		€1,754.52

For Conor's application, this means income of €4,000.00 less reasonable living expenses of €2,245.48, giving a net disposable income of €1,754.52 a month.

Conor is living beyond his means. The PIP will likely advise Conor that he will need to consider reducing his spending so as to enable the PIP to put forward a proposal more likely to achieve creditor support while keeping Conor in his home. The PIP, in formulating a proposal to Conor's creditors, will consider Conor's need for a car and may suggest that he should sell his car and either not replace it at all or replace it with a less expensive model.

Chapter 8

PERSONAL INSOLVENCY PRACTITIONERS

INTRODUCTION

[8.01] As we have noted in previous chapters, the PIA 2012 provides for a Personal Insolvency Practitioner, also known as a PIP for short, who will act on behalf of a debtor in respect of both the Debt Settlement Arrangement (DSA) and the Personal Insolvency Arrangement (PIA) procedures.

It is not possible to avail of either of these insolvency solutions without engaging the services of a PIP. PIPs are licensed and authorised by the Insolvency Service of Ireland (ISI).

The ISI have been accepting applications from potential practitioners to register as a PIP since 25 June 2013.

This chapter sets out the provisions for the authorisation, regulation, supervision and discipline of the PIP by the ISI.

AUTHORISATION OF PIPS

[8.02] The ISI, exercising its powers pursuant to s 3 and s 161 of the PIA 2012 and with the consent of the Minister for Justice and Equality, made regulations for the purpose of the control and supervision of PIPs to a DSA or PIA and these regulations are set out in the Personal Insolvency Act 2012 (Authorisation and Supervision of Personal Insolvency Practitioners) Regulations 2013[1] (referred to in this chapter as Regulations).

QUALIFYING CRITERIA

[8.03] Individuals entitled to make an application to carry on practice as a PIP are set out at s 4 of SI 209/2013. Such individuals must meet the following criteria:

(a) can demonstrate that the individual –

(i) is a solicitor in respect of whom a practising certificate (within the meaning of the Solicitors Acts 1954 to 2011) is in force, or

(ii) is a barrister at law called to the Bar of Ireland, or

(iii) is a qualified accountant and a member of a prescribed accountancy body (within the meaning of s 4 of the Companies (Auditing and Accounting) Act 2003), or

(iv) is a qualified financial advisor who holds a current qualification from the Life Insurance Association of Ireland (LIA), the Insurance Institute or the Institute of Bankers School of Professional Finance, or

1. Personal Insolvency Act 2012 (Authorisation and Supervision of Personal Insolvency Practitioners) Regulations 2013 (SI 209/2013).

(v) holds a qualification in either law, business, finance or other appropriate similar qualification to the satisfaction of the ISI, recognised to at least level 7 of the National Qualifications Framework by Quality and Qualifications Ireland (or equivalent); and

(b) can demonstrate to the satisfaction of the ISI that they have relevant knowledge and experience of and have completed a course of study and passed an examination on[2] –

(i) the law and practice generally as it applies in the State relating to the insolvency of individuals, and

(ii) the PIA 2012, such as would, in the opinion of the ISI, allow him or her to discharge the statutory duties and functions of a PIP under the PIA 2012, and

(iii) is not prohibited by law from acting as a PIP.

Before an individual will be allowed to carry on the practice of a PIP, the individual must satisfy the ISI that he or she:

(a) has adequate organisational capability and resources to carry on the practice of a PIP under the PIA 2012;

(b) holds, or will hold before commencing to carry on practice as a PIP, a policy of professional indemnity insurance which meets the requirements prescribed in the Regulations;

(c) can meet and comply with the requirements and obligations applicable to the practice of a PIP as set out in the PIA 2012, in the Regulations and in Regulations made under the PIA 2012;

(d) has submitted, in such manner as may be specified by the ISI, a completed application in the prescribed form together with such supporting information, documentation and mandates as the ISI has requested; and

(e) is tax compliant.

A policy of professional indemnity insurance means a policy of indemnity insurance against losses arising from claims in respect of any description of civil liability incurred by a person arising from his or her carrying on a practice as a PIP.

AUTHORISATION REQUIREMENTS TO CARRY ON PRACTICE AS PIP

[8.04] In order to qualify as a PIP it is necessary to apply to the ISI in the prescribed form[3] which has been set out in the Schedule of the Regulations. An individual who has been prohibited by virtue of being the subject of a major sanction[4] or where a person has

2. Personal Insolvency Act 2012 (Authorisation and Supervision of Personal Insolvency Practitioners) Regulations 2013 (SI 209/2013), s 4(b).

3. PIA 2012, s 163(1) and Personal Insolvency Act 2012 (Authorisation and Supervision of Personal Insolvency Practitioners) Regulations 2013 (SI 209/2013) – **Appendix 24**.

4. PIA 2012, s 159.

been suspended by order of the court[5] may not apply for authorisation to carry on as a PIP.[6]

An application for an authorisation shall be accompanied by the following:

(a) evidence of the applicant's competence (including any levels of education, training and experience specified by the ISI) and in particular that the applicant has a satisfactory knowledge of –

  (i) the provisions of the PIA 2012, and

  (ii) the law generally as it applies in the State relating to the insolvency of individuals and in particular statutory provisions to such persons;

(b) a report in the prescribed form[7] by a duly qualified accountant that appropriate financial systems and controls are or will be in place for the protection of moneys received from debtors if the applicant is authorised to carry on practice as a PIP;

(c) evidence in writing of the availability to the applicant of the required level of professional indemnity insurance if the applicant is authorised to carry on practice as a PIP;

(d) such other documents as may be prescribed by the ISI in relation to applications for authorisation to carry on practice as a PIP; and

(e) the prescribed fee of €1,500.[8]

At any time before the grant of, or refusal to grant, an authorisation, the ISI may request the applicant to clarify the information provided or to supply further information in respect of the applicant's character, competence or financial position or may make such enquiries as may be necessary for the purpose of evaluating the application properly and comprehensively.[9]

The ISI shall grant authorisations on the basis of the information provided to the ISI during the application process. All applicants, if granted an authorisation to carry on practice as a PIP, shall, when engaging in that practice, operate on a basis consistent with the information provided to the ISI in support of his or her application.

The ISI may initiate the complaints process under the PIA 2012 if it satisfies itself, on reasonable grounds, that the circumstances under which the authorisation was granted have changed to the extent that an application for authorisation would have been refused had the application been made in the changed circumstances.

5. PIA 2012, s 179(2).

6. PIA 2012, s 163(1).

7. Section G of the Prescribed Form of PIP Application Form which requires that the section is completed by a qualified accountant who is a member of a recognised accountancy body within the meaning of the European Communities (Statutory Audits) (Directive 2006/43/EC) Regulations 2010 (SI 220/2010) and who also holds a valid practising certificate.

8. Personal Insolvency Act 2012 (Personal Insolvency Practitioner Authorisation and Renewal of Authorisation Prescribed Fees) Regulations 2013 (SI 246/2013).

9. Personal Insolvency Act 2012 (Authorisation and Supervision of Personal Insolvency Practitioners) Regulations 2013 (SI 209/2013), s 5(2).

An applicant shall take all reasonable steps to ensure that the information provided in support of his or her application is accurate and complete.[10]

The ISI will notify an applicant when it has determined that an application is full and complete.

FITNESS AND PROBITY REGULATORY REQUIREMENTS

[8.05] The PIP must be in a position to demonstrate that he or she complies with the fitness and probity requirements set out in the Regulations.

Independence

[8.06] A PIP must be free from any undue influence, undue guidance or undue control of or by any other person which could affect his performance of his functions under the PIA 2012.[11] A PIP must seek to avoid conflicts of interest in his performance as a PIP. Where a PIP engages in other forms of business then they must ensure that the other business is appropriately segregated from their role as a PIP. A PIP must seek to ensure that they or any persons employed do not seek to benefit from their role as a PIP with respect to a debtor or creditor.

A PIP shall have in place and operate in accordance with a written conflicts of interest policy which complies with the Regulations. The conflicts of interest policy shall seek to identify the circumstances which constitute or may give rise to a conflict of interest entailing a risk to the interests of debtors or creditors who are, or may be, parties to a DSA or a PIA in respect of which the PIP is, or proposes to be, appointed and specify procedures to be followed and measures to be adopted to manage such conflicts.[12]

A PIP shall make a conflict of interest assessment in respect of a debtor prior to being appointed by the debtor and in respect of the debtor's creditor(s), on being notified by the debtor of the identity of the creditor(s).[13]

In the event that a conflict of interest arises, or may arise, either before or during the term of a DSA or PIA and cannot be reasonably avoided, a PIP shall disclose, in writing, the nature of the conflict of interest to the debtors and the creditors who are or may become parties to the relevant proposed DSA or PIA. Where the debtor or any creditor(s) objects in writing to the PIP's appointment, or continuation, within five working days of being notified of the conflict of interest, the PIP shall not take, or continue, the appointment.

---

10. Personal Insolvency Act 2012 (Authorisation and Supervision of Personal Insolvency Practitioners) Regulations 2013 (SI 209/2013), s 5(4).
11. Personal Insolvency Act 2012 (Authorisation and Supervision of Personal Insolvency Practitioners) Regulations 2013 (SI 209/2013), s 9.
12. Personal Insolvency Act 2012 (Authorisation and Supervision of Personal Insolvency Practitioners) Regulations 2013 (SI 209/2013), s 9(2).
13. Personal Insolvency Act 2012 (Authorisation and Supervision of Personal Insolvency Practitioners) Regulations 2013 (SI 209/2013), s 9(3).

Competent and Capable

[8.07] A PIP must be in a position to demonstrate to the satisfaction of the ISI that they:[14]

(a) are sufficiently competent, proficient and independent to undertake the role of a PIP;

(b) have the qualifications, skills, competence and capacity appropriate to the role of a PIP;

(c) have a clear and comprehensive understanding of the relevant legal, regulatory and financial environment applicable to the role of a PIP;

(d) have the organisational and financial competence, capacity and resources to undertake the role of a PIP in an independent and professional manner.

Education, Training and Experience

[8.08] A PIP must have the necessary qualification of either a solicitor, barrister, accountant, financial advisor or hold a qualification in law, business, finance or other appropriate similar qualification to the satisfaction to the ISI.[15] In addition to this the PIP must be able to demonstrate to the ISI that they have the relevant knowledge and experience and passed an exam on the law and practice of insolvency of individuals and the PIA 2012.

Honest, Ethical and Acting with Integrity

[8.09] A PIP (including when an applicant) must be able to demonstrate to the satisfaction of the ISI that his or her ability to act as a PIP under the PIA 2012 is not adversely affected to a material degree where the PIP is, or has been, in any jurisdiction:

(a) issued a warning, censure, suspension, reprimand or other administrative or judicial sanction or its equivalent;

(b) dismissed, or asked to resign and did resign, from any profession, vocation, office or employment or from any position of trust or fiduciary appointment, whether or not remunerated;

(c) a director (or equivalent) of a company that was struck off the register of companies (or its equivalent) by the Registrar of Companies (or its equivalent) on an involuntary basis;

(d) disqualified or restricted from acting as a director in any jurisdiction or have been disqualified from acting in any managerial capacity;

---

14. Personal Insolvency Act 2012 (Authorisation and Supervision of Personal Insolvency Practitioners) Regulations 2013 (SI 209/2013), s 10.

15. Personal Insolvency Act 2012 (Authorisation and Supervision of Personal Insolvency Practitioners) Regulations 2013 (SI 209/2013), s 4(1)(a).

(e) convicted of an offence either of money laundering or terrorist financing (or their equivalents);

(f) convicted of an offence which could be relevant to the PIP's ability to perform his or her functions under the PIA 2012;

(g) subject to a finding, judgment or order made against him or her by any court, tribunal or administrative enquiry involving fraud, misrepresentation, dishonesty or breach of trust or where the individual is subject to any current proceedings or investigation for fraud, misrepresentation, dishonesty or breach of trust;

(h) the subject of any civil penalty enforcement action taken by a regulatory authority under applicable law; or

(i) untruthful or provided false or misleading information to the ISI or uncooperative or misleading in any dealings with the ISI.

A PIP (including when an applicant) shall inform the ISI of the following events when making an application to practice as a PIP or, if occurring subsequently, on becoming aware of such event and shall be able to demonstrate that his or her ability to perform the role of a PIP under the PIA 2012 is not adversely affected to a material degree, where, in any jurisdiction:[16]

(a) the PIP, or any business in which the PIP held a position of responsibility, control or influence, has been or is being, in any jurisdiction, investigated, disciplined, censured, suspended or criticised by a regulatory or professional body, a court or tribunal or administrative inquiry or investigation or any similar body, whether publicly or privately; or

(b) the PIP has been found by a regulatory authority to have perpetrated or participated in any fraudulent, negligent, deceitful or otherwise discreditable business or professional practice; or

(c) the PIP is or was a sole trader or a director or partner, in or in control of a legal entity, which has been refused, prohibited, restricted or suspended from the right to carry on any trade, business or profession for which a licence, registration or other authorisation is required by the law in that jurisdiction or has had any such registration, authorisation, membership or licence revoked or suspended otherwise than on a voluntary basis.

Financial Soundness

[8.10] A PIP is obliged to manage his or her financial affairs relating to his or her practice as a PIP in a sound and prudent manner. [17] A PIP is also obliged to maintain his or her tax clearance status for the duration of his or her authorisation as a PIP.

16. Personal Insolvency Act 2012 (Authorisation and Supervision of Personal Insolvency Practitioners) Regulations 2013 (SI 209/2013), s 11.

17. Personal Insolvency Act 2012 (Authorisation and Supervision of Personal Insolvency Practitioners) Regulations 2013 (SI 209/2013), s 12.

Organisation and Management

[8.11] A PIP is required to have and to maintain an organisational structure that is clear and transparent with the appropriate management skills and adequate levels of staff and expertise to carry out the role and functions of a PIP in the interests of both debtors and creditors in accordance with the provisions of the PIA 2012.[18]

A PIP must manage his or her business affairs in accordance with sound administrative and accounting principles and should have in place, and maintain, up to date internal control and reporting arrangements and procedures to ensure that his or her business affairs are managed in accordance with all relevant legislation, including the requirements of the ISI under the PIA 2012, and in accordance with best practice.

A PIP must have policies, systems, procedures and internal control mechanisms in place to monitor compliance and these must be reviewed on a regular basis.

The PIP is also required to maintain records for six years following the conclusion of a DSA or PIA[19] and these must be kept in the State and made available to the ISI on request.

These records include (but are not limited to):

(a) identification of debtors and creditors who are, or may become, or were subject to or covered by a DSA or PIA;

(b) all communications with debtors and creditors who are, or may become, or were subject to or covered by a DSA or PIA and other persons concerned in preparing or administering a DSA or PIA;

(c) a copy of each debtor's Prescribed Financial Statement (PFS);

(d) details of all transactions entered into on behalf of debtors and creditors who are or may become subject to or covered by a DSA or PIA;

(e) details of all fees and charges charged in performing functions under the PIA 2012 as a PIP, including outlays recovered, together with documentation evidencing that the fees and charges were properly due to the PIP;

(f) minutes or any other record of a creditors' meeting; and

(g) all other records required to be maintained under the PIA 2012.

A PIP shall respect the confidentiality of debtors and creditors party to a DSA or PIA and must not disclose this information to a third party without specific authority from the provider or where there is a legal duty or entitlement to disclose.[20] The PIP must not disclose a debtor's Personal Public Service Number (PPSN) to any other person other than the ISI or where there is a legal duty or entitlement to disclose.

18. Personal Insolvency Act 2012 (Authorisation and Supervision of Personal Insolvency Practitioners) Regulations 2013 (SI 209/2013), s 14.

19. Personal Insolvency Act 2012 (Authorisation and Supervision of Personal Insolvency Practitioners) Regulations 2013 (SI 209/2013), s 14(5).

20. Personal Insolvency Act 2012 (Authorisation and Supervision of Personal Insolvency Practitioners) Regulations 2013 (SI 209/2013), s 14(9).

FEES, COSTS AND OUTLAYS

[8.12] A PIP may charge fees[21] in each of the following circumstances:

(a) for all work done by him or her at any time in performing his or her functions under the PIA 2012, Regulations or rules of court;

(b) for all work done by him or her in performing his or her functions permitted or required under the terms of a DSA or PIA.

A PIP may charge costs or seek to recover outlays in each of the following circumstances:

(a) for all costs and outlays incurred by him or her at any time in per- forming his or her functions under the PIA 2012, Regulations or rules of court;

(b) for all costs and outlays incurred by him or her in performing his or her functions permitted or required under the terms of a DSA or PIA.

The purpose for which a PIP may charge fees or costs or seek to recover outlays is where there is the need to ensure proper and ongoing administration of a DSA or PIA and for the commercial interest of the PIP.

PROFESSIONAL INDEMNITY INSURANCE

[8.13] A PIP shall have in place a policy of professional indemnity insurance[22] covering his or her practice as a PIP which complies with the Regulations. The amount insured for each claim shall not be less than €1,000,000 and a minimum of €1,500,000 in aggregate.

Where a PIP holds a policy of professional indemnity insurance, the PIP shall provide the ISI, prior to commencing to carry on the practice of a PIP and subsequently when seeking renewal of his or her authorisation, with a written confirmation to the ISI from the insurer that the policy of professional indemnity insurance covers his or her practice as a PIP and meets the level of cover specified in the Regulations.

The policy of indemnity insurance must be held on a continuing basis for the duration of the PIP's authorisation as a PIP. On the revocation of the policy of insurance on a voluntary termination of authorisation of a PIP, the PIP is obliged to ensure that the policy of professional indemnity insurance covers any claims made subsequent to the withdrawal of the authorisation.

TERMINATION OF APPOINTMENT AS PIP

[8.14] Where a PIP has been appointed by a debtor, he or she shall stand appointed and the debtor shall not appoint another PIP until such time as:

(a) where the debtor terminates the appointment of the PIP;

---

21. Personal Insolvency Act 2012 (Authorisation and Supervision of Personal Insolvency Practitioners) Regulations 2013 (SI 209/2013), s 15.

22. Personal Insolvency Act 2012 (Authorisation and Supervision of Personal Insolvency Practitioners) Regulations 2013 (SI 209/2013), s 6.

(b) where the PIP terminates their appointment; or

(c) where the PIP is replaced by reason of death or incapacity to act as a PIP.

Termination by Debtor

[8.15] A debtor who has appointed a PIP may terminate[23] that appointment by giving notice in writing to the PIP which notice shall specify the date of the termination which date shall not be less than one month after giving the notice of termination to the PIP. The debtor must notify the ISI as soon as practicable.

On termination of the appointment of a PIP, the debtor must within two months of the date of termination appoint a PIP to replace the original PIP and once appointed must notify the ISI of the appointment.

Where a replacement PIP has been appointed the replacement PIP must notify the ISI and creditors of their appointment.

In circumstances where a replacement PIP has been appointed, the validity of anything previously done under a DSA or PIA will remain unaffected. The protective certificate, DSA or PIA that is in effect shall continue to have effect.

Termination by PIP

[8.16] A PIP who has been appointed by a debtor may terminate[24] that appointment by giving notice in writing to the debtor which notice shall specify the date of the termination which date shall not be less than one month after giving the notice of termination to the debtor. The PIP must notify the ISI as soon as practicable.

On termination of the appointment of a PIP, the debtor must, within two months of the date of termination, appoint a PIP to replace the original PIP and once appointed must notify the ISI of the appointment.

Where a replacement PIP has been appointed the replacement PIP must notify the ISI and creditors of their appointment.

In circumstances where a replacement PIP has been appointed, the validity of anything previously done under a DSA or PIA will remain unaffected. The protective certificate, DSA or PIA that is in effect shall continue to have effect. There is provision for an extension of the protective certificate period for a further 40 days where a replacement PIP has been appointed.[25]

Termination by Death, Incapacity or Withdrawal of Authorisation

[8.17] Where a PIP appointed under the PIA 2012 either dies or becomes incapable through ill-health or otherwise of performing the function of a PIP or is no longer authorised to perform the functions of a PIP,[26] the debtor shall, as soon as they have

---

23. PIA 2012, s 49A as inserted by the Courts and Civil Law (Miscellaneous Provisions) Act 2013, s 62.
24. PIA 2012, s 49B as inserted by Courts and Civil Law (Miscellaneous Provisions) Act 2013, s 62.
25. See para **6.31** – Court Procedures.
26. PIA 2012, s 49C as inserted by Courts and Civil Law (Miscellaneous Provisions) Act 2013, s 62.

become aware of that fact or of being informed by the ISI or at the latest three months thereafter the fact, appoint a replacement PIP. On appointment of the replacement PIP, the debtor must notify the ISI.

Where a replacement PIP has been appointed the replacement PIP must notify the ISI and creditors of their appointment.

In circumstances where a replacement PIP has been appointed the validity of anything previously done under a DSA or PIA will remain unaffected. The protective certificate, DSA or PIA that is in effect shall continue to have effect. There is provision for an extension of the protective certificate period for a further 40 days where a replacement PIP has been appointed.[27]

APPLICATION FOR AUTHORISATION

[8.18] An application[28] must be made on the application form previously referred to and contained at **Appendix 24**.[29] The application must also be accompanied by:

(a) completed application form;

(b) registration of business name;

(c) qualification certificates;

(d) professional indemnity insurance;

(e) letter of intent from insurance undertaking;

(f) copy of Tax Clearance Certificate;

(g) PIP declaration;

(h) completed accountant's report;

(i) prescribed fee of €1,500.[30]

The qualified accountant's report must certify that the following procedures are employed by the PIP:

(a) written procedure that establishes clear accountability for the handling of funds;

(b) written procedure for all cheques and negotiable instruments;

(c) that appropriate and experienced personnel are engaged to monitor, investigate and resolve any differences that arise;

(d) that the duties of collecting/receiving funds, maintaining documentation, making deposits or payments and reconciling records is distributed between two or more appropriate experienced individuals.

---

27. See para **6.31** – Court Procedures

28. PIA 2012, s 163.

29. **Appendix 24** – Application Form for PIP.

30. Personal Insolvency Act 2012 (Personal Insolvency Practitioner Authorisation and Renewal of Authorisation Prescribed Fees) Regulations 2013 (SI 246/2013).

The ISI may also require an applicant to make a statutory declaration and provide such additional information in respect of the applicant's character, competence and financial position and it may make such enquiries and conduct such examinations as it considers necessary. The ISI is also entitled to require the applicant to provide a certificate from the Garda Síochána

AUTHORISATION BY ISI

[8.19] The ISI may authorise[31] an individual to carry on practice as a PIP and shall furnish to that individual the registration number assigned to such person for the purposes of the Register of PIPs.[32] The ISI shall take into account any information[33] supplied to it with the application form[34] and information provided by the Commissioner of the Garda Síochána or the Central Bank of Ireland.[35]

When the PIP receives the authorisation then this authorisation will remain in force for a period of one year from the date from when it is issued.[36] The authorisation will remain in force for the year unless it has been surrendered, revoked or otherwise ceases to be in force.

The authorisation does not allow an authorised PIP to transfer or assign the authorisation to any other person. The authorisation is personal to the PIP.[37] The PIA 2012 also provides that the authorisation is for a specific purpose and the authorisation does not allow a PIP to provide other financial advisory services subject to regulation by the Central Bank.[38]

REFUSAL OF AN APPLICATION FOR AUTHORISATION TO PRACTICE AS A PIP

[8.20] The ISI must refuse to authorise an individual to carry on practice as a PIP if:[39]

(a) the application form has not been accompanied by the necessary documentation as set out at para **8.18** above;

(b) the individual has not furnished sufficient evidence to show that there is available to him the required level of professional indemnity insurance;

(c) the individual is under 18 years of age or is an undischarged bankrupt;

31. PIA 2012, s 164.
32. PIA 2012, s 164(1).
33. PIA 2012, s 164(2).
34. PIA 2012, s 167.
35. PIA 2012, s 168.
36. PIA 2012, s 164(4).
37. PIA 2012, s 164(5).
38. PIA 2012, s 164(6).
39. PIA 2012, s 164(3).

(d) the ISI is satisfied that the individual –
  (i) is not a fit and proper person to carry on practice as a PIP,
  (ii) is not competent to carry on practice as a PIP or does not meet the levels of education, training and experience specified by the ISI,
  (iii) does not comply with any requirement of the PIA 2012 or of the Regulations.

If the ISI intends to refuse to authorise a person to carry on practice as a PIP then the ISI must give the person a notice in writing of the proposed refusal.[40] The written notice must contain the following:[41]

(a) the proposal;
(b) the reasons for the proposal;
(c) that the person must make representations in writing to the ISI on the proposal within 21 days from the date of the issue of the notice to the person or within such longer period as the ISI deems appropriate in the circumstances of the case.

If the ISI gives a written notice to a person of its proposal to refuse to authorise a person to carry on practice as a PIP then the ISI must, as soon as practicable after the expiration of the period to make representations and the time for consideration of such representation, do one of two things; either:

(a) issue to the person the authorisation that is the subject of the notice; or
(b) refuse to issue the authorisation that is the subject of the notice and give the person –
  (i) notice in writing of the refusal and the reasons for the refusal, and
  (ii) a copy of s 169 PIA 2012, ie the section detailing a right of appeal to the Circuit Court.

The timeframe for informing an applicant for an authorisation 'as soon as practicable' is not defined in the PIA 2012 and this will be left open to judicial interpretation. It is reasonable to assume that an applicant should be informed once a decision has been made by the ISI. Problems, however, may arise where the ISI takes some time in arriving at such a decision in light of the fact that it can seek information from the Commissioner of the Síochána or the Central Bank of Ireland. This information itself may take time to be provided which may delay any decision of the ISI.

REGISTER OF PIPS

[8.21] The ISI must establish and maintain a register,[42] which will be known as the Register of PIPs (Register). The Register must contain the names of PIPs.[43] It is also open to the ISI to include any other identifying particulars as the ISI considers

40. PIA 2012, s 165(1).
41. PIA 2012, s 165(1).
42. PIA 2012, s 162.
43. PIA 2012, s 162(2).

appropriate.[44] The Register must also contain other relevant information in respect of PIPs which will include suspended PIPs.[45] The Register will be available on the ISI's website.[46] A copy of any entry can be obtained on request on payment of such fee as may be prescribed.[47]

In the course of any legal proceedings, a certificate signed by the director or a member of staff of the ISI who is so authorised by the Director to give a certificate which states that a person is registered on the Register, or not, or was registered at a specified date or during a specified period or was not or has never been registered, will be deemed to be evidence, without proof of the signature, unless the contrary is proved. In effect there is a rebuttable presumption that the content of the certificate is proof of the matters contained therein.[48]

The ISI is obliged to ensure that the information contained in the Register is accurate.[49] If information is inaccurate then the ISI must make any necessary alterations. The ISI must then, as soon as reasonably practicable, inform the PIP in respect of whom such information is altered of any such alterations.[50]

In addition to the ISI being obliged to correct any errors contained in the Register, there is also an obligation on the PIP to give notice in writing to the ISI of any error that the person knows of in the entry.[51] Where there is any change in circumstances that is likely to have a bearing on the accuracy of the entry then the PIP is also obliged to notify the ISI of this change, which notification must be in writing.[52] It is also incumbent on the person to notify the ISI as soon as may be after the person becomes aware of the error or change in circumstances.

RENEWAL OF AN AUTHORISATION

[8.22] PIP authorisation lasts only for a period of one year and so to continue practising as a PIP it will be necessary to apply for a renewal of the authorisation.[53] A person applies to the ISI for a renewal of the authorisation. In order to obtain a renewed authorisation it will be necessary to make the application at least six weeks before the expiration of the authorisation. This renewal application must be accompanied by the prescribed documentation[54] and fee, which has been prescribed at €1,000.[55] At the time

44. PIA 2012, s 162(2).
45. PIA 2012, s 162(2)(b).
46. http://www.isi.gov.ie/en/ISI/Pages/PIPs.
47. PIA 2012, s 162(4).
48. PIA 2012, s 162(5).
49. PIA 2012, s 162(6).
50. PIA 2012, s 162(7).
51. PIA 2012, s 162(8).
52. PIA 2012, s 162(8)(b).
53. PIA 2012, s 166.
54. PIA 2012, s 166.
55. Personal Insolvency Act 2012 (Personal Insolvency Practitioner Authorisation and Renewal of Authorisation Prescribed Fees) Regulations 2013 (SI 246/2013).

of writing, there has been no prescription of documentation required for a renewal of an authorisation but one assumes that it will be prescribed by the ISI in due course. If the renewal authorisation is not received prior to the determination by the ISI for the renewal then the existing authorisation will continue in force until such a determination has been made.[56]

This period of grace is subject to the refusal of the renewal application as set out in sub-s (4) of s 166 PIA 2012. Again the ISI can refuse to renew an authorisation to carry on practice as PIP if the applicant has not applied as prescribed by the ISI or has not accompanied the application with a report of a duly qualified accountant that appropriate financial systems and controls are still in place for the protection of moneys received from debtors by the applicant.

The renewed authorisation starts on the day that the previous authorisation expires.[57] This is irrespective of whether the renewal application was made before, on or after that day. As with the initial application, if the ISI intends to refuse to renew an authorisation, then they must give the applicant notice in writing of their intention and reasons for the proposal to refuse and further that the person is entitled to make representations to the ISI within 21 days from the issue of the notice or as such longer period as the ISI deems appropriate.[58]

As with the initial application the ISI must either issue the renewal authorisation or give notice in writing of the refusal and the reasons thereof. Where the ISI refuses to renew an authorisation to carry on practice as a PIP, the ISI must publish particulars of this decision.[59] There is no clarification under the PIA 2012 as to where these particulars must be published but the authors presume that this will be on the ISI website where all other information is published.

Where the ISI has refused to renew an authorisation or in the event that the authorisation has been revoked or suspended and the ISI is of the opinion that adequate arrangements have not been made for handing over to another PIP then the ISI may request the PIP to hand the necessary documents over to a person appointed by the ISI.

If the PIP does not comply with the requirement then the ISI can apply in a summary manner to the Circuit Court, on notice to that person, for an order requiring the person to comply fully with the requirement within a period of time.[60] This application should be made to the judge of the circuit in which the PIP resides or has practised within the previous three years.[61]

When the ISI takes possession of the said documents from the PIP, it then has to notify the person who produced the documents with a notice of the particulars of the documents and the date it took possession of them. The ISI can make such enquiries as may be necessary to ascertain the person or persons entitled to the possession of the said

56. PIA 2012, s 166(3).
57. PIA 2012, s 166(5).
58. PIA 2012, s 167.
59. PIA 2012, s 185(1)(b).
60. PIA 2012, s 175.
61. PIA 2012, s 175(5).

documents.[62] If the documents are not produced by the ISI to the person then they may apply within 14 days from the date of the notice to the Circuit Court for an order directing the return of the documents to their possession. The court may make the order applied for or such order as it deems appropriate.[63]

APPEAL TO THE CIRCUIT COURT

[8.23] A person who has applied for an authorisation may, within 21 days from the date of receipt of notice of the decision, appeal to the Circuit Court against the decision.[64] There is no appeal to the Circuit Court of a refusal to renew an application and in these circumstances the only means of appealing this decision is by way of judicial review. The circuit where an appeal is held is the circuit where the appellant ordinarily resides or carries on any profession or business.[65]

The Circuit Court can either confirm the decision of the ISI or substitute its own determination for that decision.[66] A decision by the Circuit Court is final unless leave is granted for a case stated to the High Court on a point of law.[67]

GENERAL OBLIGATIONS OF PIPS

Retention of Records

[8.24] Where a PIP has been appointed for the purposes of a DSA or a PIA then they are required to retain such records[68] as may be prescribed and in such form and manner as may be prescribed of the PIP's activities in relation to the debtor for a period of not less than six years after the completion of the activity to which the records relate.[69] The PIP is required to keep the records for a period of six years after the DSA or PIA has terminated.

Professional Indemnity Insurance

[8.25] A PIP is required to have professional indemnity insurance[70] for the all times that they are acting as a PIP.[71] The ISI may prescribe the necessary requirements for such indemnity insurance which include the minimum amount of cover required.

---

62. PIA 2012, s 175(3).
63. PIA 2012, s 175(4).
64. PIA 2012, s 169.
65. See **Ch 6** – Court Procedures.
66. PIA 2012, s 169(3).
67. PIA 2012, s 169(4).
68. PIA 2012, s 170.
69. PIA 2012, s 170.
70. PIA 2012, s 171 and para **8.13** above.
71. PIA 2012, s 171.

Fees/Costs

[8.26] A PIP is not allowed to charge fees or costs[72] or seek to recover outlays which are not incurred as set out by the ISI.[73] The PIP is not entitled to claim costs and fees where they have not been provided for in the DSA or the PIA; thus it is necessary when drafting the DSA or PIA to include any costs/fees incurred in that agreement.

ACCOUNTS AND RELATED MATTERS

[8.27] The ISI is given a wide ambit in respect of making regulations for a PIP. The ISI can make regulations in respect of the kind of accounts that a PIP opens in the State for keeping money of the debtor, the opening and keeping of the accounts, the rights, duties and responsibilities of a PIP in respect of moneys received from debtors, including the transmission of money to creditors and the deduction of fees, charges and outlays due to a PIP, the accounting records to be maintained by a PIP, how money is lodged to an account, how a PIP complies with the regulations and how this is verified. The ISI can also provide regulation as to how the PIP's accounts are audited and it can also make regulation as to the enforcement of compliance with the regulation. It can also make regulation in respect of the imposition of fees on a PIP where an enquiry has been carried out and whether the ISI requires a further enquiry as the PIP did not comply with the enquiry. The fees imposed cannot be more than the cost of the further enquiry.

It is important that when the ISI makes regulations in respect of the PIP that it takes into consideration the necessity to protect both the debtor and creditor.

Regulations on Accounts and Related Matters

[8.28] Personal Insolvency Act 2012 (Accounts and Related Matters) Regulations 2013 (SI 247/2013) was enacted earlier in 2013 pursuant to s 173 PIA 2012 and applies to PIPs authorised by the ISI.[74]

Safeguarding of Funds

[8.29] A PIP shall put in place and maintain on a constant basis robust controls and arrangements to safeguard funds[75] received from or on behalf of debtors or held to the credit of debtors and to prevent the use of these funds for the own account of the PIP or any person other than the creditor or debtor so entitled.

A PIP is obliged to lodge promptly and hold all funds received from or on behalf of or to the credit of each debtor in an account with a bank authorised to carry out business in the State, solely for the purpose of receiving payments from that debtor and

72. PIA 2012, s 172 and para **8.12** above.

73. PIA 2012, s 172.

74. Personal Insolvency Act 2012 (Accounts and Related Matters) Regulations 2013 (SI 247/2013).

75. Personal Insolvency Act 2012 (Accounts and Related Matters) Regulations 2013 (SI 247/2013), s 3.

transmitting such payments to the creditors after the deduction of any fees, costs or outlays payable to the PIP under the PIA 2012 and Regulations under the PIA 2012 and in accordance with the terms of the DSA or PIA. The funds must be distributed to the creditors in accordance with their entitlements under the terms of the DSA or PIA.

All such accounts referred to in s 3(2) of the Regulations[76] above shall be designated as either a 'DSA account' or a 'PIA account', as appropriate, depending on whether the account is to be used to make and receive payments pertaining to a Debt Settlement Arrangement (in these Regulations a 'DSA account') or to a Personal Insolvency Arrangement (in these Regulations a 'PIA account'). A DSA account and a PIA account shall also contain a unique identifier that identifies the debtor that is party to the DSA or, as applicable, the PIA.

A PIP shall ensure that the funds received from or on behalf of each debtor and funds received by the PIP to which creditors are entitled under the relevant DSA or PIA are not co-mingled with those of the PIP or any other person.

The following details the specific credits or debits that may be made through a designated DSA or PIA account:

Credits (inward payments)

[8.30]

(a) funds received from or on behalf of the relevant debtor in respect of payments due under the DSA or PIA;

(b) refunds received from a creditor, the PIP or the bank for the credit of the relevant debtor in order to correct or reverse any of the debit payments outlined below.

Debits (outward payments)

[8.31]

(c) disbursements on behalf of the debtor to a creditor according to his or her entitlement under the DSA or PIA;

(d) fees, charges and other outlays due to the PIP under the PIA 2012 and Regulations pursuant to the PIA 2012 and in accordance with the DSA or PIA and for which the PIP has adequate documentary proof that the fees are properly due at the time of withdrawal;

(e) bank charges;

(f) moneys that have been transferred into the DSA or PIA account in error and for which the PIP has adequate documentary proof demonstrating the error.

A DSA or PIA account can never be overdrawn. A PIP shall ensure that the funds held in the DSA or PIA account are insulated against and not subject to claims of creditors of

76. Personal Insolvency Act 2012 (Accounts and Related Matters) Regulations 2013 (SI 247/2013).

the PIP. The PIP is required to keep adequate accounting records of his or her business practice and those other practices that are operated by the PIP or his associates.

The PIP is required to conduct reconciliations between his or her accounting records and those of the bank with whom the DSA or PIA account is held at a frequency that ensures the PIP is aware of any discrepancies. The PIP must, within one business day, notify the ISI in writing of differences identified during a reconciliation. The PIP must also notify the ISI immediately in writing where he or she has been unable to or has failed to perform a reconciliation with the necessary frequency and must provide an explanation for the failure.

The PIP must notify the bank in writing on the establishment of the account of each DSA account or PIA account that funds credited to the account do not form assets of the PIP and, for so long as the DSA account or PIA account remains open, ensure that the designation on all such accounts in the PIP's accounting records sufficiently distinguishes the funds held in those accounts from funds belonging to the PIP or other persons other than the relevant debtor.

Receipts and Statements

[8.32] A PIP shall issue a receipt to each debtor for all moneys received from or on behalf of the debtor.[77] The receipt shall include at least the following:

(a) the name of the debtor;

(b) the name of the PIP;

(c) the amount of the payment and the date it was received; and

(d) the type of the insolvency arrangement (being a DSA or PIA) to which the payment applies.

At least once every year a PIP shall issue a written statement to a debtor detailing since the beginning of the relevant insolvency arrangement or, if later, the most recent statement for the purposes of the Regulation[78] sent to the debtor:

(a) all moneys received from the debtor and the date on which they were received;

(b) the names of and the amounts paid to each creditor;

(c) the amount of fees, charges and other outlays deducted by the PIP;

(d) confirmation that the payments received and made by the PIP are in accordance with the terms of the DSA or PIA and where this is not the case the amount of and reason for any shortfall or overpayment; and

(e) the name of the PIP.

77. Personal Insolvency Act 2012 (Accounts and Related Matters) Regulations 2013 (SI 247/2013), s 8.

78. Personal Insolvency Act 2012 (Accounts and Related Matters) Regulations 2013 (SI 247/2013).

Accounting Records

[8.33] A PIP shall, on a constant basis, maintain proper records and books of account[79] pertaining to his or her role as a PIP and for each DSA or PIA under which he or she acts as a PIP.

The accounting records maintained by a PIP shall be such as to permit the ISI or any accountant or other person qualified to read or prepare accounts or financial records to readily understand:

(a) the receipts, payments and transactions with respect to each DSA or PIA for which he or she acts as a PIP, including, without limitation to the generality of the foregoing, the following information –

(i) details of all transactions representing all payments received into or disbursed from each DSA account and PIA account,

(ii) copies of all payment instructions to the bank where the DSA account(s) or PIA account(s) is or are held,

(iii) a record of all income and expenditure of the PIP in respect of each DSA or PIA with an explanation of its nature; and

(b) all assets, liabilities, income and expenditure of the business of the PIP.

The accounting records shall be maintained for a minimum period of six years (in the case of those relating to a DSA or PIA commencing after the completion or termination of the relevant insolvency arrangement) in a secure location and made available to the ISI or any person nominated in writing by the ISI in exercise of its functions. At least once each year, a PIP shall verify, in writing, to the ISI that he or she holds and maintains accounting records in accordance with the requirements of the Regulations.[80]

Financial Statements

[8.34] A PIP shall, on an annual basis and within six months of the financial year end, prepare financial statements or management accounts (if applicable) in respect of his or her practice as a PIP. The financial statements shall include an income and expenditure statement and a balance sheet or capital account statement.

If required by the ISI, the PIP shall engage an independent accountant or auditor to prepare a report confirming the accuracy of the accounts and the compliance with the Regulations[81] as set out above.

---

79. Personal Insolvency Act 2012 (Accounts and Related Matters) Regulations 2013 (SI 247/2013), s 9.

80. Personal Insolvency Act 2012 (Accounts and Related Matters) Regulations 2013 (SI 247/2013).

81. Personal Insolvency Act 2012 (Accounts and Related Matters) Regulations 2013 (SI 247/2013).

Enforcement

[8.35] The ISI is charged with monitoring compliance with the requirements set out under the Regulations as set out in para **8.27** above.[82] In cases where non-compliance comes to the attention of the ISI, the ISI may carry out an enquiry or appoint an inspector to investigate the PIP or take such other action as deemed necessary as provided for or permitted under the PIA 2012. Where the ISI has reason to believe or suspects that the financial circumstances of the PIP could affect his ability to carry out his functions as a PIP, the ISI may conduct an examination of the financial circumstances of the PIP.

The ISI may charge a fee to the PIP in these circumstances.

Protection of Debtor or Creditor

[8.36] Where the ISI determines that it is necessary to protect either a debtor or creditor who is a party to a DSA or a PIA then the ISI can apply to the High Court for an order preventing a bank from making a payment from an account in the name of a PIP.[83] A bank however may make such payment with leave of the court. The ISI can also apply to the court to prevent a PIP disposing, directing or facilitating the disposal of any assets within their possession or control or procurement[84] or reducing their assets below a specified amount or value.

These powers of the ISI equally apply to a former PIP.[85] Where the High Court makes an order upon the application of the ISI the PIP is required to immediately lodge any moneys subsequently received by them to the appropriate account unless the court orders otherwise.[86] Any application by the ISI is to be held in camera.[87] Where the High Court makes an order upon the application of the ISI, it may make a further order directing a specified bank to furnish information in its possession that the ISI requires in respect of the PIP in their capacity as a PIP.

The High Court can also require a PIP to swear an affidavit disclosing all information relating to any account held by the PIP or jointly held with third parties as a PIP. This power also extends to assets in a PIP's possession, power or procurement or which had been in their possession or control. The PIP can also be directed to attend for an oral examination in respect of the contents of the affidavit.[88]

Where the High Court is satisfied by the ISI that there is reason to believe that another person holds or has held assets on behalf of a PIP where the ISI have sought

82. Personal Insolvency Act 2012 (Accounts and Related Matters) Regulations 2013 (SI 247/2013), s 10.
83. PIA 2012, s 174.
84. PIA 2012, s 174(1)(c).
85. PIA 2012, s 174(6).
86. PIA 2012, s 174(4).
87. PIA 2012, s 174(2).
88. PIA 2012, s 174(3).

orders freezing accounts or assets then the High Court can order that person to disclose to the ISI all information as to such assets.

Complaints, Investigations and Sanctions

[8.37] The Director of the ISI is entitled to appoint persons to act as investigators from the staff of the ISI under such terms as he deems appropriate. The Director may appoint such other persons under such terms as he shall decide but subject to the approval of the Minister and the consent of the Minister for Public Expenditure and Reform.[89]

The Minister shall establish a panel of persons to act on a committee to be known as the Personal Insolvency Practitioners Complaints Committee (Complaints Committee).

Where the Complaints Committee deems the conduct of the PIP to be improper it shall determine whether the appropriate sanction is a minor sanction or a major sanction in the circumstances of the case.

Sanctions

[8.38] Minor sanction: means—

(a) the issue, to the PIP, of

- (i) advice,
- (ii) a caution,
- (iii) a warning, or
- (iv) a reprimand, or

(b) any combination of any of the sanctions specified above.

Major sanction: means—

(a) the revocation of his or her authorisation to carry on practice as a PIP and a prohibition (which may be a permanent prohibition, a prohibition for a specified period or a prohibition subject to specified conditions) against the former PIP applying for a new authorisation,

(b) the suspension for a specified period of his or her authorisation to carry on practice as a PIP or, in any case where the period of such suspension sought to be imposed is longer than the period of validity of the authorisation left to run, the suspension of the authorisation during that period and a prohibition for a specified period against the former PIP applying for a new authorisation,

(c) a direction to the PIP that the PIP pay a sum, as specified in the direction but not exceeding €30,000, to the ISI, being the whole or part of the cost to the ISI of an investigation of the PIP, or

(d) any combination of any of the sanctions specified above.

89. PIA 2012, s 176.

Improper Conduct: means –

(a) the commission by the PIP of an act which renders the PIP no longer a fit and proper person to carry on practice as a PIP,

(b) the commission by the PIP of a material contravention of a provision of the Regulations.

THE PROCESS

Initiation

[8.39] A person can make a complaint to the ISI alleging improper conduct by the PIP. This complaint must be in writing.[90]

Receipt of Complaint

[8.40] Where the ISI receives a complaint the ISI must:

(a) notify the PIP concerned in writing of the complaint;

(b) provide the PIP with a copy of the complaint and any other documents furnished in respect of the complaint;

(c) refer the PIP to any Regulations[91] and to any guidelines or codes of practice issued by the ISI;

(d) request the PIP to provide a response within a specified timeframe.

Where the PIP responds and the complaint is deemed to be frivolous

[8.41] Where the ISI receives a response to its request the ISI is then obliged to consider the response. Once it has considered the response, where it is satisfied that the complaint is (a) not made in good faith, (b) frivolous or vexatious or without substance or foundation or (c) likely to be resolved by mediation or other informal means between the parties, then the ISI may determine the complaint accordingly. In such a case the ISI shall notify, in writing, the complainant and the PIP of its decision and the reasons for its decision.[92]

Where the PIP doesn't respond or the complaint is deemed not be frivolous

[8.42] Where the ISI does not receive a response or receives a response but believes it not to be made in good faith, or does not believe the complaint is frivolous or vexatious, or does not believe that it can be determined informally then the ISI must cause an investigation of the complaint to be carried out.[93]

90. PIA 2012, s 178.

91. Personal Insolvency Act 2012 (Authorisation and Supervision of Personal Insolvency Practitioners) Regulations 2013 (SI 209/2013).

92. PIA 2012, s 178(3).

93. PIA 2012, s 178(4).

Withdrawal of complaint

[8.43] Where a complaint is withdrawn by a complainant before the investigation report has been furnished, the ISI may proceed with the complaint and the report if it is satisfied that there is good and sufficient reason for doing so.[94] Where this is the case then the investigation is to be treated as an investigation by the ISI[95] and will follow the procedures set out below.

If in the event of the complaint being dealt with by mediation or some other informal means and this process does not provide a solution then the complainant must make a fresh complaint;[96] there is nothing in the section which provides for a referral back to the Complaints Committee.

Investigations

[8.44] The ISI, following the receipt of a complaint or on its own volition, may commence an investigation[97] to identify any improper conduct by a PIP. The ISI will appoint an inspector for the purposes of carrying out the investigation. Where there are more than one investigators appointed, they will prepare a joint report. The terms of appointment of an inspector should define the scope of the investigation as respects the matters or the period to which it is to extend or otherwise and in particular limit the investigation to matters connected to particular circumstances.

On appointment the investigator shall:

(a) where the investigation is in consequence of the receipt of a complaint by the ISI –

 (i) give notice in writing to the PIP to whom the complaint relates setting out the particulars of the complaint,

 (ii) give the PIP copies of any documentation relevant to the investigation, and a copy of Ch 4 of the PIA 2012;

The investigator must give a copy of the notice to the complainant and make reasonable efforts to ensure that the complainant is kept informed of the progress of the investigation.

(b) where the investigation is on the volition of the ISI –

 (i) give notice in writing to the PIP to whom the complaint relates setting out the particulars of the complaint,

 (ii) give the PIP copies of any documentation relevant to the investigation, and a copy of Ch 4 of the PIA 2012, and afford the PIP the opportunity to respond within 21 days from the date of the notice received or such extended period as agreed with inspector but not exceeding 30 days.

---

94. PIA 2012, s 178(5).

95. PIA 2012, s 178(6).

96. PIA 2012, s 178(7).

97. PIA 2012, s 180.

An inspector may at all reasonable times enter, inspect, examine and search any premises at, or vehicles in or by means of which any activity in connection with the practice of the PIP is carried on. The inspector may also enter, inspect, examine and search any dwelling occupied by the PIP, being a dwelling which there are reasonable grounds to believe records relating to the practice of the PIP are being kept. The inspector has the power to require any person found in or on any premises, vehicle or dwelling or any person in charge of or in control of such premises, vehicle or dwelling or directing any activity relating to same to produce, or assist the inspector in any way, any records, books or accounts (whether kept in manual form or otherwise) or other documents which it is necessary for the inspector to see for the purposes of the investigation, and the inspector may inspect, examine, copy and take away any such records, books or accounts or other documents so produced or require a foregoing person to provide a copy of them or of any entries in them to the inspector. Any person who has the use or the charge of data equipment relating to any of the records, books or accounts is also obliged to assist the inspector.

The inspector is also entitled to require the PIP, the PIP's employee or the PIP's agent to give such authority in writing addressed to such bank or banks as the inspector requires for the purpose of enabling the inspection of any account or accounts opened, or caused to be opened, by the PIP at such bank or banks (or any documents relating thereto) and to obtain from such bank or banks copies of such documents relating to such account or accounts for such period or periods as the inspector deems necessary to fulfil that purpose.

The inspector is entitled to be accompanied by a member of the Garda Siochána if there is any obstruction to the exercise of his powers.

Any requirement to produce books, records or data as referred to above shall be within a specified timeframe. This also applies where the inspector believes a person who is not the PIP is in possession of the relevant information. This notice shall specify the place the information is to be delivered.

Where a person does not comply with the requirements of the inspector, the inspector is entitled to apply to the Circuit Court in a summary manner for an order requiring the person to comply. An application will be made to a judge of the court for the circuit in which the person resides or ordinarily carries on business, profession or occupation. The Circuit Court will make such an order where it is satisfied after hearing the application of the person's failure to comply. A person shall be entitled to the same immunities and privileges in respect of compliance with such requirement as if the person were a witness before the High Court. No statement made by that person will be admissible in criminal proceedings other than criminal proceedings for an offence under the provisions of s 181(17) PIA 2012 (see below).

Nothing shall be taken to compel the production by any person of any records, books or accounts (whether kept in manual form or otherwise) or other documents which he or she would be exempt from producing in proceedings in a court on the ground of legal professional privilege.

The inspector may apply to the District Court for a warrant to enter a PIP's private residence and a judge of the District Court is satisfied on the sworn evidence of the inspector that:

(a) there are reasonable grounds for suspecting that information is, or records, books, or accounts or other documents required by the inspector are, held on the premises or any part of the premises; and

(b) the inspector has been prevented from entering the premises or it is necessary to enter the private dwelling to exercise the powers under the PIA 2012.

The inspector may, if he deems it necessary to do so, conduct an oral hearing with the PIP.

A person will be guilty of an offence where the person:

(a) withholds, destroys, conceals or refuses to provide any information or records, books or accounts (whether kept in manual form or otherwise) or other documents required for the purposes of an investigation;

(b) fails or refuses to comply with any requirement of an inspector under this section; or

(c) otherwise obstructs or hinders an inspector in the performance of functions.

Where a PIP is convicted of an offence as outlined above, his authorisation to act as a PIP may be revoked by the court and a time period set before an application for a new authorisation can be made.

Preparation of Report

[8.45] Where an inspector has completed an investigation, the inspector shall prepare a draft of the investigation report of which it must give a copy to the PIP to whom the investigation relates, the complainant (where investigation is on foot of a complaint) and the ISI.[98] Each party will be invited to make written submissions within 30 days of receipt of the draft report or such longer period as the investigator agrees. Following the consideration of the submissions, the investigator shall prepare a final report and submit the finalised report to each of the parties.

Report Findings

[8.46] Where the investigation report states that the inspector is satisfied that improper conduct[99] by the PIP has occurred or is occurring, the inspector shall not make any recommendation or express any opinion as to the form of sanction he or she feels ought to be imposed in respect of the improper conduct.[100]

---

98. PIA 2012, s 182.
99. See para **8.38**.
100. PIA 2012, s 182(3).

Complaints Committee

[8.47] Where the Complaints Committee[101] receives an inspector's report it shall invite the PIP, the ISI and the complainant (where applicable) to make written submissions on the matters raised in the inspector's report within 30 days of the issue of the invitation or such further period as the Complaints Committee shall allow.

Where the Complaints Committee feels it is appropriate to do so, it may conduct an oral hearing.

Having completed its review, the Complaints Committee shall make a determination on the conduct of the PIP. In each case of a determination by the Complaints Committee, it shall furnish a copy of the determination to the PIP, the ISI and the complainant (where applicable).

Improper Conduct

[8.48] Where it considers the conduct not to be improper, it shall dismiss the complaint.

Minor Sanction

[8.49] Where the Complaints Committee considers the conduct to be improper conduct and the appropriate sanction to be a minor sanction, it shall determine which minor sanction applies in the circumstances of the case and shall impose that sanction.

Major Sanction

[8.50] Where the Complaints Committee considers the conduct to be improper conduct and the appropriate sanction to be a major sanction, it shall determine which major sanction applies in the circumstances of the case and shall refer the case to the High Court and make a recommendation as to the appropriate sanction.

High Court

[8.51] Where the matter is referred to the High Court,[102] it shall determine whether the appropriate sanction is a minor or major sanction in the circumstances of the case, having given all parties the opportunity to make submissions. Where the High Court determines that the appropriate sanction is a minor sanction, it shall determine which minor sanction applies and shall impose that sanction. Where the High Court determines that the appropriate sanction is a major sanction, it shall determine which major sanction applies and shall impose that sanction.

Appeal to High Court against a Determination by the Complaints Committee

[8.52] A PIP, the subject of a determination by the Complaints Committee[103] of improper conduct and that a minor sanction applies in respect of that improper conduct,

---

101. PIA 2012, s 182(4).
102. See para **6.20** – Court Procedures.
103. PIA 2012, s 183.

may appeal the decision to the High Court within 30 days of the notice of the determination by the Complaints Committee. The High Court may hear any evidence adduced or argument made, whether or not adduced or advanced to the inspector or the Complaints Committee.

The High Court, on hearing the appeal, may:

(a) (i) confirm the decision the subject of the appeal,

(ii) determine that the conduct concerned does not constitute improper conduct, or

(iii) confirm the determination that the conduct concerned does constitute improper conduct and impose a different sanction on the PIP, and

(b) make such order as to costs as it deems appropriate in respect of the appeal.

Matters to Be Considered in Determining the Appropriate Sanction

[8.53] The Complaints Committee and the High Court in determining whether a major or minor sanction applies shall take into account the circumstances of the improper conduct of the PIP and should have regard to:[104]

(a) the need to ensure that any sanction imposed—

(i) is appropriate and proportionate to the improper conduct, and

(ii) if applicable, will act as a sufficient deterrent to discourage improper conduct of that or a similar nature in the future;

(c) the seriousness of the improper conduct;

(d) the extent of any failure by the PIP to co-operate with the investigation concerned of the PIP;

(e) any excuse or explanation by the PIP for the improper conduct or failure to co-operate with the investigation concerned;

(f) any gain (financial or otherwise) made by the PIP or by any person in which the PIP has a financial interest as a consequence of the improper conduct;

(g) the amount of any loss suffered or costs incurred as a result of the improper conduct;

(h) the duration of the improper conduct;

(i) the repeated occurrence of improper conduct by the PIP;

(j) if applicable, the continuation of the improper conduct after the PIP was notified of the investigation concerned;

(k) if applicable, the absence, ineffectiveness or repeated failure of internal mechanisms or procedures of the PIP intended to prevent improper conduct from occurring;

104. PIA 2012, s 184.

(l) if applicable, the extent and timeliness of any steps taken to end the improper conduct and any steps taken for remedying the consequences of the improper conduct;

(m) whether a sanction in respect of similar improper conduct has already been imposed on the PIP by a court or the Complaints Committee; and

(n) any precedents set by a court or the Complaints Committee in respect of previous improper conduct.

Publication of Sanction

[8.54] The ISI is entitled to publish particulars in whatever form prescribed by it and for such period it deems appropriate of:[105]

(a) the conviction of a person of an offence;[106]

(b) a decision of the ISI refusing to renew an authorisation of a PIP;

(c) the suspension of a PIP[107]; and

(d) the imposition of a major sanction.

Suspension of a PIP

[8.55] Where the ISI considers it necessary to suspend a PIP[108] in order to protect debtors and creditors who are or may become parties to a DSA or a PIA, it may apply to the High Court for an order to suspend the PIP's authorisation to carry on practice as a PIP.[109] This application can be made in a summary manner but it must be on notice to the PIP.

The High Court has a wide discretion in this regard as it is open to the court to make 'any order that it considers appropriate, including an order suspending the authorisation of the PIP for such period or until the occurrence of such an event is specified in the order'.[110] The High Court may also give the ISI any other direction as it deems appropriate. Where the ISI is required to comply with directions of the High Court, the ISI must notify the PIP of its compliance with the direction and this notice must be in writing.[111]

Where the ISI consider that the immediate suspension of an authorisation of a PIP to carry on practice is necessary due to immediate risk of financial harm to debtors and creditors then the ISI may apply to the High Court *ex parte* for an interim order to suspend the authorisation.[112] The debtor and creditors need to be a party to a DSA or a

105. PIA 2012, s 185.
106. See para **8.39**.
107. See para **8.55**.
108. PIA 2012, s 179.
109. PIA 2012, s 179.
110. PIA 2012, s 179(2).
111. PIA 2012, s 179(3).
112. PIA 2012, s 179(4).

PIA or who may become parties to either arrangement. This means that the ISI can extend its powers to debtors and creditors who are not a party to an arrangement but may become a party, which extends the scope for such an order being made. This application must be grounded on an affidavit sworn on behalf of the ISI.[113]

The High Court can make an interim order to suspend an authorisation having had regard to the circumstances of the case and where the court deems it necessary to make such an order for the protection of debtors and creditors who are or may become parties to an arrangement.[114] If the High Court does make an interim order then a copy of the order and the affidavit grounding the application must be sent to the PIP as soon as is practicable.[115] The interim order made shall have effect for a period not exceeding 14 days. The order must specify the period for which the order is to have effect, which is to be less than 14 days.[116] If the time has not elapsed and the High Court makes a determination pursuant to an application on notice, ie s 179(1) PIA 2012, then the interim order will cease to have effect.[117]

Applications for suspension shall be heard in camera unless the High Court considers it appropriate to hear the application in public.[118]

Unauthorised Person acting as PIP

[8.56] A person shall not act as a PIP or hold himself or herself out as available to act as a PIP or represent himself or herself by advertisement as available as a PIP unless that person is authorised to do so under the PIA 2012.[119] Any person who acts in contravention of this shall be guilty of an offence.

113. PIA 2012, s 179(4)(b).
114. PIA 2012, s 179(5).
115. PIA 2012, s 179(6)(b).
116. PIA 2012, s 179(6)(c).
117. PIA 2012, s 179(6)(c).
118. PIA 2012, s 179(6).
119. PIA 2012, s 160.

Chapter 9

OFFENCES

INTRODUCTION

[9.01] The Personal Insolvency Act 2012 (PIA 2012) makes provision for a number of offences. The majority of offences are particular to prospective or specified debtors during the term of an insolvency arrangement. However, there are sections that are not so restrictive in their application and Approved Intermediaries (AIs) and Personal Insolvency Practitioners (PIPs) would need to be aware of the potential to commit an offence under these sections and take any necessary precautions to ensure that there is no inadvertent offence committed.

OFFENCES

False and Misleading Information[1]

[9.02] A person who knowingly or recklessly provides information which information is false or misleading in a material respect and is used in an application for a Debt Relief Notice[2] (DRN) or an application for a protective certificate in a Debt Settlement Arrangement[3] (DSA) or a Personal Insolvency Arrangement[4] (PIA) will be guilty of an offence.

There is no definition of what constitutes 'in a material respect' in determining whether an individual is guilty of an offence under this section. It is the view of the authors that this section is seeking to capture false or misleading information that would affect the debtor's entitlement to apply for a DRN or a protective certificate in a DSA or PIA.

The section is not specific to the debtor and therefore where an AI, a PIP or a creditor knowingly or recklessly provides false or misleading information they may be guilty of an offence under this section. In seeking protection against inadvertently committing an offence under this section, an AI or a PIP should ensure that all information provided by the debtor has been verified or statutorily declared.

Breach of Debtor's Obligations

[9.03] It is only the specified debtor and not an AI or a PIP that can be found guilty of an offence under this section.[5] A specified debtor is a debtor who is engaged in one of the three insolvency processes.

---

1. PIA 2012, s 26.
2. PIA 2012, s 29.
3. PIA 2012, s 59.
4. PIA 2012, s 93.
5. PIA 2012, s 127.

A specified debtor who breaches his obligations in applying for a DRN will be guilty of an offence if he (a) intentionally fails to comply with his obligations as required pursuant to a DRN application[6] or (b) provides information to the ISI in connection with such a duty or otherwise in connection with the performance by the ISI of its functions under a DRN application which is false or misleading in a material respect.[7]

There is no definition of what constitutes a 'in a material respect' in determining whether an individual is guilty of an offence under this section.

A specified debtor who breaches his obligations in applying for a protective certificate in a DSA will be guilty of an offence if he (a) intentionally fails to comply with his obligations as required pursuant to an application for a protective certificate in a DSA[8] or (b) provides information to the ISI in connection with such a duty or otherwise in connection with the performance by the ISI of its functions under an application for a protective certificate in a DSA which is false or misleading in a material respect.[9]

A specified debtor who breaches his obligations in applying for a protective certificate in a PIA will be guilty of an offence if he (a) intentionally fails to comply with his obligations as required pursuant to an application for a protective certificate in a PIA[10] or (b) provides information to the ISI in connection with such a duty or otherwise in connection with the performance by the ISI of its functions under an application for a protective certificate in a PIA which is false or misleading in a material respect.[11]

Concealment or Falsification of Documents

[9.04] This section provides for an offence relating to failure to provide, concealment, destruction, falsification or alteration of financial records by a debtor for the purpose of obtaining a PIA or avoiding its obligations as a debtor under the PIA 2012.[12]

A 'financial record' for the purposes of this section is defined as a book, document or record relating to that person's financial affairs.

A person who is:[13]

(a) obtaining an insolvency arrangement;

(b) avoiding an obligation under s 36 PIA 2012 (ie specified debtor obligations pursuant to a DRN);[14]

(c) obtaining a protective certificate pursuant to a DSA or PIA;

6. PIA 2012, s 36. See para **3.21** – Debt Relief Notices.
7. PIA 2012, s 127(1).
8. PIA 2012, s 81(3) and (6). See para **4.38** – Debt Settlement Arrangements.
9. PIA 2012, s 127(2).
10. PIA 2012, s 113(3) and (6). See para **5.40** – Personal Insolvency Arrangements.
11. PIA 2012, s 127(3).
12. PIA 2012, s 128.
13. PIA 2012, s 128(1).
14. See para **3.21** – Debt Relief Notices.

(d) avoiding an obligation under a DSA or PIA (ie debtor obligations under a DSA or PIA);[15]

(e) avoiding the variation or termination of a DRN, DSA or PIA;

(f) avoiding any other obligation under the PIA 2012;

is guilty of an offence where that person commits any of the following acts[16] in so doing:

(a) fails to provide at the request of the ISI all of the financial records of which he has possession or control;

(b) prevents the production to the ISI of a financial record;

(c) conceals, destroys, mutilates or makes any omission in, or causes or permits the concealment, destruction mutilation or falsification of, a financial record;

(d) makes, or causes or permits the making of, any false entries in a financial record; or

(e) disposes of, or alters or makes any omission in, or causes or permits the disposal, altering or making of any omission in, a financial record.

The section only applies to a person:[17]

(a) on whose behalf an application is made for a DRN, a DSA or a PIA;

(b) who is a specified debtor under a DRN for so long as the DRN remains in effect;

(c) who is party, as a debtor, to a DSA while the DSA remains in effect;

(d) who is a party, as a debtor, to a PIA while the PIA remains in effect.

The section appears only to have application to debtors who intend to apply for and specified debtors who are party to a DRN, DSA or PIA. The section does not extend to AIs and PIPs.

Fraudulent Disposal of Property

[9.05] This section provides for an offence where there is disposal of property by way of a gift or at an undervalue by a debtor for the purposes of obtaining an insolvency arrangement or protective certificate or avoiding its obligations as a debtor under the PIA 2012.[18] The section only applies where the value of the property is greater than €400.

The section only applies to a person:[19]

(a) on whose behalf an application is made for a DRN, a DSA or a PIA;

---

15. See para **4.38** – Debt Settlement Arrangements, and para **5.40** – Personal Insolvency Arrangements.
16. PIA 2012, s 128(2).
17. PIA 2012, s 128(3).
18. PIA 2012, s 129.
19. PIA 2012, s 129(4).

(b) who is a specified debtor under a DRN for so long as the DRN remains in effect;

(c) who is party, as a debtor, to a DSA while the DSA remains in effect;

(d) who is a party, as a debtor, to a PIA while the PIA remains in effect.

The section appears only to have application to prospective debtors and specified debtors who are party to a DRN, DSA or PIA. The section does not extend to AIs and PIPs.

A person commits an act[20] as set out in the section where he makes or causes to be made a gift of any of his property to another person, or makes or causes to be made any transfer of his property on terms where no consideration is received by him, or enters a transaction whereby his property is transferred to another person or a third party (who may or may not be a party to the transfer) for a consideration significantly lower than the value in money or money's worth of the property where, in all circumstances, the value of the property is greater than €400.[21]

A person is guilty of an offence where any of these acts are for the purpose of:

(a) obtaining an insolvency arrangement;

(b) avoiding an obligation under s 36 PIA 2012 (ie specified debtor obligations pursuant to a DRN);[22]

(c) obtaining a protective certificate pursuant to a DSA or PIA;

(d) avoiding an obligation under a DSA or a PIA (ie debtor obligations under a DSA or PIA);[23]

(e) avoiding the variation or termination of a DRN, DSA or PIA;

(f) avoiding any other obligation under the PIA 2012.

Obtaining Credit

[9.06] A specified debtor is not entitled to obtain credit[24] either alone or with any other person in an amount of more than €650 without informing the person from whom the credit is obtained of his name as specified in the DRN, DSA or PIA and of the fact that he is a specified debtor.[25]

A specified debtor is a person:[26]

(a) on whose behalf an application is made for a DRN, a DSA or a PIA;

20. PIA 2012, s 129(2).
21. PIA 2012, s 129(3).
22. See para **3.21** – Debt Relief Notices.
23. See para **4.38** – Debt Settlement Arrangements, and para **5.40** – Personal Insolvency Arrangements.
24. PIA 2012, s 130.
25. PIA 2012, s 130(1).
26. PIA 2012, s 130(2).

(b) who is a specified debtor under a DRN for so long as the DRN remains in effect;

(c) who is party, as a debtor, to a DSA while the DSA remains in effect;

(d) who is a party, as a debtor, to a PIA while the PIA remains in effect.

Obtaining credit includes situations where (a) goods are bailed to the debtor under a hire-purchase agreement or agreed to be sold to him under a conditional sale agreement, and (b) where he is paid in advance (in money or otherwise) for the supply of goods or services.[27]

Unauthorised Person Acting as an AI

[9.07] A person who acts as an AI or holds himself or herself out to be an AI or who represents himself or herself by advertisement as available to act as an AI and who is not authorised to so act is guilty of an offence.[28]

Unauthorised Person acting as a PIP

[9.08] A person shall not act as a PIP or hold himself or herself out as available to act as a PIP or represent himself or herself by advertisement as available as a PIP unless that person is authorised to do so under the PIA 2012.[29] Any person who acts in contravention of this shall be guilty of an offence.

Please see **Ch 8** – Personal Insolvency Practitioners[30] for further information on offences committed by a PIP or by other persons in obstructing an investigator when conducting an investigation into the conduct of a PIP.

Prosecution

[9.09] Where a person is convicted of an offence under this act then they can be summarily prosecuted by the ISI.[31]

Such prosecutions will take place in the District Court. Prosecutions on indictment will be brought by the Director of Public Prosecutions.[32]

Where someone is convicted of an offence under the PIA 2012 he shall be liable:

(a) on summary conviction to a Class A fine or to a period of imprisonment not exceeding 12 months or to both, or

27. PIA 2012, s 130(3).

28. PIA 2012, s 131.

29. PIA 2012, s 160.

30. Para **8.37** – Complaints, Investigations and Sanctions.

31. PIA 2012, s 132.

32. Article 30.3 of the Constitution provides that indictable offences are prosecuted at the suit of the People and this function is currently carried out by the Director of Public Prosecutions.

(b) on conviction on indictment to a fine not exceeding €100,000 or to imprisonment for a term not exceeding five years or both.

Chapter 10

BANKRUPTCY ACT AMENDMENTS

INTRODUCTION

[10.01] Part 4, Personal Insolvency Act 2012 (PIA 2012) deals with the amendments to the Bankruptcy Act 1988 required to give effect to the PIA 2012. The Bankruptcy Act 1988 (BA 1988) has been further amended by the provisions of the Courts and Civil Law (Miscellaneous Provisions) Act 2013. The Commencement Orders for Pt 4, PIA 2012 and for the amendments under the Courts and Civil Law (Miscellaneous Provisions) Act 2013 were signed into law on 3 December 2013.

The main changes to the bankruptcy legislation are the threshold to present a petition for bankruptcy has been increased from €1,900 to €20,000; the automatic period of discharge from bankruptcy has reduced from twelve years to three years and the threshold of exempted assets has been doubled to €6,000.

It is now also a requirement for a debtor presenting their own petition or a creditor presenting a petition to demonstrate that efforts to reach agreement using the other insolvency procedures under the PIA 2012 have been made (subject to the debtor meeting the qualifying criteria).

OVERVIEW OF BANKRUPTCY PROCEDURE

[10.02] Bankruptcy is a process where the property or assets of an individual who is unable or unwilling to pay their debts (called a debtor) is transferred to a person given charge of the property by the High Court (called a trustee) to be sold. In nearly all cases, the Official Assignee in Bankruptcy, an officer of the Courts Service, is the trustee to whom this property is transferred.[1] This is the person who administers the estate of bankrupt persons.

When the property or assets are sold, the costs, expenses, court fees and certain priority debts are paid. After this, the net proceeds are distributed to those owed money (the creditors).

Bankruptcy proceedings are brought in the High Court. The application for a bankruptcy order (as well as any other application for the bankruptcy list of the High Court) is filed in the Office of the Examiner of the High Court. Following this, the proceedings are dealt with by the High Court.

The High Court makes a debtor bankrupt either at the request of a creditor or at his own request. In either case, this request is made in a document called a petition. This must be filed in the Office of the Examiner of the High Court.

1. For more information please see http://www.isi.gov.ie/en/ISI/Pages/What_is_Bankruptcy.

Debtor

[10.03] A debtor may bring a petition for his or her own bankruptcy where he or she is unable to pay debts to creditors and where his or her available estate is sufficient to produce at least €1,900.00. The requirement for the debtor to prove that his estate is sufficient to produce at least €1,900 has been removed by s 148 PIA 2012.[2]

Creditor

[10.04] A creditor may petition for bankruptcy against a debtor where a debtor has committed an act of bankruptcy within the previous three months. The most common acts of bankruptcy relied upon by a creditor are:

(a) failure by the debtor to comply with a bankruptcy summons requesting payment of a specific sum due within fourteen days from service of the summons on the debtor; and

(b) the making of a return of no goods in respect of the debtor by the sheriff or county registrar.

The first step in bankruptcy proceedings is that an act of bankruptcy must be committed by the debtor and the creditor must be able to prove it to the court.

Where judgment has not been obtained by the creditor, a formal notice of demand called 'particulars of demand and notice requiring payment prior to the issue of a bankruptcy summons' form must be forwarded to the debtor. The debtor has four working days to respond to this notice.

If no response is received, the creditor may proceed to apply to the court for the issue of a bankruptcy summons. A bankruptcy summons will only be issued when it is proved that the creditor has exhausted all other means of execution of the judgement.

A bankruptcy summons must be served within 28 days of issue by delivering to the debtor a sealed copy of the summons together with a Bankruptcy Summons affidavit. The summons server must endorse in the summons the day and date of service. Following the service the debtor has a period of 14 days to make a payment or to apply to the court to have the summons dismissed.

If no such application is made and the debtor has not paid the debt within the time limit, he is deemed to have committed an 'act of bankruptcy' and the creditor is now in a position to petition to the High Court to adjudicate the debtor bankrupt.

The creditor's petition must be made within three months after the date the act of bankruptcy has taken place.

For a creditor to be entitled to petition the court to make a debtor bankrupt, a number of conditions must be met. These include:

(a) the petition must be presented within three months of the act of bankruptcy;

(b) the amount of debt owed must be set out in an affidavit;

(c) the debt owed must be at least €1,900.00;

2. See para **10.18** below.

(d) the debtor must be either resident in the State or within a year prior to presentation of the petition have ordinarily resided, had a dwelling house or place of business or carried on business within the State.

Discharge from Bankruptcy

[10.05] A bankrupt may be discharged from bankruptcy in a number of ways which are set out below. No bankrupt can be discharged unless there are enough funds to pay:

(a) the costs of the Official Assignee;

(b) High Court fees;

(c) the costs of the petitioning creditor;

(d) the preferential debts of the bankrupt.

When someone is discharged from bankruptcy, any funds or properties remaining with the Official Assignee are returned to the former bankrupt.

(a) Discharge after payment of debts in full.

This is where the bankrupt's creditors are paid in full. If the High Court so allows, interest may also be payable. Normally, interest is only paid where surplus funds are available.

(b) Discharge with the creditors' consent.

This is where all of the bankrupt's unsecured creditors consent to the discharge.

(c) Discharge after making composition with the creditors.

This is where unsecured creditors agree to accept payment of a certain percentage of their debt in settlement of the full amount. This must be supported by at least 60 per cent in number and value of those creditors who vote at a sitting of the High Court for this to be accepted. The bankrupt must provide the Official Assignee with sufficient funds to make this settlement and pay his/her unsecured creditors. This is called an Offer of Composition.

(d) Discharge after paying fifty cent in the Euro.

This is where all of the bankrupt's property has been fully sold or disposed of and his/her creditors have received fifty cent in the Euro on their debts.

(e) Discharge after five years.

This is where the bankruptcy has lasted for five years and all of the bankrupt's property has been fully sold or disposed of. The court must be satisfied that the bankrupt has disclosed any property acquired since his/her bankruptcy and that it would be reasonable and proper to discharge the debtor from bankruptcy.

(f) Automatic discharge after twelve years.

Discharge of the bankrupt person is automatic on the twelfth anniversary of the order of adjudication.

Bankruptcy Implications for Creditor

[10.06] The creditor must make a claim in the bankruptcy for payment and cannot use normal remedies to secure payment as of the date of the adjudication in bankruptcy.

In order for a creditor to have their debt included in the bankruptcy, they must prove their debt to the satisfaction of the Official Assignee. This means the creditor must provide evidence of their debt to the Official Assignee – for example, invoices, bank statements, judgment orders or affidavit of debt.

An advertisement for creditors will be placed in newspapers during the bankruptcy process which asks creditors to submit proof of their debt to the Official Assignee. Dividends to creditors will only be paid after this advertisement appears and a proof of debt sitting is held by the Official Assignee. This is where the Official Assignee decides if a debt (or the amount of a debt) is admitted.

All creditors are entitled to examine the proofs of other creditors. Only debts owed on the date of adjudication are admitted under the bankruptcy. The High Court decides on disputed debts. This is where the bankrupt and the creditor do not agree on the amount owed or the amount admitted by the Official Assignee.

The amount paid to a creditor in a bankruptcy will depend on a number of factors:

(a) the amount of funds available for distribution;

(b) the status of the creditor's debt;

(c) the value of the bankrupt's estate;

(d) the method of discharge.

A creditor may be a secured or unsecured creditor or a preferential creditor. An unsecured creditor ranks in priority with all other unsecured creditors in the bankruptcy. A secured creditor holds security such as a mortgage or judgment against a property owned by the bankrupt. A secured creditor can rely upon this security and sell the secured asset. They must account to the Official Assignee in respect of the sale and may claim for any amount (if any) still owed following the sale.

After this and payment of any other secured claims, a secured creditor must pay any surplus to the Official Assignee and/or others having an equity in the property. There can be a number of creditors holding security against a single property. Alternatively, a secured creditor may abandon their security and make a claim as an unsecured creditor for the entire debt.

A preferential creditor is a creditor whose debts have priority for payment before other creditors. These include taxes, rates and certain kinds of employee claims and benefits. These must be paid in full before a bankruptcy is discharged.

Bankruptcy Implications for the Bankrupt

[10.07] A bankrupt must co-operate fully with the Official Assignee's office in all matters relating to the bankruptcy.

Initially a bankrupt must attend an interview with the Official Assignee. A bankrupt must also file a Statement of Affairs in the Office of the Examiner of the High Court. This document sets out all of the bankrupt's financial details including assets held and all amounts owed by the bankrupt. The statutory court sitting will only be passed in the High Court when this Statement of Affairs has been filed.

The bankrupt will also have other legal obligations in connection with the administration of their estate and assets, including:

(a) the delivery of accounts or papers to the Official Assignee when requested;

(b) the delivery of title deeds to property and any other possessions to the Official Assignee;

(c) assisting the Official Assignee in the administration of the estate; and

(d) disclosing any property acquired since the date of the bankruptcy order to the Official Assignee.

All property held by the bankrupt when made bankrupt vests in the Official Assignee for the benefit of the bankrupt's creditors. The role of the Official Assignee is to realise this property and distribute the proceeds to the creditors in order of priority. A vesting certificate is lodged in the Office of the Examiner of the High Court and with the Property Registration Authority. This document records the interest of the Official Assignee in any property held by the bankrupt at the date of adjudication.

The only property that does not vest in the Official Assignee is essentials up to a value of €6,000[3] (previously €3,100.00), or more if the High Court allows. Any property acquired after the bankruptcy transfers to the Official Assignee, if and when the Official Assignee claims it. Under EU legislation, (EU Insolvency Regulations 2002), these provisions can be extended to property of the bankrupt that is owned abroad.

A bankrupt may operate a bank account but if credit of €650.00 or more is obtained without disclosing the bankruptcy, the bankrupt will be guilty of an offence.

A bankrupt may not act as a director, auditor, manager, liquidator or receiver of a company and is not entitled to hold elected representative office in local authorities, in the Dáil or in the Seanad.

The bankrupt's interest in the family home vests in the Official Assignee as with all other property.

However the Official Assignee may not sell the family home without obtaining permission from the High Court. Where the Official Assignee seeks this permission, the High Court may postpone the sale of the family home having regard to the interests of the creditors and of any spouse and dependants of the bankrupt. Where there is a secured loan against the property, the Official Assignee's interest only relates to the equity remaining in the property. Where the bankrupt owns property jointly with a spouse or partner, the bankruptcy causes the joint ownership to be split. The Official Assignee and the non-bankrupt co-owner then hold separate interests in the property.

The Official Assignee may apply to court for the appropriation of part of the bankrupt's salary, income or pension. If the High Court directs any deduction to be

3. PIA 2012, s 151.

made, it may have regard to the bankrupt's family responsibilities and personal situation.[4] Social welfare and unemployment payments are not liable to appropriation.

Bankruptcy Legislation

[10.08] The main provisions of bankruptcy law are contained in the BA 1988, as amended by the PIA 2012 (these amendments are detailed at para **10.13** below). The bankruptcy rules of court and forms are contained in Order 76 and Appendix O of the Rules of the Superior Courts 1986.

INSOLVENCY PROCESSES

[10.09] Where a debtor avails of any of the three insolvency processes under the PIA 2012 its creditors are restrained from taking certain actions which are outlined below, one of which is presenting a petition for bankruptcy. An application for adjudication in bankruptcy against the debtor may be made by a creditor or the debtor on the ending, termination or failure of a Debt Relief Notice (DRN), a Debt Settlement Arrangement (DSA) or a Personal Insolvency Arrangement (PIA).

Debt Relief Notice

[10.10] Where a debtor qualifies for a DRN, he enters a supervision period for the duration of the DRN.[5] During the supervision period[6] a specified creditor cannot:[7]

(a) initiate any legal proceedings in relation to a specified debt;

(b) take any step to prosecute any such legal proceedings already initiated;

(c) take any step to secure or recover payment of a specified debt;

(d) execute or enforce a judgment or order of a court or tribunal against the debtor in respect of a specified debt;

(e) take any step to recover goods in the possession or custody of the debtor (whether or not title to the goods is vested in the specified creditor);

(f) contact the specified debtor regarding payment of a specified debt, otherwise than at the request of the debtor;

(g) in relation to an agreement with the specified debtor, by reason only that the debtor is insolvent or that the DRN concerned is in effect –

  (i) terminate or amend that agreement, or

  (ii) claim an accelerated payment, or a forfeiture of a term, under that agreement.

---

4. See **Ch 7** – Reasonable Living Expenses.
5. See **Ch 3** – Debt Relief Notices.
6. See **Ch 3**, para **3.20**.
7. PIA 2012, s 35(1).

Furthermore a specified creditor shall not, during the supervision period, in respect of a specified debt, apply to proceed with:

(a) a bankruptcy petition relating to the debtor;

(b) a summons under s 8 of the BA 1988; or

(c) a petition to have the specified debtor concerned adjudicated a bankrupt in respect of a specified qualifying debt.

No other proceedings, execution or other legal process may be commenced or continued against the specified debtor or his property without leave of the court during the supervision period. The court can stay any such proceedings, execution or other legal processes for such period as the court deems appropriate.

The supervision period does not prevent a specified creditor pursuing any person that has guaranteed a debt of the specified debtor. The supervision period does not prohibit a specified creditor from taking action against a person who has jointly contracted with the specified debtor concerned or is jointly liable with that specified debtor to the specified creditor unless that other person has obtained the protection of a DSA or a PIA. The person who has jointly contracted may sue or be sued in respect of the contract without joining the specified debtor[8] unless the other person is under the protection of a DSA or a PIA.

The supervision period is disregarded when reckoning any period for the purposes of a limitation period under the statute of limitations for any proceedings or process in respect of a DRN.[9] It seems that the supervision period is excluded even where a person pursuing the specified debtor is unaware of that debtor being under the protection of a specified debt. Similarly the period for which any judgment against the specified debtor in relation to a specified qualifying debt has effect shall be extended by the period that the DRN is in effect – ie for the duration of the supervision period.[10]

Debt Settlement Arrangements

[10.11] Where a debtor qualifies for a DSA he is protected under a protective certificate which remains in situ until a DSA is agreed with his creditors.[11] A creditor to whom notice of the issue of a protective certificate[12] has been given shall not, whilst the protective certificate remains in force:

(a) initiate any legal proceedings in relation to a debt which is a specified debt;

(b) take any step to prosecute legal proceedings already initiated;

(c) execute or enforce a judgment held against the debtor in respect of a specified debt;

8. PIA 2012, s 35(5).
9. PIA 2012, s 35(7).
10. PIA 2012, s 35(8).
11. See **Ch 4** – Debt Settlement Arrangements.
12. See **Ch 4**, para **4.21**.

(d) take any step to recover goods in the possession or custody of the debtor (whether or not title to the goods is vested in the creditor);

(e) contact the debtor regarding payment of the debt otherwise than at the request of the debtor;

(f) in relation to an agreement with the debtor, including a security agreement, by reason only that the debtor is insolvent or that the protective certificate has been issued—

(i) terminate or amend that agreement, or

(ii) claim an accelerated payment, or a forfeiture of a term, under that agreement.

Where a creditor has been notified of the granting of a protective certificate, whilst the protective certificate remains in force no bankruptcy petition relating to the debtor may be presented by a creditor or, in a case where the petition has been presented by a creditor, may be proceeded with.

In addition to the specific provision above, there is a general protection[13] afforded to the debtor such that no other proceedings, no enforcement of security and no execution or other legal process may be commenced or continued against the debtor or his or her property, except with the leave of the court and subject to any order the court may make to stay such proceedings, enforcement or execution for such period as the court deems appropriate pending the outcome of attempts to reach a DSA.

It should be noted that the protective certification does not extend to protect any guarantor of the debts of the debtor or a person who has jointly contracted with the debtor or is jointly liable with the debtor to the creditor and that other person may sue or be sued in respect of the contract without joining the debtor.[14]

The period of protective certification and any extension to this period does not affect any period for the purposes of the Statute of Limitations 1957[15] or period in relation to any proceedings or process (ie the period of protective certification is disregarded). This may be of relevance in the event that a DSA is unsuccessful.

During the DSA, creditors are subject to certain restrictions once a DSA becomes effective.[16] Creditors cannot:

(a) initiate any legal proceedings in relation to a specified debt;

(b) take any step to prosecute such legal proceedings already initiated;

(c) take any step to secure or recover payment of a specified debt;

(d) execute or enforce a judgment or order of a court or tribunal against the debtor in respect of a specified debt;

(e) take any step to recover goods in the possession or custody of the debtor (whether or not title to the goods is vested in the creditor);

13. PIA 2012, s 62(3).
14. PIA 2012, s 62(4) and (5).
15. PIA 2012, s 62(7).
16. PIA 2012, s 79(3).

(f) otherwise initiate contact with the debtor in respect of payment of a specified debt;

(g) in relation to an agreement with the debtor, including a security agreement, by reason only that the debtor is insolvent or that a DSA is in effect—

 (i) terminate or amend that agreement, or

 (ii) claim an accelerated payment, or a forfeiture of a term, under that agreement.

Furthermore, while a DSA is in effect, a creditor of that debtor shall not apply for the issue of a summons under s 8 of the BA 1988 or present a petition to have the debtor concerned adjudicated a bankrupt in respect of a debt covered by the DSA.[17]

A creditor is not precluded from taking an action as respects a person who has jointly contracted with the debtor or is jointly liable with the debtor to the creditor and that other person may sue or be sued in respect of the contract without joining the debtor.[18]

The period in which the DSA is in effect shall be disregarded for the purpose of any applicable limitation period in relation to any proceedings or process to which this section applies (including any limitation period under the Statute of Limitations 1957).[19] Equally, the period for which any judgment against the debtor in relation to a debt which is the subject of a DSA has effect (whether under statute or rule of court) shall, subject to the provisions of this Act, be extended by the period that the DSA is in effect.[20]

Personal Insolvency Arrangements

[10.12] Where a debtor qualifies for a PIA, he is protected under a protective certificate which remains in situ until a PIA is agreed with his creditors.[21] A creditor to whom notice of the issue of a protective certificate[22] has been given shall not, whilst the protective certificate remains in force:

(a) initiate any legal proceedings in relation to a debt which is a specified debt;

(b) take any step to prosecute legal proceedings already initiated;

(c) execute or enforce a judgment held against the debtor in respect of a specified debt;

(d) take any step to recover goods in the possession or custody of the debtor (whether or not title to the goods is vested in the creditor);

(e) contact the debtor regarding payment of the debt otherwise than at the request of the debtor;

17. PIA 2012, s 79(5).
18. PIA 2012, s 79(6).
19. PIA 2012, s 79(8).
20. PIA 2012, s 79(9).
21. See **C 5** – Personal Insolvency Arrangements.
22. See **Ch 5**, para **5.21**.

(f) in relation to an agreement with the debtor, including a security agreement, by reason only that the debtor is insolvent or that the protective certificate has been issued—

(i) terminate or amend that agreement, or

(ii) claim an accelerated payment, or a forfeiture of a term, under that agreement.

Where a creditor has been notified of the granting of a protective certificate, whilst the protective certificate remains in force no bankruptcy petition relating to the debtor may be presented by a creditor or, in a case where the petition has been presented by a creditor, may be proceeded with.

In addition to the specific provision above, there is a general protection[23] afforded to the debtor such that no other proceedings, no enforcement of security and no execution or other legal process may be commenced or continued against the debtor or his or her property, except with the leave of the court and subject to any order the court may make to stay such proceedings, enforcement or execution for such period as the court deems appropriate pending the outcome of attempts to reach a PIA.

It should be noted that the protective certification does not extend to protect any guarantor of the debts of the debtor or a person who has jointly contracted with the debtor or is jointly liable with the debtor to the creditor and that other person may sue or be sued in respect of the contract without joining the debtor.[24]

The period of protective certification and any extension to this period does not affect any period for the purposes of the Statute of Limitations 1957[25] or period in relation to any proceedings or process (ie the period of protective certification is disregarded). This may be of relevance in the event that a PIA is unsuccessful.

A creditor is subject to certain restrictions once a PIA becomes effective.[26] A creditor cannot:

(a) initiate any legal proceedings in relation to a specified debt;

(b) take any step to prosecute such legal proceedings already initiated;

(c) take any step to secure or recover payment of a specified debt;

(d) execute or enforce a judgment or order of a court or tribunal against the debtor in respect of a specified debt;

(e) take any step to recover goods in the possession or custody of the debtor, unless title to the goods is vested in the creditor;

(f) otherwise initiate contact with the debtor in respect of payment of a specified debt;

23. PIA 2012, s 62(3).

24. PIA 2012, s 62(4) and (5).

25. PIA 2012, s 62(7).

26. PIA 2012, s 116(3).

(g) in relation to an agreement with the debtor, including a security agreement, by reason only that the debtor is insolvent or that a PIA is in effect—

(i) terminate or amend that agreement, or

(ii) claim an accelerated payment, or a forfeiture of a term, under that agreement.

Furthermore while a PIA is in effect, a creditor of that debtor shall not apply for the issue of a summons under s 8 of the BA 1988 or present a petition to have the debtor concerned adjudicated a bankrupt in respect of a debt covered by the PIA.[27]

A creditor is not precluded from taking an action as respects a person who has jointly contracted with the debtor or is jointly liable with the debtor to the creditor and that other person may sue or be sued in respect of the contract without joining the debtor.[28] This does not apply where the PIA is also in effect as respects the other person.[29]

The period in which the PIA is in effect shall be disregarded for the purpose of any applicable limitation period in relation to any proceedings or process to which this section applies (including any limitation period under the Statute of Limitations 1957).[30] Equally, the period for which any judgment against the debtor in relation to a debt which is the subject of a PIA has effect (whether under statute or rule of court) shall, subject to the provisions of the PIA 2012, be extended by the period that the PIA is in effect.[31]

A creditor is not precluded from taking an action against a guarantor of a debtor where the debtor's guaranteed debts form part of the specified debts of the PIA.[32]

AMENDMENTS TO THE BA 1988

Definitions

[10.13] This section deals with the amendments to s 3 of the BA 1988 to insert new definitions[33] arising from the provisions of the PIA 2012. Debt Settlement Arrangement and Personal Insolvency Arrangement have been given the same meanings as under the PIA 2012.

Under the BA 1988, the definition of a Bankruptcy Inspector previously meant a person employed in the Office of the Official Assignee.[34] This definition has been amended to provide the following:

---

27. PIA 2012, s 116(5).
28. PIA 2012, s 116(6).
29. PIA 2012, s 116(7).
30. PIA 2012, s 116(8).
31. PIA 2012, s 116(9).
32. PIA 2012, s 116(10).
33. PIA 2012, s 142 and the Courts and Civil Law (Miscellaneous Provisions) Act 2013, s 27.
34. BA 1988, s 60.

'Bankruptcy Inspector' means a person standing appointed for the time being—

(a) to the position of Bankruptcy Inspector in the Office of the Official Assignee in Bankruptcy on the day before the coming into operation of s 29 of the Courts and Civil Law (Miscellaneous Provisions) Act 2013, or

(b) to the position of Bankruptcy Inspector pursuant to s 12 of the Personal Insolvency Act 2012.

'Director' means the Director of the ISI.[35]

The 'Official Assignee' means a person standing appointed for the time being—

(a) to the position of Official Assignee in Bankruptcy in the Office of the Official Assignee in Bankruptcy on the day before the coming into operation of s 29 of the Courts and Civil Law (Miscellaneous Provisions) Act 2013, or

(b) to the position of Official Assignee pursuant to s 12 of the Personal Insolvency Act 2012.

Acts of Bankruptcy

[10.14] Section 7 of the BA 1988 which sets out acts of bankruptcy[36] has been amended to include as acts of bankruptcy the premature termination of a DSA or a PIA by application by the creditor or debtor under ss 83 and 122 PIA 2012 respectively, or due to greater than six months' arrears on payments by the debtor under the DSA or PIA.

Bankruptcy Summons

[10.15] This section amends s 8 BA 1988 which deals with the issue of a bankruptcy summons.[37] Previously, before the bankruptcy process could be availed of, the requisite minimum debt owed by the debtor was €1,900.

The amendments to s 8 BA 1988 review the minimum figure upwards from €1,900 to €20,000.

At present, the debt limit is €1,900 for a creditor and €1,300 for combined non-partner creditors to petition for bankruptcy. The new minimum amount in both circumstances must be more than €20,000. Provision is made for a 14-day notice requirement to ensure that a bankruptcy summons is not brought prematurely by a creditor, so as to allow the debtor to consider other options such as a DSA or a PIA. This notice must be in the prescribed form.[38]

Where the debt is less than €20,000 the insolvency procedures under a DRN, DSA or PIA should be used.

35. See **Ch 2**, para **2.05**.
36. PIA 2012, s 143.
37. PIA 2012, s 144.
38. The Courts and Civil Law (Miscellaneous Provisions) Act 2013, s 28(a).

Presentation of Petition for Bankruptcy

[10.16] This section amends s 11 BA 1988 which deals with the presenting of a petition for bankruptcy.[39]

The amendments provide that the liquidated debt amount which the creditor has to prove must be more than €20,000. At present, the creditor has to prove a debt of at least €1,900. The amendments to s 11 BA 1988 will require a debtor who presents a petition to swear an affidavit that he or she has made reasonable efforts to make use of alternatives to bankruptcy, such as a DSA or PIA to the extent that the debtor's circumstances allow. The debtor will also be required to present a statement of affairs, which must disclose that his or her debts exceed his or her assets by more than €20,000.

Petitioning Creditor's Costs

[10.17] This section amends s 12 BA 1988 which deals with the petitioning creditor's costs.[40] The amendment provides for the creditor to carry its own costs until the statutory sitting. After the statutory sitting the court can make an order for the payment of costs out of the estate of the bankrupt in course of priority to be settled by the rules of court. In considering whether to make an order the court must have regard to whether the petitioning creditor had unreasonably refused to accept proposals under a DSA or PIA.

The aim of the amendments is to further incentivise creditors to engage in a DSA or PIA process before petitioning for a debtor's bankruptcy.

Adjudication of Creditor's Petition

[10.18] This section amends s 14 of the BA 1988 which deals with the adjudication of the creditor's petition.[41] The amendment replaces the previous section and provides that before adjudicating a debtor bankrupt on foot of a petition presented by a creditor, the court will be required to consider the assets and liabilities of the debtor and assess whether it may be appropriate to adjourn proceedings to allow the debtor to attempt to enter into a DSA or PIA. Where the court makes an order adjourning the creditor's petition to allow the debtor enter an insolvency arrangement as specified by the court, a copy of the order shall be served on the debtor, either personally or by leaving it at his residence or place of business in the State. The debtor may be required to attend court and make full disclosure of his assets and liabilities to the court by way of a statement of affairs.

Adjudication of Debtor's Petition

[10.19] This section amends s 15 of the BA 1988 which deals with the adjudication of a debtor's petition.[42] The amendment replaces the current section and provides that where

39. PIA 2012, s 145.
40. PIA 2012, s 146.
41. PIA 2012, s 147.
42. PIA 2012, s 148.

the petition is presented by a debtor the court shall, on proof that the debtor is insolvent and unable to meet his or her engagements with his or her creditors, by order adjudicate the debtor a bankrupt. There will no longer be a requirement for a debtor who wishes to present a petition to possess assets capable of raising at least €1,900. The court will be required to consider the assets and liabilities of the debtor and assess whether it may be appropriate to adjourn proceedings to allow the debtor to attempt to enter into a DSA or PIA. The court may make an order adjourning the proceedings to allow the debtor to attempt to enter into a DSA or PIA.

Offers of Composition

[10.20] This section amends s 39 BA 1988 which deals with offers of composition.[43]

The amendment provides for technical amendments to s 39 BA 1988. The first amendment provides that where a stay on the realisation of the estate of the bankrupt has been granted under s 38 BA 1988 or where the Official Assignee has otherwise consented in writing to suspend the realisation of the bankrupt's estate on such terms as the Official Assignee may specify in such consent, the bankrupt shall call a meeting of his creditors before the court for the purpose of making an offer of composition to the creditors.

The second amendment provides that a creditor whose debt is less than €500 shall not be entitled to vote.

Excepted Articles

[10.21] This section amends s 45 of the BA 1988 which deals with a bankrupt's excepted articles (ie articles that are not subject to the bankruptcy process).[44]

This section currently provides that a bankrupt shall be entitled to retain, as excepted articles, such articles of clothing, household furniture, bedding, tools or equipment of his trade or occupation or other like necessaries for himself, his wife, children and dependent relatives residing with him as he may select, not exceeding in value €3,100 or such further amount as the court on an application by the bankrupt may allow.

The amendment increases the value of excepted articles that a bankrupt may retain from €3,100 to €6,000.

Fraudulent Preferences

[10.22] This section amends s 57 BA 1988 which deals with the avoidance of fraudulent preferences.[45] The amendment extends the current time period of one year to three years in regard to the avoidance of certain preferences made before adjudication in bankruptcy.

The section currently provides that every conveyance or transfer of property or charge made thereon, every payment made, every obligation incurred and every judicial

43. PIA 2012, s 149.
44. PIA 2012, s 151.
45. PIA 2012, s 152.

proceeding taken or suffered by any person unable to pay his debts as they become due from his own money in favour of any creditor or of any person in trust for any creditor, with a view to giving such creditor, or any surety or guarantor for the debt due to such creditor, a preference over the other creditors, shall, if the person making, incurring, taking or suffering the same is adjudicated bankrupt within one year after the date of making, incurring, taking or suffering the same, be deemed fraudulent and void as against the Official Assignee; but this section shall not affect the rights of any person making title in good faith and for valuable consideration through or under a creditor of the bankrupt.

The amendment extends the period from one year to a period of three years.

Avoidance of Transactions

[10.23] This section amends s 58 BA 1988 which deals with the avoidance of certain transactions.[46] The amendment extends the current time period of one year to three years in regard to the avoidance of certain transactions made before adjudication in bankruptcy.

The section currently provides that, if within one year before he is adjudicated bankrupt a debtor commits an act of bankruptcy and thereafter either sells any of his property at a price which, in the opinion of the court, is substantially below its market value or enters into or is a party to any other transaction which, in the opinion of the court, has the effect of substantially reducing the sum available for distribution to the creditors, such transaction shall be void as against the Official Assignee, unless the transaction was bona fide entered into and the other party had not at the time of the transaction notice of any prior act of bankruptcy committed by the bankrupt.

The amendment extends this period from one to three years.

Settlements of Property

[10.24] This section amends s 59 of the BA 1988 which deals with certain settlements of property.[47] The amendment extends the relevant time periods from two years to three years in regard to certain voluntary settlements of property made before adjudication in bankruptcy.

The section currently provides for the voiding of certain transactions settling property in the two years prior to the adjudication of the bankrupt. This has now been extended to three years.

Power of the Official Assignee to Appropriate the Bankrupt's Income

[10.25] This section inserts a new s 65A to BA 1988. This section relates to the application for an order for the Official Assignee to appropriate a bankrupt's income.[48] This section repeals s 65 BA 1988 except in respect to orders already in force and an

46. PIA 2012, s 153.
47. PIA 2012, s 154.
48. PIA 2012, s 155.

application is sought under s 65(2) BA 1988 for a variation of the order having regard to any changes in the family responsibilities or personal situation of the bankrupt.

Preferential Payments

[10.26] This section amends s 81 BA 1988 which deals with preferential payments[49] of the BA 1988 to align the date of assessment of tax owed by a bankrupt with the calendar tax year. Prior to 2001, the tax year ran from 6 April to the following 5 April. In 2001, the tax year changed to the calendar year 1 January to 31 December. The amendment substitutes 31 December for 5 April to correctly align an assessment of tax to the tax year.

Discharge and Annulment

[10.27] This section amends s 85 of the BA 1988 which deals with the discharge and annulment of the bankrupt.[50] The entire section is substituted with a new section and also inserts four new sections into the BA 1988.

The new text of s 85 provides for automatic discharge from bankruptcy after three years from the date of adjudication. Section 85 BA 1988, as amended by s 30 of the Civil Law (Miscellaneous Provisions) Act 2011, currently provides for automatic discharge from bankruptcy after 12 years.

The new text of s 85 also provides that where an order of adjudication was made more than three years prior to the coming into effect of this section, the bankruptcy shall stand discharged six months after that day unless the bankruptcy has been otherwise discharged. This six month period will allow time for creditor objections in such cases.

The bankrupt's unrealised property will remain vested in the Official Assignee after discharge from bankruptcy and the discharged bankrupt will be under a duty to co-operate with the Official Assignee in the realisation and distribution of such of his property as is vested in the Official Assignee.

The new s 85A (Objection to automatic discharge from bankruptcy) permits the Official Assignee or a creditor to apply to court to object to the discharge of a person from bankruptcy. The grounds for such an objection are that the debtor has failed to co-operate with the Official Assignee or has hidden or failed to disclose income or assets. The court may suspend the discharge pending further investigation or extend the period before discharge of the bankrupt to a date not later than the eighth anniversary of the making of the adjudication order.

The new s 85B (Entitlement to discharge from bankruptcy) restates the existing law in ss 85(3) and (4) BA 1988, as amended by s 30 of the Civil Law (Miscellaneous Provisions) Act 2011. This section has been further amended to provide that an Order of Discharge shall provide that any property of the bankrupt then vested in the Official Assignee shall be revested in or returned to the bankrupt and that the order, for that

49. PIA 2012, s 156.

50. PIA 2012, s 157.

purpose, shall be deemed to be a conveyance, assignment or transfer of that property to the bankrupt and shall be registered accordingly.[51]

This is in contrast to the amended s 85 BA 1988 which provides for the automatic discharge of a bankrupt after three years. Section 85(3) BA 1988 provides for the unrealised property of bankrupt to remain vested in the Official Assignee in contrast to being revested in the bankrupt, the reasoning being that under s 85B BA 1988 the bankrupt will have paid either a euro in the euro, obtained a waiver from his creditors or had the adjudication discharged thus there is no need for the Official Assignee to retain the vested property as there would at that stage be no outstanding creditors.

The new s 85C (Annulment of adjudication in bankruptcy) restates the current provisions in relation to annulment of bankruptcy contained in ss 85(8) and 85(9) of the 1988 act.

The new s 85D (Bankruptcy payment orders) permits the court to order a bankrupt to make payments from his income or other assets to the Official Assignee or trustee in bankruptcy for the benefit of his creditors. In making such an order, the court must have regard to the reasonable living expenses of the bankrupt and his family.

The court may also have regard to any guidelines on reasonable expenditure and essential income published by the Official Assignee or by the ISI. The ISI has published regulations relating to a debtor's reasonable living expenses and the court must have regard to these regulations.[52] The court may vary a bankruptcy payment order where there has been a material change in the circumstances of the discharged bankrupt. A material change is generally viewed as a change to the income or assets or liabilities or debts of the bankrupt that may affect his ability to meet agreed repayments.

Pension of a Bankrupt

[10.28] The treatment of pensions has been amended and brought into line with the UK where a pension is not treated as an asset.[53]

Where a person is adjudicated bankrupt and he or she is, or may become entitled to, payments under a relevant pension arrangement, assets relating to the arrangement (other than payments already received by the bankrupt, or that the bankrupt was entitled to receive, under the arrangement) shall not vest in the Official Assignee for the benefit of the creditors of the bankrupt.

However, where a bankrupt has an interest in or entitlement under a relevant pension arrangement which would, if the bankrupt performed an act or exercised an option, cause that debtor to receive from or at the request of the person administering that relevant pension arrangement:

(a) an income; or

(b) an amount of money other than income;

51. Courts and Civil Law (Miscellaneous Provisions) Act 2013, s 34.

52. See **Ch 7** – Reasonable Living Expenses.

53. PIA 2012, s 150.

in accordance with the relevant provisions of the Taxes Consolidation Act 1997, that bankrupt shall be considered as being in receipt of such income, and such amount of money shall vest in the Official Assignee or the trustee in bankruptcy.

This applies where the bankrupt is entitled at the date of adjudication, or was entitled at any date before the adjudication but had not exercised an option, or becomes entitled within a period of five years from the date of the adjudication to exercise the option.

Where the OA or the trustee in bankruptcy considers that it would be beneficial to the creditors of the bankrupt they may exercise the option in the circumstances above in place of the bankrupt.

Relevant pension arrangements means:

(a) a retirement benefits scheme, within the meaning of s 771 of the Taxes Consolidation Act 1997, for the time being approved by the Revenue Commissioners for the purposes of Ch 1 of Pt 30 of that act;

(b) an annuity contract or a trust scheme or part of a trust scheme for the time being approved by the Revenue Commissioners under s 784 of the Taxes Consolidation Act 1997;

(c) a PRSA contract, within the meaning of s 787A of the Taxes Consolidation Act 1997, in respect of a PRSA product, within the meaning of that section;

(d) a qualifying overseas pension plan within the meaning of s 787M of the Taxes Consolidation Act 1997;

(e) a public service pension scheme within the meaning of s 1 of the Public Service Superannuation (Miscellaneous Provisions) Act 2004;

(f) a statutory scheme, within the meaning of s 770(1) of the Taxes Consolidation Act 1997, other than a public service pension scheme referred to in para (e);

(g) such other pension arrangement as may be prescribed by the Minister, following consultation with the Ministers for Finance, Social Protection and Public Expenditure and Reform.

Where a bankrupt or a person on his or her behalf has made relevant pension arrangements within the three years prior to the adjudication and which contributions:

(a) were excessive in view of the bankrupt's financial circumstances when those contributions were made; and

(b) had the effect of—

    (i) materially contributing to the bankrupt's inability to pay his or her debts, or

    (ii) substantially reducing the sum available for distribution to the creditors,

the court may make an order in relation to the excessive amount so that it be vested in the Official Assignee to be made available for distribution to the creditors.

The financial circumstance of the bankrupt must be taken into consideration in determining whether the contributions were excessive and in particular:

(a) whether the bankrupt made payments to his or her creditors in respect of debts due to those creditors on a timely basis at or about the time when the bankrupt made the contribution concerned;

(b) whether the bankrupt was obliged to make contributions of the amount or percentage of income as the payments actually made under his or her terms and conditions of employment and, if so obliged, whether the bankrupt or a person who as respects the bankrupt is a relative could have materially influenced the creation of such obligation;

(c) the amount of the contributions paid, including the percentage of total income of the bankrupt in each tax year concerned which such contributions represent;

(d) the amount of the contributions paid in each of the six years prior to the making of the adjudication, including the percentage of total income of the bankrupt which such contributions represent in each of those years;

(e) the age of the bankrupt at the relevant times;

(f) the percentage limits which applied to the bankrupt in relation to relief from income tax for the purposes of making contributions to a relevant pension arrangement in each of the six years prior to the adjudication; and

(g) the extent of provision made by the bankrupt in relation to any relevant pension arrangement prior to the making of the contributions concerned.

'Relative' for these purposes includes a brother, sister, parent, spouse or civil partner of the person or a child of the person or of the spouse or civil partner.

Appendix 1

PRESCRIBED FINANCIAL STATEMENT

SI 326 of 2013

SCHEDULE 1

PRESCRIBED FINANCIAL STATEMENT

Debt Relief Notice

Name of Debtor:

Address:

Assets & Liabilities – Summary

Assets	**Total** €
Principal Private Residence (PPR)	
Investments (real property)	
Investments (other than real property)	
Plant, Equipment,Tools	
Vehicles	
Stock in trade	
Money owed to you	
Bank/Building Society Accounts	
Credit Union (net asset)	
Cash on hand	
Prospective assets	
Contingent assets	
Other	
Total Assets	

Liabilities (debts)	**Qualifying debts** €	**Non-Qualifying debts** €	**Total** €
PPR lender			
Financial Institutions			
Credit Union (net liability)			
Excludable Debts - Revenue			
Excludable Debts - Other than Revenue			
Employees			
Equipment Lessors/Hire Purchase			
Trade creditors			
Connected creditors			
Other debts			
Prospective debts			
Contingent debts			
Excluded debts			
Total debts			
Assets Less Liabilities			

All assets/debts are stated net of offsets

Income & Expenditure - Summary	
Income (monthly)	**€**
Salary/Wages	
Pension income	
Income from self employment (before tax)	
Rental income (net of expenses)	
Investment income	
Household members	
Income from boarders/lodgers	
Income from State agencies	
Department of Social Protection	
Other	
Total income	
Expenditure (monthly)	**€**
Income Tax & Social Insurance	
Reasonable Living Expenses - set costs per guide	
Reasonable Living Expenses - rent/mortgage	
Reasonable Living Expenses - childcare costs	
Reasonable Living Expenses - special circumstances	
Payments in respect of Excluded Debts	
Payments in respect of Excludable Debts not permitted	
Total Monthly Expenditure Before Debt Repayment	
Net disposable income	

Assets – Detail

1 Principal Private Residence

1.1 Address (note 1)
1.2 Original cost
1.3 Purchase date
1.4 Current market value
1.5 Debtor ownership %
1.6 Debtor's interest (derived field)
1.7 Comment

2 Investment Property

2.1 Description/Type*
2.2 Address (note 1)
2.3 Title - Freehold/Leasehold/Other
2.4 Original cost
2.5 Purchase date
2.6 Current market value
2.7 Debtor ownership %
2.8 Debtor's interest (derived field)
2.9 Monthly income
2.10 Monthly expenditure
2.11 Comment

Description/Type*
Residential buy to let - apartment
Residential buy to let - house
Commercial buy to let
Commercial premises
Holiday home
Land
Other - provide details

3 Investments (other than real property)

3.1 Description/Type*
3.2 Name of security issuer
3.3 Address (note 1)
3.4 Original cost
3.5 Purchase date
3.6 Current market value
3.7 Debtor ownership %
3.8 Debtor's interest (derived field)
3.9 Monthly income
3.10 Is the asset located in the State? Yes ☐ No ☐
3.11 Comment

Description/Type*
Stocks/shares
Bonds
Endowment policies
Pension
Antiques
Precious metals/Jewellery
Prize Bonds
Livestock
Other - provide details

4 Plant, Equipment, Tools

4.1 Description
4.2 Original cost
4.3 Purchase date
4.4 Current market value
4.5 Debtor ownership %
4.6 Debtor's interest (derived field)
4.7 Is the asset located in the State? Yes ☐ No ☐
4.8. Comment

5	Vehicles	
5.1	Make	
5.2	Model	
5.3	Year	
5.4	Registration number	
5.5	Mileage	
5.6	Need for vehicle	
5.7	Original cost	
5.8	Purchase date	
5.9	Current market value	
5.10	Subject to finance?	Yes ☐ No ☐
5.11	Balance outstanding	
5.12	Monthly instalment	
5.13	Adapted for disabled use?	Yes ☐ No ☐
5.14	Is the asset located in the State?	Yes ☐ No ☐
5.15	Comment	

6	Stock in trade	
6.1	Current market value	
6.2	Is the asset located in the State?	Yes ☐ No ☐
6.3	Comment	

7	Money owed to you
7.1	Name of debtor
7.2	Address (note 1)
7.3	Book value
7.4	Realisable amount
7.5	Comment

8	Bank/Building Society Accounts
8.1	Name of bank/building society
8.2	Address (note 1)
8.3	Account Name
8.4	Account Number
8.5	IBAN/BIC Number
8.6	Balance
8.7	Debtor ownership %
8.8	Debtor's interest (derived field)
8.9	Comment

9	Credit Union Shares/Investment
9.1	Name of credit union
9.2	Address (note 1)
9.3	Account Name
9.4	Account Number
9.5	Current market value (less loan)
9.6	Debtor ownership %
9.7	Debtor's interest (derived field)
9.8	Comment

10	Cash on hand

10.1 Amount
10.2 Is the asset located in the State? Yes ☐ No ☐
10.3 Comment

11	Prospective assets

11.1 Description
11.2 Estimated value
11.3 Estimated date of receipt
11.4 Is the asset located in the State? Yes ☐ No ☐
11.5 Comment

12	Contingent assets

12.1 Description
12.2 Estimated value
12.3 Estimated date of receipt
12.4 Is the asset located in the State? Yes ☐ No ☐
12.5 Comment

13	Other

13.1 Description
13.2 Estimated value
13.3 Is the asset located in the State? Yes ☐ No ☐
13.4 Comment

Liabilities – Detail

Questions common across all debt headings (except excluded debts):

1 Is this debt secured? Yes ☐ No ☐
If yes, security type:
Mortgage/Charge
Other - if other please give details
What is the debt secured on?

2 Has any of this debt been incurred within 6 months of the application date? Yes ☐ No ☐
If yes, please state amount.

1 Principal Private Residence Lender

1.1 Account Number
1.2 IBAN/BIC Number
1.3 Account Name
1.4 Contact details (note 2)
1.5 Monthly repayments - per contract
1.6 Monthly repayments - actual
1.7 Remaining term (months)
1.8 Original amount borrowed
1.9 Purpose of loan
1.10 Amount due
1.11 Of the amount due, how much is qualifying debt with reference to section 25 of the Personal Insolvency Act 2012?
1.12 Is the liability joint and several? Yes ☐ No ☐
1.13 If no, state % of liability
1.14 Amount of debtor's liability (derived field)
1.15 Arrears included in amount due
1.16 Restructured? Yes ☐ No ☐
If yes, please provide details
1.17 Current interest rate
1.18 Comment

2 Financial Institutions

2.1 Account Number
2.2 IBAN/BIC Number
2.3 Account Name
2.4 Contact details (note 2)
2.5 Account Type*
2.6 Monthly repayments - per contract
2.7 Monthly repayments - actual
2.8 Remaining term (months)
2.9 Original amount borrowed
2.10 Purpose of loan
2.11 Amount due
2.12 Of the amount due, how much is qualifying debt with reference to section 25 of the Personal Insolvency Act 2012?
2.13 Is the liability joint and several? Yes ☐ No ☐
2.14 If no, state % of liability
2.15 Amount of debtor's liability (derived field)
2.16 Arrears included in amount due
2.17 Restructured? Yes ☐ No ☐
If yes, please provide details
2.18 Current interest rate
2.19 Comment

Account Type*
Mortgage
Personal loan
Overdraft
Credit card
Store card
Other – provide details

3	Credit Union
3.1	Account Number
3.2	Account Name
3.3	Contact details (note 2)
3.4	Monthly repayments - per contract
3.5	Monthly repayments - actual
3.6	Remaining term (months)
3.7	Original amount borrowed
3.8	Purpose of loan
3.9	Amount due
3.10	Of the amount due, how much is qualifying debt with reference to section 25 of the Personal Insolvency Act 2012?
3.11	Is the liability joint and several? Yes ☐ No ☐
3.12	If no, state % of liability
3.13	Amount of debtor's liability (derived field)
3.14	Arrears included in amount due
3.15	Restructured? Yes ☐ No ☐ If yes, please provide details
3.16	Interest rate
3.17	Comment

4	Excludable Debts - Revenue
4.1	Description/Type*
4.2	Contact details (note 2)
4.3	Permitted? Yes ☐ No ☐
4.4	If yes, creditor consent or deemed consent
4.5	If creditor consents, please scan letter of consent
4.6	If deemed consent, scan proof of letter requesting consent
4.7	Amount due
4.8	Of the amount due, how much is qualifying debt with reference to section 25 of the Personal Insolvency Act 2012?
4.9	Preferential amount included in amount due (where known)
4.10	Instalment arrangement? Yes ☐ No ☐
4.11	Amount of instalment
4.12	Comment

Description/Type*
Income Tax
VAT
PAYE/PRSI
Relevant contracts tax
Local Property Tax
Interest & penalties
Other – provide details

5	Excludable Debts - Other than Revenue
5.1	Description/Type*
5.2	Contact details (note 2)
5.3	Permitted? Yes ☐ No ☐
5.4	If yes, creditor consent or deemed consent
5.5	If creditor consents, please scan letter of consent
5.6	If deemed consent, scan proof of letter requesting consent
5.7	Amount due
5.8	Of the amount due, how much is qualifying debt with reference to section 25 of the Personal Insolvency Act 2012?
5.9	Preferential amount included in amount due (where known)
5.10	Comment

Description/Type*
Local Government (Charges) Act 2009
Rates - Local Government Act 2001
HSE (Nursing Homes Support Scheme Act 2009)
Service charges/contributions under MUD Act 2011
Social Welfare Consolidation Act 2005
Other – provide details

6	Employees

6.1 Description/Type*
6.2 Contact details (note 2)
6.3 Amount due
6.4 Of the amount due, how much is qualifying debt with reference to section 25 of the Personal Insolvency Act 2012?
6.5 Preferential amount included in amount due (where known)
6.6 Comment

Description/Type*
Arrears of wages
Minimum notice
Holiday pay
Redundancy

7	Equipment Lessors/Hire Purchase

7.1 Description/Type*
7.2 Contact details (note 2)
7.3 Account Number
7.4 Amount due
7.5 Of the amount due, how much is qualifying debt with reference to section 25 of the Personal Insolvency Act 2012?
7.6 Comment

Description/Type*
Lease
Hire purchase
Other – provide details

8	Trade creditors

8.1 Contact details (note 2)
8.2 Amount due
8.3 Of the amount due, how much is qualifying debt with reference to section 25 of the Personal Insolvency Act 2012?
8.4 Comment

9	Connected creditors

9.1 Contact details (note 2)
9.2 Purpose of loan
9.3 Amount due
9.4 Of the amount due, how much is qualifying debt with reference to section 25 of the Personal Insolvency Act 2012?
9.5 Please specify the connection
9.6 Comment

10	Other debts

10.1 Description
10.2 Contact details (note 2)
10.3 Purpose of loan
10.4 Amount due
10.5 Of the amount due, how much is qualifying debt with reference to section 25 of the Personal Insolvency Act 2012?
10.6 Comment

11	Prospective debts

11.1 Description
11.2 Contact details (note 2)
11.3 Amount due
11.4 Of the amount due, how much is qualifying debt with reference to section 25 of the Personal Insolvency Act 2012?
11.5 Payment date
11.6 Comment

12	Contingent debts
12.1	Description
12.2	Contact details (note 2)
12.3	Estimated amount
12.4	Estimated payment date
12.5	Comment

13	Excluded debts
13.1	Amount due
13.2	Comment

Note 1
Address
Country
Street (line 1)
Street (line 2)
Street (line 3)
Town
Zip/Postal code
County

Note 2
Contact details:
Legal name of creditor
Country
Street (Line 1)
Street (Line 2)
Street (Line 3)
Town
Zip/Postal Code
County
Email Address
Telephone Number

Monthly Income - Detail		
	Type of income	€ Amount
1	Salary/Wages – gross Comment	
2	Pension income Comment	
3	Income from self employment (before tax) Comment	
4	Rental income (net of expenses) Comment	
5	Income from investments Comment	
6	Contribution from household members Comment	
7	Income from boarders/lodgers Comment	
8	Income from State agencies Comment	
9	Department of Social Protection	
9.1	Jobseekers Allowance/Benefit Comment	
9.2	Disability Allowance Comment	
9.3	Carer's Allowance Comment	
9.4	Family Income Supplement Comment	
9.5	Rent Supplement Comment	
9.6	One Parent Family Payment Comment	
9.7	Child Benefit Comment	
9.8	Mortgage Interest Supplement Comment	
9.9	Other – Please specify Details Comment	

10	Child or Spousal Maintenance Comment
11	Other Comment **Total monthly income**

Monthly Expenditure - Detail

	Type of expenditure	€ Amount
1	Income Tax & Social Insurance	
1.1	Income Tax Comment	
1.2	PRSI Comment	
1.3	Universal Social Charge Comment	
1.4	Other – please specify Details Comment	
2	Reasonable Living Expenses - set costs (derived)	
3	Reasonable Living Expenses - rent/mortgage	
4	Reasonable Living Expenses - childcare costs	
5	Reasonable Living Expenses - special circumstances	
6	Payments in respect of Excluded Debts Comment	
7	Payments in respect of Excludable Debts not permitted Comment	
	Total monthly expenditure	

Signature of Debtor ____________________________

Printed Name of Debtor ____________________________

Date ____________________________

Note: This document will be completed in electronic format on such electronic platform that the Insolvency Service may from time to time make available or otherwise specify for such purpose, following which, the information will be processed into an output format which may be in electronic form or printed on paper. Where any item in this document is completed to the effect of 'no', or any item in this document is not completed, that information may not appear on such output format and any person reviewing the output format should proceed on the basis that, where the output format does not refer to such information, the relevant item was either completed by selecting 'no' or the relevant item was not applicable in that instance. In this document, where an asterisk (*) is used and a choice is provided of the appropriate response, the response selected will appear in the output format. This note will not appear on the output format.

SCHEDULE 2

PRESCRIBED FINANCIAL STATEMENT

Debt Settlement Arrangement/Personal Insolvency Arrangement

Name of Debtor(s):

Address:

Assets & Liabilities - Summary

	Total €
Assets	
Principal Private Residence (PPR)	
Investments (real property)	
Investments (other than real property)	
Plant, Equipment,Tools	
Vehicles	
Stock in trade	
Money owed to you	
Bank/Building Society Accounts	
Credit Union (net asset)	
Cash on hand	
Prospective assets	
Contingent assets	
Other	
Total Assets	

Liabilities (debts)	**Specified Debts** €	**Unspecified Debts** €	**Total** €
PPR lender			
Financial Institutions			
Credit Union (net liability)			
Excludable Debts - Revenue			
Excludable Debts - Other than Revenue			
Employees			
Equipment Lessors/Hire Purchase			
Trade creditors			
Connected creditors			
Other debts			
Prospective debts			
Contingent debts			
Excluded debts			
Total debts			
Assets Less Liabilities			

All assets/debts are stated net of offsets

Income & Expenditure - Summary

Income (monthly)	**€**
Salary/Wages	
Pension income	
Income from self employment (before tax)	
Rental income (net of expenses)	
Investment income	
Household members	
Income from boarders/lodgers	
Income from State agencies	
Department of Social Protection	
Other	________
Total income	________

Expenditure (monthly)	**€**
Income Tax & Social Insurance	
Utilities	
Household	
Transport Costs	
Principal Primary Residence Costs	
Education	
Medical	
Social Inclusion	
Other	________
Total Monthly Expenditure before debt repayment	________
	________
Net disposable income/available for debt service/arrears	________
Payments in relation to debt repayments/arrears	________

Assets – Detail

1	Principal Private Residence
1.1	Address (note 1)
1.2	Original cost
1.3	Purchase date
1.4	Current market value
1.5	Debtor ownership %
1.6	Debtor's interest (derived field)
1.7	Comment

2	Investment Property
2.1	Description/Type*
2.2	Address (note 1)
2.3	Title - Freehold/Leasehold/Other
2.4	Original cost
2.5	Purchase date
2.6	Current market value
2.7	Debtor ownership %
2.8	Debtor's interest (derived field)
2.9	Monthly income
2.10	Monthly expenditure
2.11	Comment

Description/Type*
Residential buy to let - apartment
Residential buy to let - house
Commercial buy to let
Commercial premises
Holiday home
Land
Other - provide details

3	Investments (other than real property)
3.1	Description/Type*
3.2	Name of security issuer
3.3	Address (note 1)
3.4	Original cost
3.5	Purchase date
3.6	Current market value
3.7	Debtor ownership %
3.8	Debtor's interest (derived field)
3.9	Monthly income
3.10	Is the asset located in the State? Yes ☐ No ☐
3.11	Comment

Description/Type*
Stocks/shares
Bonds
Endowment policies
Pension
Antiques
Precious metals/Jewellery
Prize Bonds
Livestock
Other - provide details

4	Plant, Equipment, Tools
4.1	Description
4.2	Original cost
4.3	Purchase date
4.4	Current market value
4.5	Debtor ownership %
4.6	Debtor's interest (derived field)
4.7	Is the asset located in the State? Yes ☐ No ☐
4.8	Comment

5	Vehicles	
5.1	Make	
5.2	Model	
5.3	Year	
5.4	Registration number	
5.5	Mileage	
5.6	Need for vehicle	
5.7	Original cost	
5.8	Purchase date	
5.9	Current market value	
5.10	Subject to finance?	Yes ☐ No ☐
5.11	Balance outstanding	
5.12	Monthly instalment	
5.13	Adapted for disabled use?	Yes ☐ No ☐
5.14	Is the asset located in the State?	Yes ☐ No ☐
5.15	Comment	

6	Stock in trade	
6.1	Current market value	
6.2	Is the asset located in the State?	Yes ☐ No ☐
6.3	Comment	

7	Money owed to you
7.1	Name of debtor
7.2	Address (note 1)
7.3	Book value
7.4	Realisable amount
7.5	Comment

8	Bank/Building Society Accounts
8.1	Name of bank/building society
8.2	Address (note 1)
8.3	Account Name
8.4	Account Number
8.5	IBAN/BIC Number
8.6	Balance
8.7	Debtor ownership %
8.8	Debtor's interest (derived field)
8.9	Comment

9	Credit Union Shares/Investment
9.1	Name of credit union
9.2	Address (note 1)
9.3	Account Name
9.4	Account Number
9.5	Current market value (less loan)
9.6	Debtor ownership %
9.7	Debtor's interest (derived field)
9.8	Comment

10	Cash on hand	
10.1	Amount	
10.2	Is the asset located in the State?	Yes ☐ No ☐
10.3	Comment	

11	Prospective assets	
11.1	Description	
11.2	Estimated value	
11.3	Estimated date of receipt	
11.4	Is the asset located in the State?	Yes ☐ No ☐
11.5	Comment	

12	Contingent assets	
12.1	Description	
12.2	Estimated value	
12.3	Estimated date of receipt	
12.4	Is the asset located in the State?	Yes ☐ No ☐
12.5	Comment	

13	Other	
13.1	Description	
13.2	Estimated value	
13.3	Is the asset located in the State?	Yes ☐ No ☐
13.4	Comment	

Liabilities - Detail

Questions common across all debt headings (except excluded debts):

1 Is this debt secured? Yes ☐ No ☐

If yes, security type:

Mortgage/Charge

Other - if other give details

What is the debt secured on?

2 Has any of this debt been incurred within 6 months of the application date? Yes ☐ No ☐

If yes, please state amount.

1 Principal Private Residence Lender

1.1	Account Number	
1.2	IBAN/BIC Number	
1.3	Account Name	
1.4	Contact details (note 2)	
1.5	Monthly repayments - per contract	
1.6	Monthly repayments - actual	
1.7	Remaining term (months)	
1.8	Original amount borrowed	
1.9	Purpose of loan	
1.10	Amount due	
1.11	Is the liability joint and several?	Yes ☐ No ☐
1.12	If no, state % of liability	
1.13	Amount of debtor's liability (derived field)	
1.14	Arrears included in amount due	
1.15	Restructured?	Yes ☐ No ☐
	If yes, please provide details	
1.16	Current interest rate	
1.17	Comment	

2 Financial Institutions

2.1	Account Number	
2.2	IBAN/BIC Number	
2.3	Account Name	
2.4	Contact details (note 2)	
2.5	Account Type*	
2.6	Monthly repayments - per contract	
2.7	Monthly repayments - actual	
2.8	Remaining term (months)	
2.9	Original amount borrowed	
2.10	Purpose of loan	
2.11	Amount due	
2.12	Is the liability joint and several?	Yes ☐ No ☐
2.13	If no, state % of liability	
2.14	Amount of debtor's liability (derived field)	
2.15	Arrears included in amount due	
2.16	Restructured?	Yes ☐ No ☐
	If yes, please provide details	
2.17	Current interest rate	
2.18	Comment	

Account Type*
Mortgage
Personal loan
Overdraft
Credit card
Store card
Other – provide details

3	Credit Union	
3.1	Account Number	
3.2	Account Name	
3.3	Contact details (note 2)	
3.4	Monthly repayments - per contract	
3.5	Monthly repayments - actual	
3.6	Remaining term (months)	
3.7	Original amount borrowed	
3.8	Purpose of loan	
3.9	Amount due	
3.10	Is the liability joint and several?	Yes ☐ No ☐
3.11	If no, state % of liability	
3.12	Amount of debtor's liability (derived field)	
3.13	Arrears included in amount due	
3.14	Restructured?	Yes ☐ No ☐
	If yes, please provide details	
3.15	Interest rate	
3.16	Comment	

4	Excludable Debts - Revenue	
4.1	Description/Type*	
4.2	Contact details (note 2)	
4.3	Permitted?	Yes ☐ No ☐
4.4	If yes, creditor consent or deemed consent	
4.5	If creditor consents, please scan letter of consent	
4.6	If deemed consent, scan proof of letter requesting consent	
4.7	Amount due	
4.8	Preferential amount included in amount due (where known)	
4.9	Instalment arrangement?	Yes ☐ No ☐
4.10	Amount of instalment	
4.11	Comment	

Description/Type*
Income Tax
VAT
PAYE/PRSI
Relevant contracts tax
Local Property Tax
Interest & penalties
Other-provide details

5	Excludable Debts - Other than Revenue	
5.1	Description/Type*	
5.2	Contact details (note 2)	
5.3	Permitted?	Yes ☐ No ☐
5.4	If yes, creditor consent or deemed consent	
5.5	If creditor consents, please scan letter of consent	
5.6	If deemed consent, scan proof of letter requesting consent	
5.7	Amount due	
5.8	Preferential amount included in amount due (where known)	
5.9	Comment	

Description/Type*
Local Government (Charges) Act 2009
Rates - Local Government Act 2001
HSE (Nursing Homes Support Scheme Act 2009)
Service charges/contributions under MUD Act 2011
Social Welfare Consolidation Act 2005
Other – provide details

6	Employees

6.1 Description/Type*
6.2 Contact details (note 2)
6.3 Amount due
6.4 Preferential amount included in amount due (where known)
6.5 Comment

Description/Type*
Arrears of wages
Minimum notice
Holiday pay
Redundancy

7	Equipment Lessors/Hire Purchase

7.1 Description/Type*
7.2 Contact details (note 2)
7.3 Account Number
7.4 Amount due
7.5 Comment

Description/Type*
Lease
Hire purchase
Other-provide details

8	Trade creditors

8.1 Contact details (note 2)
8.2 Amount due
8.3 Comment

9	Connected creditors

9.1 Contact details (note 2)
9.2 Purpose of loan
9.3 Amount due
9.4 Please specify the connection
9.5 Comment

10	Other debts

10.1 Description
10.2 Contact details (note 2)
10.3 Purpose of loan
10.4 Amount due
10.5 Comment

11	Prospective debts

11.1 Description
11.2 Contact details (note 2)
11.3 Estimated amount
11.4 Estimated payment date
11.5 Comment

12	Contingent debts

12.1 Description
12.2 Contact details (note 2)
12.3 Estimated amount
12.4 Estimated payment date
12.5 Comment

13	Excluded debts
13.1	Amount due
13.2	Comment

Note 1
Address
Country
Street (line 1)
Street (line 2)
Street (line 3)
Town
Zip/Postal Code
County

Note 2
Contact details:
Legal name of creditor
Country
Street (Line 1)
Street (Line 2)
Street (Line 3)
Town
Zip/Postal Code
County
Email Address
Telephone Number

Monthly Income - Detail		
	Type of income	**€ Amount**
1	Salary/Wages - gross Comment	
2	Pension income Comment	
3	Income from self employment (before tax) Comment	
4	Rental income (net of expenses) Comment	
5	Income from investments Comment	
6	Contribution from household members Comment	
7	Income from boarders/lodgers Comment	
8	Income from State agencies Comment	
9	Department of Social Protection	
9.1	Jobseekers Allowance/Benefit Comment	
9.2	Disability Allowance Comment	
9.3	Carer's Allowance Comment	
9.4	Family Income Supplement Comment	
9.5	Rent Supplement Comment	
9.6	One Parent Family Payment Comment	
9.7	Child Benefit Comment	
9.8	Mortgage Interest Supplement Comment	
9.9	Other –Please specify Details Comment	

10	Child or Spousal Maintenance Comment
11	Other Comment **Total income**

	Monthly Expenditure - Detail	
	Type of expenditure	**€ Amount**
1	**Income Tax & Social Insurance**	
1.1	Income Tax Comment	
1.2	PRSI Comment	
1.3	Universal Social Charge Comment	
1.4	Other - *please specify* Details Comment	
2	**Utilities**	
2.1	Electricity Comment	
2.2	Gas /Oil Comment	
2.3	Phone/Internet Comment	
2.4	TV/Cable Comment	
2.5	Mobile Phone Comment	
2.6	Refuse Charges Comment	
2.7	TV Licence Comment	
2.8	Other - *please specify* Details Comment	
3	**Household**	
3.1	Childcare Comment	
3.2	Elderly care (e.g., carer, nursing home fees etc) Comment	
3.3	Food/Housekeeping/Personal Care Comment	
3.4	Clothing and Footwear Comment	

3.5 Household Repairs/Maintenance
Comment

3.6 Other - *please specify*
Details
Comment

4 **Transport Costs**
4.1 Petrol
Comment

4.2 Motor Insurance /Tax/NCT
Comment

4.3 Rail/Bus/Taxi Costs (including school transport costs for children)
Comment

4.4 Car Maintenance/Repairs
Comment

4.5 Car Parking and Tolls
Comment

4.6 Other - *please specify*
Comment

5 **Principal Primary Residence Costs**
5.1 Rent/Mortgage
Comment

5.2 Mortgage Protection/Endowment Premium
Comment

5.3 Payment Protection
Comment

5.4 House Insurance
Comment

5.5 Property Service/Management Charges
Comment

5.6 Other - *please specify*
Details
Comment

6 **Education**
6.1 Books
Comment

6.2 School/ College Fees
Comment

6.3 Uniforms
Comment

6.4 Extra Curricular activities (e.g. school outings)
Comment

6.5 Other - *please specify*
Details
Comment

7 **Medical**
7.1 Medical Expenses and Prescription Charges
Comment

7.2 Health Insurance
Comment

7.3 Other - *please specify*
Details
Comment

8 **Social Inclusion**
8.1 Lifestyle Expenses (e.g., family events, Christmas, Birthdays, eating out etc.)
Comment

8.2 Club membership
Comment

8.3 Other - *please specify*
Details
Comment

9 **Other**
9.1 Life Assurance
Comment

9.2 Pension Contribution
Comment

9.3 Maintenance paid to spouse/child
Comment

9.4 Other - *please specify*
Comment

9.5 Monthly expenditure on property assets
Comment

9.6 Monthly Savings
Comment

Total Monthly Expenditure before debt repayment/arrears

10 **Payments in relation to Debt repayments/arrears**
10.1 PPR Mortgage
Comment

10.2 Credit Union
Comment

10.3 Credit/Store card
Comment

10.4 Personal loan
Comment

10.5 Loan from family/friends
Comment

10.6 Payments in respect of Excluded Debts
Comment

10.7 Payments in respect of Excludable Debts not permitted
Comment

10.8 Other - *please specify*
Comment

Signature of Debtor ______________________________

Printed Name of Debtor ___________________________

Date ______________

Note: This document will be completed in electronic format on such electronic platform that the Insolvency Service may from time to time make available or otherwise specify for such purpose, following which, the information will be processed into an output format which may be in electronic form or printed on paper. Where any item in this document is completed to the effect of 'no', or any item in this document is not completed, that information may not appear on such output format and any person reviewing the output format should proceed on the basis that, where the output format does not refer to such information, the relevant item was either completed by selecting 'no' or the relevant item was not applicable in that instance. In this document, where an asterisk (*) is used and a choice is provided of the appropriate response, the response selected will appear in the output format. This note will not appear on the output format.

Appendix 2

APPLICATION FOR DEBT RELIEF NOTICE

SI No 333 of 2013

Schedule

APPLICATION FOR DEBT RELIEF NOTICE

AN CHÚIRT CHUARDA

THE CIRCUIT COURT

[........................] CIRCUIT COUNTY OF [........................]

IN THE MATTER OF AN APPLICATION UNDER SECTION 31 OF THE PERSONAL INSOLVENCY ACT 2012

AND IN THE MATTER OF [.......................................] OF [..],

A DEBTOR

I ....

of ....

County of ....

HEREBY APPLY for the making of an order for the issue under section 31(2)(*a*) of the Personal Insolvency Act 2012 of a Debt Relief Notice in respect of the debts specified in the application under section 29 of the said Act which the Court is satisfied are qualifying debts.

Dated ....20.....

Important Information and Statements

1. Unless otherwise defined in this application form, terms used herein have the same meaning as under the Personal Insolvency Act 2012 (the "Act").

2. This application form has been prescribed by the Insolvency Service for the purposes of Section 29(2) of the Act.

3. The Insolvency Service may request any further information it requires from an approved intermediary and defer further consideration of the application until such information is furnished to the Insolvency Service. Failure to furnish such information, within 14 days or such longer period as the Insolvency Service may (at its discretion) permit, will mean that the application shall be deemed to have been withdrawn.

4. Where a debtor (the "Debtor") becomes aware of any inaccuracy or omission in this application or any document accompanying this application, or any material change in his or her circumstances between the date of the application and the date on which the application is reviewed by the appropriate court, he or she is required under section 29(3) of the Act to inform the approved intermediary of these facts as soon as practicable. An approved intermediary who receives such information is required under section 29(4) of the Act to furnish that information to the Insolvency Service without delay.

5. The Insolvency Service hereby agrees to the Debtor communicating with the Insolvency Service by electronic means for the purposes of any communication or notice required or permitted to be sent or given by the Debtor to the Insolvency Service, from time to time, in connection with this Act including for the purpose of any notice referred to in section 134 of the Act. Any such communication or notice should be sent to drn@isi.gov.ie.

6. Notwithstanding any agreement by the Debtor to receiving electronic communication and notices, there may be circumstances in which the Insolvency Service will send documents, information and other communications to the Debtor in hard copy rather than electronically, in which case the Insolvency Service reserves the right to do so, including for the purpose of giving the Debtor any notice referred to in section 134 of the Act.

7. This application may be withdrawn at any time prior to the issue of a Debt Relief Notice in accordance with section 29(5) of the Act.

8. This application shall be accompanied by the prescribed fee and the following documentation—

(*a*) a copy of the statement made by the approved intermediary under section 27(6) of the Act;

(*b*) the Debtor's signed confirmation that he or she satisfies the eligibility criteria specified in section 26(2) of the Act;

(*c*) the Prescribed Financial Statement completed under section 27 of the Act and a statutory declaration of the Debtor confirming that the statement is a complete and accurate statement of the Debtor's assets, liabilities, income and expenditure;

(*d*) a schedule of the creditors of the Debtor and the debts concerned, stating in relation to each such creditor the information specified in section 29(2)(*d*) of the Act;

(*e*) the Debtor's written consent to the disclosure and processing of his or her personal data as specified in section 29(2)(*e*) of the Act;

(*f*) the Debtor's written consent to the making of any enquiry under section 30 of the Act relating to the Debtor by the Insolvency Service;

(*g*) the Debtor's signed statement stating whether, to the best of his or her knowledge, there is any judgment or court order in force against him or her which relates to a debt which is a qualifying debt;

(*h*) such other documentation as may be requested in this application.

Application Form

DEBTOR'S DETAILS — Initial Information	
Has the Debtor confirmed in writing to the approved intermediary that he or she wishes to apply for a Debt Relief Notice?	Yes ☐ No ☐
Does the Debtor agree to receiving by electronic means communications or notices required or permitted to be sent or given to the Debtor by the Insolvency Service, from time to time, in connection with the Act or related rules of court? Electronic communications or notices will be sent to the Debtor's email address provided in this application form.	Yes ☐ No ☐
The Courts Service may wish to communicate with the Debtor, from time to time, by electronic means in connection with the Act or related rules of court. If such circumstances arise, does the Debtor agree to receiving by electronic means communications or notices required or permitted to be sent or given to the Debtor by the Courts Service in connection with the Act or related rules of court? Electronic communications or notices will be sent to the Debtor's email address and/or mobile telephone number provided in this application form.	Yes ☐ No ☐

DEBTOR'S DETAILS — Personal Details	
Surname:	
First name:	
Name as it appears on birth certificate:	
Is the Debtor or has the Debtor been known by any other name? If yes, please supply name(s):	Yes ☐ No ☐ Name(s):
Title:*	Mr Mrs Miss Ms Other (please specify)
Gender:*	Male Female Other
PPS number:	
Date of birth:	
Country of birth:	
Nationality:	
Current Marital Status:*	Single (never married) Married (first marriage, no previous annulment) Married (following previous annulment) Re-married (following death of spouse) Re-married (following divorce/annulment) Civil partnership Separated Divorced Widow/Widower
Current Address:	
Home telephone number:	
Mobile telephone number:	
Email address:	

DEBTOR'S DETAILS — Previous Addresses	
Has the Debtor had any previous addresses in the last 5 years? If yes, please supply address(es):	Yes ☐ No ☐ Address(es): Start date and end date:

DEBTOR'S DETAILS — Employment Status	
What is the Debtor's current employment status?*	Employed Self-employed/Trading Unemployed Retired Student Housewife/husband Other (please specify)
If "Employed" is chosen the following questions must be answered:	
Occupation:	
Name of employer:	
Address of employer:	
Length of Service with employer: *Please specify in years and months.*	
If "Self-employed/Trading" is chosen the following questions must be answered:	
Occupation:	
Type of Business:	
Trading/Business Name:	
Address of Business:	
Was/Is the business registered for VAT? If yes, please supply VAT number.	Yes ☐ No ☐ VAT number:
Is the Debtor a sole trader? If not, what is the percentage of the Debtor's ownership of the business?	Yes ☐ No ☐ Percentage:
When did the business start trading? *Please specify a year and a month.*	

DEBTOR'S DETAILS — Previous Businesses	
Has the Debtor ever carried on a business, other than that referred to in the Employment Status section, under a trading/business name or any other name other than the Debtor's current name? If yes, please supply all previous name(s) and address(es).	Yes ☐ No ☐ Name(s) and Address(es): Start date and end date:

DEBTOR'S DETAILS — Insolvency Status	
Is the Debtor, as a debtor, as of the date of this application, a party to a Debt Settlement Arrangement or a Personal Insolvency Arrangement which is in effect?	Yes ☐ No ☐
Is the Debtor as of the date of this application a discharged bankrupt subject to a bankruptcy payment order?	Yes ☐ No ☐
Is the Debtor, as a debtor, as of the date of this application, subject to an arrangement under the control of the court under Part IV of the Bankruptcy Act 1988?	Yes ☐ No ☐

DEBTOR'S DETAILS — Prior Insolvency Processes	
Has the Debtor ever been a specified debtor with respect to a Debt Relief Notice?	Yes ☐ No ☐
Has the Debtor applied for a protective certificate (under Chapter 3 or 4 of the Act) within the period of 12 months ending on the date of this application?	Yes ☐ No ☐
Has the Debtor successfully completed a Debt Settlement Arrangement or a Personal Insolvency Arrangement within the period of 5 years ending on the date of this application?	Yes ☐ No ☐
Has the Debtor applied for bankruptcy and the petition has not been adjudicated before the date of this application? If yes, does section 26(9) of the Act apply and if so, please provide details.	Yes ☐ No ☐ Yes ☐ No ☐ Details:
Has a creditor of the Debtor before the date of this application petitioned to make the Debtor bankrupt but the hearing concerned has not yet taken place? If yes, does section 26(10) of the Act apply and if so, please provide details.	Yes ☐ No ☐ Yes ☐ No ☐ Details:
Has the Debtor, before the date of this application, been adjudged bankrupt and the adjudication has not been annulled or discharged?	Yes ☐ No ☐
Has the Debtor been discharged from bankruptcy within the period of 5 years ending on the date of this application?	Yes ☐ No ☐

DEBTOR'S DETAILS — Other Eligibility Criteria	
Does the Debtor have qualifying debts that amount to €20,000 or less?	Yes ☐ No ☐
Does the Debtor have a net disposable income, calculated in accordance with section 26(5) of the Act, of €60 or less a month?	Yes ☐ No ☐
Does the Debtor have assets, calculated in accordance with section 26(6) of the Act, worth €400 or less?	Yes ☐ No ☐
Is the Debtor domiciled in the State, or within one year before the date of this application, has the Debtor ordinarily— (i) resided in the State, or (ii) had a place of business in the State?*	Yes ☐ No ☐ Domiciled Resided Business
Is the Debtor, taking into account the factors set out in section 26(7) of the Act, insolvent within the meaning of the Act and has no likelihood of becoming solvent within a period of 3 years from the date of this application, while also maintaining a reasonable standard of living for himself or herself and his or her dependants?	Yes ☐ No ☐
Has the Debtor, during the period of two years ending on the date of this application, entered into a transaction with a person at an undervalue that has materially contributed to the Debtor's inability to pay his or her debts (other than any debts due to the person with whom the Debtor entered the transaction at an undervalue)?	Yes ☐ No ☐
Has the Debtor, during the period of two years ending on the date of this application, given a preference to a person that has had the effect of substantially reducing the amount available to the Debtor for the payment of his or her debts (other than a debt due to the person who received the preference)?	Yes ☐ No ☐
Has 25% or more of the Debtor's qualifying debts been incurred during the period of 6 months ending on the date of this application?	Yes ☐ No ☐

REASONABLE LIVING EXPENSES (RLE)	
For the purposes of calculating the monthly total set costs under the guidelines on a reasonable standard of living and reasonable living expenses issued under Section 23 of the Act (the "Reasonable Living Expenses Guidelines"), is this a one adult household or a two adult household?*	One adult household Two adult household
Does the Debtor have any dependent children (under 19 years of age) living with him or her? *If yes, complete —Reasonable Living Expenses — Children.*	Yes ☐ No ☐
Does the Debtor own a motor vehicle?	Yes ☐ No ☐
If yes, does the Debtor require a motor vehicle?	Yes ☐ No ☐
The monthly total set costs under the Reasonable Living Expenses Guidelines for the Debtor's typical household are:	€
Does the Debtor have any childcare costs? If yes, please give the monthly expenditure amount assessed to be reasonable by the approved intermediary in accordance with the Reasonable Living Expenses Guidelines.	Yes ☐ No ☐ Monthly amount: €
How much is the Debtor's monthly rent, mortgage repayment or other accommodation costs assessed to be reasonable by the approved intermediary in accordance with the Reasonable Living Expenses Guidelines?	€
Does the Debtor have any expenditure in relation to special circumstances, which is required to be taken into account when calculating his or her reasonable living expenses? *If yes, complete —Reasonable Living Expenses — Special Circumstances.*	Yes ☐ No ☐
In the case of a two adult household, has the Debtor rebutted the presumption of an equal split of the reasonable living expenses between them?	Yes ☐ No ☐
What percentage of the Debtor's household reasonable living expenses should be attributed to the Debtor?	Percentage:
The Debtor's reasonable living expenses are:	€

REASONABLE LIVING EXPENSES — Children	
For the purposes of calculating the Debtor's reasonable living expenses under the Reasonable Living Expenses Guidelines, which of the following age categories does the Debtor's child(ren) fall into?*	Infant (0-2) Pre-school (3) Primary school (4-11) Secondary school (12-18)

REASONABLE LIVING EXPENSES — Special Circumstances	
Please give the monthly expenditure amount and details of this expenditure.	Monthly amount: € Details:

JURISDICTION	
With reference to section 5(2) of the Act, please specify relevant County of the Debtor:	
Circuit Court:	
Reason for specifying County:*	Debtor residing at the time of this application Debtor resided within one year of the time of this application Debtor has a place of business at the time of this application Debtor had a place of business within one year of the time of this application

Signature of Debtor:	
Printed Name of Debtor:	
Date:	

Note: This document will be completed in electronic format on such electronic platform that the Insolvency Service may from time to time make available or otherwise specify for such purpose, following which, the information will be processed into an output format which may be in electronic form or printed on paper. Where any item in this document is completed to the effect of 'no', or any item in this document is not completed, that information may not appear on such output format and any person reviewing the output format should proceed on the basis that, where the output format does not refer to such information, the relevant item was either completed by selecting 'no' or the relevant item was not applicable in that instance. In this document, where an asterisk (*) is used and a choice is provided of the appropriate response, the response selected will appear in the output format. This note will not appear on the output format.

Appendix 3

APPLICATION FORM FOR AI

SI No 216 of 2013

APPROVED INTERMEDIARY APPLICATION FORM

Part A — Details of Applicant

1. Full legal name of company / partnership / other

2. Trading Name, if different from 1 above (please submit a copy of your Registration of Business Name Certificate, if applicable)

3. Contact Details

Telephone Number of Principal Business	
Mobile number of person responsible	
Fax Number	
Postal Address	
Direct e-mail address (all correspondence from the Insolvency Service of Ireland will be sent to this address)	
Website Address	

4. Type of legal entity (e.g. limited company, partnership, charitable society or other)

5. Companies Registration Office Number

6. Date of establishment

7. Nature of your primary business

8. Name of all Directors (including non-executive Directors) or Partners

First Name	Surname	Date of Appointment	Director Type

9. Details of Shareholders who directly hold shares or other interests representing 10% or more of the voting or capital rights of the applicant

First Name	Surname	% held	Date Acquired DD/MM/YY

Part B — Details of applicant, if an individual or the person who will provide approved intermediary services for the applicant who is a body corporate (responsible person)

1. Full name of individual or responsible person

2. Date of Birth

Day		Month		Year	

3. Private Address

4. Personal Public Service Number (PPSN) (if any)

Please complete Q. 5 and/ or Q. 6

5. Passport

Passport Number	
Country of Issue	
Expiry Date (dd/mm/yyyy)	

Or

6. Driving Licence

Driving Licence Number	
Country of Issue	
Expiry Date (dd/mm/yyyy)	

7. Contact Details

Telephone Number of Principal Business	
Mobile Number of Responsible Person	
Fax Number	
Direct e-mail address (all correspondence from the Insolvency Service of Ireland will be sent to this address)	
Website address	

Part C — Fitness & Probity

To be completed by an individual applicant and responsible person for approved intermediary services on behalf of a corporate body

1. Current Employment Details

Name of Employer	Address	Position Held	Start Date

2. Previous employer if changed in the last 12 months

3. Qualifications

Please give the following details of any qualifications you have acquired (including membership of professional bodies/associations and the course of study you have completed and passed in relation to the insolvency of individuals and the Personal Insolvency Act 2012):

Nature of Qualification	Name of awarding institution/ professional association	Country	Date Obtained (mm/yyyy)

4. Relevant Training or Experience

Please give similar details in relation to any relevant training or experience you have in the provision of financial advice to persons in arrears:

Name of Training/ Experience	Name of Institution/ professional association/Employer	Duration of training/ Length of experience	Date Completed (mm/yyyy)

5. The following questions are to be answered by entering a tick in the appropriate box. Where the response to a question is YES the individual applicant and/or responsible person should provide the following on a separate sheet and referenced to the appropriate question:

(a) full details;

(b) a submission on why such act will not adversely affect, to a material degree, his or her ability to act as an approved intermediary or provide approved intermediary services for the applicant.

	Are you or have you ever been:	Yes	No
A	subject to any disciplinary proceedings or issued with a warning, censure, suspension, reprimand or other administrative or judicial sanction or its equivalent?		
B	dismissed or asked to resign and did not resign from a fiduciary appointment or a position of trust whether or not remunerated?		
C	a director (or equivalent) of a company that was struck off the register of companies (or equivalent) by the Registrar of Companies (or its equivalent) on an involuntary basis?		
D	disqualified or restricted from acting as a director in any jurisdiction or disqualified from acting in any managerial capacity?		
E	convicted of an offence which could be relevant to an approved intermediary's ability to perform his, her or its functions under the Act?		
F	subject to a finding, judgment or order made against you by any court, tribunal or administrative enquiry involving fraud, misrepresentation, dishonesty or breach of trust or are you currently subject to any proceedings or investigation for fraud, misrepresentation, dishonesty or breach of trust?		
G	in the course of your employment or profession been the subject of enforcement action taken by a regulatory authority under applicable law?		

Part D — Approved Intermediary Declaration

I, ____________________(applicant name / responsible person for Approved Intermediary services on behalf of applicant company) apply for authorisation under section 47 of the Personal Insolvency Act 2012 on the basis of information supplied on this form and any additional information supplied to the Insolvency Service of Ireland in the course of this application.

I acknowledge that the Insolvency Service of Ireland may process and disclose such information in the performance of its statutory functions or otherwise as may be specifically authorised by law.

I warrant that I have truthfully and fully answered the relevant questions in this application form and disclosed any other information which might reasonably be considered relevant for the purpose of this application.

I am aware that it may be grounds for refusal of my application and/or grounds for revocation of an authorisation approval granted on foot of this application to knowingly or recklessly:

a. Provide false or misleading information and/or to make a false or misleading statement (which I acknowledge may include the withholding by me of relevant information) in this application for approval and/or;

b. Fail to inform and/or withhold from the Insolvency Service of Ireland details of any material change in circumstances/new information which is relevant and/or material to this application.

I warrant that I will promptly notify the Insolvency Service of Ireland of any changes in the information I have provided, and supply any other relevant information which may come to light in the period during which the application is being considered by the Insolvency Service of Ireland.

I hereby give permission to the Insolvency Service of Ireland to contact my employer during the period this application is being considered to confirm my employment status and also that I am fit and proper to practise as an approved intermediary.

Signed: ____________________ (Applicant/responsible person)

Print Name: ____________________ (Applicant/responsible person)

Signed: ____________________ (on behalf of Employer)

Print Name: ____________________ (on behalf of Employer)

Date: ____________________

Part E — Checklist

The Insolvency Service of Ireland will NOT commence the processing of any application if it deems the application to be incomplete. Applications will be deemed incomplete unless all applicable supporting documentation (as outlined in the checklist below) has been received. Incomplete applications will be returned to you as invalid. An application that has to be re-submitted will be dealt with as a brand new application.

	Applicant	ISI USE ONLY
Completed Application Form (signed and all questions answered)	☐	☐
Registration of Business Name Certificate (Part A)	☐	☐
If applicable, a business name registration certificate issued by the Companies Registration Office must be supplied in relation to all trading names (if different to the legal name) that the applicant wishes to use in relation to approved intermediary practice. Please contact the Companies Registration Office (www.cro.ie) if you have any queries in relation to your business name registration certificate.		
Qualification Certificates (Part C)		
Signed Declaration (Part D)		

Appendix 4

FIRST SCHEDULE BANKRUPTCY ACT 1988

Proof of Debts

General

(New)

1. Every creditor shall prove his debt and a creditor who does not do so is not entitled to share in any distribution that may be made.

2.

(*a*) A creditor may prove his debt by delivering or sending by post to the Official Assignee particulars of his debt (in this Schedule referred to as a "***proof of debt***").

(*b*) *Subparagraph (a)* is without prejudice to the entitlement of a creditor to prove his debt at a sitting of the Court.

3. The Official Assignee may fix a time within which proofs of debt shall be sent to him. A proof submitted thereafter shall not be allowed except by order of the Court.

4. Proof of debt may be furnished by way of a detailed statement of account, an affidavit of debt or other prescribed means.

5. The creditor shall specify the vouchers or any other evidence by which the debt can be substantiated. He shall also give particulars of any counterclaim that, to his knowledge, the bankrupt or arranging debtor may have, and he shall indicate whether or not he is a secured creditor.

6. Proof of debt in respect of money lent by a moneylender shall have annexed thereto the particulars required by section 16 (2) of the Moneylenders Act, 1933 .

7. An affidavit shall be required in any case where the debt is disputed or the Court or the Official Assignee thinks fit.

(1857, s. 246)

8. Proof of debt may be given by the oath or affidavit of the creditor himself or by the oath or affidavit of some person authorised by or on behalf of the creditor and, if made by a person so authorised, shall state his authority and means of knowledge.

9. Subject to *paragraph 24 (5)*, a creditor may, with the consent of the Official Assignee, amend his proof of debt.

10. Every creditor who has lodged a proof of debt is entitled to see and examine the proofs of other creditors.

11. A husband and wife may prove a debt against each other as if they were not married.

(New)

12. A sole trustee (including a personal representative) who is a bankrupt or an arranging debtor shall be entitled, without leave of the Court, to prove in his own

bankruptcy or arrangement in respect of a debt due from him to the trust estate. Any dividend in respect of such a debt shall be paid to the Accountant of the High Court for credit of the trust estate.

(1872, s. 48)

13. If any bankrupt or arranging debtor, at the date of the adjudication or order for protection, is liable in respect of distinct contracts, as a member of two or more distinct firms, or as a sole contractor, and also as member of a firm, the circumstance that such firms are, in whole or in part, composed of the same individuals, or that the sole contractor is also one of the joint contractors, shall not prevent proof in respect of such contracts against the properties respectively liable upon such contracts.

(*cf.* 1857, s. 260)

14. On any debt or sum certain, payable at a certain time or otherwise, whereon interest is not reserved or agreed for, and which is overdue at the date of the adjudication, the creditor may prove for interest at the rate currently payable on judgment debts to that date from the time when the debt or sum was payable, if the debt or sum is payable by virtue of a written instrument at a certain time, and if payable otherwise, then from the time when a demand in writing has been made, giving notice that interest will be claimed from the date of the demand until the time of payment.

(*cf.* 1857, s. 252)

15. In respect of debts due after the adjudication or order for protection, the liability for which existed at the date of such adjudication or order for protection, a creditor may prove for the value of the debt at that date.

16. Where a person who is liable to make any periodical payment (including rent) is adjudicated bankrupt or is granted an order for protection on a day other than the day on which such payment becomes due, the person entitled to the payment may prove for a proportionate part of the payment for the period from the date when the last payment became due to the date of the adjudication or order for protection as if the payment accrued due from day to day.

(1857, s. 251)

17. (1) Where there are mutual credits or debts as between a bankrupt and any person claiming as a creditor, one debt or demand may be set off against the other and only the balance found owing shall be recoverable on one side or the other.

(2) Section 36 of the Civil Liability Act, 1961 (which provides for the set-off of claims), as amended by section 5 of the Civil Liability (Amendment) Act, 1964 , shall apply with the substitution in section 36 (3) of a reference to subparagraph (1) for the reference to section 251 of the Irish Bankrupt and Insolvent Act, 1857.

18. This Schedule is without prejudice to section 61 of the Civil Liability Act, 1961 (which provides for proof of claims for damages or contribution in respect of a wrong) and section 62 of the said Act (which provides for the application of moneys payable under certain policies of insurance where the insured becomes a bankrupt).

19. A creditor shall, unless the Court otherwise orders, bear his own costs of proving a

debt.

(1857, s. 246)

20. Any person seeking to prove a debt or from whom additional proof is required, or any other person, may be examined by the Court in relation thereto.

21. Where a creditor or other person with intent to defraud makes any false claim or any proof, declaration or statement of account before the Court or in his affidavit which is untrue in any material particular in connection with the proof of debts, the Court may, in addition to any other penalty provided in this Act, disallow the claim in whole or in part.

22. Before deciding on a claim, the Official Assignee may require a creditor to furnish additional information or proof or to attend before him.

23. The Official Assignee shall deal in the following manner with claims:

(*a*) He shall prepare a list certified by him of the claims.

(*b*) This list shall record—

(i) the claims allowed by him, which shall be deemed to be admitted, and

(ii) the claims either disallowed by him or which he considers should not be admitted without reference to the Court.

(*c*) He shall refer disputed debts to the Court for adjudication.

(*d*) The decision of the Official Assignee in regard to a claim shall be confirmed in writing to the creditor.

(*e*) Any person aggrieved by the decision of the Official Assignee may appeal to the Court.

(*f*) The Official Assignee shall place a copy of the list on the Court file.

(*g*) The list shall be open to public inspection on payment of a prescribed fee but no fee shall be charged to creditors inspecting the list.

Secured Creditors

(1872, s. 21)

24. (1) If a secured creditor realises his security, he may prove for the balance due to him after deducting the net amount realised and receive dividends thereon but not so as to disturb any dividend then already declared. If he surrenders his security for the general benefit of the creditors, he may prove for his whole debt.

(2) If a secured creditor does not either realise or surrender his security, he shall, before ranking for dividend, state in his proof the particulars of his security, the date on which it was given and the value at which he assesses it, and he shall be entitled to receive a dividend only in respect of the balance due to him after deducting the value so assessed.

(3) A secured creditor shall not be entitled to surrender his security after the time fixed by the Official Assignee for receipt of proofs of debt, except by order of the Court.

(4) (*a*) Where a security is valued by the creditor, the Official Assignee may at any time redeem it on payment to the creditor of the assessed value. If the Official

Assignee is dissatisfied with the assessed value he may require that the property comprised in any security so valued be offered for sale at such time and on such terms and conditions as may be agreed upon between him and the creditor or, in default of agreement, as the Court may direct. If the sale be by public auction the creditor, or the Official Assignee on behalf of the estate, may bid or purchase.

(*b*) The creditor may, however, at any time by notice in writing require the Official Assignee to elect whether he will or will not exercise his power of redeeming the security or requiring it to be offered for sale, and if the Official Assignee does not, within three months after receiving the notice, signify in writing to the creditor his election to exercise the power, he shall not be entitled to exercise it; and the equity of redemption, or any other interest in the property comprised in the security which is vested in the Official Assignee, shall vest in the creditor and the amount of his debt shall be reduced by the amount at which the security has been valued.

(5) Where a creditor has valued his security he may at any time amend the valuation and proof on showing to the satisfaction of the Official Assignee, or the Court, that the valuation and proof were made *bona fide* on a mistaken estimate, but every such amendment shall be made at the cost of the creditor, and upon such terms as the Court shall order, unless the Official Assignee allows the amendment without application to the Court.

(6) Where a valuation has been amended in accordance with *subparagraph (5)*, the creditor shall forthwith repay any surplus dividend which he may have received in excess of that to which he would have been entitled on the amended valuation or, as the case may be, shall be entitled to be paid, out of any money for the time being available for dividend, any dividend or share of dividend which he has not received by reason of the inaccuracy of the original valuation before that money is made applicable to the payment of any future dividend but he shall not be entitled to disturb the distribution of any dividend declared before the date of the amendment.

(7) If a creditor having valued his security subsequently realises it, or if it is realised under the provisions of *subparagraph (4)*, the net amount realised shall be substituted for the amount of any valuation previously made by the creditor, and shall be treated in all respects as an amended valuation made by the creditor.

(8) If it is found at any time that the affidavit made by or on behalf of a secured creditor has omitted to state that he is a secured creditor, such creditor shall surrender his security to the Official Assignee for the general benefit of the creditors unless the Court on application otherwise orders, and the Court may allow the affidavit to be amended upon such terms as to repayment of any dividend or otherwise as the Court may consider just.

(9) If a secured creditor does not comply with *subparagraph (8)*, he shall be excluded from all share in any dividend.

(10) Subject to the provisions of *subparagraph (4)*, the creditor shall in no case receive more than one pound in the pound and interest, where the creditor is entitled to prove for interest.

(11) Where a mortgagee holds as security a policy of assurance on the life of a bankrupt or an arranging debtor which in the event of the non-payment of premiums provides for their automatic discharge out of moneys payable under the policy, the value of the policy for the purpose of proving in the bankruptcy or arrangement shall be taken to be not less than the value as at the date of adjudication or order for protection; provided that, if the bankrupt or arranging debtor dies before the policy is surrendered, the mortgagee may apply to the Court for the purpose of revaluing his security.

Appendix 5

DSA APPLICATION FORM

SI No 332 of 2013

Schedule

APPLICATION FOR PROTECTIVE CERTIFICATE
(DEBT SETTLEMENT ARRANGEMENT)

*AN CHÚIRT CHUARDA

*[THE CIRCUIT COURT] *[THE HIGH COURT]

*PERSONAL INSOLVENCY ACT 2012

*[...................] CIRCUIT *COUNTY OF [...................]

IN THE MATTER OF AN APPLICATION UNDER SECTION 61 OF THE PERSONAL INSOLVENCY ACT 2012

AND IN THE MATTER OF ....]

OF [..],

A DEBTOR

*I/*We ....

of ....

County of ....

*and ....

of ....

County of ....

HEREBY APPLY for the making of an order for the issue under section 61(2)(*a*) of the Personal Insolvency Act 2012 of a protective certificate.

Dated.............20.....

* Delete where inapplicable

Important Information and Statements

1. Unless otherwise defined in this application form, terms used herein have the same meaning as under the Personal Insolvency Act 2012 (the "Act").

2. This application form has been prescribed by the Insolvency Service for the purposes of Section 59(2) of the Act.

3. The Insolvency Service may request any further information it requires from a debtor (the "Debtor") or personal insolvency practitioner and defer further consideration of the application until such information is furnished to the Insolvency Service. Failure to furnish such information, within 14 days or such longer period as the Insolvency Service may (at its discretion) permit, will mean that the application shall be deemed to have been withdrawn.

4. Where the personal insolvency practitioner becomes aware of any inaccuracy or omission in this application or any document accompanying this application, he or she is required under section 59(4) of the Act to inform the Insolvency Service of this fact as soon as practicable.

5. The Insolvency Service hereby agrees to the Debtor communicating with the Insolvency Service by electronic means for the purposes of any communication or notice required or permitted to be sent or given by the Debtor to the Insolvency Service, from time to time, in connection with this Act including for the purpose of any notice referred to in section 134 of the Act. Any such communication or notice should be sent to dsa@isi.gov.ie

6. Notwithstanding any agreement by the Debtor to receiving electronic communications and notices, there may be circumstances in which the Insolvency Service will send documents, information and other communications to the Debtor in hard copy rather than electronically, in which case the Insolvency Service reserves the right to do so, including for the purpose of giving the Debtor any notice referred to in section 134 of the Act.

7. This application may be withdrawn at any time prior to the issue of a protective certificate in accordance with section 59(3) of the Act.

8. This application shall be accompanied by the prescribed fee and the following documentation:

(*a*) a statement of the personal insolvency practitioner prepared under section 54 of the Act;

(*b*) the Debtor's signed confirmation that he or she satisfies the eligibility criteria specified in section 57 of the Act;

(*c*) the Prescribed Financial Statement;

(*d*) the statutory declaration of the Debtor referred to in section 57(1)(*c*) of the Act;

(*e*) a schedule of creditors of the Debtor and the debts concerned, stating in relation to each such creditor the information specified in section 59(2)(*e*) of the Act;

(*f*) the Debtor's written consent to the disclosure and processing of his or her personal data of the Debtor as specified in section 59(2)(*f*) of the Act;

(*g*) the Debtor's written consent to the making of any enquiry under section 60 of the Act relating to the Debtor by the Insolvency Service;

(*h*) such other documentation as may be requested in this application

Application Form

APPLICATION QUESTIONS	
Is this an individual application or a joint application? If this is a joint application each Debtor must complete the "Debtor's Details" sections.	Individual ☐ Joint ☐
Are the total liabilities of the Debtor determined on the basis of the Prescribed Financial Statement completed by the Debtor in respect of this application in excess of €2,500,000?	Yes ☐ No ☐
Have 25% or more of the Debtor's debts (other than excluded debts and secured debts) been incurred during the period of 6 months ending on the date of this application?	Yes ☐ No ☐

(DEBTOR'S DETAILS sections to be completed by all debtors in the case of a joint application)

DEBTOR'S DETAILS — Initial Information	
Has the Debtor received advice from the personal insolvency practitioner on the matters set out in section 52 of the Act?	Yes ☐ No ☐
Was the advice referred to in section 52(1)(c) of the Act confirmed in writing by the personal insolvency practitioner to the Debtor?	Yes ☐ No ☐
Has the Debtor instructed the personal insolvency practitioner in writing to make a proposal for a Debt Settlement Arrangement in accordance with Chapter 3 of the Act?	Yes ☐ No ☐
Does the Debtor agree to receiving by electronic means communications or notices required or permitted to be sent or given to the Debtor by the Insolvency Service, from time to time, in connection with the Act or related rules of court? Electronic communications or notices will be sent to the Debtor's email address provided in this application form.	Yes ☐ No ☐

DEBTOR'S DETAILS — Initial Information	
The Courts Service may wish to communicate with the Debtor, from time to time, by electronic means in connection with the Act or related rules of court. If such circumstances arise, does the Debtor agree to receiving by electronic means communications or notices required or permitted to be sent or given to the Debtor by the Courts Service in connection with the Act or related rules of court? Electronic communications or notices will be sent to the Debtor's email address and/or mobile telephone number provided in this application form.	Yes ☐ No ☐

DEBTOR'S DETAILS — Personal Details	
Surname:	
First name:	
Name as it appears on birth certificate:	
Is the Debtor or has the Debtor been known by any other name? If yes, please supply name(s):	Yes ☐ No ☐ Name(s):
Title:*	Mr Mrs Miss Ms Other (please specify)
Gender:*	Male Female Other
PPS number:	
Date of birth:	
Country of birth:	
Nationality:	

DEBTOR'S DETAILS — Personal Details	
Current Marital Status:*	Single (never married) Married (first marriage, no previous annulment) Married (following previous annulment) Re-married (following death of spouse) Re-married (following divorce/annulment) Civil partnership Separated Divorced Widow/Widower
Current Address:	
Home telephone number:	
Mobile telephone number:	
Email address:	

DEBTOR'S DETAILS — Previous Addresses	
Has the Debtor had any previous addresses in the last 5 years? If yes, please supply address(es):	Yes ☐ No ☐ Address(es): Start date and end date:

DEBTOR'S DETAILS — Employment Status	
What is the Debtor's current employment status?*	Employed Self-employed/Trading Unemployed Retired Student Housewife/husband Other (please specify)
If "Employed" is chosen the following questions must be answered:	
Occupation:	
Name of employer:	
Address of employer:	
Length of Service with employer: *Please specify in years and months.*	
If "Self-employed/Trading" is chosen the following questions must be answered:	
Occupation:	
Type of Business:	
Trading/Business Name:	
Address of Business:	
Was/Is the business registered for VAT? If yes, please supply VAT number.	Yes ☐ No ☐ VAT number:
Is the Debtor a sole trader? If not, what is the percentage of the Debtor's ownership of the business?	Yes ☐ No ☐ Percentage:
When did the business start trading? *Please specify a year and a month.*	

DEBTOR'S DETAILS — Previous Businesses	
Has the Debtor ever carried on a business, other than that referred to in the Employment Status section above, under a trading/business name or any other name other than the Debtor's current name? If yes, please supply all previous name(s) and address(es)	Yes ☐ No ☐ Name(s) and Address(es): Start date and end date:

DEBTOR'S DETAILS — Insolvency Status	
Is the Debtor an undischarged bankrupt?	Yes ☐ No ☐
Is the Debtor a discharged bankrupt subject to a bankruptcy payment order?	Yes ☐ No ☐
Is the Debtor a person who is a specified debtor as respects a Debt Relief Notice which is in effect?	Yes ☐ No ☐
Is the Debtor a person who, as a debtor, is subject to a Personal Insolvency Arrangement which is in effect?	Yes ☐ No ☐
Is the Debtor a person who, as a debtor, is subject to an arrangement under the control of the court under Part IV of the Bankruptcy Act 1988?	Yes ☐ No ☐

DEBTOR'S DETAILS — Prior Insolvency Processes	
Has the Debtor been the subject of a protective certificate issued under section 61 of the Act less than 12 months prior to the date of this application?	Yes ☐ No ☐
Has the Debtor had his or her debts discharged pursuant to section 46(1) of the Act less than 3 years prior to the date of this application?	Yes ☐ No ☐
Has the Debtor had his or her debts discharged pursuant to a Personal Insolvency Arrangement less than 5 years prior to the date of this application?	Yes ☐ No ☐
Has the Debtor been discharged from bankruptcy less than 5 years prior to the date of this application?	Yes ☐ No ☐
Has the appropriate court made an order referred to in section 57(2) of the Act stating that it is satisfied that the current insolvency of the Debtor arises by reason of exceptional circumstances or other factors which are substantially outside the control of the Debtor and that it would be just to permit the Debtor to make a proposal for a Debt Settlement Arrangement? If yes, please provide a copy of the order with this application. *Only to be answered if any of the previous four questions are answered in the positive.*	Yes ☐ No ☐
Has the Debtor ever entered into a Debt Settlement Arrangement?	Yes ☐ No ☐

DEBTOR'S DETAILS — Other Eligibility Criteria	
Is the Debtor domiciled in the State, or within one year before the date of this application, has the Debtor ordinarily— (i) resided in the State, or (ii) had a place of business in the State?*	Yes ☐ No ☐ Domiciled Resided Business
Is the Debtor insolvent within the meaning of the Act?	Yes ☐ No ☐

REASONABLE LIVING EXPENSES (RLE)	
For the purposes of calculating the monthly total set costs under the guidelines on a reasonable standard of living and reasonable living expenses issued under Section 23 of the Act (the "Reasonable Living Expenses Guidelines"), is this a one adult household or a two adult household?*	One adult household Two adult household
Does the Debtor have any dependent children (under 19 years of age) living with him or her? *If yes, complete —Reasonable Living Expenses — Children.*	Yes ☐ No ☐
Does the Debtor own a motor vehicle?	Yes ☐ No ☐
If yes, does the Debtor require a motor vehicle?	Yes ☐ No ☐
The monthly total set costs under the Reasonable Living Expenses Guidelines for the Debtor's typical household are:	€
Does the Debtor have any childcare costs? If yes, please give the monthly expenditure amount assessed to be reasonable by the personal insolvency practitioner in accordance with the Reasonable Living Expenses Guidelines.	Yes ☐ No ☐ Monthly amount: €
How much is the Debtor's monthly rent, mortgage repayment or other accommodation costs assessed to be reasonable by the personal insolvency practitioner in accordance with the Reasonable Living Expenses Guidelines?	€
Does the Debtor have any expenditure in relation to special circumstances, which is required to be taken into account when calculating his or her reasonable living expenses? *If yes, complete —Reasonable Living Expenses — Special Circumstances.*	Yes ☐ No ☐
In the case of a two adult household, has the Debtor rebutted the presumption of an equal split of the reasonable living expenses between them?	Yes ☐ No ☐
What percentage of the Debtor's household reasonable living expenses should be attributed to the Debtor?	Percentage:
The Debtor's reasonable living expenses are:	€

REASONABLE LIVING EXPENSES — Children	
For the purposes of calculating the Debtor's reasonable living expenses under the Reasonable Living Expenses Guidelines, which of the following age categories does the Debtor's child(ren) fall into?*	Infant (0-2) Pre-school (3) Primary school (4-11) Secondary school (12-18)

REASONABLE LIVING EXPENSES — Special Circumstances	
Please give the monthly expenditure amount and details of this expenditure.	Monthly amount: € Details:

JURISDICTION **Only applicable if Circuit Court Application**	
With reference to section 5(2) of the Act, please specify relevant County of the Debtor:	
Circuit Court:	
Reason for specifying County:*	Debtor residing at the time of this application Debtor resided within one year of the time of this application Debtor has a place of business at the time of this application Debtor had a place of business within one year of the time of this application

Signature of Debtor:	
Printed Name of Debtor:	
Date:	

Note: This document will be completed in electronic format on such electronic platform that the Insolvency Service may from time to time make available or otherwise specify for such purpose, following which, the information will be processed into an output format which may be in electronic form or printed on paper. Where any item in this document is completed to the effect of 'no', or any item in this document is not completed, that information may not appear on such output format and any person reviewing the output format should proceed on the basis that, where the output format does not refer to such information, the relevant item was either completed by selecting 'no' or the relevant item was not applicable in that instance. In this document, where an asterisk (*) is used and a choice is provided of the appropriate response, the response selected will appear in the output format. This note will not appear on the output format.

Appendix 6

SECTION 81 BANKRUPTCY ACT 1988

81.—(1) In the distribution of the property of a bankrupt there shall be paid in priority to all other debts—

(a) all local rates due from the bankrupt at the date of the order of adjudication, and having become due and payable within twelve months next before that date, and all property or income tax assessed on the bankrupt up to the 5th day of April next before the date of the order of adjudication, and not exceeding in the whole one year's assessment;

(b) all wages or salary (whether or not earned wholly or in part by way of commission) of any clerk or servant in respect of services rendered to the bankrupt during the four months next before the date of the order of adjudication not exceeding £2,500;

(c) all wages not exceeding £2,500 of any labourer or workman (whether payable for time or for piece work) in respect of services rendered to the bankrupt during the four months next before the date of the order of adjudication: provided that, where any farm labourer has entered into a contract for the payment of a portion of his wages in a lump sum at the end of the year or other shorter term of hiring, the priority under this section shall extend to the whole of such sum, or a part thereof, as the Court may decide to be due under the contract proportionate to the time of service up to the date of the order of adjudication;

(d) all accrued holiday remuneration becoming payable to any clerk, servant, workman or labourer (or in the case of his death to any other person in his right) on the termination of his employment before or by the effect of the adjudication order;

(e) all sums due to any employee pursuant to any scheme or arrangement for the provision of payments to the employee while he is absent from employment owing to ill health;

(f) any payments due by the bankrupt pursuant to any scheme or arrangement for the provision of superannuation benefits to or in respect of employees of the bankrupt whether such payments are due in respect of the bankrupt's contribution to that scheme or under that arrangement or in respect of such contributions payable by the employees to the bankrupt under any such scheme or arrangement which have been deducted from the wages or salaries of employees;

(g) any debt, payment or contribution which by virtue of any provision in any enactment in operation before the commencement of this Act was included in the debts to which section 4 of the Preferential Payments in Bankruptcy (Ireland) Act, 1889, gave priority; and any reference to the said section 4 in any such enactment shall be construed as a reference to this subsection.

(2) The foregoing debts shall rank equally between themselves and be paid in full unless the property of the bankrupt is insufficient to meet them, in which case they shall abate in equal proportions between themselves.

(3) Subject to the retention of such sums as may be necessary for the costs and expenses of administration or otherwise, the foregoing debts shall be discharged forthwith so far as the property of the bankrupt is sufficient to meet them.

(4) In the event of a landlord or other person distraining or having distrained on any goods or effects of the bankrupt within three months next before the date of the order of adjudication, the debts to which priority is given by this section shall be a first charge on the goods or effects so distrained on, or the proceeds of sale thereof; provided that in respect of any money paid under any such charge the landlord or other person shall have the same rights of priority as the person to whom the payment is made.

(5) Any remuneration in respect of a period of holiday or absence from work through good cause shall be deemed to be wages in respect of services rendered to the bankrupt during that period.

(6) Notwithstanding section 4, this section shall not apply where the order of adjudication was made before the commencement of this Act, and in such a case, the provisions relating to preferential payments which would have applied if this Act had not been passed shall be deemed to remain in full force.

(7) Subsections (1), (2), (3), (5) and (6) shall apply in the case of an arranging debtor under the provisions of this Act as if he were a bankrupt, and as if the date of the filing of the petition for arrangement were substituted for the date of the order of adjudication.

(8) Any creditor who, in the case of an arrangement, votes in respect of any debt to which priority is given by this section for or against the acceptance of the debtor's proposal or any modification thereof or, in the case of a composition after bankruptcy, votes in respect of any such debt for or against the acceptance of the bankrupt's offer of composition or any modification thereof shall by so voting be deemed to have abandoned any rights under subsection (1) and shall be remitted to such rights (if any) in respect of any of the debts therein mentioned as such creditor would have had apart from that subsection.

(9) This section shall apply in the case of a deceased person who dies insolvent as if he were a bankrupt and as if the date of his death were substituted for the date of the order of adjudication.

(10) Nothing in this section shall alter the effect of section 3 of the Partnership Act, 1890, or shall prejudice the provisions of section 14 of the Trustee Savings Banks Act, 1863, or the provisions of the Friendly Societies Act, 1896.

Appendix 7

INSTRUMENT APPOINTING A PROXY

SI No 335 of 2013

IN THE MATTER OF A CREDITORS' MEETING PURSUANT TO THE PERSONAL INSOLVENCY ACT 2012 AND THE PERSONAL INSOLVENCY ACT 2012 (PROCEDURES FOR THE CONDUCT OF CREDITORS' MEETINGS) REGULATIONS 2013

AND IN THE MATTER OF [name of debtor] OF [address of debtor], A DEBTOR

____________________ [name of proxy] of _________________________[address of proxy] is hereby appointed agent and proxy for the undersigned in the above matter, to represent and vote for the undersigned [in favour of (Yes)]/ [against (No)] / [in favour of (Yes) or against (No) as such proxy in his or her discretion shall determine]* the approval of a proposal at the creditors' meeting to be held in respect thereof on ____/____/____ [insert date of meeting], or at any adjournment of such meeting.

....[Signature of creditor]

.... [Name in block capitals]

.... [Signature of Witness]

.... [Witness Name in block capitals]

Dated ....

*Strike out whatever is not desired.

Appendix 8

APPLICATION FOR PROTECTIVE CERTIFICATE

SI No 331 of 2013

Schedule

APPLICATION FOR PROTECTIVE CERTIFICATE

(PERSONAL INSOLVENCY ARRANGEMENT)

*AN CHÚIRT CHUARDA

*[THE CIRCUIT COURT] *[THE HIGH COURT]

*THE PERSONAL INSOLVENCY ACT 2012

*[....] CIRCUIT *COUNTY OF [....]

IN THE MATTER OF AN APPLICATION UNDER SECTION 95 OF THE PERSONAL INSOLVENCY ACT 2012

AND IN THE MATTER OF [...]
OF [..],

A DEBTOR

*I/*We ....

of ....

County of ....

*and ....

of ....

County of ....

HEREBY APPLY for the making of an order for the issue under section 95(2)(*a*) of the Personal Insolvency Act 2012 of a protective certificate.

Dated .... 20 ....

* delete where inapplicable

Important Information and Statements

1. Unless otherwise defined in this application form, terms used herein have the same meaning as under the Personal Insolvency Act 2012 (the "Act").

2. This application form has been prescribed by the Insolvency Service for the purposes of Section 93(2) of the Act.

3. The Insolvency Service may request any further information it requires from a debtor (the "Debtor"), or personal insolvency practitioner and defer further consideration of the application until such information is furnished to the Insolvency Service. Failure to furnish such information, within 14 days or such longer period as the Insolvency Service may (at its discretion) permit, will mean that the application shall be deemed to have been withdrawn.

4. Where the personal insolvency practitioner becomes aware of any inaccuracy or omission in this application or any document accompanying this application, he or she is required under section 93(4) of the Act to inform the Insolvency Service of this fact as soon as practicable.

5. The Insolvency Service hereby agrees to the Debtor communicating with the Insolvency Service by electronic means for the purposes of any communication or notice required or permitted to be sent or given by the Debtor to the Insolvency Service, from time to time, in connection with this Act including for the purpose of any notice referred to in section 134 of the Act. Any such communication or notice should be sent to pia@isi.gov.ie.

6. Notwithstanding any agreement by the Debtor to receiving electronic communications and notices, there may be circumstances in which the Insolvency Service will send documents, information and other communications to the Debtor in hard copy rather than electronically, in which case the Insolvency Service reserves the right to do so, including for the purpose of giving the Debtor any notice referred to in section 134 of the Act.

7. This application may be withdrawn at any time prior to the issue of a protective certificate in accordance with section 93(3) of the Act.

8. This application shall be accompanied by the appropriate fee and the following documentation:

(*a*) a statement of the personal insolvency practitioner prepared under section 54 of the Act;

(*b*) the Debtor's signed confirmation that he or she satisfies the eligibility criteria specified in section 91 of the Act;

(*c*) the declaration in writing of the Debtor referred to in section 91(1)(*g*) of the Act or in the alternative, the personal insolvency practitioner's written confirmation as referred to in section 91(2) of the Act;

(*d*) the Prescribed Financial Statement;

(*e*) the statutory declaration of the Debtor referred to in section 91(1)(*e*) of the Act;

(*f*) a schedule of creditors of the Debtor and the debts concerned, stating in relation to each such creditor the information specified in section 93(2)(*e*) of the Act;

(*g*) the Debtor's written consent to the disclosure and processing of his or her personal data of the Debtor as specified in section 93(2)(*f*) of the Act;

(*h*) the Debtor's written consent to the making of any enquiry under section 94 of the Act relating to the Debtor by the Insolvency Service;

(*i*) such other documentation as may be requested in this application.

Application Form

APPLICATION QUESTIONS	
Is this an individual application or a joint application? If this is a joint application each Debtor must complete the "Debtor's Details" sections.	Individual ☐ Joint ☐
If an individual application, is it proposed that this application will be administered in common with one or more other Personal Insolvency Arrangements pursuant to Section 89(4) of the Personal Insolvency Act 2012? If yes, provide ISI case reference number(s) for the relevant arrangement(s).	Yes ☐ No ☐ Case Reference No(s).:
Are the total liabilities of the Debtor as determined on the basis of the Prescribed Financial Statement completed by the Debtor in respect of this application in excess of €2,500,000?	Yes ☐ No ☐
Has 25% or more of the Debtor's debts (other than excluded debts) been incurred during the period of 6 months ending on the date of this application?	Yes ☐ No ☐
Is the aggregate of the debts of the Debtor which are secured debts less than €3,000,000? If no, have all of the creditors who are secured creditors consented in writing so that the limit of €3,000,000 shall not apply? If yes, please provide a copy of the consent with this application.	Yes ☐ No ☐ Yes ☐ No ☐
Is at least one of the creditors of the Debtor a secured creditor holding security over an interest in property (real or personal) of the Debtor situate in the State?	Yes ☐ No ☐

(DEBTOR'S DETAILS sections to be completed by all debtors in the case of a joint application)

DEBTOR'S DETAILS — Initial Information	
Has the Debtor received advice from the personal insolvency practitioner on the matters set out in section 52 of the Act?	Yes ☐ No ☐
Was the advice referred to in section 52(1)(c) of the Act confirmed in writing by the personal insolvency practitioner to the Debtor?	Yes ☐ No ☐
Has the Debtor instructed the personal insolvency practitioner in writing to make a proposal for a Personal Insolvency Arrangement in accordance with Chapter 4 of the Act?	Yes ☐ No ☐
Does the Debtor agree to receiving by electronic means communications or notices required or permitted to be sent or given to the Debtor by the Insolvency Service from time to time in connection with the Act or related rules of court? Electronic communications or notices will be sent to the Debtor's email address provided in this application form.	Yes ☐ No ☐
The Courts Service may wish to communicate with the Debtor, from time to time, by electronic means in connection with the Act or related rules of court. If such circumstances arise, does the Debtor agree to receiving by electronic means communications or notices required or permitted to be sent or given to the Debtor by the Courts Service in connection with the Act or related rules of court? Electronic communications or notices will be sent to the Debtor's email address and/or mobile telephone number provided in this application form.	Yes ☐ No ☐

DEBTOR'S DETAILS — Personal Details	
Surname:	
First name:	
Name as it appears on birth certificate:	
Is the Debtor or has the Debtor been known by any other name? If yes, please supply name(s):	Yes ☐ No ☐ Name(s):
Title:*	Mr Mrs Miss Ms Other (please specify)
Gender:*	Male Female Other
PPS number:	
Date of birth:	
Country of birth:	
Nationality:	
Current Marital Status:*	Single (never married) Married (first marriage, no previous annulment) Married (following previous annulment) Re-married (following death of spouse) Re-married (following divorce/annulment) Civil partnership Separated Divorced Widow/Widower
Current Address:	
Home telephone number:	
Mobile telephone number:	
Email address:	

DEBTOR'S DETAILS — Previous Addresses	
Has the Debtor had any previous addresses in the last 5 years? If yes, please supply address(es):	Yes ☐ No ☐ Address(es): Start date and end date:

DEBTOR'S DETAILS — Employment Status	
What is the Debtor's current employment status?*	Employed Self-employed/Trading Unemployed Retired Student Housewife/husband Other (please specify)
If "Employed" is chosen the following questions must be answered:	
Occupation:	
Name of employer:	
Address of employer:	
Length of Service with employer: *Please specify in years and months.*	
If "Self-employed/Trading" is chosen the following questions must be answered:	
Occupation:	
Type of Business:	
Trading/Business Name:	
Address of Business:	
Was/Is the business registered for VAT? If yes, please supply VAT number.	Yes ☐ No ☐ VAT number:
Is the Debtor a sole trader? If not, what is the percentage of the Debtor's ownership of the business?	Yes ☐ No ☐ Percentage:
When did the business start trading? *Please specify a year and a month.*	

DEBTOR'S DETAILS — Previous Businesses	
Has the Debtor ever carried on a business, other than that referred to in the Employment Status section above, under a trading/business name or any other name other than the Debtor's current name? If yes, please supply all previous name(s) and address(es)	Yes ☐ No ☐ Name(s) and Address(es): Start date and end date:

DEBTOR'S DETAILS — Insolvency Status	
Is the Debtor an undischarged bankrupt?	Yes ☐ No ☐
Is the Debtor a discharged bankrupt subject to a bankruptcy payment order?	Yes ☐ No ☐
Is the Debtor a person who is a specified debtor as respects a Debt Relief Notice which is in effect?	Yes ☐ No ☐
Is the Debtor a person who, as a debtor, is subject to a Debt Settlement Arrangement which is in effect?	Yes ☐ No ☐
Is the Debtor a person who, as a debtor, is subject to an arrangement under the control of the court under Part IV of the Bankruptcy Act 1988?	Yes ☐ No ☐

DEBTOR'S DETAILS — Prior Insolvency Processes	
Has the Debtor been the subject of a protective certificate issued under section 95 of the Act less than 12 months prior to the date of this application?	Yes ☐ No ☐
Has the Debtor had his or her debts discharged pursuant to a final Debt Relief Notice less than 3 years prior to the date of this application?	Yes ☐ No ☐
Has the Debtor had his or her debts discharged pursuant to a Debt Settlement Arrangement less than 5 years prior to the date of this application?	Yes ☐ No ☐
Has the Debtor been discharged from bankruptcy less than 5 years prior to the date of this application?	Yes ☐ No ☐
Has the appropriate court made an order referred to in section 91(3) of the Act stating that it is satisfied that the current insolvency of the Debtor arises by reason of exceptional circumstances or other factors which are substantially outside the control of the Debtor and that it would be just to permit the Debtor to make a proposal for a Personal Insolvency Arrangement? If yes, please provide a copy of the order with this application. *Only to be answered if any of the previous four questions are answered in the positive.*	Yes ☐ No ☐
Has the Debtor ever entered into a Personal Insolvency Arrangement?	Yes ☐ No ☐

DEBTOR'S DETAILS — Other Eligibility Criteria	
Is the Debtor domiciled in the State, or within one year before the date of this application, has the Debtor ordinarily— (i) resided in the State, or (ii) had a place of business in the State?*	Yes ☐ No ☐ Domiciled Resided Business
Is the Debtor insolvent within the meaning of the Act?	Yes ☐ No ☐

REASONABLE LIVING EXPENSES (RLE)	
For the purposes of calculating the monthly total set costs under the guidelines on a reasonable standard of living and reasonable living expenses issued under Section 23 of the Act (the "Reasonable Living Expenses Guidelines"), is this a one adult household or a two adult household?*	One adult household Two adult household
Does the Debtor have any dependent children (under 19 years of age) living with him or her? *If yes, complete — Reasonable Living Expenses — Children.*	Yes ☐ No ☐
Does the Debtor own a motor vehicle?	Yes ☐ No ☐
If yes, does the Debtor require a motor vehicle?	Yes ☐ No ☐
The monthly total set costs under the Reasonable Living Expenses Guidelines for the Debtor's typical household are:	€
Does the Debtor have any childcare costs? If yes, please give the monthly expenditure amount assessed to be reasonable by the personal insolvency practitioner in accordance with the Reasonable Living Expenses Guidelines.	Yes ☐ No ☐ Monthly amount: €
How much is the Debtor's monthly rent, mortgage repayment or other accommodation costs assessed to be reasonable by the personal insolvency practitioner in accordance with the Reasonable Living Expenses Guidelines?	€
Does the Debtor have any expenditure in relation to special circumstances, which is required to be taken into account when calculating his or her reasonable living expenses? *If yes, complete — Reasonable Living Expenses — Special Circumstances.*	Yes ☐ No ☐
In the case of a two adult household, has the Debtor rebutted the presumption of an equal split of the reasonable living expenses between them?	Yes ☐ No ☐
What percentage of the Debtor's household reasonable living expenses should be attributed to the Debtor?	Percentage:
The Debtor's reasonable living expenses are:	€

REASONABLE LIVING EXPENSES — Children	
For the purposes of calculating the Debtor's reasonable living expenses under the Reasonable Living Expenses Guidelines, which of the following age categories does the Debtor's child(ren) fall into?*	Infant (0-2) Pre-school (3) Primary school (4-11) Secondary school (12-18)

REASONABLE LIVING EXPENSES — Special Circumstances	
Please give the monthly expenditure amount and details of this expenditure.	Monthly amount: € Details:

JURISDICTION **Only applicable if Circuit Court Application**	
With reference to section 5(2) of the Act, please specify relevant County of the Debtor.	
Circuit Court:	
Reason for specifying County:*	Debtor residing at the time of this application Debtor resided within one year of the time of this application Debtor has a place of business at the time of this application Debtor had a place of business within one year of the time of this application

Signature of Debtor:	
Printed Name of Debtor:	
Date:	

Note: This document will be completed in electronic format on such electronic platform that the Insolvency Service may from time to time make available or otherwise specify for such purpose, following which, the information will be processed into an output format which may be in electronic form or printed on paper. Where any item in this document is completed to the effect of 'no', or any item in this document is not completed, that information may not appear on such output format and any person reviewing the output format should proceed on the basis that, where the output format does not refer to such information, the relevant item was either completed by selecting 'no' or the relevant item was not applicable in that instance. In this document, where an asterisk (*) is used and a choice is provided of the appropriate response, the response selected will appear in the output format. This note will not appear on the output format.

Appendix 9

FORM NO 52A

Form 52A Certificate under the Personal Insolvency Act 2012, ss 31, 61 and 95

AN CHÚIRT CHUARDA

THE CIRCUIT COURT

[......] CIRCUIT COUNTY OF [......]

IN THE MATTER OF PART 3, *[CHAPTER 1] *[CHAPTER 3] *[CHAPTER 4] OF THE PERSONAL INSOLVENCY ACT 2012

AND IN THE MATTER OF [.......] OF [.........], A DEBTOR

CERTIFICATE UNDER SECTION *[31] *[61] *[95] OF THE PERSONAL INSOLVENCY ACT 2012

*The Insolvency Service of Ireland, having considered the application for a Debt Relief Notice by the above named debtor, a copy of which is furnished together with this certificate, HEREBY CERTIFIES that the application is in order.

*The Insolvency Service of Ireland, having considered the application for a protective certificate by the above named Debtor, a copy of which is furnished with this certificate, HEREBY CERTIFIES that the application is in order.

Dated this .... day of ...... 20 ....

*Signed:

*Director of the Insolvency Service of Ireland

*member of staff of the Insolvency Service of Ireland duly authorised by the Director of the Insolvency Service of Ireland

To: The *County Registrar, ... Circuit Court Office at .....

*Combined Court Office at ....

*office of the Courts Service at ......

[*Note: this certificate, if furnished by electronic means to the Court, does not require to be authenticated by the signature of the person issuing it on behalf of the Insolvency Service of Ireland.*]

**Delete where inapplicable.*

Appendix 10

FORM NO 52B

SI No 317 of 2013

Form: 52B Debt Relief Notice

AN CHÚIRT CHUARDA

THE CIRCUIT COURT

[......] CIRCUIT COUNTY OF [......]

Record number ....

IN THE MATTER OF PART 3, CHAPTER 1 OF THE PERSONAL INSOLVENCY ACT 2012

AND IN THE MATTER OF [.......] OF [........], A DEBTOR

Before Judge ......

DEBT RELIEF NOTICE

The Court

1. Being satisfied that the above entitled proceedings may be brought in the Circuit Court for this Circuit because it is the Circuit of the Circuit Court in which

*the above-named debtor to whom the application relates was residing at the time of the making of the application or has resided within one year of the time of the making of the application

*the above-named debtor to whom the application relates had a place of business at the time of the making of the application or has had a place of business within one year of the time of the making of the application

2. Having considered:

(i) the application dated the .... 20 ..... for the issue of a Debt Relief Notice in respect of the said debtor furnished to the Court on .... 20 ..... by the Insolvency Service of Ireland

(ii) the certificate of the Insolvency Service of Ireland, having performed its functions under the Personal Insolvency Act 2012 in relation to the said application, that the application to the Insolvency Service of Ireland under section 29 of the Personal Insolvency Act 2012 on behalf of the said debtor is in order

(iii) copies of the supporting documentation for the application (other than the documents referred to in section 29(2)(e) and (f) of the Act)

*(iv) further *information *evidence provided to it

3. Being satisfied that the criteria specified in section 26(2) of the Personal Insolvency Act 2012 have been satisfied

hereby issues in accordance with section 31(2) of the Personal Insolvency Act 2012 a Debt Relief Notice in respect of the said debtor and in respect of the debts specified in the application under section 29 of the said Act which the Court is satisfied are qualifying debts, as set out hereunder:

Specified qualifying debts		
Reference/Number (if any) as per Prescribed Financial Statement	Value of the debt on the application date (€)	Specified creditor to whom it is owed
	€......	........of ....

Given by the Court on .... 20 ....

Registrar [Name]

**Delete where inapplicable*

Appendix 11

FORM NO 51

SI No 316 of 2013

No 51

O. 76A, r. 7(1)

THE HIGH COURT

PERSONAL INSOLVENCY ACT 2012

IN THE MATTER OF PART 3, *[CHAPTER 3] *[CHAPTER 4] OF THE PERSONAL INSOLVENCY ACT 2012

AND IN THE MATTER OF [.......] OF [.......], A DEBTOR

CERTIFICATE UNDER SECTION *[61] *[95] OF THE PERSONAL INSOLVENCY ACT 2012

The Insolvency Service of Ireland, having considered the application for a protective certificate by the above named Debtor, a copy of which is furnished with this certificate, HEREBY CERTIFIES that the application is in order.

Dated this .... day of .... 20..

*Signed:

*Director of the Insolvency Service of Ireland

*member of staff of the Insolvency Service of Ireland duly authorised by the Director of the Insolvency Service of Ireland

To: The Registrar,

Central Office,

Four Courts,

Dublin 7

[*Note: this certificate, if furnished by electronic means to the Court, does not require to be authenticated by the signature of the person issuing it on behalf of the Insolvency Service of Ireland.*]

The total liabilities of the debtor, determined on the basis of the Prescribed Financial Statement completed by the debtor concerned in respect of the application concerned, are in excess of €2,500,000.

**Delete where inapplicable*

Appendix 12

FORM NO 52

SI No 316 of 2013

No 52

O. 76A, r. 7(3)

THE HIGH COURT

PERSONAL INSOLVENCY ACT 2012

IN THE MATTER OF PART 3, CHAPTER 3 OF THE PERSONAL INSOLVENCY ACT 2012

AND IN THE MATTER OF [.........] OF [.........], A DEBTOR

Before Mr/Ms Justice .....

PROTECTIVE CERTIFICATE

(DEBT SETTLEMENT ARRANGEMENT)

The Court

1. Being satisfied that the total liabilities of the debtor, determined on the basis of the Prescribed Financial Statement completed by the debtor concerned in respect of the application concerned, are in excess of €2,500,000

2. Having considered:

(i) the application dated the ...... 20... for the issue of a protective certificate in respect of the said debtor furnished to the Court on ...... 20.... by the Insolvency Service of Ireland

(ii) the certificate of the Insolvency Service of Ireland, having performed its functions under the Personal Insolvency Act 2012 in relation to the said application, that the application to the Insolvency Service of Ireland under section 59 of the Personal Insolvency Act 2012 on behalf of the said debtor is in order

(iii) copies of the supporting documentation for the application (other than the documents referred to in section 59(2)(f) and (g) of the Act)

*(iv) further *information *evidence provided to it

3. Being satisfied that the criteria specified in section 57 of the Personal Insolvency Act 2012 have been satisfied to the extent that the said criteria have not been disapplied by an order made under section 57(2) of the said Act

4. Being satisfied that the other relevant requirements relating to an application for the issue of a protective certificate have been met

hereby issues in accordance with section 61(2) of the Personal Insolvency Act 2012 a protective certificate in respect of the said debtor and in respect of the debts as set out hereunder:

Specified debts		
Reference/Number (if any) as per Prescribed Financial Statement	Value of the debt on the application date (€)	Creditor to whom debt is owed
	€ ……	…… of ….

Given by the Court on ..... 20.....

Registrar [Name]

**Delete where inapplicable*

Appendix 13

FORM NO 52C

SI No 317 of 2013

Form: 52C Protective certificate (debt settlement arrangement)

AN CHÚIRT CHUARDA

THE CIRCUIT COURT

[......] CIRCUIT COUNTY OF [......]

Record number ......

IN THE MATTER OF PART 3, CHAPTER 3 OF THE PERSONAL INSOLVENCY ACT 2012

AND IN THE MATTER OF [......] OF [........], A DEBTOR

Before Judge .....

PROTECTIVE CERTIFICATE

(DEBT SETTLEMENT ARRANGEMENT)

The Court

1. Being satisfied that the above entitled proceedings may be brought in the Circuit Court for this Circuit because the total liabilities of the above named debtor determined on the basis of the Prescribed Financial Statement completed by the said debtor for the purpose of the proceedings do not exceed €2,500,000 and that the proceedings are brought in the Circuit of the Circuit Court in which

*the said debtor to whom the application relates was residing at the time of the making of the application or has resided within one year of the time of the making of the application

*the said debtor to whom the application relates had a place of business at the time of the making of the application or has had a place of business within one year of the time of the making of the application

2. Having considered:

(i) the application dated the ...... 20 .... for the issue of a protective certificate in respect of the said debtor furnished to the Court on .... 20 ..... by the Insolvency Service of Ireland

(ii) the certificate of the Insolvency Service of Ireland, having performed its functions under the Personal Insolvency Act 2012 in relation to the said application, that the application to the Insolvency Service of Ireland under section 59 of the Personal Insolvency Act 2012 on behalf of the said debtor is in order

(iii) copies of the supporting documentation for the application (other than the documents referred to in section 59(2)(f) and (g) of the Act)

*(iv) further *information *evidence provided to it

3. Being satisfied that the criteria specified in section 57 of the Personal Insolvency Act 2012 have been satisfied to the extent that the said criteria have not been disapplied by an order made under section 57(2) of the said Act

4. Being satisfied that the other relevant requirements relating to an application for the issue of a protective certificate have been met

hereby issues in accordance with section 61(2) of the Personal Insolvency Act 2012 a protective certificate in respect of the said debtor and in respect of the debts as set out hereunder:

	Specified debts	
Reference/Number (if any) as per Prescribed Financial Statement	Value of the debt on the application date (€)	Creditor to whom debt is owed
	€......	........of ....

Given by the Court on .... 20 ....

Registrar [Name]

**Delete where inapplicable*

Appendix 14

FORM NO 53

SI No 316 of 2013

No 53

O. 76A, r. 11(1)

THE HIGH COURT

PERSONAL INSOLVENCY ACT 2012

IN THE MATTER OF PART 3, *[CHAPTER 3] *[CHAPTER 4] OF THE PERSONAL INSOLVENCY ACT 2012

AND IN THE MATTER OF [..........] OF [.............], A DEBTOR

NOTICE OF OBJECTION

TAKE NOTICE that .... of ......, being a creditor of the above named debtor, in the amount of €....,

having received on the .... day of ..... 20... a notice sent on the .... day of .... 20... pursuant to

*section 75(2) of the Personal Insolvency Act 2012 concerning a proposed *(variation of a) Debt Settlement Arrangement

*section 112(2) of the Personal Insolvency Act 2012 concerning a proposed *(variation of a) Personal Insolvency Arrangement

in respect of the said debtor,

hereby gives notice of objection under *[section 75(3)] *[section 112(3)] of the Personal Insolvency Act 2012 to the coming into effect of the said proposed *(variation of a) *Debt Settlement Arrangement *Personal Insolvency Arrangement.

The grounds of objection are as follows

[*specify succinctly the grounds on which objection is made, as set out in*

**section 87 of the Personal Insolvency Act 2012 in the case of a Debt Settlement Arrangement*

**section 120 of the Personal Insolvency Act 2012, in the case of a Personal Insolvency Arrangement.*]

Dated the ..... day of ..... 20....

Creditor/Solicitor for creditor

To: The Registrar,

Central Office,

Four Courts,

Dublin 7

And to: the Insolvency Service of Ireland at ....

And to: .... of ...... personal insolvency practitioner appointed by the debtor.

**Delete where inapplicable*

Appendix 15

FORM NO 52D

SI No 317 of 2013

Form: 52D Notice of objection

AN CHÚIRT CHUARDA

THE CIRCUIT COURT

[......] CIRCUIT COUNTY OF [......]

Record number ....

IN THE MATTER OF PART 3, *[CHAPTER 3] *[CHAPTER 4] OF THE PERSONAL INSOLVENCY ACT 2012

AND IN THE MATTER OF [..........] OF [.........], A DEBTOR

NOTICE OF OBJECTION

TAKE NOTICE that ...... of ..... , being a creditor of the above named debtor, in the amount of € ...., having received on the ...... day of .... 20 .... a notice sent on the

..... day of .... 20 .... pursuant to

*section 75(2) of the Personal Insolvency Act 2012 concerning a proposed *(variation of a) Debt Settlement Arrangement

*section 112(2) of the Personal Insolvency Act 2012 concerning a proposed *(variation of a) Personal Insolvency Arrangement

in respect of the said debtor,

hereby gives notice of objection under *[section 75(3)] *[section 112(3)] of the Personal Insolvency Act 2012 to the coming into effect of the said proposed *(variation of a) *Debt Settlement Arrangement *Personal Insolvency Arrangement.

The grounds of objection are as follows

[*specify succinctly the grounds on which objection is made, as set out in*

**section 87 of the Personal Insolvency Act 2012 in the case of a Debt Settlement Arrangement*

**section 120 of the Personal Insolvency Act 2012, in the case of a Personal Insolvency Arrangement.*]

Dated the .... day of ..... 20 .....

____

Creditor/Solicitor for creditor

To: The *County Registrar, ... Circuit Court Office at ......

*Combined Court Office at .....

*office of the Courts Service at ....

And to: the Insolvency Service of Ireland at .....

And to: .... of ...... personal insolvency practitioner appointed by the debtor.

**Delete where inapplicable*

Appendix 16

FORM NO 54

SI No 316 of 2013

No 54

O. 76A, rr. 11(2), 20(2)

THE HIGH COURT

PERSONAL INSOLVENCY ACT 2012

IN THE MATTER OF PART 3, *[CHAPTER 3] *[CHAPTER 4] OF THE PERSONAL INSOLVENCY ACT 2012

AND IN THE MATTER OF [.......] OF [...........], A DEBTOR

NOTIFICATION TO COURT BY INSOLVENCY SERVICE OF IRELAND UNDER SECTION *[76] *[113] OF THE PERSONAL INSOLVENCY ACT 2012

The Insolvency Service of Ireland hereby notifies the Court that it has received notification from .... of ....,

the personal insolvency practitioner appointed by the above named debtor, that

a *[Debt Settlement Arrangement] *[Personal Insolvency Arrangement] has been approved at a meeting of the creditors of the debtor

and that it has recorded such approval in the Register of *[Debt Settlement Arrangements] *[Personal Insolvency Arrangements].

This notification is accompanied by:

a true copy of the certificate provided for under *section 75(1)(a) *section 112(1)(a) of the Act with the result of the vote taken at the creditors' meeting

a true copy of the approved *[Debt Settlement Arrangement] *[Personal Insolvency Arrangement] and

a true copy of the statement provided for under *section 75(1)(c) *section 112(1)(c) of the Act.

Dated this … day of …… 20.....

*Signed:

*Director of the Insolvency Service of Ireland

*member of staff of the Insolvency Service of Ireland duly authorised by the Director of the Insolvency Service of Ireland

To: The Registrar,

Central Office,

Four Courts,

Dublin 7

[Note: this notification, if furnished by electronic means to the Court, does not require to be authenticated by the signature of the person issuing it on behalf of the Insolvency Service of Ireland.]

**Delete where inapplicable*

Appendix 17

FORM NO 52E

SI No 317 of 2013

Form 52E Notification to court by Insolvency Service of Ireland under the Personal Insolvency Act 2012, ss 76 and 113

AN CHÚIRT CHUARDA

THE CIRCUIT COURT

[......] CIRCUIT COUNTY OF [......]

IN THE MATTER OF PART 3, *[CHAPTER 3] *[CHAPTER 4] OF THE PERSONAL INSOLVENCY ACT 2012

AND IN THE MATTER OF [......] OF [.......], A DEBTOR

NOTIFICATION TO COURT BY INSOLVENCY SERVICE OF IRELAND UNDER SECTION *[76] *[113] OF THE PERSONAL INSOLVENCY ACT 2012

The Insolvency Service of Ireland hereby notifies the Court that it has received notification from ...... of ......,

the personal insolvency practitioner appointed by the above named debtor,

that

a *[Debt Settlement Arrangement] *[Personal Insolvency Arrangement] has been approved at a meeting of the creditors of the debtor

and that it has recorded such approval in the Register of *[Debt Settlement Arrangements] *[Personal Insolvency Arrangements].

This notification is accompanied by:

a true copy of the certificate provided under *section 75(1)(a) *section 112(1)(a) of the Act with the result of the vote taken at the creditors' meeting

a true copy of the approved *[Debt Settlement Arrangement] *[Personal Insolvency Arrangement] and

a true copy of the statement provided under *section 75(1)(c) *section 112(1)(c) of the Act.

Dated this ... day of ..... 20 ...

*Signed:

*Director of the Insolvency Service of Ireland

*member of staff of the Insolvency Service of Ireland duly authorised by the Director of the Insolvency Service of Ireland

To: The *County Registrar, ... Circuit Court Office at ....

*Combined Court Office at ....

*office of the Courts Service at ....

[*Note: this notification, if furnished by electronic means to the Court, does not require to be authenticated by the signature of the person issuing it on behalf of the Insolvency Service of Ireland.*]

**Delete where inapplicable*

Appendix 18

FORM NO 55

SI No 316 of 2013

No 55

O. 76A, rr.11(5), 20(5)

HIGH COURT

PERSONAL INSOLVENCY ACT 2012

CERTIFICATE UNDER *[SECTION 75(1)(a)] *[SECTION 112(1)(a)] OF THE PERSONAL INSOLVENCY ACT 2012 WITH THE RESULT OF THE VOTE TAKEN AT THE CREDITORS' MEETING

*I, ... of ...., personal insolvency practitioner, being the personal insolvency practitioner appointed by the above-named debtor to act as *his/* her personal insolvency practitioner for the purposes of Chapter 3 of Part 3 of the said Act HEREBY CERTIFY pursuant to section 75(1)(a) of the said Act that the result of the vote taken at the creditors' meeting concerning the proposed Debt Settlement Arrangement for the above-named debtor, held at .... on the .... day of ..... 20... is as follows:

		Percentage of total
Number of votes in value of the creditors present and voting		100%
Number of votes in value of the creditors present and voting in favour of the proposed Debt Settlement Arrangement		
Number of votes in value of the creditors present and voting against the proposed Debt Settlement Arrangement		

The requisite percentage of creditors referred to in section 73(6) of the said Act has approved the proposal for a Debt Settlement Arrangement.

OR

*I, ... of ......, personal insolvency practitioner, being the personal insolvency practitioner appointed by the above-named debtor to act as *his/* her personal insolvency practitioner for the purposes of Chapter 4 of Part 3 of the said Act HEREBY CERTIFY pursuant to section 112(1)(a) of the said Act that the result of the vote taken at the creditors' meeting concerning the proposed Personal Insolvency Arrangement for the above-named debtor, held at ..... on the .... day of ...... 20... is as follows:

Secured		Percentage of total
Number of votes in value of the secured creditors who are entitled to vote and have voted		100%
Number of votes in value of the secured creditors who are entitled to vote and have voted in favour of the proposed Personal Insolvency Arrangement		
Number of votes in value of the secured creditors who are entitled to vote and have voted against the proposed Personal Insolvency Arrangement		
Unsecured		Percentage of total
Number of votes in value of the unsecured creditors who are entitled to vote and have voted		100%
Number of votes in value of the unsecured creditors who are entitled to vote and have voted in favour of the proposed Personal Insolvency Arrangement		
Number of votes in value of the unsecured creditors who are entitled to vote and have voted against the proposed Personal Insolvency Arrangement		
Total		Percentage of total
Total number of votes in value of the creditors present and voting		100%
Total number of votes in value of the creditors present and voting in favour of the proposed Personal Insolvency Arrangement		
Total number of votes in value of the creditors present and voting against the proposed Personal Insolvency Arrangement		

The requisite percentage of creditors referred to in section 110(1) of the said Act has approved the proposal for a Personal Insolvency Arrangement.

Dated this ..... day of ..... 20......

Signed:

**Delete where inapplicable*

Appendix 19

FORM NO 52F

SI No 317 of 2013

Form 52F Certificate under the Personal Insolvency Act 2012, ss 75(1)(a) and 112(1)(a)

AN CHÚIRT CHUARDA

THE CIRCUIT COURT

[......] CIRCUIT COUNTY OF [......]

IN THE MATTER OF PART 3, *[CHAPTER 3] *[CHAPTER 4] OF THE PERSONAL INSOLVENCY ACT 2012

AND IN THE MATTER OF [........] OF [........], A DEBTOR
CERTIFICATE UNDER *[SECTION 75(1)(a)] *[SECTION 112(1)(a)] OF THE PERSONAL INSOLVENCY ACT 2012 WITH THE RESULT OF THE VOTE TAKEN AT THE CREDITORS' MEETING

*I, ... of ...... , personal insolvency practitioner, being the personal insolvency practitioner appointed by the above-named debtor to act as *his/* her personal insolvency practitioner for the purposes of Chapter 3 of Part 3 of the said Act HEREBY CERTIFY pursuant to section 75(1)(a) of the said Act that the result of the vote taken at the creditors' meeting concerning the proposed Debt Settlement Arrangement for the above-named debtor, held at .... on the .... day of .... 20 .... is as follows:

		Percentage of total
Number of votes in value of the creditors present and voting		100%
Number of votes in value of the creditors present and voting in favour of the proposed Debt Settlement Arrangement		
Number of votes in value of the creditors present and voting against the proposed Debt Settlement Arrangement		

The requisite percentage of creditors referred to in section 73(6) of the said Act has approved the proposal for a Debt Settlement Arrangement.

OR

*I, ... of ...., personal insolvency practitioner, being the personal insolvency practitioner appointed by the above-named debtor to act as *his/* her personal insolvency practitioner for the purposes of Chapter 4 of Part 3 of the said Act HEREBY CERTIFY pursuant to section 112(1)(a) of the said Act that the result of the vote taken at the creditors' meeting concerning the proposed Personal Insolvency Arrangement for the above-named debtor, held at ..... on the ..... day of ...... 20 ... is as follows:

Secured		Percentage of total
Number of votes in value of the secured creditors who are entitled to vote and have voted		100%
Number of votes in value of the secured creditors who are entitled to vote and have voted in favour of the proposed Personal Insolvency Arrangement		
Number of votes in value of the secured creditors who are entitled to vote and have voted against the proposed Personal Insolvency Arrangement		
Unsecured		Percentage of total
Number of votes in value of the unsecured creditors who are entitled to vote and have voted		100%
Number of votes in value of the unsecured creditors who are entitled to vote and have voted in favour of the proposed Personal Insolvency Arrangement		
Number of votes in value of the unsecured creditors who are entitled to vote and have voted against the proposed Personal Insolvency Arrangement		
Total		Percentage of total
Total number of votes in value of the creditors present and voting		100%
Total number of votes in value of the creditors present and voting in favour of the proposed Personal Insolvency Arrangement		
Total number of votes in value of the creditors present and voting against the proposed Personal Insolvency Arrangement		

The requisite percentage of creditors referred to in section 110(1) of the said Act has approved the proposal for a Personal Insolvency Arrangement.

Dated this .... day of ..... 20 .....

Signed:

To: The *County Registrar, ... Circuit Court Office at ....

Combined Court Office at ......

*office of the Courts Service at ....

**Delete where inapplicable*

Appendix 20

FORM NO 56

SI No 316 of 2013

No 56

O. 76A, rr.11(5), 20(5)

THE HIGH COURT

PERSONAL INSOLVENCY ACT 2012

STATEMENT UNDER *[SECTION 75(1)(c)] *[SECTION 112(1)(c)] OF THE PERSONAL INSOLVENCY ACT 2012

1. I, ... of ...., personal insolvency practitioner, being the personal insolvency practitioner appointed by the above-named debtor to act as *his/*her personal insolvency practitioner for the purposes of *Chapter 3/* Chapter 4 of Part 3 of the said Act HEREBY CONFIRM

*for the purposes of section 78(2) and (5) of the said Act that I am of the opinion that—

(i) the said debtor satisfies the eligibility criteria for the proposal of a Debt Settlement Arrangement specified in section 57 of the said Act,

(ii) the approved Debt Settlement Arrangement complies with the mandatory requirements referred to in section 65(2) of the said Act, and

(iii) the approved Debt Settlement Arrangement does not contain any terms that would release the said debtor from an excluded debt, an excludable debt (other than a permitted debt) or a secured debt or otherwise affect such a debt.

*for the purposes of section 115(2) and (5) of the said Act that I am of the opinion that—

(i) the said debtor satisfies the eligibility criteria for the proposal of a Personal Insolvency Arrangement specified in section 91 of the said Act,

(ii) the approved Personal Insolvency Arrangement complies with the mandatory requirements referred to in section 99(2) of the said Act, and

(iii) the approved Personal Insolvency Arrangement does not contain any terms that would release the said debtor from an excluded debt or an excludable debt (other than a permitted debt) or otherwise affect such a debt

Dated this ...... day of .... 20....

Signed:

**Delete where inapplicable*

Appendix 21

FORM NO 52G

SI No 317 of 2013

Form 52G Statement under the Personal Insolvency Act 2012, s 75(1)(c) and 112(1)(c)

AN CHÚIRT CHUARDA

THE CIRCUIT COURT

[......] CIRCUIT COUNTY OF [......]

IN THE MATTER OF PART 3, *[CHAPTER 3] *[CHAPTER 4] OF THE PERSONAL INSOLVENCY ACT 2012

AND IN THE MATTER OF [......] OF [..........], A DEBTOR

STATEMENT UNDER *[SECTION 75(1)(c)] *[SECTION 112(1)(c)] OF THE PERSONAL INSOLVENCY ACT 2012

1. I, ... of ......, personal insolvency practitioner, being the personal insolvency practitioner appointed by the above-named debtor to act as *his/* her personal insolvency practitioner for the purposes of *Chapter 3/*Chapter 4 of Part 3 of the said Act HEREBY CONFIRM

*for the purposes of section 78(2) and (5) of the said Act that I am of the opinion that—

(i) the said debtor satisfies the eligibility criteria for the proposal of a Debt Settlement Arrangement specified in section 57 of the said Act,

(ii) the approved Debt Settlement Arrangement complies with the mandatory requirements referred to in section 65(2) of the said Act, and

(iii) the approved Debt Settlement Arrangement does not contain any terms that would release the said debtor from an excluded debt, an excludable debt (other than a permitted debt) or a secured debt or otherwise affect such a debt.

*for the purposes of section 115(2) and (5) of the said Act that I am of the opinion that—

(i) the said debtor satisfies the eligibility criteria for the proposal of a Personal Insolvency Arrangement specified in section 91 of the said Act,

(ii) the approved Personal Insolvency Arrangement complies with the mandatory requirements referred to in section 99(2) of the said Act, and

(iii) the approved Personal Insolvency Arrangement does not contain any terms that would release the said debtor from an excluded debt or an excludable debt (other than a permitted debt) or otherwise affect such a debt

Dated this ..... day of ...... 20 ....

Signed:

To: The *County Registrar, ... Circuit Court Office at ......

*Combined Court Office at ......

*office of the Courts Service at .....

**Delete where inapplicable*

Appendix 22

FORM NO 57

SI No 316 of 2013

No 57

O. 76A, r. 16(3)

THE HIGH COURT

PERSONAL INSOLVENCY ACT 2012

IN THE MATTER OF PART 3, CHAPTER 4 OF THE PERSONAL INSOLVENCY ACT 2012

AND IN THE MATTER OF [.........] OF [..........], A DEBTOR

Before Mr/Ms Justice .....

PROTECTIVE CERTIFICATE

(PERSONAL INSOLVENCY ARRANGEMENT)

The Court

1. Being satisfied that the total liabilities of the debtor, determined on the basis of the Prescribed Financial Statement completed by the debtor concerned in respect of the application concerned, are in excess of €2,500,000

2. Having considered:

(i) the application dated the ...... 20.. for the issue of a protective certificate in respect of the said debtor, furnished to the Court on .... 20.. by the Insolvency Service of Ireland

(ii) the certificate of the Insolvency Service of Ireland, having performed its functions under the Personal Insolvency Act 2012 in relation to the said application, that the application to the Insolvency Service of Ireland under section 93 of the Personal Insolvency Act 2012 on behalf of the said debtor is in order

(iii) copies of the supporting documentation for the application (other than the documents referred to in section 93(2)(f) and (g) of the Act)

*(iv) further *information *evidence provided to it

3. Being satisfied that the criteria specified in section 91 of the Personal Insolvency Act 2012 have been satisfied to the extent that the said criteria have not been disapplied by an order made under section 91(3) of the said Act

4. Being satisfied that the other relevant requirements relating to an application for the issue of a protective certificate have been met

hereby issues in accordance with section 95(2) of the Personal Insolvency Act 2012 a protective certificate in respect of the said debtor and in respect of the debts as set out hereunder:

Specified debts		
Reference/Number (if any) as per Prescribed Financial Statement	Value of the debt on the application date (€)	Creditor to whom debt is owed
	€......	........of ....

Given by the Court on .... 20.....

Registrar [Name]

**Delete where inapplicable*

Appendix 23

FORM NO 52H

SI No 317 of 2013

Form: 52H Protective certificate (personal insolvency arrangement)

AN CHÚIRT CHUARDA

THE CIRCUIT COURT

[......] CIRCUIT COUNTY OF [......]

Record number ......

IN THE MATTER OF PART 3, CHAPTER 4 OF THE PERSONAL INSOLVENCY ACT 2012

AND IN THE MATTER OF [........] OF [.......], A DEBTOR

Before Judge ....

PROTECTIVE CERTIFICATE

(PERSONAL INSOLVENCY ARRANGEMENT)

The Court

1. Being satisfied that the above entitled proceedings may be brought in the Circuit Court for this Circuit because the total liabilities of the above named debtor determined on the basis of the Prescribed Financial Statement completed by the said debtor for the purpose of the proceedings do not exceed €2,500,000 and that the proceedings are brought in the Circuit of the Circuit Court in which

*the above-named debtor to whom the application relates was residing at the time of the making of the application or has resided within one year of the time of the making of the application

*the above-named debtor to whom the application relates had a place of business at the time of the making of the application or has had a place of business within one year of the time of the making of the application

2. Having considered:

(i) the application dated the .... 20 .... for the issue of a protective certificate in respect of the said debtor, furnished to the Court on ..... 20 .... by the Insolvency Service of Ireland

(ii) the certificate of the Insolvency Service of Ireland, having performed its functions under the Personal Insolvency Act 2012 in relation to the said application, that the application to the Insolvency Service of Ireland under section 93 of the Personal Insolvency Act 2012 on behalf of the said debtor is in order

(iii) copies of the supporting documentation for the application (other than the documents referred to in section 93(2)(f) and (g) of the Act)

*(iv) further *information *evidence provided to it

3. Being satisfied that the criteria specified in section 91 of the Personal Insolvency Act 2012 have been satisfied to the extent that the said criteria have not been disapplied by an order made under section 91(3) of the said Act

4. Being satisfied that the other relevant requirements relating to an application for the issue of a protective certificate have been met

hereby issues in accordance with section 95(2) of the Personal Insolvency Act 2012 a protective certificate in respect of the said debtor and in respect of the debts as set out hereunder:

Specified debts		
Reference/Number (if any) as per Prescribed Financial Statement	Amount of the debt on the application date (€)	Creditor to whom debt is owed
	€......	........of ....

Given by the Court on .... 20 ....

Registrar [Name]

**Delete where inapplicable*

Appendix 24

APPLICATION FORM PIP

SI No 209 of 2013

SCHEDULE

PRESCRIBED FORM OF PERSONAL INSOLVENCY PRACTITIONER APPLICATION FORM

Part A — Details of Applicant

1. Full Name

2. Previous Name(*s*) if any

3. Date of Birth

Day		Month		Year	

4. Place of Birth

5. Nationality

6. Private Address

7. PPSN (if applicable)

8. Passport

Passport Number:	
Country of Issue:	
Expiry Date (dd/mm/yyyy)	

9. Trading Name or business name of the Applicant (if different to above)

10. Address of your proposed principal place of business (i.e. the main place you will operate from/ the contact address)

11. State whether you would be self-employed or employed when practicing as a personal insolvency practitioner

12. If employed, please provide the name of your employer

13. Contact details of applicant

Telephone Number of Principal Business	
Mobile Number	
Fax Number	
Direct e-mail address (to be used in future correspondence) *	
Website Address	

* All correspondence from the Insolvency Service of Ireland will be sent to this e-mail address

14. Where the business will operate from:

Home ☐

Separate Office ☐

15. If you are currently authorised and/or supervised by a regulatory authority inside or outside of the State please provide the following details:

Regulatory Authority (including relevant country where it is not the State)	Regulated Activity	Details of licence/ authorisation held	Period for which authorisation is held

Part B — Fitness & Probity

1. Employment History for the last ten years

Employer Name	Address	Position Held	Start & End Date	Reason for Leaving

2. Please explain any professional timeline gap exceeding 12 weeks between employments within the last 10 years.

3. Qualifications and Memberships

Please give the following details of any qualification you have acquired (including memberships of professional associations):
(See Part H — Checklist for a list of acceptable qualifications and please submit copies of all certificates listed.)

Nature of Qualification/ Membership	Name of awarding institution/ professional association	Country	Date Obtained (mm/yyyy)

4. Relevant Training

Please give similar details in relation to any other training received that may be relevant to the role of personal insolvency practitioner:

Name of Training	**Name of institution/ professional association**	**Country**	**Duration of training**	**Date completed (mm/yyyy)**

5. Details of experience relevant to the role of a personal insolvency practitioner:

Name of Employer	**Position Held**	**Dates/Duration**	**Details of Experience**

6. The following questions are to be answered by entering a tick in the appropriate box. In any case where the response to a question is YES, full details should be given on a separate sheet and referenced to the appropriate question.

		Yes	No
A	Have you been convicted of any offence involving fraud, dishonesty, breach of trust, tax offences or of aiding and abetting tax evasion in the State or elsewhere, including any conviction related to financial crime or breach of statutory or regulatory requirements?		
B	Have you been a director or manager of an entity or business that was, during your period as a director or manager, convicted of an offence involving fraud, dishonesty, breach of trust, tax offences or of aiding and abetting tax evasion in the State or elsewhere, including any conviction related to financial crime or breach of statutory or regulatory requirements?		
C	Have you at any time, in the State or elsewhere, been adjudicated bankrupt, or entered into any compromise with your creditors related to bankruptcy or insolvency or are you currently the subject of bankruptcy or insolvency related proceedings or measures? Are you aware of any such proceedings or measures pending?		
D	Have you at any time failed to satisfy a judgment debt under a court order made in the State or elsewhere within one year of the making of the order?		
E	Have you ever been disqualified or restricted, in the State or elsewhere, by a court from acting as a director of a company or equivalent, or from acting in the management or conduct of the affairs or control of any company, partnership, or unincorporated association?		
F	Have you ever been refused entry to any profession or been dismissed or compelled to resign from any office or position or trust, whether or not remunerated?		
G	Have you ever been prohibited, suspended, refused or restricted in the right, in the State or elsewhere, to carry on any trade, business or profession for which a specific licence, registration or other authority is required?		
H	In the last ten years, have you been the director or equivalent of an entity, in the State or elsewhere, which has gone into liquidation, receivership or examinership or similar or analogous measures or steps in any other country and, in such circumstances, entered into any arrangements with its creditors which gave rise to a loss to the creditors either while you were a director or equivalent or within one year of your ceasing to be a director or equivalent?		

		Yes	No
I	Has any entity with which you were associated as a director, manager or shareholder during the last ten years been compulsorily wound up or equivalent in the State or elsewhere, either whilst you were associated with it or within one year after you ceased to be associated with it?		
J	Have you ever been concerned with the management, conduct of affairs or control of any entity that, by reason of any matter relating to a time when you were so concerned, has been censured, disciplined, restricted, sanctioned, fined, convicted or publicly criticised, by any enquiry, by any governmental, judicial or statutory authority, by any professional body or by a similar body overseas?		
K	Have you ever been concerned with the management, conduct of affairs, or control of any entity which applied for regulatory approval in respect of any business in the State or elsewhere and, by reason of any matter relating to a time when you were so concerned, was refused the application or had the approval subsequently withdrawn, suspended or restricted?		

Part C
Professional Indemnity Requirements

Please note that it is a mandatory requirement, set out in section 171 of the Act, that all personal insolvency practitioners hold a policy of professional indemnity insurance ('PII'), which meets the requirements prescribed by the Insolvency Service of Ireland under section 161 of the Act.

Do you have PII in place?

Yes ☐ **No** ☐

If **'No'** you must submit written confirmation from an insurer authorised to carry on business in the State that it will provide the necessary required level of PII cover to you, should you be authorised as a personal insolvency practitioner.

If **'Yes'**, indicate what PII cover you maintain, the excess amount and include a copy of your PII policy schedule.

PII cover
Indicate what PII cover you maintain

Excess Amount	Per Claim Cover	Aggregate Cover

Effective date of PII cover: ________________

Expiry date of PII cover: ________________

Name of insurer: ________________

Number of the policy that includes your PII cover: ________________

You must provide written evidence from the relevant insurer that the PII covers your practice as a personal insolvency practitioner and meets the level of cover specified in these Regulations.

Accountant's Report
As per section 163 (2)(*b*) of the Act, you must submit a report from a qualified accountant (see Part G) confirming that the appropriate financial systems and controls are or will be in place for the protection of moneys received from debtors if you are authorised to act as a personal insolvency practitioner.

Tax Clearance Certificate
Please provide a copy of your current Tax Clearance Certificate.

Part D — General Business Information

1. Do you or any person on your behalf have back-up and disaster recovery procedures in place for maintaining debtor files?

Yes ☐ **No** ☐

Please provide details:

2. Please detail how you propose to market or advertise your services as a personal insolvency practitioner.

3. Please advise if you will provide any other business services other than your acting as a personal insolvency practitioner. If 'Yes' please outline the services provided/ to be provided.

4. If you have answered 'Yes' to question 3 above, you must ensure that the different business areas are appropriately segregated.

Please set out the arrangements you (including, where applicable, any arrangements through your employer with your agreement) have in place to ensure the segregation of the personal insolvency practitioner role and its records and accounts from the other areas of your business or, as applicable, that of your employer.

5. Please confirm that you have adequate resources (including financial capacity), policies, procedures, systems and controls in place necessary to comply with your obligations under the Act and the regulations.

Yes ☐ **No** ☐

6. Set out the number of full time equivalent employees anticipated to be involved in the management or establishment of debt settlement arrangements or personal insolvency arrangements in respect of which you anticipate to be appointed in the first year of acting as a personal insolvency practitioner.

Number of employees: ________________

7. Set out whether the employees will be employed by you or by your employer (if any) and if the latter, provide an explanation, on a separate sheet, as to how such arrangement will permit you to carry on effectively the functions of a personal insolvency practitioner under the Act.

By me, as employer ☐

By my employer ☐

8. Provide an estimate of the number of debtors for whom you anticipate acting as a personal insolvency practitioner in the first year of trading.

Number of debtors: ________________

9. Please provide an estimate of your projected turnover from your activities as a personal insolvency practitioner in your first year of operating.

Turnover: € ________________

Part E — Banking Arrangements & Professional Advisors

1. Please provide the following details in relation to your main business bank account(*s*):

Bank Name & Address	Account Number	Sort Code	Date Opened

Please note that a business bank account must be opened prior to authorisation.

2. Give the name and address of the bank you intend to operate your DSA/PIA accounts from.

Bank Name	Address

3. Give the name of the authorised signatories on the DSA/PIA accounts.

Title	First Name	Surname	Position Held

4. Will your accounting records and other practice records be held at your principal business address?

Yes ☐ **No** ☐

If No, please provide the address where the records will be held.

5. Give the name, address and telephone number of your accountants/auditors, the date of their appointment and the name of your contact person within the firm.

Name of Auditors	
Address Line 1	
Address Line 2	
Address Line 3	
Address Line 4	
Telephone Number	
Name of Contact Person	
Date of Appointment	________________ (dd/mm/yyyy)

6. Give the name, address and telephone number of your legal advisors, the date of their appointment and the name of your contact person within the firm.

Name of Solicitor's Firm	
Address Line 1	
Address Line 2	
Address Line 3	
Address Line 4	
Telephone Number	
Name of Contact Person	
Date of Appointment	________________ (dd/mm/yyyy)

Part F– Personal Insolvency Practitioner Declaration

I, ______________________, (insert your name) apply under section 163 of the Personal Insolvency Act 2012 for authorisation under section 164 of the Personal Insolvency Act 2012 on the basis of information supplied on this form and any additional information supplied to the Insolvency Service of Ireland in connection with this application.

I acknowledge that the Insolvency Service of Ireland may process and disclose such information in the performance of its statutory functions or otherwise as may be specifically authorised by law.

I warrant that I have truthfully and fully answered the relevant questions in this application and disclosed any other information which might reasonably be considered relevant for the purpose of this application.

I am aware that it may be an offence and/or grounds for refusal of my application and/or grounds for revocation of an authorisation granted on foot of this application to knowingly or recklessly:

a. provide false or misleading information and/or to make a false or misleading statement (which I acknowledge may include the withholding by me of relevant information) in this application for approval and/or;

b. fail to inform and/or withhold from the Insolvency Service of Ireland details of any material change in circumstances/new information which is relevant and/or material to this application.

I undertake that I will promptly notify the Insolvency Service of Ireland of any changes in the information I have provided and supply any other relevant information, which may come to light in the period during which the application is being considered and, if this application is accepted, thereafter.

I am aware of the provisions of the Personal Insolvency Act 2012 and reasonably believe that I can meet the requirements of that Act and the Regulations made under it.

Signed: ______________________

Print Name: ______________________

Dated: ______________________

Part G — Application to be authorised as a personal insolvency practitioner: Accountant's report to the Insolvency Service of Ireland

Please note this report is to be completed by a qualified accountant who is a member of a recognised accountancy body within the meaning of the European Communities (Statutory Audits) (Directive 2006/43/EC) Regulations 2010 (S.I. No. 220 of 2010) and holds a valid practising certificate.

To: The Insolvency Service of Ireland

This report is given for the purposes of section 163(2) (*b*) of the Personal Insolvency Act 2012.

PART I — Applicant's Declaration

1. ______________________________ [Full name of the applicant]

2. ____

____

____[Address]

I, ______________________________, am aware that appropriate financial systems and controls are required to be in place for the protection of moneys received from debtors.

I acknowledge the requirement—

(*a*) that there is in place a written procedure that establishes clear accountability for the handling of funds, which ensures that receipt of funds from debtors is properly accounted for, are protected, and the funds are identifiable to specific debtors;

(*b*) that there is a written procedure to ensure that all cheques and other negotiable instruments are promptly endorsed and a follow-up system has been established to ensure that post-dated cheques are always deposited on the date of the cheque or within appropriate time frames;

(*c*) that appropriate experienced personnel are engaged to monitor, on a constant basis, funds received versus funds due and payments made and they have the ability to investigate and resolve any differences that arise;

(*d*) that the duties of collecting / receiving funds, maintaining documentation, making deposits or payments and reconciling records is distributed between two or more appropriate experienced individuals.

I hereby declare that appropriate financial systems and controls, as set out in matters (*a*) to (*d*) above, are/will be in place for the protection of moneys received from debtors before any personal insolvency services are provided by me.

Signed: ______________________________

Print Name: ______________________________

Dated: ______________________________

PART II — Accountant's Declaration

This report is given for the purposes of section 163 (2) (*b*) of the Personal Insolvency Act 2012.

________________ [Name of accountant or accountancy firm], a qualified accountant who is a member of a recognised accountancy body within the meaning of the European Communities (Statutory Audits) (Directive 2006/43/EC) Regulations 2010 (S.I. No. 220 of 2010) and holds a valid practising certificate, has examined the above declaration and matters (*a*) to (*d*) above and supporting documentation in respect of matters (*a*) to (*d*).

The applicant is responsible for making an application that is correct in all material particulars.

The applicant is also responsible for operating effective and appropriate financial systems and controls for the protection of moneys received from debtors. An appropriate framework of financial systems and controls provides reasonable, but not absolute, assurance that the moneys received from debtors are protected.

My/Our responsibility is to examine the declaration and the supporting evidence; and to express an opinion as to whether the applicant has or intends to have in place appropriate financial systems and controls as set out in matters (*a*) to (*d*) in the above declaration.

In my/our opinion, based on my/our examination, the applicant (has/ on the basis of representations made to me/us by the applicant, is intending to have) in place appropriate financial systems and controls, as set out in (*a*) to (*d*) above for the protection of moneys received from debtors, before any personal insolvency services are provided.

I/we have received all the explanations and information I/we require to form my/our opinion.

Signed: ____________________________ Date: ________________
Accountant (for and on behalf of [name of accountancy firm])

Particulars of accountant

(Firm's) Name:

(Firm's) Address:

Accountancy body of which a member:

Membership Number:

Note for applicant:
Please note that the application will only be processed once this report is complete and received.

Part H — Checklist

The Insolvency Service of Ireland will NOT commence the processing of any application if it is not complete in all respects. Applications will be treated as incomplete unless all questions raised in the application form are fully answered and all applicable supporting documentation (as outlined in the checklist below) has been received by the Insolvency Service of Ireland. Incomplete applications will be returned to you as invalid. Applications that have to be re-submitted will be treated as a new application.

	Applicant	ISI USE ONLY
Completed Application Form (signed and all questions answered)	☐	☐
Registration of Business Name Certificate (Part A) If applicable, a business name registration certificate issued by the Companies Registration Office must be supplied in relation to all trading names (if different to the legal name) that the applicant wishes to use in relation to acting as a personal insolvency practitioner. Please contact the Companies Registration Office (www.cro.ie) if you have any queries in relation to your business name registration certificate. An authorisation will only be granted to an individual and not a company or partnership.	☐	☐
Qualification Certificates (Part B)		
1. Qualified accountant and a member of a prescribed accountancy body	☐	☐
2. Qualification as a barrister at law	☐	☐
3. Solicitor's practicing certificate	☐	☐
4. Qualified Financial Adviser Diploma	☐	☐
5. Copy of certificate/diploma from a relevant professional educational body confirming satisfactory completion of a course on personal insolvency law and practice in the State	☐	☐
6. Copy of any educational qualification/certificate which you believe is applicable to the role of a personal insolvency practitioner	☐	☐
PII Cover (Part C) Written evidence of PII cover (copy of policy or similar) or that cover will be available upon authorisation.	☐	☐
Letter of Intent from Insurance Undertaking (Part C)	☐	☐
Copy of your current Tax Clearance Certificate (Part C)	☐	☐
Signed Declaration (Part F)	☐	☐
Completed Accountants Report (Part G)	☐	☐

INDEX

[*all references are to paragraph number*]